D1062664

THE
PROSE WORKS OF
JOHN DONNE

To the Noblest knight
Sr Edward Herbert.

Sr

I make account that thys Booke hath enough per=
formd wch yt undertooke, both by Argument and
Example. Itt shall therfore the lesse neede to bee
ytt selfe another Example of ye Doctrine. Itt shall
not therfore kyll ytt selfe; that ys, not bury itselfe.
for if ytt should do so, those reasons by wch that
Act should bee defended or excusd, were also lost
wt ytt. Since ytt ys content to liue, ytt cannot
chuse a wholsomer ayre then yor Library, where
Autors of all complexions are presrud. If any
of them grudge thys Booke a roome, and sus=
pect ytt of new or dangerous Doctrine, yow, who
know us all, can best Moderate. To those reasons
wch I know yor Loue to mee wyll make in my fauer,
and discharge, yow may add thys, That though
thys Doctrine hath not beene tought nor defen=
ded by writers, yet they, most of any sorte of Men
in the world, haue practisd ytt. — —

Yor very true and earnest
frnde, and Seruant
and Louer

J. Donne

Reduced Facsimile of Donne's Letter in the Bodleian Manuscript of 'Biathanatos'
(*MS. e Musaeo 131*)

A Study of the
PROSE WORKS OF
JOHN DONNE

BY

EVELYN M. SIMPSON

SECOND EDITION

OXFORD
AT THE CLARENDON PRESS
1948

Oxford University Press, Amen House, London E.C.4
GLASGOW NEW YORK TORONTO MELBOURNE WELLINGTON
BOMBAY CALCUTTA MADRAS CAPE TOWN
Geoffrey Cumberlege, Publisher to the University

74176
827.35
S613S

FIRST EDITION 1924

PRINTED IN GREAT BRITAIN

PREFACE

SINCE the first edition of this book was published in 1924, more than four hundred books, pamphlets, and articles on Donne have appeared. Not only have new estimates been made of Donne as a writer, but my fellow workers and I have discovered a number of seventeenth-century manuscripts which have added materially to our knowledge of his work. The sifting of this material has taken a considerable time, and the result has been that much of the book has been rewritten, especially Chapters III, IV, V, VI, and IX. All through the book, moreover, small changes and additions have been made in order to keep abreast of modern research. The main plan, however, has been kept unchanged, and the arrangement and numbering of the chapters are the same.

The changes in Chapters III and V are made with the object of presenting Donne as a man of the Renaissance more clearly than was done in the first edition. In the new pages which I have added to Chapter III I have dealt briefly with Donne's indebtedness to Latin, French, Italian, and Spanish authors. The quotations which I have given are representative, and the list is not meant to be exhaustive. Here I must thank Professor C. J. Sisson, Editor of the *Modern Language Review*, for permission to reprint some material from my article 'Donne's Spanish Authors' in that journal, which appeared too late for me to insert a footnote at the appropriate place.

Chapter VI contains much additional material on the manuscripts of the *Juvenilia*. It has also been enlarged by an entire section devoted to Donne's prose satire, *Catalogus Librorum Aulicorum*. This was first published by his son in 1650 in a few extra leaves inserted, oddly enough, in a new edition of the *Poems*. It was reprinted with the poems in the editions of 1654, 1669, and 1719, and was then forgotten for more than two hundred years. In 1930 I edited it for the Nonesuch Press with an account of the revised manuscript draft of it which I had found in a seventeenth-century commonplace book in the Library of Trinity College,

Cambridge. Only 750 copies were published, and the edition was sold out within a fortnight. Hence there has been little opportunity for it to become widely known among Donne students. I am much indebted to the Nonesuch Press for their generosity in giving me permission to reprint a large part of my introduction to that edition, and also a number of items of the *Catalogus* in the English translation which was supplied by my husband. This little satire with its Rabelaisian flavour gives us by far the fullest account which we possess of Donne's attitude towards his contemporaries, legal, literary, and political. It contains a wonderful picture of some of the most prominent figures of Elizabethan London. Donne the satirist is here seen at his bitterest and most incisive.

The new matter which has been added to Chapter IX is of quite a different kind. It is the result of prolonged study, which has made me realize the importance of the *Essays in Divinity* in the history of Donne's thought. I have shown the close connexion of the book with the two verse *Anniversaries* and with the *Divine Poems* as well as with some of the earlier sermons. Donne the poet is the best commentator on Donne the prose-writer.

Chapter XI has been enlarged by the addition of a selection of Coleridge's notes on Donne's sermons. Appendix A, which formerly contained the sermon on Psalm xxxviii. 9 from Mr. Wilfred Merton's manuscript, now contains a list of the available seventeenth-century manuscripts of Donne's works. Professor G. R. Potter's edition of the sermon from a manuscript in Harvard College Library has provided a better text than that in the Merton manuscript.

My thanks are due to the Principal and Fellows of Newnham College, Cambridge, for the grant of a Research Fellowship to enable me to produce an edition of Donne's sermons and also to complete the revision of the present work. The first edition contained my acknowledgements to those who helped me a quarter of a century ago. In the correction of past mistakes and the addition of new material I have been helped by many others, and in particular by the late Dr. F. E. Hutchinson, whose unfailing kindness I shall always gratefully remember. My indebtedness to Sir Herbert Grierson's two-volume edition of Donne's *Poems* is apparent on almost every page, and I must also acknowledge important help received from him in tracking down manuscripts of the *Juvenilia*. Dr. G. L. Keynes has helped me with bibliographical problems, and I have had useful discussions with Mr. John Sparrow. Miss H. L. Gardner, Fellow of St. Hilda's College, has given me valuable help with Chapter IV. I must also acknowledge help received from Professor H. W. Garrod, Professor F. P. Wilson, the Rev. Canon R. F. Fellowes who lent me his copy of the *XXVI Sermons*, Father Luke Walker, O.P., who sent me some useful corrections, Miss Mahood, Tutor of St. Hugh's College, and the Librarians of Christ Church and Worcester College, Oxford, and of Trinity College, Cambridge, as well as from Mr. G. W. Henderson, Sub-Librarian and Archivist of St. Paul's Cathedral Library.

From across the Atlantic I have received valuable help from Professor R. C. Bald of Cornell University, U.S.A., Professor C. M. Coffin of Kenyon College, Gambier, Ohio, Professor W. A. Jackson of Harvard College, and Dr. Roger E. Bennett. I must thank the Librarians of Harvard College Library, the Henry E. Huntington Library, and the New York Public Library (Henry W. and Albert A. Berg Collection) for permission to describe and quote from manuscripts in their libraries.

Finally, my best thanks are due to my husband, Percy Simpson, whose advice and encouragement have been an unfailing source of inspiration to me.

E. M. S.

CONTENTS

I

INTRODUCTION

DURING the last half-century there has been a remarkable revival of Donne's fame. This was heralded by the publication in 1899 of Sir Edmund Gosse's *Life and Letters of John Donne*, followed in 1912 by Sir Herbert Grierson's two-volume edition of the *Poems*. At first attention was concentrated on the poems and on Donne's life, but gradually the importance of his prose works began to be realized. Logan Pearsall Smith's anthology of passages from the *Sermons* attracted the attention of many, and this was followed by John Sparrow's edition of the *Devotions*, the Nonesuch editions of *Ten Sermons* and *Paradoxes and Problems*, and the facsimile reproductions of *Juvenilia*, *Biathanatos*, and *Ignatius his Conclave*. John Hayward's Nonesuch *Donne: Complete Poems and Selected Prose* carried the process a stage farther by including large portions of the prose with a popular edition of the poems.

As all this material became available, men began to realize that Donne was a master of language both in verse and prose. There is a vital energy which makes his words memorable: 'A bracelet of bright hair about the bone', or '... all Divinity Is love or wonder'—these are winged arrows which stick fast in the mind. Prose is less terse, less arresting, but Donne has many sentences which can hardly be forgotten. 'Our life is a warfare; God would not chuse Cowards.' 'And therefore never send to know for whom the *bell* tolls; It tolls for *thee*.' Side by side with these brief pregnant phrases there are images of curious felicity. 'No Man is an Iland, intire of it selfe; every man is a peece of the *Continent*, a part of the *maine*; if a *Clod* bee washed away by the *Sea*, *Europe* is the lesse, as well as if a Promontorie were. . . . Any Mans *death* diminishes *me*, because I am involved in *Mankinde*.' Of the everlasting day of eternity he writes:

'*Methusalem*, with all his hundreds of yeares, was but a Mushrome of a nights growth, to this day, And all the foure Monarchies, with all their thousands of yeares, And all the powerfull Kings, and all the beautifull Queenes of this world, were but as a bed of flowers, some gathered at six, some at seaven, some at eight, All in one Morning, in respect of this Day.'

Again,

'like a Lily in Paradise, out of red earth, I shall see my soule rise out of his blade, in a candor, and in an innocence, contracted there, acceptable in the sight of his Father.'

Any man who can speak like this is sure of an audience, in the twentieth century as well as in the seventeenth. And Donne is not merely a maker of verbal spells; he has something to say. It is true that much of his prose is occupied with outworn controversies, and lumber inherited from the Fathers and the Schoolmen. *Pseudo-Martyr* is a striking example of an almost unreadable book written by a man of genius. Yet in the *Essays in Divinity*, the *Devotions*, and the *Sermons*, though we may become fatigued at times, we are conscious throughout of a live mind dealing with problems of fundamental importance. When he chooses, he can go straight to the point. 'Even humility itself is a pride, if we think it to be our own', 'Nothing hinders our owne salvation more than to deny it to all but our selves', 'Death comes equally to us all, and it makes us all equall when it comes.'

The present volume is concerned chiefly with the prose works, but in estimating their value it is impossible to separate them entirely from Donne's poetry. Much of their value lies in the fact that they are the expression in another medium of the personality of a great poet. But their interest is not simply that of a commentary on the *Poems*. They are complementary, not merely supplementary; in them Donne achieved the same sort of success as in his poetry—that is to say, the *Sermons*, like the *Songs and Sonnets* and the *Second Anniversary*, are great, though not flawless, works of art. In fact, the prose works present a curious parallel to the *Poems* in their successes and failures, their power of rising to the most astounding heights of imagination and their inability to remain for any length of time, not only at such a height—which would hardly be surprising—but even at the level of the ordinary second-class writer. Ben Jonson's criticism of Donne's poetry, 'That he esteemeth John Done the first poet in the world in some things. . . . That Done for not keeping of accent deserved hanging. . . . That Done himself for not being understood would perish', would apply, with the change of a few words, equally to Donne's prose, which produces in most readers exactly the same alternation of wondering delight with extreme exasperation. No single prose work, not even a single sermon, attains the perfection of literary form. There is always some tedious excursus which we would wish away, or some frigid and tasteless conceit which repels our sympathy, even in the finest of Donne's discourses. Yet none of the greatest of our prose-writers—not Browne, nor Bacon, nor Taylor, nor Lamb, nor De Quincey—has ever surpassed him at his best moments. He is at the opposite pole from Andrea del Sarto, 'the faultless painter', or Tennyson's Maud—'Faultily faultless, icily regular, splendidly null, Dead perfection, no more.' He is compact of contradictions—sinner and saint, philosopher and buffoon, the most passionate of lovers, the most cynical of sensualists, with the God and the Devil within him always striving for mastery. It is this that gives him in part his perennial attraction. All men can see in him some aspect of their own nature, and can sympathize with one or other of his moods. Moreover, the study of his works reveals to us a living thing, a personality not yet rigid and fixed, but always changing, expanding, struggling, growing gradually in love and purity and devotion, but retaining all the force of a passionate energy which cannot be content to flow in the recognized channels—poetic, literary, ecclesiastic—of the day, but must fashion for itself new ways of expression and find new outlets, however tortuous, however difficult.

This complex nature of Donne's genius has been recognized by most of the later critics. Rupert Brooke alluded to it in the characteristically brilliant review of Grierson's edition which he contributed to the *Nation* in 1913:

'In his [Donne's] own words he "loved to be subtle to plague himself". He would startle the soul from her lair with unthinkable paradoxes, and pursue her, with laughter and tears, along all the difficult coasts between sense and madness. At one moment he knows the most unworldly ecstasy of the communion of two souls:

> And whilst our souls negotiate there,
> We like sepulchral statues lay,
> All day the same our postures were,
> And we said nothing all the day.

At another he contemplates the consummation of human love within the black, bright walls of a flea. He compares his lady to a primrose, an angel, the number five, Mary Magdalen, a gingerbread figure, Newfoundland, the stationary leg of a compass, God. And one can never doubt his sincerity. . . .'[1]

Gosse ends his account of Donne's life with the words:

'And so we leave him, surely the most undulating, the most diverse of human beings, as Montaigne would say. Splendid and obscure he was, in the extreme versatility and passion, the profoundity, the saintliness, the mystery of his inscrutable character. No one, in the history of English Literature, as it seems to me, is so difficult to realise, so impossible to measure, in the vast curves of his extraordinary and contradictory features. Of his life, of his experiences, of his opinions, we know more now than it has been vouchsafed to us to know of any other of the great Elizabethan and Jacobean galaxy of writers, and yet how little we fathom his contradictions, how little we can account for his impulses and his limitations. Even those of us who have for years made his least adventures the subject of close and eager investigation must admit at last that he eludes us. He was not the crystal-hearted saint that Walton adored and exalted. He was not the crafty and redoubtable courtier whom the recusants suspected. He was not the prophet of the intricacies of fleshly feeling whom the young poets looked up to and worshipped. He was none of these, or all of these, or more. What was he? It is impossible to say, for, with all his superficial expansion, his secret died with him. We are tempted to declare that of all great men he is the one of whom least is essentially known. Is not this, perhaps, the secret of his perennial fascination?'[2]

It is difficult, however, to be satisfied with any view of Donne's character, which, while admitting the contradictions in his nature, makes no attempt to resolve them. And a close study of his works, prose as well as poetry, makes it

[1] *Nation*, xii. 825.
[2] Gosse, *Life and Letters of John Donne*, ii. 290–1.

clear that his was no case of dual personality. He was not a Jekyll–Hyde in Jacobean dress, except in the sense that the allegory is true of all of us. It was not one personality who wrote the cynical *Elegies* or *Paradoxes and Problems*, and another who during the same years 'began seriously to survey and consider the body of divinity, as it was then controverted betwixt the Reformed and the Roman Church', and a little later embodied the results of his reading in the learned and temperate *Pseudo-Martyr*. Nothing in Donne's works is more noticeable than the intensely individual and personal flavour which marks all he produced. There is an essential unity underlying the flagrant and manifold contradictions of his temperament.

A distinction has sometimes been drawn between his poetry and his prose. It has been claimed that the poems were the work of 'Jack Donne', and the sermons and devotions that of the grave Dean of St. Paul's. This, however, is merely a rough classification, intended to describe the majority of the writings in each division. It cannot be pressed far, as any examination of Donne's work will prove that there are many poems—the third *Satire*, *La Corona*, the *Litany*, the *Holy Sonnets*—which belong to the thinker and the theologian, while there are prose works—the *Paradoxes and Problems*, or even *Ignatius his Conclave*—which belong to the witty and dissolute Jack Donne.

Even a division of his life into periods, to which different classes of work can be assigned, does not altogether remove the difficulty, for these contradictory elements often exist side by side in a single poem or prose work, and on the other hand there is a close connexion between the earlier and the later work, so that the third *Satire* (written when Donne was in the twenties) anticipates certain passages in the *Essays in Divinity* and the *Sermons*, and the conceits of the *Songs and Sonnets* reappear in the *Hymn to God, my God, in my sickness*, written late in his life. Donne's conversion did not mark a sharp distinction between two periods, each with its appropriate quota of prose and poetry. To say this is not to deny the reality or the importance of the change. A true development can be traced in Donne's character and inner life. From the theological point of view the Dean of St. Paul's was actually 'a new creature'. The unregenerate Jack Donne could never have written the wonderful Easter sermon with its rapture of mystical contemplation, nor the last hymns with their yearning penitence and devotion. But Donne's conversion was not a lightning transformation. It represented on one side the culmination of a process which had begun in childhood and had lasted nearly forty years, and on the other it was the starting-point of another long process of purification and sanctification which continued till his death. Thus there is a psychological unity in Donne's career. Through all his conflicting moods we can trace a thread of purpose which binds together his youth, manhood, and later years. He was always the seeker, who pursued Truth from the early days when he depicted her standing 'on a huge hill, Cragged and steep', forcing her lovers to wind backwards and forwards in their efforts to reach her,[1] to the storm-tossed middle years when he cried:

> Thirst for that time, O my insatiate soule,
> And serve thy thirst, with Gods safe-sealing Bowle.
> . . . Forget this rotten world; And unto thee
> Let thine owne times as an old storie bee.[2]

He was still seeking, when a few years later he implored:

> Show me deare Christ, thy spouse, so bright and clear.
> What! is it She, which on the other shore
> Goes richly painted? or which rob'd and tore
> Laments and mournes in Germany and here?[3]

Even in his last days, when he could say with 'a modest assurance' that he doubted not of his own salvation, he was still the seeker, though now one with a joyous sight of his goal. 'Not as though I had already attained' was his motto, as it was St. Paul's, and on his death-bed he reached forward earnestly to what lay before him, saying in his last hour, 'I were miserable if I might not die', and repeating again and again, 'Thy kingdom come, Thy will be done.'

[1] *Third Satire* (Grierson, *Poems*, i. 157).
[2] *Second Anniversary* (ibid. 252).
[3] *Holy Sonnet XVIII* (ibid. 330).

This constant search for a Truth which was also Beauty and Goodness is the explanation of much that is puzzling in Donne's life. He began the quest, as Walton tells us, in early youth, but for a time the senses led him astray. Baffled and disappointed, he refused to follow the poetical conventions of the day and to praise in glowing sonnets a beauty which had proved treacherous and unsatisfying. He flung bitter gibes at women and at himself:

> I am two fooles, I know,
> For loving, and for saying so
> In whining Poetry;[1]

> Now thou hast lov'd me one whole day,
> To morrow when thou leav'st, what wilt thou say?
> Wilt thou then Antedate some new made vow?[2]

He vented the same disappointment in the cynical *Paradoxes*, but he did not cease his search. Then in his love for his wife part of his nature found satisfaction, but the intellect continued its eager quest, seeking truth in the folios of the controversialists, while his ambition led him to try one profession after another, only to be disappointed in each. His restless energy made him study everything in turn—law, politics, medicine, theology, poetry—but all withered at his touch. The fruit of the tree of the knowledge of good and evil was but an apple of Sodom to his taste.

It is characteristic of the man that the most successful of the poems of his middle period are not to be found among the verses which he addressed to brilliant courtly patronesses like the Countess of Bedford or Lady Huntingdon, but in the two *Anniversaries* which he composed on the death of Elizabeth Drury, a girl of fifteen, whom he had never seen. The best commentary on these is Donne's own remark, quoted in Ben Jonson's *Conversations*. Jonson declared 'That Dones Anniversarie was profane and full of Blasphemies: that he told Mr. Donne, if it had been written of the Virgin Marie it had been something; to which he

[1] *The triple Foole* (ibid. 16).
[2] *Woman's constancy* (ibid. 9).

answered that he described the Idea of a Woman, and not as she was.' It was ideas, not forms or colours or sounds, that excited Donne's imagination and fired his fancy. He was the most intellectual of poets, and the least dependent on his sense-impressions.

Donne's contemporaries were fully aware of the fact that his conversion did not change the habit of his mind, but provided new channels into which his passionate energy could flow. Chudleigh observed this in his *Elegy* on Donne:

> He kept his loves, but not his objects; wit
> Hee did not banish, but transplanted it,
> Taught it his place and use, and brought it home
> To Pietie, which it doth best become.[1]

Thomas Carew's epitaph expresses a similar thought:

> Here lies a King, that rul'd as hee thought fit
> The universall Monarchy of wit;
> Here lies two Flamens, and both those, the best,
> Apollo's first, at last, the true Gods Priest.[2]

This continuity of purpose saves Donne's later life from the dullness which sometimes overtakes the old age of poets who in their youth were passionate enough, but in whom the fires have early died down. The latter years of Wordsworth, peaceful and honourable as they were, seem to many to belong to a different being from the ardent revolutionary of the seventeen-nineties. But the divine fire burned as intensely, and more purely, in Donne's *Holy Sonnets* as in the *Songs and Sonnets* of his youth. He went on struggling, aspiring, craving for a vision of Truth and Beauty and Goodness which should satisfy his desire and re-make him in its own image. The ascent was not uninterrupted; there were falls and mistakes on the way. Long after his outward life had become pure and regular, he was tormented by the impurity of his own imagination, recurring to the forbidden

[1] *On Dr. John Donne* (Grierson, i. 394). Quoted with approval by Izaak Walton in his *Life of Dr. John Donne* (1670), p. 39.

[2] *An Elegie upon the death of the Deane of Pauls, Dr. John Donne* (Grierson, i. 380).

pleasures of earlier years. As he grew in holiness, sin became more distasteful to him, and the blackness of his own heart appalled him, so that there were times when he doubted of his share in the mercy of God. The constitutional melancholy and morbidity which had marked him from his youth distracted him also in his later years. He was like Bunyan's Christian in the Valley of the Shadow of Death,[1] tormented by evil suggestions of which he could not discern the origin. The agony of his mind is reflected in the prayers in the *Essays in Divinity*, in the *Devotions*, even in certain parts of the *Sermons*. The terrible passage on damnation which has been so often quoted derives its force not from any gloating of Donne's mind over the tortures of others but from the half-expressed fear that it may be his own fate which he is describing.[2] He sees the essence of Hell in no physical or material torments but in the agony of a soul cast out from the presence of God, which might have been its life and light.

Yet these dark moments did not last. Donne pressed on, in spite of fears and forebodings, to the goal of his pilgrimage. We learn from many passages that he found inexpressible

[1] *Pilgrim's Progress.* The whole passage might be quoted as an almost exact description of certain periods of Donne's life: 'When he sought, in the dark, to shun the ditch on the one hand, he was ready to tip over into the mire on the other; also when he sought to escape the mire, without great carefulness he would be ready to fall into the ditch. Thus he went on, and I heard him here sigh bitterly; for, besides the dangers mentioned above, the pathway was here so dark, that ofttimes, when he lift up his foot to set forward, he knew not where or upon what he should set it next. . . . Also he heard doleful voices, and rushings to and fro, so that sometimes he thought he should be torn in pieces, or trodden down like mire in the streets. . . . I took notice that now poor Christian was so confounded, that he did not know his own voice; and thus I perceived it. Just when he was come over against the mouth of the burning pit, one of the wicked ones got behind him, and stepped up softly to him, and whisperingly suggested many grievous blasphemies to him, which he verily thought had proceeded from his own mind.'

[2] This is made clearer by the sentences which follow: 'Especially to us, for as the perpetuall losse of that is most heavy, with which we have been best acquainted, and to which wee have been most accustomed; so shall this damnation, which consists in the losse of the sight and presence of God, be heavier to us then others, because God hath so graciously, and so evidently, and so diversly appeared to us.' *LXXX Sermons*, 76. 777.

comfort for his own soul in ministering the consolations of God to others. His experience resembled that of Bunyan, who relates that he was often weighed down to despair by the thought of his own sins till he entered the pulpit, and then the load was lifted from his heart as he preached the message of God to repentant sinners.[1]

The marks of conflict are still visible at the close of Donne's life. *Death's Duel*, his last sermon, is a strange mingling of intense devotion to Christ with a gloomy morbidity of fancy which delights in picturing the physical corruption of the body, with the accompaniment of worms and dust. The effigy on his monument, which was saved from the fire which destroyed old St. Paul's, was fashioned according to his own instructions from a drawing made of him in his shroud during his last illness, and in its horrible suggestion of mortality contrasts curiously enough with the hopeful note of the epitaph, also inscribed by Donne's own orders, which in its last lines speaks of him as 'though set in dust', yet 'looking towards Him Whose name is the Rising'.[2]

At the very end the clouds seem to have rolled away from Donne's troubled soul. Walton was confident 'that he had now a modest assurance that his prayers were then heard, and his petition granted'. To the friends who stood around his bedside it seemed that his soul had already 'some Revelation of the Beatifical Vision', as he exclaimed 'I were miserable if I might not die', and then repeated over and over again 'Thy Kingdom come, Thy Will be done'. There is no sign of doubt or fear in the poem written on his death-bed, the *Hymn to God my God, in my sickness*, though in it his agile fancy still delights in paradoxes and conceits. He is tuning his instrument at the door of the room where he will be part of God's music in the choir of saints for evermore.

1 Bunyan, *Grace Abounding*, p. 84 (Cambridge English Classics, ed. 1907).

2 *Hic licet in occiduo cinere aspicit eum*
Cujus nomen est Oriens.

In a letter to Sir Robert Ker (Tobie Mathew Collection, p. 305) Donne had used this phrase of Christ, *Oriens nomen ejus*, quoting the Vulgate rendering of Zechariah, vi. 12. For a full description of the monument, and the circumstances under which the drawing was made, see Walton, *Life* (1670), pp. 75, 76.

He thinks that Christ's cross and Adam's tree grew once in the same place, and he prays that, as he shares in the mortality of the first Adam, so the second Adam's blood may wash his soul. The Tree of the Knowledge of Good and Evil has become for him at last the Tree of Life, whose leaves are for the healing of the nations.

II

SKETCH OF DONNE'S LIFE

THE study of the life-history of a writer like Donne, whose personality is reflected so clearly in his work, is a necessary preliminary to a right understanding of the work itself. He stands at the opposite pole from a dramatist like Shakespeare, whose individuality is merged for most readers in that of his creations. An unusually large amount of material for such a study is to be found in Donne's letters,[1] and in the famous *Life of Dr. John Donne* by Donne's personal friend, Izaak Walton, written originally to be prefixed to the 1640 edition of Donne's *LXXX Sermons*, and much enlarged by Walton when it was issued separately in 1658. Dr. Augustus Jessopp used some of this material for his short biography of Donne in the 'Leaders of Religion' series, and it was handled at much greater length, and supplemented from various manuscript sources, in Sir Edmund Gosse's *Life and Letters of John Donne* (1899). More recently fresh light has been thrown on the facts of Donne's life in articles by H. W. Garrod, F. P. Wilson, John Sparrow, I. A. Shapiro, and R. E. Bennett. In the succeeding pages I have tried to lay stress on those aspects of Donne's life which are particularly important in connexion with his prose works, and would refer readers to the above-mentioned books for a fuller treatment of his career as a whole.

John Donne was born in London in the latter half of 1571 or in the first half of 1572. From a document discovered by F. P. Wilson[2] in the Guildhall Records, we know that on 19 June 1593 Donne was 'of full age of xxi years and upwards'. This makes it certain that he was born before 19 June 1572. Walton was therefore in error in stating that

[1] *Letters to Severall Persons of Honour written by John Donne*, edited by his son, 1651. See also Sir Tobie Mathew's *Collection of Letters* (published 1660), which contains a number of Donne's letters.

[2] 'Notes on the Early Life of John Donne', *Review of English Studies*, iii. 276–7.

he was born in 1573. The engraving by William Marshall of Donne as a young man bears the date 'Anno Dni 1591. Aetatis suae 18.' This would imply that Donne was born either in 1572 or 1573. On the engraving by Pieter Lombart he is said to have been 'Anno Ætatis suae 59' when he died on 31 March 1631, and this would give us a birth-date in 1571 or the first half of 1572. H. W. Garrod has brought forward some further evidence[1] which may mean that Donne was born on 16 August 1571, but I cannot feel that it is altogether conclusive.[2]

Donne's father was a prosperous tradesman who became Warden of the Ironmongers' Company in 1574. According to Walton he was 'lineally descended from a very ancient family in Wales'—perhaps the Dwnns of Dwynn in Radnorshire, but more probably the Dwnns of Kidwelly.[3] Donne came, however, of a distinguished family on his mother's side. She was the daughter of John Heywood, epigrammatist and interlude-writer, and his wife Joan, the sister of William Rastell, the famous jurist, who was the son of John Rastell, controversialist and interlude-writer. Rastell's wife was Elizabeth, sister of Sir Thomas More, and thus Donne was connected with some of the staunchest Roman Catholic families in England. The Mores, Rastells, and Heywoods had all suffered for their faith, and Donne was justified in the claim which he put forward in his *Pseudo-Martyr* that no family 'which is not of farre larger extent and greater branches, hath endured and suffered more in their persons and fortunes, for obeying the teachers of Romane Doctrine'.[4]

Donne's father died in 1575/6. Walton says that 'his mother and those to whose care he was committed were watchful to improve his knowledge, and to that end appointed him

[1] *Times Literary Supplement*, 30 Dec. 1944.

[2] See W. Milgate, 'The Date of Donne's Birth', *N. and Q.*, 16 Nov. 1946.

[3] Gosse, *Life and Letters of John Donne*, i. 4, 5. Gosse observes that Donne, when Dean of St. Paul's, bore as his arms, 'a wolf salient, and a chief argent', a fact which might be adduced in support of his descent from the Duns or Dwnns of Kidwelly in Carmarthenshire, who use the same arms.

[4] *Pseudo-Martyr*, Sig. ¶ 1.

tutors both in the mathematics,[1] and in all the other liberal sciences, to attend him. But with these arts they were advised to instil into him particular principles of the Romish Church; of which those tutors professed, though secretly, themselves to be members.' In 1581 Mrs. Donne's brother, Jasper Heywood, an Oxford scholar, who had been obliged, soon after Elizabeth's accession, to resign his Fellowship at All Souls and retire to the Continent, returned to England as head of the Jesuit mission. He was a clever but eccentric man, who in his Oxford days had translated three of Seneca's tragedies into English verse,[2] and afterwards had taught philosophy and theology in the Jesuit colleges at Rome and Dillingen. His behaviour on this mission was foolishly ostentatious, and he quarrelled with some of the English priests. He was recalled and set out for France, but the boat in which he sailed was driven back to the English coast by a storm, and he and his companions were seized by the civil authorities and imprisoned. Five of Heywood's party were executed, but he himself was released in January 1584/5, after he had spent seventeen months in prison, and was exiled on pain of death if he should set foot in England again.

Donne's mother remained an ardent Roman Catholic all her life. His younger brother, Henry, died in 1593, of a fever contracted in the prison into which he was thrown for having concealed in his room a secular priest called Harrington. Thus the atmosphere in which Donne grew up was one of persecution and intrigue. In later life he suggested that one of the causes of his own morbid inclination to suicide might have been the fact that he had his 'first breeding and conversation with men of a suppressed and afflicted Religion, accustomed to the despite of death, and hungry of an imagin'd Martyrdome'.[3] The influence of Donne's early

[1] To this early training we probably owe the large use which Donne makes of geometrical imagery in his poems (e.g. *A Valediction: forbidding Mourning*, *Upon the translation of the Psalms*).

[2] His translation of Seneca's *Troades* (or *Troas*, as the name appears on Heywood's title-page) was published in 1559, that of *Thyestes* in 1560, and of *Hercules Furens* in 1561.

[3] *Biathanatos*, p. 17.

training persisted all through his life. Although he soon rejected certain dogmas of the Roman Church and later attacked the Jesuits with particular vigour, his mind always showed the marks of the school of thought in which it had been formed. He remained a disciple of the philosophy of St. Augustine and St. Thomas Aquinas, both of whom he constantly quoted in the sermons of his later years.

In 1584 Donne was sent to Hart Hall, Oxford. According to Walton he stayed there for three years, and was then transferred to Cambridge, where he spent another three years, but took no degree at either university, owing to religious difficulty about the oath required at graduation. He was admitted as a law student at Thavies Inn, London, not later than May 1591, and was transferred to Lincoln's Inn on 6 May 1592.[1] The records show that he was in London at various dates between 1592 and November 1594.

Walton tells us that at this time Donne, though naturally inclined to the religion of his 'dear and pious parents', had as yet 'betrothed himself to no religion that might give him any other denomination than a Christian', and that he soon began seriously to study the points at issue between the Roman and Anglican communions. The result was that Donne abandoned the Roman Church, but it was some years before we find him as a convinced Anglican. Gosse's statement of the case is probably correct:

> 'As soon as Donne found himself free from his mother's tutelage, his attachment to the Catholic faith began to decline; presently his indifference to its practice, combined with an intellectual scepticism as to its tenets, led him away from any Christian communion, yet all the while he nourished a kind of dormant religiosity, ready to break forth into flame as soon as the tumult of the senses and the enraged curiosity of life had been somewhat assuaged by experience.'[2]

The years between 1590 and 1601 were largely occupied by Donne in this 'enraged curiosity of life'. Nominally his study was the law, but though he quickly gathered wide

[1] I. A. Shapiro published the results of his detailed study of the Black Books and Admission Registers of Lincoln's Inn in two articles, 'John Donne and Lincoln's Inn 1591–94', in *T.L.S.* 16 and 23 Oct. 1930.

[2] Gosse, i. 27, 28.

and profound legal knowledge, his mind could not rest content within the bounds of his profession.[1] He mastered the 'grounds and use of physic',[2] he was keenly interested in the scientific discoveries of the day, and he studied foreign literature, especially French, Italian, and Spanish.[3] It was not, however, books alone that interested him; it was life itself. We can discern in his poems a feverish craving for sensation and experience. In his lyrics, satires, and elegies he gives us glimpses of his adventures of divers kinds in love intrigues, friendship, and travel.

Walton states that Donne spent 'a convenient time', later altered to 'some years', in Italy and Spain, and that he spent the greater part of his patrimony 'in many and chargeable travels'. There has been much discussion about the date of these travels, which were assigned by Jessopp to the period 1587–90, and by Gosse to 1592–6. John Sparrow has fully examined the evidence available to him, and has decided in favour of the period between November 1594 and June 1596.[4] At any rate, in June 1596 Donne engaged himself for foreign service in the expedition to Cadiz, and he was present at the battle in which the Spanish Fleet was defeated. In the next year he took part in the naval expedition to intercept the Spanish plate-ships off the Azores, and it is to this voyage that we owe the poems of *The Storm* and *The Calm*. They were written to Christopher Brooke, Donne's best friend at Lincoln's Inn, and in them Donne enumerates his reasons for volunteering for this expedition—the hope of prize-money, the desire to escape from 'the queasy pain of being beloved and loving', and the craving to satisfy the adventurous 'thirst of honour or fair death'.[5]

[1] See Donne's letter to Sir H. Goodyer: '. . . I begun early, when I understood the study of our laws: but was diverted by the worst voluptuousnes, which is an Hydroptique immoderate desire of humane learning and languages.' *Letters* (1651), p. 51.

[2] Walton, *An Elegie upon Dr. Donne*, l. 46 (Grierson, i. 377). See also *Letters* (1651), pp. 14, 15.

[3] A detailed account of these studies will be found *infra*, chap. iii.

[4] 'The Date of Donne's Travels', in *A Garland for John Donne*, pp. 123–51. Professor R. C. Bald has lately discovered some new facts which may, when published, modify Sparrow's conclusions.

[5] Grierson, i. 179.

It is possible, but not certain, that for a few months at the beginning of 1598 Donne was employed by Cecil as a confidential messenger in the course of his negotiations with Henri IV of France.[1] Early in 1598 Donne became secretary to Sir Thomas Egerton, the Lord Keeper, afterwards Lord Chancellor Ellesmere, with whom he remained for almost four years.

A large number of Donne's secular poems and also most of his prose *Paradoxes and Problems* belong to the years between 1590 and 1601,[2] though it is impossible to date them with any certainty. They mirror for us Donne's inner life at this period with amazing clearness. One of the most striking features of Donne's mind was its sincerity, which amounts at times to an almost brutal candour; and another was its ingenuity, delighting perpetually in paradox and metaphor, in strained allusion and far-fetched conceit. Both these characteristics are evident in the *Paradoxes and Problems* and in the poems, which are full of the so-called metaphysical 'wit' which was to become so popular in the early seventeenth century, and yet have an extraordinary directness, laying bare before us the recesses of Donne's heart cynically unabashed. Some are frankly sensual, in places immoral, and nearly all of them are permeated with arrogant cynicism. Donne was a rebel against the Petrarchan convention which had lingered on in Elizabethan poetry, and had made of every woman a goddess, fair and cold, whose lover served her in trembling adoration. No poet has derided more than Donne the inconstancy, the shallowness of women. He cries

at their best
Sweetnesse and wit, they'are but *Mummy*, possest.[3]

[1] See the articles by Sir Edmund Chambers and Sir Herbert Grierson in *Modern Language Review*, v. 492; vi. 153, 397, and Grierson, *Poems*, ii. 141. Sparrow (op. cit. 125–7) sums up the results of their discussion.

[2] Ben Jonson affirmed that Donne wrote 'all his best pieces (of poetry) ere he was twenty-five years old'. See his *Conversations with Drummond of Hawthornden*, § 7.

[3] *Loves Alchymie* (Grierson, i. 40).

Or again:

If thou beest borne to strange sights,
  Things invisible to see,
Ride ten thousand daies and nights,
  Till age snow white haires on thee,
Thou, when thou retorn'st, wilt tell mee
All strange wonders that befell thee,
    And sweare
    No where
Lives a woman true, and faire.

If thou find'st one, let mee know,
Such a Pilgrimage were sweet;
Yet doe not, I would not goe,
  Though at next doore we might meet,
Though shee were true, when you met her,
  And last, till you write your letter,
    Yet shee
    Will bee
False, ere I come, to two, or three.[1]

Arresting as such poems may be in their cynicism, they have the merit of sincerity, and thus illustrate, on one side of Donne's nature, that search for truth which was characteristic of the man. The old chivalrous ideal had become a mockery by this time, and it had to be dethroned before a new one, truer to the facts of experience, could be set up. And, withal, the true spirit of poetry blows, though in fitful gusts, through the *Songs and Sonnets* and *Elegies* and *Satires*. Here and there are lines and phrases that are unforgettable, such as the beginning of *The Good-morrow*:

I wonder by my troth, what thou, and I
Did, till we lov'd?[2]

or the description of the opened grave and the skeleton that is found with

A bracelet of bright haire about the bone.[3]

Passion and melancholy are the keynotes of this poetry; Love and Death are the two absorbing themes to which

[1] Grierson, i. 8. [2] Ibid. 7. [3] Ibid. 62.

Donne continually recurs. Underneath this varied, exciting, riotous outward life, there was a deep undercurrent of melancholy in Donne. The thought of death haunted him—death who turns this warm flesh, so capable of exquisite sensation, into a mere handful of dust, death whose dark shadow falls always athwart the lighted vista of love and happiness.

To the year 1601 belongs a longer and more ambitious poem, *The Progress of the Soul*, which was never completed. It is based on the Pythagorean theory of metempsychosis, which Donne extends to the vegetable world as well as the animal. The poem follows the history of the soul of the apple which Eve plucked, and according to Ben Jonson Donne intended to trace this soul, after it had inhabited certain vegetable and animal forms, to its abode 'in all the bodies of the Hereticks from the soul of Cain', and to have left it in the body of Calvin.[1] The poem itself indicates, however, that at one time Donne intended Queen Elizabeth to be the last recipient of this strange guest, but in the five hundred lines which he composed he carried the action no farther than finding the soul a human habitation within Siphatecia, Adam's daughter and Cain's wife, so that, as Gosse remarks, 'we have not yet advanced out of sight of the Garden of Eden, and at this rate of progress it would have taken millions of verses to bring us safely down to Queen Elizabeth.'[2]

De Quincey is the solitary critic of note who has praised this poem. 'Massy diamonds compose the very substance of his poem on the Metempsychosis, thoughts and descriptions which have the fervent and gloomy sublimity of Ezekiel or Aeschylus, whilst a diamond dust of rhetorical brilliancies is strewed over the whole of his occasional verses and his prose.'[3] Most readers, however, will agree with Grierson: 'In no poem is the least attractive side of Donne's mind so clearly revealed, that aspect of his wit which to some readers is more repellent, more fatal to his claim to be a poet, than too subtle ingenuity or misplaced erudition—the vein of sheer

[1] Ben Jonson, *Conversations with Drummond of Hawthornden*, § 8.

[2] Gosse, i. 138.

[3] De Quincey (*Works*, ed. Masson, x. 39).

ugliness which runs through his work, presenting details that seem merely and wantonly repulsive.'[1]

Along with his literary pursuits Donne tried to lay the foundations of a political career. I. A. Shapiro[2] has shown that Donne was probably the 'John Dunn, Esquier' who on 1 October 1601 was elected one of the members for Brackley, Northants. Parliament assembled on 27 October and was dissolved on 19 December 1601. Apparently Donne took no part in any debate during the short life of this parliament. Several friends of his were members, such as Richard Martin, Robert Cotton, and also his future father-in-law, Sir George More.

Donne's marriage in December 1601 changed the whole course of his life. Lady Egerton's favourite niece, Ann More, spent much of her time at her aunt's house, and was in fact considered almost as an adopted daughter. When Lady Egerton died in January 1600, Ann remained at York House and managed the establishment, though she was then only sixteen years old. Donne was on terms of considerable intimacy with the Egerton family; Sir Thomas had a great liking for his brilliant young secretary, and always used him 'with much courtesie, appointing him a place at his own Table, to which he esteemed his Company and Discourse a great Ornament'.[3] When Lady Egerton died, Donne and Ann were naturally thrown much together, and since Ann's mother had been dead some years the girl was largely her own mistress. The two fell in love with each other, and their courtship progressed rapidly.

In the autumn of that year, Sir Thomas announced his intention of marrying again, and Ann was recalled to her father's house at Losely, but by this time she and Donne had exchanged 'such faithful promises as never to be violated

[1] Grierson, ii, p. xx.

[2] *T.L.S.*, 10 Mar. 1932, p. 172, 'Was Donne a Member of the 1601 and 1614 Parliaments?' Shapiro points out that Brackley belonged to Ferdinand, fifth Earl of Derby, on whose death in 1594 the manor and borough of Brackley were assigned to Frances, his second daughter. In Oct. 1600 Ferdinand's widow married Egerton, Donne's employer, and in 1601 Egerton's influence would be all-powerful at Brackley.

[3] Walton, *Life* (1670), p. 17.

by either party'. During 1601 Ann came up to town several times, and Donne contrived to meet her in private. At last they decided to tempt fortune by a secret marriage, trusting that when Ann's father, Sir George More, realized that the deed was done, he would bow to the inevitable. They were married in December; Christopher Brooke, Donne's best friend, gave away the bride, and his brother, Samuel, who had only just taken orders, performed the ceremony.

The task of informing Sir George of the marriage was a very delicate one. It was entrusted finally, after numerous hints had only made Sir George angry and suspicious, to the Earl of Northumberland,[1] an eccentric and learned man who had a love for intrigue of all kinds. His intervention was, however, unsuccessful; Sir George, who was a vain man and at this time stood high in the queen's favour, was furiously angry, and not only succeeded in inducing Egerton to dismiss Donne from his service, but also caused Donne and the two Brookes to be arrested and thrown into prison on the charge of breaking the civil and the canon law by marrying a girl without her father's consent. There followed a wretched period of uncertainty for Donne. Sir George tried to secure a legal decree rendering the marriage null and void, but Donne's penitence and entreaties at last caused him to withdraw his opposition, and after some months the marriage was confirmed by the ecclesiastical courts, and in process of time Ann, who had been kept in durance at her father's house, was allowed to join her husband.

Their prospects, however, were not bright. Donne's reckless living had squandered most of his property and involved him in heavy debts; Sir George refused to give his daughter anything more substantial than his blessing: Donne had lost his post as the Lord Keeper's secretary, and though Sir George, now that his anger was appeased, besought his brother-in-law to take back the culprit, Egerton only answered that it was at Sir George's request that he had discharged Donne, and sorry as he had been to part with his

[1] Dr. John Sampson suggests that George Gerrard, who was a close friend of Donne's, may have formed the link between Donne and the Earl (*Essays and Studies*, vii. 94).

brilliant secretary, 'yet it was inconsistent with his place and credit, to discharge and re-admit servants at the request of passionate petitioners'.

For some time Sir Francis Woolley, a kinsman of Ann's and a friend of Donne's, gave them a home at his own house. After a while Donne rented a small house at Mitcham and divided his time between it and rooms in the Strand, where he collected material from canon law and the Fathers for the use of Thomas Morton, afterwards Bishop of Durham, who was then engaged in controversy with the Roman party.

Donne's letters give us a vivid picture of his troubles at this time.[1] He and his wife had both been used to ease and comfort; now they were to a certain extent dependent on the charity of friends, and as children were born to them in rapid succession it became increasingly difficult to make both ends meet. The house at Mitcham was small and damp.

[1] 'I write from the fire side in my Parler, and in the noise of three gamesome children; and by the side of her, whom because I have transplanted into a wretched fortune, I must labour to disguise that from her by all such honest devices, as giving her my company, and discourse, therefore I steal from her, all the time which I give this Letter, and it is therefore that I take so short a list, and gallop so fast over it.' *Letters* (1651), pp. 137, 138.

'Sir you would pity me if you saw me write, and therefore will pardon me if I write no more: my pain hath drawn my head so much awry, and holds it so, that mine eie cannot follow mine hand: I receive you therefore into my prayers, with mine own weary soul, and commend myself to yours.' Ibid., pp. 36, 37.

'It is (I cannot say the waightyest, but truly) the saddest lucubration and nights passage that ever I had. For it exercised those hours, which, with extreme danger of her, whom I should hardly have abstained from recompensing for her company in this world, with accompanying her out of it, encreased my poor family with a son.' Ibid., p. 147.

'I have occasion to sit late some nights in my study, (which your books make a prety library) and now I finde that that room hath a wholesome emblematique use: for having under it a vault, I make that promise me, that I shall die reading, since my book and a grave are so near. But it hath another as unwholesome, that by raw vapors rising from thence, (for I can impute it to nothing else) I have contracted a sicknesse which I cannot name nor describe. For it hath so much of a continuall Cramp, that it wrests the sinews, so much of a Tetane, that it withdraws and puls the mouth, and so much of the Gout, (which they whose counsell I use, say it is) that it is not like to be cured, though I am too hasty in three days to pronounce it.' Ibid., pp. 31, 32.

Donne suffered from frequent illness, and heads some of his letters 'from my hospital at Mitcham'.

There came at last a chance of escape from these straitened circumstances. In 1607 Morton was made Dean of Gloucester, and on his preferment he at once sought to help Donne out of these difficulties. He suggested that Donne should take orders, promising to give him a comfortable benefice. Donne was given three days to consider the proposal, and at the end of that time he refused it in words to this effect, as reported by Morton himself:[1]

'My most worthy and most deare friend . . . my refusall is not for that I think my self too good for that calling, for which Kings, if they think so, are not good enough: nor for that my education and learning, though not eminent, may not, being assisted with Gods grace and humility, render me in some measure fit for it: but I dare make so dear a friend as you are my Confessor; some irregularities of my life, have been so visible to some men, that though I have, I thank God, made my peace with him by penitentiall resolutions against them, and by the assistance of his grace banish'd them my affections; yet this, which God knows to be so, is not so visible to man, as to free me from their censures, and it may be that sacred calling from a dishonour. And besides, whereas it is determined by the best of *Casuists* that *Gods glory should be the first end, and a maintenance the second motive to embrace that calling;* and though that each man may propose to himself both together; yet the first may not be put last without a violation of conscience, which he that searches the heart will judge. And truly my present condition is such, that if I ask my own conscience whether it be reconcilable to that rule, it is at this time so perplexed about it, that I can neither give myself nor you an answer. . . .'

Gosse points out that the wording of this speech has not the peculiar ring of Donne's style, but no doubt need therefore be thrown on the general trustworthiness of the narrative. The speeches which Walton records are clearly not reported verbatim, but represent the general substance of Donne's conversations reproduced in Walton's own phrases, though the use of the first person is retained throughout.

[1] The account of this incident did not appear in Walton's first draft of his *Life of Donne*, prefixed to the *LXXX Sermons* of 1640. Walton added it in the 1658 edition, stating that he had received the narrative from Morton himself, who was then the 'most learned and laborious Bishop of Durham'.

Gosse thinks Donne's refusal of Morton's offer so extraordinary that it can only be explained by a lingering attachment to the Roman Church.[1] This was probably one of the factors which led Donne to decline the offer, but in a mind so complex as Donne's, there must have been a number of motives at work. Doubtless, his lingering hope of secular promotion was another factor, and this must be coupled with his own sense of unworthiness, and of a lack of vocation for the ministry.

On this subject some additional information can be given from a little-known account of Morton entitled 'The Life of Dr. Thomas Morton, Late Bishop of Duresme. Begun by R. B. Secretary to his Lordship. And Finished by J. N. D.D. his Lordships Chaplain. York. . . . 1669.'

R. B.'s full name is given in the Bodleian Catalogue as Richard Baddily.[2] He must not be confounded with the 'R. B.' who wrote an elegy on Donne, and who has been identified as Richard Busby, the famous headmaster of Westminster.[3] In the preface (sig. A 5 verso) to this *Life* of Morton he states that he had been Morton's 'Servant and Secretary for the space of 50 years', and that having lost his employment during the Commonwealth, he thought that he could not better bestow some part of his 'still-decaying old Age' than in recollecting and laying together some such memorable particulars as he had observed during his attendance on Bishop Morton. He sent these recollections to Morton himself, wishing to attempt nothing of that kind without his liking and approbation. 'And to his Lordship it was committed, and with him left; but by him the less minded, for that his thoughts were *upwards*, and Heavenly fixed. And here (as it seemeth) Dr. *Barwick*, who then and

[1] Gosse, i. 161, 162.

[2] In 1621 a certain 'Ryc. Baddeley' dedicated Molle's translation of the *Walking Librarie* of Camerarius 'To the Right Honorable and Reuerend Father in God Iohn Lo. Bishop of Lincolne Elect'. He must be distinguished from the R. B. (Richard Badiley) 'a seaman of the Trinity House' who wrote *The Seaman Undeceived*. J. N. was Dr. Joseph Naylor, Prebendary of Durham and Rector of Sedgfield.

[3] See Dr. John Sampson's article 'A Contemporary Light upon John Donne', *Essays and Studies*, vii. 105.

there attended on his Lordship, as Chaplain, did furnish himselfe with such passages, as (after) he had use of in the Writing of his Life, whereof he could not be better Informed.'

This is a reference to the official biography of Morton by Dean Barwick, which contains a good deal of material found also in R. B.'s *Life*. Barwick, however, has nothing to say about Donne, whereas R. B. has a long passage which adds some details to Walton's account.

'For his (i.e. Morton's) Judgement of the due deserts of Learning, take one instance; when he was *Deane of Glocester*, and Mr. *John Donne* had cast himselfe into a Sea of misery, by the marriage of the Daughter of Sir *George Moore* Knight, whereby he was exuted of his Secretaries place under the Lord Chancellor *Egerton*, and had spent most of his own means in the pursuit of his said marriage, whereby he was brought to a low ebb and debility in his Estate; and knowing no wayes, or means whereby he could subsist, Children especially encreasing yearly; then did *Deane Morton* earnestly and seriously move him to take the holy Ministery on him, whereby the better to support and maintain that Charge; and for his better incouragement, he willingly and freely offered to resigne unto him the *Rectory of Long Marston* in *York-shire* being of the yearly value (*plus minus*) of two hundred pounds *per Annum*; yet to this friendly motion he would not (then) give his assent, but put it by, in hope (as it should seem) of some other preferment, for which he thought himselfe more fit.

'And long after, the said Mr. *Donne*, having grapled with many extremities at home, he passed over into *France*, where he gave himself to the Study of the Laws: And from *Amiens*, (as I remember) he writ a Letter to his alwayes true friend *Deane Morton*, wherein he requested his advice, Whether taking the Degree of a *Doctor* in that Profession of the Laws, it might not be conducible and advantagious unto him to Practice at home in the *Arches London*.[1] Unto whom the *Deane* then returned him answer, That in his Judgement, he thought the Ministry in the Church of God would be safer, and fitter for him: Whereupon he desisted from further prosecution of those Studies.

'For doubtless the holy Spirit had the greatest stroak and power to incline, and draw him to that sacred Profession: For my selfe have long since seen his Picture in a dear friends Chamber of his in *Lincolnes Inne*, all envelloped with a darkish shadow, his face and feature hardly discernable, with this ejaculation and wish written thereon; *Domine*

[1] Gosse (op. cit. i. 304) quotes this sentence from 'And long after . . .', but takes no notice of its context.

illumina tenebras meas: which long after was really accomplished, when (by King *James* his weighty and powerfull perswasions) he took holy Orders at the hands of the right Reverend Father *John* Lord Bishop of *London*, and so became a learned and assiduous Preacher. Whereupon His gracious Majesty King *James* bestowed the *Deanary* of St. *Pauls London* upon him: where what profitable pains he took, and els where, the large Book of his *Sermons*, and other Learned Labors, (which are Published, both before, and after he had been *Dean*) do most sufficiently attest and demonstrate.

'For a Close, concerning this Learned Gentleman, I will add one instance of his ripe and sudden wit, For at one time when Bishop *Morton* gave him a good quantity of Gold (then a usefull token) saying, *Here Mr.* Donne, *take this, Gold is restorative*: He presently answered, *Sir, I doubt I shall never restore it back again*: and I am assured that he never did.'[1]

A little later Donne seems to have fallen into a state of acute depression. From his youth up he had meditated on the idea of suicide as a possible escape from the troubles of life. He now compiled a treatise on this subject, considering most carefully on what grounds suicide was condemned as mortal sin by theologians and casuists, and came to the conclusion that in certain circumstances a man might lawfully kill himself, if the glory of God remained his guiding motive.

This treatise, which Donne entitled *Biathanatos*, was clearly intended at first for publication. Two sections of the preface are entitled, 'Why I make it publique' and 'What reader I desire to have'. He was aware, however, while writing it, of the dangers of misinterpretation to which he laid himself open,[2] and when the book was finished, he went no farther than to send the manuscript to 'some particular friends in both Universities', who answered that there was

[1] pp. 97–104. Donne makes the same play on *restorative* and *restore* in his eleventh *Elegie*, *The Bracelet*, l. 112 (Grierson, i. 100): 'Gold is Restorative, restore it then.'

[2] *Biathanatos*, p. 216. 'I abstained purposely from extending this discourse to particular rules, or instances, both because I dare not professe my self a Maister in so curious a science, and because the limits are obscure, and steepy, and slippery, and narrow, and every errour deadly, except where a competent diligence being fore-used, a mistaking in our conscience may provide an excuse.'

certainly a false thread in the argument, but one not easily to be found.

Emigration also seems to have suggested itself to Donne's mind as a possible way out of his difficulties. A letter written in February 1609 tells us 'News is here none at all, but that John Dunn seeks to be Secretary at Virginia'.[1] Fortunately, a better solution of his difficulties was found. Sir George was induced by friends to pay his daughter's dowry, and Donne, released from his immediate embarrassment, was able to find in literature a means of support. His pen was very active for the next few years. The study of controversial theology, which he had undertaken in his work for Morton, now furnished him with material for a treatise of his own entitled *Pseudo-Martyr*, in which he tried to persuade the Romanists to take the oath of allegiance to the king. It was a learned and temperately worded discussion of the question, and it won the approval of King James.

Pseudo-Martyr was published in 1610, and was followed in 1611 by another controversial work, *Ignatius his Conclave*—a much more bitter, and also much livelier, attack on the Jesuits. Donne was evidently by this time a convinced Anglican, and in *Pseudo-Martyr* he assures us that he had reached this position as the result of much study, accompanied by humility and prayer. To this period belong also a number of sacred poems, such as *The Litany* and *The Cross*. All these writings produce one impression—that Donne's pride and scepticism had now disappeared, but that his faith was chiefly an intellectual matter and awakened no deep emotion. The poems are largely an exercise in ingenuity. They abound in the 'conceits' for which Donne has become famous, and many of these are tasteless in the extreme. There was need for the prayer which Donne uttered in one verse of his *Litany*:

> When wee are mov'd to seeme religious
> Only to vent wit, Lord deliver us.[2]

Yet there had been real and deep advance since the time

[1] *Calendar of Domestic State Papers, James I*, 1609, xliii. 76.
[2] Grierson, i. 345.

of the voluptuous *Elegies* and the cynical *Progress of the Soul.* Trouble had softened Donne's hardness and arrogance, and his love for his wife had purified his nature. Grierson has pointed out that there are three distinct strains in Donne's love-poetry—the turbid, cynical, sensual vein of his earlier period, the calm, philosophical, somewhat artificial note of Platonic friendship in poems addressed to various high-born ladies who were his patronesses, and another strain, both pure and passionate, which pervades a number of poems which we may reasonably conclude were addressed to his wife. There is the famous *Valediction: forbidding Mourning*, written on the eve of a journey abroad, and the less famous but almost more beautiful *Valediction: of Weeping*:

O more then Moone,
Draw not up seas to drowne me in thy spheare,
Weepe me not dead, in thine armes, but forbeare
To teach the sea, what it may doe too soone.[1]

or there is the delightful *Song*:

Sweetest love, I do not goe,
For wearinesse of thee,
Nor in hope the world can show
A fitter Love for mee;

But since that I
Must dye at last, 'tis best,
To use my selfe in jest
Thus by fain'd deaths to dye.[2]

In 1611 Donne wrote and published his *Anatomy of the World*, an elegy on the death of Elizabeth Drury, the fifteen-year-old daughter of Sir Robert Drury of Hawstead, Suffolk. He followed this up in 1612 by *The Second Anniversary*, or the *Progress of the Soul*, a further commemoration of Elizabeth Drury. Sir Robert was now Donne's patron, and in November 1611 he took Donne with him on a journey to the Continent. They returned to England in August 1612, after visiting Amiens, Paris, Spa, and Brussels.

Like most of the other poets of the time, Donne composed

[1] Grierson, i. 39.

[2] Ibid. 18.

a funeral elegy on the death of Prince Henry in the winter of 1612, and he also wrote an epithalamion for the marriage of the Princess Elizabeth to the Elector Palatine in February 1612/13. About this time he placed himself under the protection of the king's favourite, Viscount Rochester, and declared his intention of taking holy orders. In a letter to Rochester, he said: 'For, having obeyed at last, after much debatement within me, the Inspirations (as I hope) of the Spirit of God, and resolved to make my Profession Divinitie: I make account, that I do but tell your Lordship, what God hath told me, which is, That it is in this course, if in any, that my service may be of use to this Church and State.'[1] His purpose, however, was not yet definitely fixed, for in a later letter he asked Sir Robert Ker to use his influence with Rochester to secure for him a diplomatic post.[2]

It has repeatedly been stated that Donne took an active part in the proceedings of the divorce suit which the Countess of Essex brought against her husband in 1613 in order that she might marry Rochester. This statement is due to a confusion of John Donne with Sir Daniel Donne or Dunne, D.C.L., who was then Dean of Arches, and was one of the commissioners who tried the Essex divorce case. In the Harleian Manuscripts (MS. 39, fol. 416–31) there is a 'Discourse written by Sr Daniell Dunn doctor of the civell Lawe of the whole prosecution of the Nullitie betweene the Earle of Essex and his wife the Lady Frauncis Howard'. There is also a paper in the Stowe MSS. Parliamentary Record, no. 95, 'Miscellaneous legal collections' (*Hist. MSS. Comm.*, Report 8, part iii, p. 226), headed 'Dr. Donne's compendium of the whole course of proceeding in the nullity of the marriage of the Earl of Essex and the Lady Frances Howard'. Dr. Donne is here Daniel Donne again; John Donne did not receive the doctorate till 1615. Gosse ascribed both these papers to John Donne, and devoted a number of pages (vol. ii. 19–28) to what he thought to be Donne's complicity in a shameful intrigue, although he described it as 'a subject which the biographer of Donne would willingly

[1] *Letters*, Tobie Mathew Collection, pp. 319, 320.
[2] *Letters* (1651), pp. 297, 298.

pass over in silence'.[1] The error was pointed out in a review of Gosse's book,[2] but it has been frequently repeated.

It is true that Donne, in a letter to a friend,[3] mentioned that 'some appearances have been here of some treatise concerning this nullity, which are said to proceed from Geneva', and remarked that 'it may prove possible that my weak assistance may be of use in this matter', but nothing came of this suggestion. It is also true that Donne composed an epithalamion for the marriage of Rochester, now Earl of Somerset, with the Countess in December 1613, but in this he is no more blameworthy than Ben Jonson or Campion, who wrote similar poems for the same occasion. Nothing was then known of the infamous murder of Sir Thomas Overbury by the countess. Even the saintly Bishop Andrewes had acquiesced in the divorce, and the king and the whole court favoured the marriage. It was not till 1615 that the truth came to light, and Somerset was disgraced and his wife condemned to death, but reprieved.

Shapiro[4] has shown that 'John Dun, esq' is mentioned as the first member for Taunton in a list of members of the Parliament which met on 5 April 1614, and was dissolved on 7 June 1614. It appears from a letter[5] to Goodyer that Donne's constituency was offered him by the Master of the Rolls, Sir Edward Phelips, and that Sir Edward Herbert had also offered him a seat. During the short life of this parliament Donne was a member of several committees, but there is no record of his taking part in a debate. The speedy dissolution of Parliament was a blow to Donne's political hopes. His rather servile expressions of devotion to Somerset failed to procure him any office. According to Walton, the favourite asked King James to bestow on Donne the post of a clerk of the Council who had lately died, but the king refused his request, saying: 'I know Mr. Donne is a learned

[1] Gosse went so far as to conjecture (ii. 87) that Donne's supposed activity in the nullity suit might have hindered his preferment to a bishopric in later years.

[2] *Athenæum*, 11 Nov. 1899, followed by a note in the same, 16 Dec. 1899.

[3] *Letters* (1651), p. 180.

[4] *T.L.S.*, 10 Mar. 1932, p. 172.

[5] *Letters* (1651), pp. 169–71. Shapiro has given the first satisfactory explanation of a passage which had puzzled Donne's biographers.

man, has the abilities of a learned Divine; and will prove a powerful Preacher; and my desire is to prefer him that way.'[1]

Donne had long been intellectually convinced of the truth of Christianity, but he had had no wish to enter the Anglican priesthood, preferring a secular career. In 1612–13 he had considered the possibility of taking Orders, but had decided to make another attempt at securing political office. With the dissolution of Parliament in June 1614 it became clear that these hopes were vain. It was probably during the second half of 1614 that he wrote the little book of *Essays in Divinity*, published in 1651, twenty years after Donne's death, by his son, who described the contents as 'the voluntary sacrifices of severall hours, when he had many debates betwixt God and himself, whether he were worthy, and competently learned to enter into Holy Orders'. This contains sufficient proof of Donne's learning, but in beauty of style it cannot be compared with his later devotional works. It is, however, interesting for the light it throws on Donne's theological position at the date of his entrance into the ministry. The divided state of Christ's Church still troubles him, but it no longer drives him into unbelief, as at the time of his writing the third *Satire*. For himself he has thrown in his lot with the Church of England, but he will not condemn the members of other churches. Rome and Geneva, though they may have erred in different directions, are still branches of the One Church, 'journying to one *Hierusalem*, and directed by one guide, Christ Jesus'. Uniformity in non-essentials no longer seems to him a necessity, but at the same time he longs for unity, that the Church 'discharged of disputations, and misapprehensions, and this defensive warr, might contemplate Christ clearly and uniformely. . . . For then, that *savour of life unto life* might allure and draw those to us, whom our dissentions, more then their own stubbornness with-hold from us.'[2]

It is in the prayers which form an integral part of this little book[3] that we find the clearest expression of Donne's

[1] Walton, *Life* (1670), p. 34. [2] *Essays in Divinity*, pp. 110–12.

[3] Gosse wished to separate the prayers from the rest of the *Essays in Divinity* and to assign them to 1617, when Donne's wife died. He believed

struggles of heart and will, and of the change which was taking place within him. Here are two characteristic passages:

'O keep and defend my tongue from misusing that Name [i.e. the Name of God] in lightnesse, passion, or falshood; and my heart, from mistaking thy Nature, by an inordinate preferring thy Justice before thy Mercy, or advancing this before that. And as, though thy self hadst no beginning thou gavest a beginning to all things in which thou wouldst be served and glorified; so, though this soul of mine, by which I partake thee, begin not now, yet let this minute, O God, this happy minute of thy visitation, be the beginning of her conversion, and shaking away confusion, darknesse, and barrennesse; and let her now produce Creatures, thoughts, words, and deeds agreeable to thee. And let her not produce them, O God, out of any contemplation, or (I cannot say, *Idæa*, but) *Chimera* of my worthinesse, either because I am a man and no worme, and within the pale of thy Church, and not in the wild forrest, and enlightned with some glimerings of Naturall knowledge; but meerely out of Nothing: Nothing pre[e]xistent in her selfe, but by power of thy Divine will and word.'[1]

'O Lord, I most humbly acknowledg and confesse, that I have understood sin, by understanding thy laws and judgments; but have done against thy known and revealed will. Thou hast set up many candlesticks, and kindled many lamps in mee; but I have either blown

that it was not until after this event that Donne's inner life underwent a real change. He stated: 'There is abundant evidence to show that this condition or crisis [i.e. conversion] was passed through by Donne in the winter of 1617; that at that time he became 'converted' in the intense and incandescent sense. At that juncture, under special conditions, and at the age of forty-four, he dedicated himself anew to God with a peculiar violence of devotion, and witnessed the dayspring of a sudden light in his soul' (Gosse, ii. 99). The 'abundant evidence' to which Gosse refers was to be found, according to his own account, in the two sonnet sequences, *La Corona* and the *Holy Sonnets*, and in the prayers in the *Essays in Divinity*, which seemed to him 'to have no connection with the rest' of the book (ibid. ii. 102), and might therefore be assigned to a later period. The *La Corona* sonnets are, however, assigned by Grierson to a much earlier date, 'in or before 1609', and the evidence from the *Holy Sonnets* is derived from Sonnet xvii, which refers specifically to Ann Donne's death. Miss H. L. Gardner in her forthcoming edition of Donne's *Divine Poems* argues that the main body of the *Holy Sonnets* (nos. i–xvi) is earlier than the three detached sonnets (xvii–xix) which are found in the Westmoreland MS. alone. For the vital connexion of the prayer which Gosse quotes, with the rest of the *Essays in Divinity*, see *infra*, chapter ix, pp. 224–5.

[1] *Essays in Divinity* (1651), pp. 77–8.

them out, or carried them to guide me in by and forbidden ways. Thou hast given mee a desire of knowledg, and some meanes to it, and some possession of it; and I have arm'd my self with thy weapons against thee: Yet, O God, have mercy upon me, for thine own sake have mercy upon me. Let not sin and me be able to exceed thee, nor to defraud thee, nor to frustrate thy purposes: But let me, in despite of Me, be of so much use to thy glory, that by thy mercy to my sin, other sinners may see how much sin thou canst pardon.'[1]

Ever afterwards Donne spoke with gratitude of the king, whose advice to enter the ministry led him to the self-examination and struggle of soul which resulted in his dedication to the will of God. 'I date my life from my Ministery', he said in one of his sermons, 'for I received mercy, as I received the Ministery, as the Apostle speaks.'[2] To Charles I, when Prince of Wales, he wrote in 1623: 'In my second Birth, your Highness Royall Father vouchsafed mee his Hand, not onely to sustaine mee in it, but to lead mee to it.'[3] In a letter written long afterwards to a friend these words occur: 'When I sit still and reckon all my old Master's Royall favours to me, I return evermore to that, that he first enclined me to be a Minister.'[4]

Donne was ordained in January 1615, by the Bishop of London.[5] 'Now', says Izaak Walton,

'the *English Church* had gain'd a second St. *Austine*, for, I think, none was so like him before his Conversion: none so like St. *Ambrose* after it: and if his youth had the infirmities of the one, his age had the excellencies of the other, the learning and holiness of both. And now all his studies which had been occasionally diffused, were all concentred in Divinity. Now he had a new calling, new thoughts, and a new imployment for his wit and eloquence. Now all his earthly affections were changed into divine love; and all the faculties of his own soul were ingaged in the Conversion of others: In preaching the glad

[1] Ibid., pp. 216–17.

[2] *L Sermons*, 27. 234.

[3] Dedicatory epistle to *Devotions upon Emergent Occasions*.

[4] *Letters*, Tobie Matthew's Collection, p. 308.

[5] A letter to Sir Edward Herbert, first printed by John Hayward in the Nonesuch *Donne*, shows that the exact date was 23 Jan. The Bishop of London was John King, father of Henry King, who later became Donne's friend and poetic disciple.

tidings of Remission to repenting Sinners; and peace to each troubled soul. To these he applyed himself with all care and diligence; and now, such a change was wrought in him, that he could say with David, *Oh how amiable are thy Tabernacles, O Lord God of Hosts!* Now he declared openly, *that when he required a temporal, God gave him a spiritual blessing.* And that, *he was now gladder to be a door-keeper in the house of God, then he could be to injoy the noblest of all temporal imployments.*'[1]

His first sermon was preached at Paddington, then a village outside London. It has not been preserved, and the earliest of Donne's sermons which we possess was that preached on 30 April 1615, before the queen at Greenwich.[2] In the spring of 1616 he was presented to the living of Keyston, a small village in Huntingdonshire, and later in the same year he became rector of Sevenoaks in Kent. He did not, however, reside in either parish. He loved London and hated the country,[3] and in the autumn of 1616 he obtained a much more congenial appointment, that of Reader in Divinity to the Benchers of Lincoln's Inn.[4] This was no sinecure, for it involved, as Dr. Jessopp points out, preaching nearly fifty sermons a year to a learned and critical audience, who expected no hasty and improvised addresses, but carefully thought-out discourses, each occupying an hour to deliver. It was, moreover, a hard test of the sincerity of Donne's conversion, for the Benchers had been the friends and companions of his youth; they had known him in his wildest days as a law-student, and they would have readily detected the slightest taint of hypocrisy in his sermons. He acquitted himself triumphantly in a very difficult post, and the love and esteem which the Benchers felt for him were expressed in many ways.[5] Though Donne had not yet reached the full height of his power as a preacher, his

[1] Walton, *Life* (1670), p. 37.

[2] *XXVI Sermons*, no. 11.

[3] This is evident from the *Letters*, e.g. p. 63, where Donne speaks of 'the barbarousnesse and insipid dulnesse of the Country'.

[4] Walton has misdated this appointment, placing it after Mrs. Donne's death in 1617. See Gosse, ii. 91.

[5] Walton, *Life* (1670), pp. 43, 44; Gosse, ii. 110, 154, 155.

Lincoln's Inn sermons have a peculiar interest for us.[1] There are personal touches in them which are absent from the more elaborate discourses which he afterwards delivered at St. Paul's or Whitehall, and there is never the slightest attempt to place himself on a pedestal apart from his audience. He speaks of sin as a thing of which he himself has known the bondage, and can still feel at times the attraction, though he loathes it now from the bottom of his heart. The world, the flesh, and the devil have had as much power over him as over any of his hearers. He has known ambition, pride, hatred, lust as well as they. He is no cloistered recluse who has lived apart from his fellows—he is a man who has sinned and suffered and struggled, who has groped his way through darkness and the shadow of death, till at last the day-spring from on high has visited him, to guide his feet into the way of peace.

In this connexion his devotion to St. Augustine is significant. Out of the mass of authorities, patristic and medieval, to whom his sermons constantly refer, one name stands out above all others as that of a living force in his life and work. There is scarcely a sermon of Donne's which has not at least one reference to St. Augustine, and many contain four or five quotations from 'that blessed and Sober Father'. Like Augustine, Donne cried to God, 'Too late have I sought Thee, oh Beauty old yet ever new.' It was in phrases caught from Augustine that he lamented that he had wasted on lower things the praises which should belong to the eternal loveliness.[2]

This penitence was no passing emotion, but lasted to the end of his life. Long after he had become Dean of St. Paul's, famous for his holiness and austerity, and the greatest preacher of his day, he encouraged those who were diffident as to their salvation by his own example: 'I doubt not of mine own salvation; and in whom can I have so much

[1] At least sixteen of these have been preserved, viz. *LXXX Sermons*, no. 42; *L Sermons*, nos. 11 to 23 inclusive; *XXVI Sermons*, nos. 19 and 23. Elsewhere I have given reasons for thinking that four more sermons (*LXXX*, nos. 38–41) belong to this period (see Appendix B).

[2] *LXXX Sermons*, 12. 123.

occasion of doubt, as in my self? When I come to heaven, shall I be able to say to any there, Lord! how got you hither? Was any man less likely to come thither then I?'[1]

Soon after Donne's appointment to Lincoln's Inn the great sorrow of his life fell on him in the death of his wife in 1617. Walton has left us a vivid picture of his grief when she, 'who had long been the delight of his eyes, the Companion of his youth . . . with whom he had divided so many pleasant sorrows and contented fears, as Common-people are not capable of', was now removed from him by death. 'His very soul was elemented of nothing but sadness; now grief took so full a possession of his heart, as to leave no place for joy: If it did, it was a joy to be alone, where like a *Pelican in the wilderness*, he might bemoan himself without witness or restraint, and pour forth his passions like *Job* in the days of his affliction, *Oh that I might have the desire of my heart! Oh that God would grant the thing that I long for!*'[2]

Donne himself has given us in his seventeenth *Holy Sonnet* a description of his own state of mind after her death, and his increased longing for holiness:

> Since she whom I lov'd hath payd her last debt
> To Nature, and to hers, and my good is dead,
> And her Soule early into heaven ravished,
> Wholly on heavenly things my mind is sett.
> Here the admyring her my mind did whett
> To seeke thee God; so streames do shew their head;
> But though I have found thee, and thou my thirst hast fed,
> A holy thirsty dropsy melts mee yett.
> But why should I begg more Love, when as thou
> Dost wooe my soule for hers; offring all thine:
> And dost not only feare least I allow
> My Love to Saints and Angels things divine,
> But in thy tender jealosy dost doubt
> Least the World, Fleshe, yea Devill putt thee out.[3]

Ann Donne had borne her husband twelve children, of whom seven survived her, the remaining five having died in

[1] *LXXX Sermons*, 24, 241.
[2] Walton, *Life* (1670), pp. 41, 42.
[3] Grierson, i. 330.

infancy. On her death Donne gave them 'a voluntary assurance never to bring them under the subjection of a stepmother; which promise he kept most faithfully, burying with his tears all his earthly joyes in his most dear and deserving wives grave; betaking himself to a most retired and solitary life.'[1] Of these children one, Lucy, died unmarried in 1626/7; the others survived their father.[2]

In 1619 Donne was sent by the king to Germany as a member of Lord Doncaster's embassy, which was intended to promote peace among the warring German princes. The Emperor Matthias, who was also King of Bohemia, had appointed his kinsman, the Archduke Ferdinand of Styria, as his heir to the Bohemian crown. Ferdinand was an uncompromising Catholic, and the Bohemian nobles, who were strongly Protestant, refused to accept him as their ruler.

[1] Walton, *Life* (1670), p. 41.

[2] Constance, the eldest, married Edward Alleyn, the founder of Dulwich College, in 1623, and after his death married Samuel Harvey in 1630, by whom she had three sons. John, Donne's elder son, became his father's editor, and prepared the *LXXX*, *L*, and *XXVI Sermons* for the press, besides issuing certain other writings, such as the *Essays in Divinity* and *Paradoxes, Problems*, about which Donne had apparently left no instructions, and *Biathanatos*, of which he had said expressly that it was not to be published. This son was intended for the Church, and it was for his benefit that a large number of the sermons were carefully written out by Donne during the autumn of 1625 (see letter quoted by Gosse, op. cit. ii. 225). At the time of his father's death he was a graduate of Christ Church, Oxford. He afterwards took the degree of D.C.L. at Padua, and in 1638 was ordained, and became rector of High Roding in Essex. In 1639 he was presented to the livings of Fulbeck in Lincolnshire, and of Ufford in Northamptonshire. During the Civil War he was deprived of his benefices and came to London, and by 1648 he had become chaplain to the Earl of Denbigh, to whom he dedicated the 1649 edition of his father's sermons. He died in London 1662. Anthony à Wood says of him that he was 'an atheistical buffoon, a banterer, and a person of over free thoughts'.

George, the younger surviving son, became a soldier, and was taken prisoner in the retreat from the Isle of Rhé in 1627. He was still a prisoner when his father died, but was subsequently released, and returned to England about 1634. He died in 1639.

Bridget Donne married a certain Thomas Gardiner of Barstowe. Margaret married Sir William Bowles of Chislehurst, and left a large family, of whom descendants still survive. Elizabeth married Cornelius Laurence, Doctor of Physic (Gosse, ii. 297).

The Emperor Matthias died in the spring of 1619, and a proposal was made that James I of England should arbitrate between Ferdinand and his subjects. Doncaster's embassy set out in May 1619, and on its arrival at Heidelberg early in June Donne preached twice before the Prince and Princess Palatine.[1] The embassy also visited Ulm, Augsburg, Munich, Salzburg, Nuremberg, Maestricht, and in December it was at The Hague, where Donne preached before the States General and was presented by them with a gold medal which had been struck as a memorial of the Synod of Dort, which had recently dispersed. Doncaster did not succeed in fulfilling the king's hopes of mediation. The Bohemian nobles had invited the Elector Palatine to become their sovereign, and after some hesitation he accepted. He was crowned at Prague late in 1619, but his reign in Bohemia lasted only a year.

Doncaster's embassy returned to England early in 1620, and in 1621 Donne became Dean of St. Paul's. Here his sermons attracted crowds of hearers, and his fame as a preacher steadily increased. In the winter of 1623 a serious illness brought him near death. During his recovery he composed *Devotions upon Emergent Occasions*, a curious little book of meditations and prayers which was published in the spring of 1624.

In 1624 Donne was appointed to the vicarage of St. Dunstan's in the West. Izaak Walton was one of his new parishioners, and it is from this period that the intimacy between Donne and Walton dates. Walton speaks of himself as Donne's convert,[2] and depicts in the most vivid language the impression which Donne's preaching produced on his congregation.

Donne's friendship with George Herbert and his mother was one of the chief pleasures of these later days. To Magdalen Herbert (who married Sir John Danvers as her second

[1] The Princess was Elizabeth, daughter of James the First. Donne had celebrated her marriage with the Elector Palatine in his *Epithalamion* (Grierson, i. 127–31). One of the sermons preached before her has been preserved in Donne's *XXVI Sermons* as no. 20.

[2] Walton, *An Elegie upon Dr. Donne* (Grierson, i. 377).

husband) Donne addressed some poems in a tone of courtly compliment, and it was at the Danvers's house in Chelsea that he spent three months while the plague raged in 1625. With George Herbert he had 'a long and dear friendship, made up of such a sympathy of inclinations that they coveted and joyed to be in each other's company'. He encouraged Herbert in the writing of sacred verse, and shortly before Donne's death the two men exchanged poems in English and Latin.

Another close friend was Henry King, Bishop of Chichester, who became Donne's executor. Among the many admirers who after Donne's death wrote elegies in his praise were such different men as Edward Hyde,[1] Thomas Carew, Lord Falkland, and Dr. Corbet, Bishop of Oxford. Donne's circle of acquaintances was a wide one, but as years went by he withdrew himself more and more from society, giving up himself entirely to the duties of his calling. He generally preached once a week, if not more often, and immediately after the delivery of one sermon he would choose a text for the next and plan out the heads under which he would consider the subject. During the week he would consult the Fathers, and cast his study and meditation into suitable form. On Saturday he gave himself a rest, and visited his friends or otherwise diverted his thoughts, saying 'that he gave both his body and mind that refreshment, that he might be enabled to do the work of the day following, not faintly, but with courage and cheerfulness'.

In this time of his prosperity he did not forget those who had helped him in his misfortunes. He was able to send gifts of money to some who had formerly shown him kindness, and were now impoverished by extravagance, and he was 'a continual giver to poor scholars, both of this and foreign nations'. At all the festivities of the year, especially at Christmas and Easter, he sent a bounty to the prisons of London, and by his gifts many who were imprisoned for small debts

[1] It has been disputed whether this was Edward Hyde, Earl of Clarendon, or the Rev. Edward Hyde, Fellow of Trinity College, Cambridge. See Grierson, ii. 255, 256. Dr. Sampson has given strong reasons for assigning the verses to Clarendon (*Essays and Studies*, vii. 98–103).

were released. His life was full of charity and holiness, so that Lord Falkland could say of him,

> His words work'd much, but his example more,
> That preach't on worky dayes.[1]

Meanwhile he did not entirely give up poetry, the delight of his youth. He repented, indeed, sincerely of many of his earlier poems, and they were never published till after his death, though they had been so widely circulated in manuscript that it was impossible for him to destroy all trace of them. His poetical style—the metaphysical strain admired and imitated by Herbert, Vaughan, and Crashaw—did not change on his conversion; only his themes were different.

While Donne thus showed himself a sincere Christian, he can hardly be called a saint. Walton's biography gives us an exquisite portrait, but it omits the flaws in Donne's character, and the admixture of worldliness which we detect in his letters. The marriage he arranged for his eldest daughter was strangely mercenary in view of Donne's own romantic marriage. Doubtless he wished to save her from the struggle with poverty and hardship which his wife had been obliged to face, but his letters[2] on the subject, while they show his care for his daughters, seem to treat money and social position as the chief things to be desired in marriage.

Thus the years passed by, marked only by changes at home—the marriage of one daughter, the death of another, the launching of his sons in different professions—or by occasional attacks of illness, or by visits to friends in the country, or by attendance at ecclesiastical commissions, on two of which he sat.[3] Gosse has produced evidence to show

[1] *An Elegie on Dr. Donne* (Grierson, i. 381).

[2] *Letters* (1651), pp. 185–6. See also Gosse, ii. 192, 193, 217.

[3] Both of these dealt with matters in which Donne's early legal training must have been useful. In a letter in *T.L.S.*, 1 Aug. 1942, 'Donne the Lawyer', W. Milgate showed that in the summer of 1628 Donne was associated with the Bishops of Ely and St. Davids, and with Sir Charles Caesar and others who were commissioned to examine the proceedings of a Prerogative Court of Canterbury in a lawsuit. In June 1629 'he sat at Lambeth on a commission consisting of Laud, himself, and the Bishops of Winchester and Norwich, to decide a dispute which had broken out between the Bishop of Salisbury and the Dean and Chapter of that diocese' (Gosse, ii. 262–3).

that in 1630 it was decided that Donne should be made a bishop, but just at this moment his health finally broke down. Whilst staying with his married daughter he was seized by a severe illness, and though he recovered sufficiently to return to London, it was clear that his days were numbered.

It was in the spring of 1630/1 that he was appointed, for the last time, to preach before the king on the first Friday in Lent. This was an office which he had many times performed, and though he was now wasted with sickness he refused to let his weakness hinder him from preaching. 'Many of his friends', says Walton, '(who with sorrow saw his sickness had left him onely so much flesh as did onely cover his bones) doubted his strength to perform that task, and did therefore disswade him from undertaking it, assuring him however, it was like to shorten his life; but he passionately denied their requests; saying, *he would not doubt that that God who in so many weaknesses had assisted him with an unexpected strength, would not withdraw it in his last employment; professing an holy ambition to perform that sacred work.*'[1]

When he appeared in the pulpit, it became evident that he was a dying man. There were 'faint pauses' in his prayer, and the hearers wondered if he would have strength to fulfil his task. The text seemed prophetically chosen, 'Unto God the Lord belong the issues of death', and in the last words of the sermon Donne took leave for ever of his congregation. He had spoken of the horrors of death, of corruption, and of the worm, and then turned to speak of the death of Christ, how God the Lord, even the Lord of life, had Himself borne the pains of death, and on this note he bade farewell. 'As God breath'd a soul into the first *Adam*, so this second *Adam* breath'd his soul into God, into the hands of God. There we leave you, in that blessed dependancy, to hang upon him, that hangs upon the cross. There bath in his tears, there suck at his wounds, and lie down in peace in his grave, till he vouchsafe you a Resurrection, and an ascension into that Kingdome which he hath purchas'd for you, with the inestimable price of his incorruptible blood.'[2]

[1] Walton, *Life* (1670), p. 71.
[2] *XXVI Sermons*, 26. 411. (*Deaths Duell*, pp. 42, 43.)

Walton has given us a vivid picture of the days that followed. Donne had still enough strength for a few last employments. He directed the construction of his own monument, sent for his friends to give them parting messages, and wrote his last poem,[1] full as ever of quaint conceits, but with a haunting beauty which makes itself felt from the first stanza to the last.

> Since I am comming to that Holy roome,
> Where, with thy Quire of Saints for evermore,
> I shall be made thy Musique; As I come
> I tune the Instrument here at the dore,
> And what I must doe then, thinke here before.
>
> . . . .
>
> So, in his purple wrapp'd receive mee Lord,
> By these his thornes give me his other Crowne;
> And as to others soules I preach'd thy word,
> Be this my Text, my Sermon to mine owne,
> Therefore that he may raise the Lord throws down.[2]

'Now he had nothing to doe but die; To doe which, he stood in need of no more time, for he had long studied it, and to such a perfection, that in a former sicknesse he called God to witnesse, he was that minute prepared to deliver his soule into his hands, if that minute God would accept of his dissolution. In that sicknesse he begged of his God, (the God of constancy) to be preserved in that estate for ever. And his patient expectation to have his immortall soule disrobed from

[1] Professor G. C. Moore Smith and Mr. John Sparrow have argued that this poem was written during Donne's sickness in the winter of 1623. See *Modern Language Review*, xix. 462–6. In my article 'The Date of Donne's *Hymne to God my God, in my Sicknesse*' (*M.L.R.* xli. 9–15, Jan. 1946) I have produced additional evidence in support of the later date. Walton's statement is confirmed by the evidence of Henry King, who was present at Donne's bedside in Mar. 1630/1. An examination of the MSS. of Donne's poems supports the view that this *Hymne* was written considerably later than the *Hymne to God the Father*, which was composed in 1623. The latter found its way into seven MS. collections, whereas the former is found only in MS. Stowe 961. These collections were mostly made before 1631, as the impulse to form them ceased when it became known soon after Donne's death that a volume of his poems would soon be published by Marriott. Moreover, the tone of the *Hymne to God my God* differs markedly from that of the *Hymne to God the Father*, and of the *Devotions*, written in 1623, while it agrees closely with the end of *Deaths Duell*.

[2] Grierson, i. 368, 369.

her garment of mortality, makes me confident he now had a modest assurance, that his prayers were then heard, and his petition granted. He lay fifteene dayes earnestly expecting his hourely change; And in the last houre of his last day, (as his body melted away, and vapoured into spirit) his soule having (I verily beleeve) some revelation of the Beatifical Vision, he said, *I were miserable*, *if I might not die:* And after those words, closed many periods of his faint breath with these words, *Thy kingdome come*, *Thy will be done.* His speech which had long been his faithfull servant, remained with him till his last minute; and then forsook him, not to serve another master, but died before him, for that it was uselesse to him, who now conversed with God on earth, (as Angels are said to doe in heaven) onely by thoughts and looks. Being speechlesse, he did (as S. *Stephen*) *look stedfastly towards heaven*, till he saw the Sonne of God standing at the right hand of his Father; And being satisfied with this blessed sight, (as his soule ascended, and his last breath departed from him) he closed his owne eyes, and then disposed his hands and body into such a posture, as required no alteration by those that came to shroud him.'[1]

[1] Walton, *Life* (prefixed to the *LXXX Sermons*, 1640), sig. B 6, verso.

III

DONNE AS A MAN OF LETTERS

OF all the great Elizabethan and Jacobean writers, Donne is the one of whose life, tastes, and habits we know the most. His outward appearance at different stages of his life is familiar to us, since we have portraits of him at eighteen, at forty-two, in his later years, and finally on his death-bed. Much of his correspondence has been preserved, and his life-history was narrated by one of his personal friends, who was also the most exquisite of seventeenth-century biographers. His published works fill six large volumes of several hundred pages each, and though we have lost certain of his writings (for instance, 'the resultance of 1400. Authors, most of them abridged and analysed with his own hand', and the 'copies of divers Letters and cases of Conscience that had concerned his friends, with his observations and solutions of them'[1]) there is no reason to think that these would have added materially to our knowledge of the man himself. If mystery still clings to the figure of Donne, this is due not to any lack of information about him but to the presence of the indefinable quality of genius in his work. Talent is comparatively easy to analyse and assess, but in the last resort genius always eludes the industrious commentator or biographer. And with all his lack of artistry, with all his flaws and incompleteness, Donne has that touch of greatness which lifts him far above such painstaking contemporaries as Samuel Daniel or George Wither, above his faithful disciple, George Herbert, and which places him for us beside Ben Jonson or Bacon as one of the chief forces in seventeenth-century literature.

If, however, we admit frankly that we shall never solve the ultimate riddle of Donne's genius, we can yet learn much from the study of his mental development and of the books, persons, and events which influenced him. As a man of letters he is a fascinating figure. He came of a literary

[1] Walton, *Life* (1670), p. 62.

stock on his mother's side. The families of More, Rastell, and Heywood were honourably known in the sixteenth century for their devotion to learning. Donne inherited this devotion, and he is a typical Renaissance scholar in his desire for knowledge of all kinds—the 'sacred hunger of science' as he called it in one of his poems,[1] or the 'hydroptique immoderate desire of humane learning', as he described it when feeling dissatisfied with the small material reward which his studies had brought him.

His earliest efforts in prose show the influence of contemporary foreign literature. In the *Paradoxes and Problems*, the two *Characters*, and the *Essay on Valour*, he attempted forms strange to English, which had recently been introduced from Italy and France. The results do not seem markedly successful to us. The *Paradoxes and Problems* are poor stuff compared with the poems which Donne was writing at approximately the same time. Nevertheless, the same impulse which made him an eager innovator in verse drove him also to try new kinds of prose, and he went direct to continental models instead of imitating his contemporaries who were attempting the same thing. He was interested, however, in seeing what his friends thought of this kind of writing, and we find him sending his paradoxes to Wotton and explaining that they are not to be taken at their face value. 'If they make you to find better reasons against them, they do their office: for they are but swaggerers: quiet enough if you resist them . . . they are rather alarums to truth to arme her, then enemies.'[2] Similarly he exchanges 'problems' with Sir Henry Goodyer,[3] while Cornwallis on his side dedicates some of his paradoxes to Donne.[4]

Donne had travelled in France, Spain, and Italy, and knew something of the language and literature of all these countries. He was one of the few Jacobean writers who read Dante in the original, and he commented at length on a passage of the *Inferno* in a letter[5] written probably to

[1] *To Mr. B. B.* (Grierson, i. 212).
[2] Letter in the Burley MS. printed on p. 316 of this volume.
[3] *Letters* (1651), p. 108. [4] Bodleian Library, MS. Rawlinson D. 718.
[5] Letter in the Burley MS. printed on p. 314 of this volume.

Wotton. There is another reference, much less definite, in Satire IV, lines 157–9, and there is a distinct resemblance between the lines in *Ignatius his Conclave* beginning 'As a flower wet with last nights dew, and then Warm'd with the new Sunne, doth shake off agen . . .',[1] and lines 127–30 of Canto III of the *Inferno*. Dante is mentioned by Donne in *The Courtier's Library*,[2] and a phrase there may be a reminiscence of lines 121–3 of Canto V of the *Inferno*. Donne possessed a copy of an edition of the *Convivio* printed at Venice in 1531, which later became the property of Selden, and is now in the Bodleian Library.[3] From Petrarch (Canz. XIX, st. 7, l. 1) he took the motto 'Per Rachel ho servito e non per Lea' which he wrote on the title-pages of the books in his own library.[4] He discussed and condemned the works of Pietro Aretino in a letter to Wotton printed at the end of the present volume.[5] He possessed a copy of the *Prediche* of Bernardino Ochino da Siena, and one of the *Più Consigli ed Avvertimenti* of Guicciardini.[6] There are traces of the influence of Ortensio Lando's *Paradossi* on the *Paradoxes and Problems*.[7]

French literature also had a considerable effect on Donne's earlier work. *An Essay of Valour* is a poor attempt at a form which Montaigne[8] had made popular. In the *Essays in Divinity* the account of Raymond of Sebund may have been inspired by Montaigne's account of that writer. It was from

[1] *Ignatius his Conclave* (1611), sig. G 4^{v}. This resemblance was first pointed out by Mario Praz in *Secentismo e Marinismo in Inghilterra* (1925), p. 51. See also F. P. Wilson, *A Supplement to Toynbee's 'Dante in English Literature'*, *Italian Studies*, iii, p. 58.

[2] See p. 37 and note on p. 74 of that work.

[3] Keynes, *Bibliography of Donne*, no. 295.

[4] There is a quotation from Petrarch in the sentences (undoubtedly genuine) which MS. Ashmole 826 adds to *Problem iv*. See my article 'More MSS. of Donne's *Paradoxes and Problems*', *Review of English Studies*, x. 297.

[5] pp. 316–17.

[6] Keynes, op. cit., no. 317, and Harvard College Library. Sotheby has advertised a copy of Guicciardini's *Propositioni di stato* as having belonged to Donne's library.

[7] Mario Praz, op. cit., p. 13.

[8] Donne has a reference to '*Michel Montaige*' [read '*Montaigne*'] in *Letters* (1651), p. 106.

Rabelais that Donne took the idea of a mock library which is the basis of *Catalogus Librorum Aulicorum*,[1] and there are references to Rabelais in the *Satires*, the letters to Wotton, and the lines which Donne contributed to Coryat's *Crudities*.[2] The form and method of *Ignatius his Conclave* seem to have been derived in part from *La Satire Ménippée*,[3] published anonymously in Paris in 1594, and frequently reprinted during the next twenty years. Grierson[4] suggests that the first four lines of Donne's Fourth Satire owe something to Régnier's imitation of Horace. There is a reference to Ronsard in the additional sentences found in one of the manuscripts of the *Problems*.[5] Donne owned a few French books which are still in existence, among them the old farce *Fou et Sage*,[6] and *Histoire remarquable et véritable de ce qui s'est passé par chacun iour au siège de la ville d'Ostende* (1604).[7]

This bald summary suggests that it was chiefly the satirists and the essayists who influenced Donne's work. Rabelais, Montaigne, the *Satire Ménippée*, and Régnier in French, and Lando in Italian provided models for his imitation, while his preference for Dante over Petrarch, and his use of the *Inferno* in preference to the other parts of the *Divina Commedia*, are due to the strongly marked satiric quality of that work. The only contemporary English work which he singled out for praise was Ben Jonson's fiercely satiric comedy of *Volpone*. For this he wrote commendatory Latin verses in which he praised Jonson as one who, though following the ancients, struck out a new path of his own.[8] The references

[1] See my introduction to *The Courtier's Library*, pp. 1–3.

[2] For the *Satires*, see Grierson, i. 161; for the letters, pp. 310, 319 of the present volume; and for the lines to Coryat, *Crudities* (1611), sig. f. 5, verso (ll. 11–13).

[3] C. M. Coffin, *John Donne and the New Philosophy*, p. 197.

[4] *Poems*, ii. 117–18. In an undated letter Donne writes: 'I make shift to think that I promised you this book of French Satyrs. If I did not, yet it may have the grace of acceptation . . .' (*Letters*, 1651, p. 294). Was this a copy of Régnier's work?

[5] *Review of English Studies*, x. 296.

[6] British Museum (shelf-mark C. 22. a. 42). It has the signature 'J. Donne'.

[7] *Bodleian Library Record*, vol. i, no. 9, Apr. 1940.

[8] Grierson, i. 398:

Tam nemo veterum est sequutor, ut tu
Illos quod sequeris novator audis.

to contemporary English writers in *Catalogus* are all satirical. Donne pokes fun at the posies and anagrams of Sir John Davies, the projects of Sir Hugh Plat, and the *Ajax*, a treatise on sanitary reform by Sir John Harrington.[1]

It has often been said that Donne was more powerfully influenced by Spanish literature than by that of any other country. Those who hold this view base it mainly on a letter written by Donne to Buckingham when the latter was in Spain in 1623 on the occasion of the projected Spanish marriage for Charles, then Prince of Wales.

> 'I can thus far make myselfe beleeve that I ame where your Lordship ys, in Spaine, that in my poore Library, where indeed I am, I can turne myne Ey towards no shelfe, in any profession, from the Mistresse of my youth, Poetry, to the wyfe of myne age Diuinity, but that I meet more Autors of that nation, then of any other. Theyr autors in Diuinity, though they do not show us the best way to heaven, yet they thinke they doe: And so, though they say not true, yet they do not ly, because they speake theyr Conscience.'[2]

After printing this letter Gosse comments:

> 'It is curious to see Donne turning resolutely away from the literature of his native country, which we know he contemned, while expending his full attention on that of Spain. He stands in a singular position therefore; he is an Englishman of the late Elizabethan and early Jacobean age, wholly indifferent to Shakespeare, but eager to read the elegies of Herrera, perfectly languid in the presence of Bacon, but an ardent admirer of Luis de Granada and Jorge de Montemôr. Yet we must remember that he went, in response to an imperious instinct, where his peculiarly southern and Catholic intellect found the food that it required.'[3]

As yet only one Spanish book owned by Donne has been discovered.[4] The great preponderance of Latin books from

[1] See my notes on these authors on pp. 56, 61, 65 of *The Courtier's Library*.

[2] Bodleian Library, Tanner MS. 73. 305 (Gosse, ii. 176–7).

[3] Gosse, *Life and Letters of Donne*, ii. 177–8.

[4] This is the *Iosephina* of Geronimo Gracian (Brussels, 1609) of which a copy with Donne's autograph and motto is in the British Museum. See J. A. Muñoz Rojas, 'Un libro español en la biblioteca de Donne', *Revista de Filología Española*, xxv. 108–11.

Donne's library which have been preserved reflects the ascendancy of Latin writers in the marginal references supplied by Donne for his prose works. As far as I can discover, Donne never mentions Herrera, Luis of Granada, or St. John of the Cross. Miss M. P. Ramsay thinks that she has discovered an echo of St. Teresa in one of Donne's letters to Goodyer: 'Rappelons aussi une lettre de 1608, dans laquelle se retrouvent comme des échos des écrits de la mystique espagnole Sainte Thérèse',[1] and adds a footnote, 'Cf. Ste Thérèse, *Vie. Degrés de l'Oraison*, ch. xiii. *et seq*.' She also points out that some phrases in Donne's poem *The Ecstasie* remind us of St. Teresa's description of mystical union,[2] but these, as Grierson has observed, may be derived from Plotinus, whom Donne knew in Latin.

The references to Spanish vernacular literature in Donne's works are few in number. In one letter he writes, 'The Spanish proverb informes me, that he is a fool which cannot make one Sonnet, and he is mad which makes two.'[3] In another letter he alludes to 'a little ragge of *Monte Magor* [read, *Monte Mayor*], which I read last time that I was in your Chamber . . . that Death came so fast towards mee, that the over-joy of that recovered mee.'[4] This suggests that Donne possessed no copy of Montemayor's work, which indeed was old-fashioned by the time that Donne wrote, and was unlikely, in its blend of chivalry and pastoral romance, to appeal to Donne's taste. In one of his sermons Donne remarks: 'I remember a vulgar Spanish Author, who writes the *Iosephina*, the life of *Ioseph*, the husband of the blessed Virgin *Mary*. . . .'[5]

This list of quotations is not impressive, and compares poorly with the considerable number of references to French and Italian works. I suggest that Donne's letter to Bucking-

[1] *Les Doctrines médiévales chez Donne*, p. 80.

[2] Ibid., p. 256.

[3] *Letters* (1651), pp. 103–4. This proverb is found in the *Floresta Española* of Melchior de Santa Cruz, as was pointed out by E. G. Mathews in a letter to the *Times Literary Supplement*, 12 Sept. 1936, which quotes the proverb from the 1614 edition printed at Brussels.

[4] *Letters* (1651), p. 299.

[5] *LXXX Sermons*, 18. 176.

ham has been misunderstood. He does not say that he had more books *in Spanish*, but that he had 'more authors of that nation' than of any other on his shelves. As far as divinity, philosophy, and canon law are concerned he was thinking, I believe, of the many Spanish theologians and lawyers who wrote in Latin, and whom he quotes repeatedly in *Biathanatos*, *Essays in Divinity*, and the *Sermons*. I have drawn up a list of no less than forty of these, and I append a brief account of a few of the most important authors who wrote in Latin to whom Donne makes definite reference. One of these is Raymond of Sebund, born at Barcelona in the fourteenth century, on whose great work *Theologica Natura sive Liber Creaturarum* Donne draws in the *Essays in Divinity*.[1] Ignatius Loyola, the founder of the Jesuits, is introduced into *Ignatius his Conclave* only to be satirized as a puppet villain, but he is mentioned more seriously in the *Sermons*. Tostatus, or Alonso Tostado (1400–55), a Spanish bishop who wrote voluminously both in Latin and Spanish, is quoted in the *Essays in Divinity* and the *Sermons*.[2] Azorius, or Juan Azor (1533–1603), a Spanish Jesuit who wrote *Institutiones Morales*, is quoted repeatedly in *Biathanatos*.[3] Two other Spanish Jesuits are quoted in *Biathanatos*: Mariana[4] notorious for his advocacy of regicide in his *De Rege et Regis Institutione*, and Alfonso de Castro,[5] who wrote *Variae materiae morales inchoatae*. Acosta, a Spanish Jesuit, is quoted in the *Essays in Divinity*[6] for his work on the evangelization of the American Indians, and Alfonso Barcena, a Spanish Jesuit missionary who died in Peru, is mentioned in the same volume. In the *Sermons* Donne made considerable use of a number of Latin commentaries by Spanish writers, such as Luis Alcazar, who wrote *Investigatio arcani sensus in Apocalypsi*,[7] Ribera,[8] a Jesuit doctor of Salamanca, who also wrote on the Apoca-

[1] 1651 edition, pp. 7, 8.

[2] Ibid., p. 51 and *LXXX*, 32. 314.

[3] pp. 30, 42, 44. [4] pp. 132, 135. [5] p. 68.

[6] *Essays*, p. 186. Marginal reference *Jo. Acosta de procur. Jud.* [read, *Ind.*] *sal. l.* 2. *c.* 9.

[7] *LXXX*, 19. 184.

[8] Ibid. and *L*, 15. 126.

lypse, Gasper Sanctius[1] (1554–1628), whom Donne describes as 'a learned Jesuit', Alfonso Salmeron of Toledo[2] (1516–85), a companion of Loyola, and Turrecremata[3] or Torquemada (1388–1468), the Dominican who became a Cardinal. These names represent only one-third of the total number to whom Donne refers, but their many works would occupy a considerable amount of room on his shelves. It should be noted that they were not writers of the mystical school of St. Teresa and St. John of the Cross, and if Donne really made as much use of these latter writers as some critics suggest, is it curious that he should have suppressed all reference to the mystics while adding marginal references to the works of these Jesuits and Dominicans.

On the other hand, the Spanish poets whose works were on Donne's shelves were probably poets who wrote in the vernacular. The use of a Spanish motto on the engraving by Marshall of a portrait of Donne at the age of 18 suggests that the poet was familiar in early life with the Spanish tongue. There is a close kinship of spirit between Donne's earlier poems and those of Gongora, and the whole question of Donne's possible indebtedness to Spanish poets needs careful investigation.

As a man of letters Donne was strongly influenced by the Latin classical writers. He knew something at least of the work of Lucretius, Virgil, Horace, Ovid, Juvenal, Martial, Cicero, Plautus, Terence, Livy, Tacitus, Seneca, the elder and the younger Pliny, Aulus Gellius, Varro, Valerius Maximus, Ausonius, and Lactantius.[4] We need not assume that Donne was thoroughly familiar with all these authors because he quotes from them. Lucretius was an author little

[1] *LXXX*, 15. 151.   [2] Ibid. 49. 489.

[3] I am indebted to M. P. Ramsay (op. cit., Appendixes i–v) for the dates of these writers, and for some brief notes on their lives.

[4] Jack Lindsay in a letter 'Donne and the Roman Poets' (*T.L.S.*, 19 Feb. 1931, p. 135) says of Donne's poetry, 'Ovid was undoubtedly the most diffused influence; but Donne had clearly read, and been strongly affected by, Catullus, Propertius, Petronius, Martial and Juvenal.' As this is a study of the prose works I have confined my remarks to those authors who influenced Donne's prose as well as his poetry.

read by the Elizabethans, and Donne has two quotations from him in the *Essays in Divinity*,[1] which come from the first two books of the *De Rerum Natura*. These two books may have been all that he knew of Lucretius, but it was otherwise with Virgil, Horace, Juvenal, Martial, and Seneca. He possessed a copy of an Italian version of the Æneid into *terza rima* by Giovanpaolo Vasio,[2] but his quotations from Virgil are naturally always from the Latin. His highest praise was given to Virgil, whom he calls 'the King of the Poets',[3] and again 'the greatest Poet'[4]—a judgement which reminds us of Ben Jonson's admiration of Virgil, and of the fact that he cast Donne for the role of Criticus in the lost dialogue which should have preceded his translation of Horace's *Ars Poetica*. Most of Donne's quotations are from the *Æneid*, but he also knew the Virgilian Appendix.

Horace, Martial, and Juvenal influenced Donne strongly both in poetry and prose. We see the example of Horace at work in the *Fourth Satire*, where Donne describes his meeting with a bore in the manner of Horace's 'Ibam forte via Sacra'. It is not a translation but an adaptation of Horace's theme to Donne's own time and circumstances.[5] In his earliest known letter[6] Donne quotes a scrap from Horace, *Epode* xv. 24, 'ast ego vicissim risero'. In the *Essays in Divinity* he quotes a line from Horace's *Satires*,[7] and in the *Sermons* he introduces two lines from the Odes with the words 'sayes the

[1] 1651 edition, p. 57: 'Nec bene promeritis capitur, nec tangitur ira' from *De Rerum Nat.* ii. 651, and 'Nil semine egeret... ferre omnes omnia possent... subito exorirentur... incerto spatio' (ibid. i. 160–81).

[2] W. H. Robinson's Catalogue 71, 1940.

[3] *L Sermons*, 31, 273. Here Donne quotes the famous line 'Mens agitat molem, et magno se corpore miscet' (*Æn.* vi. 727).

[4] *LXXX*, 48. 482; 'The greatest Poet layes the greatest levity and charge that can be laid, to this kinde of people, that is, *In contraria*, that they change even from one extreme to another; *Scinditur incertum studia in contraria vulgus* [*Æn.* ii. 39].... Neither was that Poet ever bound up by his words, that hee should say *In contraria*, because a milder or more modified word would not stand in his verse; but hee said it, because it is really true.'

[5] Grierson, i. 158, 159. See also the note in ii. 117.

[6] See p. 303 *infra*.

[7] *Sat.* II. iii. 295, quoted in *Essays*, p. 57, and also in *LXXX Sermons*, 39. 386.

Poet',[1] and elsewhere quotes him as 'the learned Poet'.[2] As for Martial, he is quoted seven times in the *Paradoxes and Problems*, once in the *Essays in Divinity*, and at least twice in the *Sermons*.[3] Donne admired him for his wit, his brevity, his hatred of shams, and perhaps also for his less admirable qualities, his coarseness and brutality. The influence of Juvenal is apparent in Donne's *Satires*, especially in v. 35–8, which contain a reminiscence of *Sat*. xiii. 28–31:

> O Age of rusty iron! Some better wit
> Call it some worse name, if ought equall it;
> The iron Age *that* was when justice was sold; now
> Injustice is sold dearer farre. . . .[4]

A passage in Juvenal to which Donne refers again and again is the description in *Sat*. xv. 10–11:

> O sanctas gentes quibus haec nascuntur in hortis
> Numina. . . .

This appears in *Essays in Divinity* as 'For the *Egyptians*, most abundant in Idolatry, were from thence said to have Gods grow in their gardens'.[5] The reference is to the sacredness of '*Onions*, and *Garlike*' which Donne mentions in the preceding sentence, and this is also found in *The Second Anniversary*, ll. 427–8:

> For as the Wine, and Corne, and Onions are
> Gods unto them, so Agues bee, and Warre.

Juvenal is also quoted in the *Sermons*, as, for example:

> 'And the naturall man hath his sweet singer too, a learned Poet that tels him, that seldome any enormous Malefactor enjoyes *siccam mortem*, (as he calls it) a dry, an un-bloody death.'[6]

It was the satiric quality of Horace, Martial, and Juvenal

[1] *LXXX Sermons*, 30. 297, quoting *Odes* IV. ix. 29, 30.

[2] *LXXX*, 57. 579.

[3] For the full list of references see my appendix 'Donne's Reading of Martial' following my article 'Donne's *Paradoxes and Problems*', in *A Garland for John Donne*, ed. T. Spencer, pp. 44–9. Donne's verse epigrams are strongly reminiscent of Martial.

[4] Grierson, i. 169.

[5] p. 41.

[6] *LXXX*, 48. 478. This is from *Sat*. x. 112, 113. See also *L*, 20. 172, where the famous 'Maxima debetur pueris reverentia' is quoted.

that attracted the young Donne. As he grew older, however, he began to choose other classical authors for his reading. Seneca's moral maxims recur constantly in the *Sermons*, and such other prose-writers as Cicero and the two Plinies make their appearance on his pages.[1]

Donne had also some knowledge of the by-ways of Latin literature. John Sparrow has given an account in 'A Book from Donne's Library'[2] of the volume *Epigrammata et Poemata Vetera*, edited by the French scholar Pithou, which is now in the Bodleian Library. It consists of two parts, the first of which contains four books of miscellaneous epigrams, while the second contains the *Ciris*, the *Culex*, the *Moretum*—works belonging to the Virgilian Appendix—as well as the Eclogues of Calpurnius, the *Panegyricus* of Optatianus Porfyrius, and the Elegies of Maximian. Donne has marked a number of lines in the two latter works, and Sparrow suggests that the third Elegy of Maximian may have had some influence on Donne's fourth and twelfth Elegies, which describe a somewhat similar situation.

Donne's knowledge of Greek authors was confined to those whom he knew in Latin translations. Chief among these were Plato, Aristotle, Plotinus, Plutarch, Lucian, with a smattering of Aelian, Artemidorus, Epictetus, Diogenes Laertius, Dion Cassius, and others. In *Biathanatos* there is a long quotation from Plato's *Laws*, where 'the English reproduces word by word the Latin of Ficino's translation'.[3] On the other hand, in *Pseudo-Martyr* Donne uses the Latin translation by Serranus (*Opera Platonis ex novo J. Serrani interpretatione*) printed in 1578.[4] The treatise of Plato which had the greatest effect on Donne's mind was the *Timaeus* with the doctrine of Ideas. He refers specifically to this in *Essays in Divinity*:

[1] For Seneca see *LXXX*, 39. 387; 70. 713; *XXVI*, 2. 19; 6. 75 *et passim*. For Cicero, *Essays in Divinity*, p. 69, and *LXXX*, 48. 478. For Pliny's Natural History, *LXXX*, 61. 617 and *L*, 50, 466.

[2] *The London Mercury*, xxv. 171–80 (Dec. 1931).

[3] M. P. Ramsay, op. cit., p. 295. The passage is on p. 74 of *Biathanatos*, and the marginal reference is '*De leg.* 9'.

[4] Ramsay, op. cit., p. 295.

'The greatest Dignity which we can give this world, is, that the *Idæa* of it is eternall, and was ever in God . . . and therefore these *Idæas* and eternall impressions in God, may boldly be said to be *God*; for nothing understands God of it self, but God; and it is said, *Intellectæ Jynges à patre, intelligunt et ipsæ*: And with *Zoroaster* (if I misconceive not) *Jynx* is the same as *Idæa* with *Plato*.'[1]

The Platonic doctrine of Ideas had passed into Christian philosophy through Augustine, as Donne recognizes in passages of the *Sermons*:

'Of which Ideaes . . . S. *Augustine* pronounces, *Tanta vis in Ideis constituitur*, There is so much truth, and so much power in these Ideaes, as that without acknowledging them, no man can acknowledge God, for he does not allow God Counsaile, and Wisdome, and deliberation in his Actions . . . . And therefore he, and others of the Fathers read that place, (which we read otherwise) *Quod factum est, in ipso vita erat*; that is, in all their Expositions, whatsoever is made, in time, was alive in God, before it was made, that is, in that eternall Idea, and patterne which was in him.'[2]

The Platonic doctrine of 'remembrance' is also alluded to in the *Sermons*: '*Plato* plac'd *all learning* in the memory . . . . All knowledge, that seems new to day, sayes *Plato*, is but a remembring of *that*, which your soul knew before.'[3] The *Republic* is alluded to in *Pseudo-Martyr*.[4] Plato's insistence on the importance of geometry was thoroughly congenial to Donne's mind. The symbolism of geometry, which to some seems so dry and uninspiring, was to Donne a constant source of poetic imagery. 'One of the most convenient Hieroglyphicks of God, is a Circle; and a Circle is endlesse',[5] he says in one of his sermons, while in the *Obsequies to the Lord Harrington* he devotes eighteen lines to a comparison of the soul as a circle with the 'great circles' of the heavens and 'the tropique circles' and the smaller polar circles. In

[1] *Essays in Divinity*, i, pp. 58, 59. There is a marginal reference '*Zoroastr. Oracul.* 4.' to which Jessopp adds 'apud F. Patricium "Jynges Ideæ Principia"'.

[2] *LXXX Sermons*, 66. 667, 668. The marginal reference is to John i. 3, 4. See also *LXXX*, 79. 700.

[3] *L Sermons*, 20. 164.

[4] Cap. i, par. 6.

[5] *LXXX Sermons*, 2. 13.

the *Second Anniversary* he describes the perfection of Elizabeth Drury's soul by saying of it:

> To whose proportions if we would compare
> Cubes, th'are unstable; Circles, Angular.[1]

Aristotle was almost as important as Plato for the development of Donne's mind, but it is difficult to assess exactly how much came to Donne directly from the reading of Aristotle in Latin, and how much through the medium of St. Thomas Aquinas and the other Schoolmen. For the direct use of Aristotle we note Donne's reference to the *Ethics* in *Biathanatos*:

> 'Of such reasons [against suicide] derived from the rules of Morall vertue, *Aristotle* insinuates two. For observing that this kinde of death caught men by two baits, *Ease* and *Honour*. Against them who would dy to avoid *Miserie*, Hee teaches *Death to be the greatest misery which can fall upon us* [marginal reference, *Arist. Eth. E.* 3. *c.* 6] . . . . And then, that Honour and Fame might draw none, he sayes, *It is Cowardlinesse, and Dejection, and an argument of an unsufferable and impatient minde* [marginal reference, *Cap.* 7.].'[2]

The influence of Aristotle through Aquinas and the Schoolmen will be discussed in a later chapter.

Similarly with Plotinus, we find direct quotations such as that in *LXXX Sermons*, 79. 812, '*Deus est quod ipse voluit*' [marginal reference, *Plotinus*], together with much indirect indebtedness through the numerous Christian writers such as the pseudo-Dionysius, who had absorbed neoplatonic ideas.

Donne brought to these studies a mind which, though trained in medieval methods, was in some ways strikingly modern. He was by nature bold, restless, rebellious, impatient of convention, and he had also that ardent love of truth which is the property of no particular age, but which always distinguishes its owner from the mass of writers who

[1] Grierson, i. 255. C. M. Coffin enlarges on the geometric nature of Donne's imagery, op. cit., pp. 177–80.

[2] p. 114. For references to Aristotle in the *Sermons*, see *LXXX*, 39. 388 and 61. 617.

are content to repeat parrot-like the fashionable catchword of the day. Originality and audacity are two of the marks of his poetry, and in a less degree they distinguish his prose, though here he founded no new school and exerted much less influence on the literary development of his successors. Alike in poetry and prose he took the medieval philosophy which was the groundwork of his thought, and let the searchlight of his genius play on it till it assumed new and fantastic forms.

Professor Courthope has shown that much of Donne's wit, which was admired so greatly by his contemporaries, consists in the application of philosophical terms and images to the emotions of love and religion. The breakdown of the medieval system of thought is closely connected with the sudden outburst of 'metaphysical' conceits in the poetry of Donne and his followers. There is no need here to labour the point, but it is worth noticing that these conceits are found in Donne's best prose as well as in his poetry. His duller works, such as *Pseudo-Martyr*, are comparatively free from them; but where he is most truly himself, as in the *Devotions* or the greater sermons, the far-fetched images which displeased Dr. Johnson make their appearance once more. This habit of mind, so alien from the ordered thinking of the eighteenth century, was natural to Donne, to whom anything in heaven or earth could be used to illustrate anything else. The reader of the sermons is constantly surprised by some brilliant comparison which seems at first merely fanciful, but on examination proves to be really illuminating. Donne had the poet's eye, which can discern a world of meaning in the most apparently trivial object, and he rejected the hackneyed comparisons of professional writers in favour of a new set of images coined in the mint of his own powerful imagination. The sonneteers had written perpetually of cheeks like roses, lips like cherries, starry eyes, and hair like gold, but Donne disdained this obvious imagery. It was an inner resemblance rather than an outer which he sought. It is remarkable how little use he makes in his poetry of comparisons drawn from flowers or fruits or any other of the beautiful things in nature. In his sermons, too, he differed from Jeremy Taylor, whose luscious and ornate style is seen to advantage in the famous description of the rose.[1] Donne has one or two passages in which he shows that he was alive to the beauty of flowers,[2] but most of the comparisons in the sermons are drawn from circles, maps, engravings, elephants, whales, fleas, discoveries in the West Indies, scholastic theories of the nature of angels, and so forth.[3] Thus he speaks of the life of a righteous man as an engraving:

'Bee pleased to remember that those Pictures which are deliver'd in a minute, from a print upon a paper, had many dayes, weeks, Moneths time for the graving of those Pictures in the Copper; So this Picture of that dying Man, that dies in Christ, that dies the death of the Righteous, that embraces Death as a Sleepe, was graving all his life; All his publique actions were the lights, and all his private the shadowes of this Picture.'[4]

Again he compares preaching to the harpooning of whales:

'The rebuke of sin, is like the fishing of *Whales*; the Marke is great enough; one can scarce misse hitting; but if there be not *sea room* and line enough, and a dexterity in letting out that line, he that hath fixed his harping Iron, in the Whale, endangers himselfe, and his boate; God hath made us *fishers of Men*; and when we have struck a *Whale*, touch'd the conscience of any person, which thought himselfe above rebuke, and increpation, it struggles, and strives, and as much as it can, endeavours to draw fishers, and boate, the Man and his fortune into contempt, and danger. But if God tye a *sicknesse*, or any other calamity, to the end of the line, that will winde up this Whale againe, to the boate, bring back this rebellious sinner better advised, to the mouth of the Minister, for more counsaile, and to a better souplenesse, and inclinablenesse to conforme himselfe, to that which he shall after receive from him; onely calamity makes way for a rebuke to enter.'[5]

It would be easy to make a long string of such examples and to emphasize the grotesqueness of many of them, but it is a mistake to think of Donne's imagery as merely quaint.

[1] *Holy Dying*, chap. i, sect. 2.

[2] For instance, *LXXX Sermons*, 30. 297; *L Sermons*, 31. 272.

[3] This list, though it may seem a haphazard one, has been chosen to include most of Donne's favourite images. For circles, see *LXXX Sermons*, 2. 14; maps, *LXXX*, 55. 558; elephants, *L*, 40. 372; whales, *LXXX*, 69. 702.

[4] *XXVI Sermons*, 15. 218.

[5] *L Sermons*, 10. 74, 75.

He is not quaint as Quarles of the *Emblems* was quaint. There is generally a profound metaphysical significance beneath his choice of imagery which seems trivial or ludicrous. It is true that sometimes his ingenuity betrays him, as in the well-known couplet in his *Elegie upon the untimely death of the incomparable Prince Henry*:

> For whom, what Princes angled, when they tryed,
> Met a Torpedo, and were stupified.[1]

This is grotesque, and nothing more. But there are few passages in the *Sermons* which fail as badly as this, for Donne does not try to display his cleverness in the pulpit, as he had done in the *Elegie*. Mere cleverness is the bane of Donne's worst poems, as it is also of his *Paradoxes and Problems*, but in the *Sermons* Donne tries to come to grips with his hearers, many of them ignorant and uncultured, and he finds imagery of the greatest help. He tells us himself that no comparison is too high or too low for him, if by it he may reach the understanding of some poor soul.[2] But the image, though it may be a homely one, is nearly always surprising in its context. Take an example where Donne makes use of an ordinary metaphor, and gives it freshness and vividness by one or two turns of phrase:

> 'There is Ayre enough in the world, to give breath to every thing, though every thing doe not breath. If a tree, or a stone doe not breathe, it is not because it wants ayre, but because it wants meanes to receive it, or to returne it. All egges are not hatched that the hen sits upon; neither could Christ himselfe get all the chickens that were hatched, to come, and to stay under his wings.'[3]

[1] Grierson, i. 268.

[2] *L Sermons*, 26. 228: 'We need not call that a *Fable*, but a *Parable*, where we heare, That a Mother to still her froward childe told him, she would cast him to the Wolf, the Wolf should have him; and the Wolf which was at the doore, and within hearing, waited, and hoped he should have the childe indeed: but the childe being still'd, and the Mother pleased, then she saith, so shall we kill the Wolf, the Wolf shall have none of my childe, and then the Wolf stole away. No metaphor, no comparison is too high, none too low, too triviall, to imprint in you a sense of Gods everlasting goodnesse towards you.'

[3] *LXXX Sermons*, 7. 70.

In spite, however, of the originality of most of Donne's imagery, there is a good deal of repetition in his work. He does not plagiarize from others, but he has no scruple in borrowing from himself. This was perhaps inevitable in the sermons. No man could hope to preach hundreds of elaborate discourses, each of them an hour long, without making use again and again of ideas and images which he had employed before. Sometimes he deliberately inserts a long passage which had done duty in a slightly different context in an earlier sermon.[1] But when the sermons are set side by side with the other prose works or with the poems, we still find that we are moving in the same circle of imagery. There is a certain narrowness about Donne's range of metaphor and simile, when he is contrasted with a master like Milton. Thus the famous comparison of the circle made by the pair of compasses in the *Valediction: forbidding Mourning* reappears in the 'Sermon preached at the Earl of Bridgewater's House' in 1627, though the application is a different one.

> If they be two, they are two so
> As stiffe twin compasses are two,
> Thy soule the fixt foot, makes no show
> To move, but doth, if the'other doe.
>
> And though it in the center sit,
> Yet when the other far doth rome,
> It leanes, and hearkens after it,
> And growes erect, as that comes home.
>
> Such wilt thou be to mee, who must
> Like th'other foot, obliquely runne;
> Thy firmnes makes my circle just,
> And makes me end, where I begunne.[2]

'First then, Christ establishes a Resurrection, *A Resurrection there shall be*, for, that makes up *Gods circle*. The *Body* of Man was the first point that the foot of Gods Compasse was upon: First, he created the body of *Adam*: and then he carries his Compasse round, and shuts

[1] The most striking example of this is the passage quoted on pp. 272–4.
[2] Grierson, i. 50, 51.

up where he began, he ends with the *Body of man* againe in the glorification thereof in the Resurrection.'[1]

Again, the opening lines of the 'Obsequies to the Lord Harrington, brother to the Lady Lucy, Countesse of Bedford' find their echo in the sermon 'Preached at Paul's Cross . . . March 24, 1616':

> Faire soule, which wast, not onely, as all soules bee,
> Then when thou wast infused, harmony,
> But did'st continue so; and now dost beare
> A part in Gods great organ, this whole Spheare.[2]

'Is the world a great and harmonious Organ, where all parts are play'd, and all play parts; and must thou only sit idle and hear it?'[3]

The comparison of God to a circle, which men foolishly attempt to square, is found both in the poems and the sermons.

> Eternall God, (for whom who ever dare
> Seeke new expressions, doe the Circle square,
> And thrust into strait corners of poore wit
> Thee, who art cornerlesse and infinite). . . .[4]

'God is a circle, himselfe, and he will make thee one; Goe not thou about to square eyther circle, to bring that which is equall in it selfe, to Angles, and Corners, into dark and sad suspicions of God, or of thy selfe, that God can give, or that thou canst receive no more Mercy, then thou hast had already.'[5]

In all these instances, the thought had been already expressed by Donne in poetry before it found a way into his prose, so that, as Professor Saintsbury says, 'he did but transprose his verse and trans-hallow his profanities', but in at least one example, poem and sermon were written on the same occasion, and once or twice the sermon preceded the poem. The 'Sermon of Valediction at My Going into Germany' and the 'Hymne to Christ, at the Authors last going into Germany', give us the outpouring of Donne's soul at once in verse and in prose, and the comparison of the two modes of expression makes an interesting study. The resemblance is particularly close in one passage.

[1] *L Sermons*, 1. 3. [2] Grierson, i. 271. [3] *XXVI Sermons*, 24. 343.
[4] Grierson, i. 348. [5] *LXXX Sermons*, 2. 14.

'Christ Jesus remember us all in his Kingdome, to which, though we must sail through a sea, it is the sea of his blood, where no soul suffers shipwrack; though we must be blown with strange winds, with sighs and groans for our sins, yet it is the Spirit of God that blows all this wind, and shall blow away all contrary winds of diffidence or distrust in Gods mercy.'[1]

In what torne ship soever I embarke,
That ship shall be my embleme of thy Arke;
What sea soever swallow mee, that flood
Shall be to mee an embleme of thy blood;
Though thou with clouds of anger do disguise
Thy face; yet through that maske I know those eyes,
Which, though they turne away sometimes,
They never will despise.[2]

When Donne, a little before his death, sent George Herbert a seal on which was engraven the figure of Christ crucified on an anchor, he accompanied the gift with some verses in Latin and English, explaining that a sheaf of snakes, his family crest, used formerly to be the mark of his seal. These lines contain conceits about the serpent which Donne had previously employed in a sermon preached at St. Dunstan's.

A Sheafe of Snakes used heretofore to be
My Seal, The Crest of our poore Family.
Adopted in Gods Family, and so
Our old Coat lost, unto new armes I go . . . .
Yet may I, with this, my first Serpents hold,
God gives new blessings, and yet leaves the old;
The Serpent, may, as wise, my pattern be;
My poison, as he feeds on dust, that 's me.
And as he rounds the Earth to murder sure,
My death he is, but on the Crosse, my cure.
Crucifie nature then, and then implore
All Grace from him, crucified there before.[3]

'I may say to the Serpent, Your meat is dust; and I was dust; but *Deposui terram*, I have shak'd off my dust, by true repentance, for I have shak'd off my self, and am a new creature, and am not now meat

[1] *XXVI Sermons*, 19. 281.

[2] Grierson, i. 352.

[3] Ibid. 399. For an account of the circumstances of the composition of these verses, see Walton, *Life of Donne* and *Life of George Herbert*.

for your Table. . . . The creeping Serpent, the groveling Serpent, is Craft; the exalted Serpent, the crucified Serpent, is Wisdome. . . . That creeping Serpent, Satan, is war, and should be so; The crucified Serpent Christ Jesus is peace, and shall be so for ever. The creeping Serpent eats our dust, the strength of our bodies, in sicknesses, and our glory in the dust of the grave: The crucified Serpent hath taken our flesh, and our blood, and given us his flesh, and his blood for it.'[1]

Again, the *Hymne to God my God, in my sicknesse*, contains imagery which was also employed in the 'Sermon Preached upon Easter-Day 1629', and in an undated sermon on the penitential psalms.

> Whilst my Physitians by their love are growne
> Cosmographers, and I their Mapp, who lie
> Flat on this bed, that by them may be showne
> That this is my South-west discoverie
> *Per fretum febris*, by these streights to die,
>
> I joy, that in these straits, I see my West;
> For, though theire currants yeeld returne to none,
> What shall my West hurt me? As West and East
> In all flatt Maps (and I am one) are one,
> So death doth touch the Resurrection.
>
> Is the Pacifique Sea my home? Or are
> The Easterne riches? Is *Ierusalem?*
> *Anyan*, and *Magellan*, and *Gibraltare*,
> All streights, and none but streights, are wayes to them,
> Whether where *Iaphet* dwelt, or *Cham*, or *Sem*.[2]

'Who ever amongst our Fathers, thought of any other way to the Moluccaes, or to China, then by the Promontory of *Good hope*? Yet another way opened it self to *Magellan*; a Straite; it is true; but yet a way thither; and who knows yet, whether there may not be a North-East, and a North-West way thither, besides?'[3]

'In a flat Map, there goes no more, to make West East, though they be distant in an extremity, but to paste that flat Map upon a round body, and then West and East are all one. In a flat soule, in a dejected conscience, in a troubled spirit, there goes no more to the making of that trouble, peace, then to apply that trouble to the body of the

[1] *L Sermons*, 47. 443–5.
[2] Grierson, i. 368.
[3] *LXXX Sermons*, 24. 241.

Merits, to the body of the Gospel of Christ Jesus, and conforme thee to him, and thy West is East.'[1]

The examples just given illustrate how much use Donne made of imagery drawn from sea-faring. The *Sermons* and the *Essays in Divinity*, like the *Hymns*, are full of nautical metaphors. The strong sea-wind of the Elizabethan voyages blows through them, and scatters the cobwebs of scholastic subtlety.

'A Prince is Pilot of a great ship, a Kingdome; we of a pinnace, a family, or a less skiff, our selves: and howsoever we be tossed, we cannot perish; for our haven (if we will) is even in the midst of the Sea; and where we dy, our home meets us.'[2] 'Therefore, as in violent tempests, when a ship dares bear no main sayl, and to lie still at hull, obeying the uncertain wind and tyde, puts them much out of their way, and altogether out of their account, it is best to put forth such a small ragg of sail, as may keep the bark upright, and make her continue near one place, though she proceed not; So in this question, where we cannot go forward . . . and to ly hulling upon the face of the waters, and think nothing, is a stupid and lazy inconsideration.'[3]

The two characteristics of Donne's poetry which have most impressed the popular mind are its metaphysical 'wit' and its morbidity, and both of these are evident in his prose work also. In fact, the few passages of his prose which are generally included in anthologies have evidently been chosen for these particular qualities. But just as it is easy to mistake the nature of his wit, so the popular mind often errs in its description of Donne's work as morbid. Morbid many passages undoubtedly are. The close of the sermon on 'falling *out* of the hands of God', the description of the corruption of the dead body in *Death's Duel*—these and many others like them are almost insane in their emphasis on the horrible. The misfortune is that those who form their judgement of Donne from anthologies only can have no idea of the sanity and beauty of much of his writing. To read the huge folio volume of the *LXXX Sermons* is to realize that here was a

[1] *LXXX Sermons*, 55. 558.

[2] *Essays in Divinity* (1651), p. 74.

[3] Ibid., pp. 19, 20. For passages from the *Sermons* see *LXXX*, 35. 341, and 61. 610; *L*, 5. 37; 18. 150; 28. 241 and 247; 29. 250; 30. 270.

man pre-eminently wise and gifted, with a marvellous faculty of clear thought, lovable, too, and tolerant above most of his contemporaries. But there were certain flaws in a mind which was otherwise sane and healthy. Chief of these was a morbid obsession with the idea of death, especially the physical decay which attends death. One is tempted to think that Donne had seen some horrible sight in childhood which left its mark on his highly sensitive nature. All his poetry and his prose, from the earliest to the latest, has traces of this obsession. Closely allied to it is a certain delight in ugliness which reminds us occasionally of Swift. Some of his finest passages are marred by offensive lines or phrases, out of keeping with the general tone of his work.[1] The witty depravity of the early poems is, of course, a different matter, but this bad taste is found here and there in his more serious work. Though Donne may lay stress on the 'inglorious and contemptible vilification' of man in the grave, and may unveil with scorn the rottenness of human grandeur, he never forgets that man as man is worthy of honour, for the Divine spark still burns in him. He loves to remind his hearers that Christ took not on Him the nature of angels, but took on Him the seed of Abraham.[2] Like Pascal, he knows that man is greater than the external universe, though it should overwhelm him.

'Man is an abridgement of all the world; and as some *Abridgements* are greater, then some other authors, so is one man of more dignity, then all the earth. . . . Sinne hath diminished man shrowdly, and brought him into a narrower compasse; but yet, his *naturall immortality*, (his soule cannot dye) and his *spirituall possibility*, even to the last gaspe, of spending that immortality in the kingdome of glory, and living for ever with God, (for otherwise, our immortality were the heaviest part of our curse) exalt this valley, this clod of earth to a noble heighth. . . . Consider the dignity of man in his *nature*, and then, in the *Sonne of God* his assuming that nature, which gave it a new dignity and this will beget in thee a *Pride* that God loves, a valuing of thy selfe above all the tentations of this world.'[3]

[1] On this subject see Grierson, ii. 87, '. . . that strange bad taste, some radical want of delicacy, which mars not only Donne's poems and lighter prose, but even at times the sermons'.

[2] *LXXX Sermons*, 28. 284.

[3] *L Sermons*, 38. 352.

The morbidity of Donne's fancy has its own importance. It is like the mists which rise at evening from the fens and produce the marvellous colours of the fenland sunsets. The mists are unhealthy and have no beauty in themselves, but the light of the setting sun, as it struggles through them, is refracted into the strangest harmonies of orange, crimson, and copper. Donne's work has about it something of the sinister glories of such a sunset. The dying splendour of the Elizabethan age—nay, more, the break-up of a whole system of thought, is reflected in his pages. 'And new Philosophy calls all in doubt', as he said of the Copernican theory of the universe,[1] and in such a period of change and uncertainty it is not marvellous that men's minds turned more and more to the certainty of death. Bitterness and disillusionment mark the literature of the last few years of Elizabeth's reign. After the chivalrous romantic poetry of Spenser and Sidney comes the satiric note of Hall, Donne, and Marston. Men began to weary of the worship of beauty and the poetry of emotional delight, and to seek literature with a sharper flavour instead of the sweetness which had begun to cloy. The harsh ugliness of certain parts of Donne's work did not repel his readers. They admired his prodigious display of wit, whether he showed it in season or out of season. But his fame would have perished, as Ben Jonson predicted, if he had not possessed higher qualities than those which attracted attention to him at the moment. There is some resemblance between Donne's position at the end of the Elizabethan age and the position of Wilde, Shaw, and others at the end of the Victorian. In both periods there was a reaction from a literature which had been romantic and emotional in its appeal, and a desire for more intellectual display, showing itself in a love of witty paradox. Along with this went a craving for the cynical and the morbid, which both Donne and Wilde were able to satisfy. But Donne was immeasurably Wilde's superior as a man and as a writer. He had passion, imagination, and a sure grip of the facts of life which Wilde lacked. As Gosse says of Donne's treatment of *Biathanatos*, 'His conscience was healthy, if his nerves

[1] *The First Anniversary* (Grierson, i. 237).

were not.'[1] It was in his prose-writings especially that he showed how sound was his judgement and how broad his outlook on the main issues of life. The sermons are full of the ripe wisdom of experience gathered in many different walks of life. Donne had been a traveller, a law-student, a soldier, a poet, before he became a preacher, and as secretary to the Lord Chancellor he had met many of the most notable men of the day. It was his rash marriage, not any lack of capacity, which had caused his failure in political life. His true greatness does not become apparent till we study all sides of his work. 'Books', said Dr. Johnson, 'without a knowledge of life are useless, for what should books teach but the art of living?' Donne had this knowledge in large measure, and in his sermons he gave of it generously to his hearers.[2] He did not inflict on them the trite homilies which are all that many people expect from the pulpit. He believed with the Preacher that God 'hath no pleasure in fools'. But it was the pompous and self-satisfied, not the simple or ignorant, whom he regarded as fools.[3] He had plenty of sound advice for young and old, for those about to marry, for those in business, for those distressed by religious doubts and scruples about their election or their assurance of salvation. Nothing could be kinder or wiser than his treatment

[1] Gosse, i. 260.

[2] No short extracts can give any adequate idea of this side of Donne's genius, but I add a few sentences as samples. Further illustrations will be found in Chap. XI.

'A man is thy Neighbor, by his Humanity, not by his Divinity; by his Nature, not by his Religion: a Virginian is thy Neighbor, as well as a Londoner; and all men are in every good mans Diocess, and Parish.' *XXVI Sermons*, 25. 375.

'Man is not all soule, but a body too; and, as God hath married them together in thee, so hath he commanded them mutuall duties towards one another; and God allowes us large uses of *temporall blessings*, and of recreations too.' *L Sermons*, 38. 351. 'And this is one strange and incurable effect of this opinion of wit, and knowledge, that whereas every man murmurs, and sayes to himself, such a man hath more land then I, more money then I, more custome, more practise then I, (when perchance, in truth it is not so) yet every man thinks, that he hath more wit, more knowledge, then all the world beside, when, God knows it is very far from being so.' *LXXX Sermons*, 30. 296.

[3] *LXXX Sermons*, 30. 296.

of those timid souls who were troubled by the harsh Calvinistic doctrines of many of the Puritan divines.[1] His own conviction that it is wrong to ascribe conduct to God which we should unhesitatingly condemn in man saved him from acquiescing in the theory of 'reprobation'. His theology was sometimes illogical, but perhaps it was none the worse for that. The attempt to treat man's knowledge of God as an exact science has led to countless troubles in religion. Donne was content to own that life is full of unsolved mysteries, while basing his faith on a God 'whose judgements may be unsearchable, but they cannot be unjust'.

The same qualities of sanity and broad-mindedness are seen in the letters. There is a delightful verse epistle to Sir Henry Goodyer, who was living extravagantly at court. Donne tactfully suggests a journey abroad in order that his friend may give up some of his expensive habits:

Who makes the Past, a patterne for next yeare,
  Turnes no new leafe, but still the same things reads,
Seene things, he sees againe, heard things doth heare,
  And makes his life, but like a paire of beads.

. . . The noble Soule by age growes lustier,
  Her appetite, and her digestion mend,
Wee must not sterve, nor hope to pamper her
  With womens milke, and pappe unto the end.

Provide you manlyer dyet; you have seene
  All libraries, which are Schools, Camps, and Courts;
But aske your Garners if you have not beene
  In harvests, too indulgent to your sports.

[1] Ibid. 33. 322: 'This very scruple was the voyce and question of God in him; to come to a doubt, and to a debatement in any religious duty, is the voyce of God in our conscience: Would you know the truth? Doubt, and then you will inquire: And *facile solutionem accipit anima, quæ prius dubitavit*, sayes S. *Chrysost.* As no man resolves of any thing wisely, firmely, safely, of which he never doubted, never debated, so neither doth God withdraw a resolution from any man, that doubts with an humble purpose to settle his owne faith, and not with a wrangling purpose to shake another mans.' Cf. *Satire* iii. 77.

Would you redeeme it? then your selfe transplant
A while from hence. Perchance outlandish ground
Beares no more wit, then ours, but yet more scant
Are those diversions there, which here abound.

To be a stranger hath that benefit,
Wee can beginnings, but not habits choke.
Goe; whither? Hence; you get, if you forget;
New faults, till they prescribe in us, are smoake.

. . . However, keepe the lively tast you hold
Of God, love him as now, but feare him more,
And in your afternoones thinke what you told
And promis'd him, at morning prayer before.

Let falshood like a discord anger you,
Else be not froward. But why doe I touch
Things, of which none is in your practice new,
And Tables, or fruit-trenchers teach as much;

But thus I make you keepe your promise Sir,
Riding I had you, though you still staid there,
And in these thoughts, although you never stirre,
You came with mee to Micham, and are here.[1]

Friendship played an important part in Donne's life. He called it his 'second religion', and he has been amply repaid for the devotion which he gave it. To his friends we owe all our knowledge of the gentler, more urbane side of his nature. Walton's *Life* alone would have served to keep his memory green, and the *Letters* of 1651 are a proof of the intimate affection which Donne felt for his friends, and also of the way in which they treasured his letters. We might have expected so original and independent a genius to be as isolated in life as he was in poetry, but on the contrary he seems to have been one of the most sociable of men. He charmed and delighted courtiers like Sir Henry Wotton and Sir Henry Goodyer, divines like Morton, great ladies like the Queen of Bohemia and the Countesses of Bedford and Huntingdon, as well as simple men like Izaak Walton the linen-draper. His literary friends were generally younger

[1] Grierson, i. 183, 184. Goodyer does not seem to have taken Donne's advice, for we hear later of his debts and difficulties.

poets such as Herbert and Henry King, who looked up to him as their master, but of the men of his own generation, Ben Jonson was his warm friend and admirer, as well as his candid critic. Walton has left an inimitable description of his personal appearance, as his friends saw it:

'He was of Stature moderately tall, of a strait and equally-proportioned body, to which all his words and actions gave an unexpressible addition of Comeliness.

'The melancholy and pleasant humor were in him so contempered, that each gave advantage to the other, and made his Company one of the delights of Mankind.

'*His fancy* was unimitably high, equalled only by his great wit, both being made useful by a commanding judgement.

'*His aspect* was chearful, and such as gave a silent testimony of a clear knowing soul, and of a Conscience at peace with it self.

'*His melting eye* shewed that he had a soft heart, full of noble compassion; of too brave a soul to offer injuries, and too much a Christian not to pardon them in others . . . .

'He was by nature highly passionate, but more apt to reluct at the excesses of it. A great lover of the offices of humanity, and of so merciful a spirit, that *he never beheld the miseries of Mankind without pity and relief*.'[1]

This account seems at first to suit ill with the poet of the *Satires* and the cynical *Progress of the Soul*, but at bottom, Donne was always a lover of his kind. His fierceness was due to the occasional exasperation of a particularly sensitive temperament. Cynicism was the cloak with which, as a young man, he tried to hide his feelings, but as age approached he dropped the disguise. Mankind—including womankind—was always his proper study. He was no poet of Nature; like Dr. Johnson and Charles Lamb, he was never so happy anywhere as in London. In his youth he frequented theatres and amusements of all kinds,[2] and though later he denounced

[1] Walton, *Life* (1670), pp. 80, 81.

[2] See Grierson, ii. 172: 'This letter and that to Mr. E. G. show that Donne was a frequenter of the theatre in these interesting years, 1593 to 1610, the greatest dramatic era since the age of Pericles. Sir Richard Baker, in his *Chronicle of the Kings of England*, recalls his "Old Acquaintance . . . Mr. John Dunne, who leaving Oxford, liv'd at the Inns of Court, not dissolute but very neat: a great Visiter of Ladies, a great Frequenter of Plays, a great Writer of conceited Verses".'

comedies, wine, and women as 'Job's miserable comforters' to the downcast soul, his friendship with Ben Jonson shows that he did not dislike the serious drama, while in his sermons he took up the position, in contrast to the Puritans, of a champion of all innocent amusements.

Donne's attitude towards women is characteristic of the man in its superficial inconsistency and its underlying fixity. He is a sensualist and an idealist, and his poems contain some of the most cynical censures and the most extravagant eulogies that have ever been offered to women. He has passion in abundance, but little tenderness, though an occasional poem like 'Sweetest Love, I do not go' is there to remind us that tenderness was not foreign to his nature. His prose works show that he despised the intellectual powers of women, and that he never regarded them as the equals and comrades of men.[1] His marriage did nothing to shake this consciousness of male intellectual superiority, though it taught him reverence for the spiritual qualities of womanhood. Few great writers have shown so little insight into the secrets of a woman's heart, and yet few have been more dependent on the friendship and sympathy of women. The supreme influences in Donne's life are those of women—his mother, his early loves, his wife, his patronesses and friends. To these he owed his early training in the Catholic faith, his disillusionment with life, the recovery of his ideals, his spiritual awakening, and finally the pleasant intimacies which formed the chief recreation of his later years. Donne's contempt for women's understanding did not prevent him from becoming a member of the literary coteries which gathered round such ladies as the Countess of Bedford or the Countess of Huntingdon, and he addressed to them the most elaborate of his verse epistles, full of learned allusions and delicate compliments. He had a long and sacred friendship with Magdalen Herbert, the 'autumnal beauty' of whose face he praised in one of the best known of his later poems,

[1] See *Juvenilia*, Problem VI: 'Why hath the Common Opinion afforded Women Soules?' quoted on p. 142, and, as an example of his later mature opinion, *L Sermons*, 2. 14 (preached at a wedding), 'She is but *Adjutorium*, but a Help: and no body values his staffe as he does his legges.'

and whose virtues he celebrated in the sermon which he preached at her grave in 1627. Among his last letters are those which he addressed to his 'noble sister', Mrs. Cokaine, to whom he wrote of his feelings and intimate thoughts with a freedom which is rare in his correspondence. In theory Donne despised women as a sex, but in practice he loved and honoured individual women, and in return they gave him a boundless devotion. He had all the virile qualities which attract a woman, and on his side he was too susceptible to be able to judge women as a whole calmly and dispassionately. 'First passion, then fatigue, and understanding slipped out between them.'[1]

Thus Donne is poles apart from such men as Richardson or Meredith, who have analysed the workings of women's minds with a skill which astounds women themselves. In spite of the important part played by his wife, we have no clear idea of her personality. He gives us no portrait of her in his poems, no hint of her tastes and habits in his letters. Perhaps she was rather colourless, save in her great love for him. She married at seventeen, and her life afterwards was a hard one, with a steadily increasing family and a perpetual lack of money. Donne himself must have been an exacting husband, nervous, morbid, and subject to frequent attacks of illness. She kept his love to the end—no small feat with so brilliant and so wayward a man. She was a woman of tender piety—so much is evident from the seventeenth *Holy Sonnet* —and her death left a gap in Donne's life which he never turned to earthly love to fill.

[1] I quote this sentence from a letter addressed to me by the late Sir Walter Raleigh, which has since been printed (*Letters*, 1926, p. 519). I should like to acknowledge the debt which I owe to the inspiration of two talks with him on the subject of Donne.

IV

DONNE AS A THEOLOGIAN

DONNE was a man of affairs, not a cloistered contemplative nor a scholar living in retirement. He produced most of his theological work when he was Dean of St. Paul's and vicar of the busy parish of St. Dunstan's. It might have been expected that the literary and intellectual quality of his prose would suffer from the necessity of adapting his thought to the comprehension of large mixed audiences, but on the contrary the *Sermons* rank far higher as literature than the *Essays in Divinity* or *Biathanatos*. Donne was a great preacher because he insisted on raising his audience to his own level by the intensity of his spiritual passion. His religion, individual as it was in its personal apprehension of God, was also emphatically social. He would not be saved alone; he stretched out imploring hands to the men and women who were sinning as he had sinned, but who were also potential members of the Communion of Saints.

Many readers of Donne's poetry have felt strongly the incongruity of his position as a religious teacher. They are willing enough to admit the sincerity of the agonized penitence of the *Holy Sonnets*, but they cannot fit the passionate, cynical, sensuous figure of the poet into the ecclesiastical garments of the Dean. They think that Donne must have felt himself to be playing a part, and that he must have subscribed to the Thirty-nine Articles with his tongue in his cheek.

It is easy to see that Donne has little in common with the typical Anglican dignitary. Respectability is supposed to be the hall-mark of a Dean and Chapter; one would hesitate to ascribe that quality to Donne even in his latest and holiest days. Respectability implies decorum and well-regulated feelings on all subjects, but Donne's emotions were always violent to excess. 'He was by nature highly passionate,' says Walton, 'but more apt to reluct at the excesses of it.' The 'naked thinking heart', of which he spoke in his poems, is evident in all his work. Compared with the gentle piety of George Herbert or Nicholas Ferrar, his religion seems highly coloured, almost over-strained. We should have felt less surprise if we had found him in a Roman monastery or a Puritan conventicle instead of the Cathedral Church of St. Paul's. Did so fiery a soul ever feel itself really at home within the Anglican fold?

It is worth while to examine Donne's mature teaching in some detail in order to see whether there is any foundation for this sense of incongruity. Did Donne preach doctrines which held for him no vital meaning? Was there a taint of insincerity about his work? Or, if the passion of the *Sermons* carries conviction of his sincerity to the reader's mind, did he interpret familiar doctrines in a way which was strange to many of his contemporaries? Is there anything in his religious teaching which bears the stamp of his own individuality?

He has left us ample material for such an investigation in the *Sermons*, the *Devotions*, and the *Letters*. It is the abundance rather than the paucity of evidence which has deterred most of his commentators. Those who, like Dr. Jessopp, have become familiar with the huge tomes of his writings have not hesitated to express their profound belief in his sincerity. They have marvelled that the English Church has taken so few pains to honour a man whom she might have regarded as one of her brightest ornaments of learning and devotion. Yet, while Donne's sincerity is unmistakable to the reader, the reason for his non-recognition as a religious teacher also becomes apparent. Apart from the scandal caused by the posthumous publication of his early poems and prose trifles, the ecclesiastical authorities must have found much that was disconcerting in Donne's work. He preached toleration in an age which demanded rigid conformity, and his controversial sermons lacked the bitterness which was demanded of a zealous defender of the faith. The Puritans suspected him of an inclination to Popery, while Laud's party at one time thought him in league with the Puritans. His theology was too medieval in some respects and too modern in others. And though his sermons were welcomed on their first publication, the tide of fashion soon turned against the whole school of Jacobean prose-writers with their fantastic conceits and their allegorical interpretations. The new age distrusted enthusiasm and mysticism in religion, and demanded good sense and plain reasoning. Even in Donne's own time there were some who thought him 'a bad edifier',[1] and the men who listened a generation later to the preaching of Barrow, South, and Tillotson would have found the style of the *LXXX Sermons* intolerably subtle and involved, spinning a web of medieval dialectic around the plain truths of religion.

An examination of the *Sermons* shows that there is nothing really heterodox in Donne's mature opinions. In his youth he had propounded certain heretical views on such doctrines as the transmigration of souls and the nature of woman.[2] In the *Sermons* he retracts these opinions, and there is no evidence to prove that he had ever held them seriously or had regarded such subjects as anything but stalking-horses for the display of his youthful wit.

The fullest exposition of Donne's theology is to be found in the great series of Christmas, Easter, Whitsuntide, and Trinity sermons, which occupy the earlier part of the *LXXX Sermons*. From these it will be seen that he held the fundamental Christian doctrines which are expressed in the Apostles' and the Nicene Creed, and that his general standpoint was that of an orthodox[3] Anglican divine of the school of Andrewes and Laud. He did not, however, lay equal stress on all parts of the Creed. The Incarnation, the Atonement, and the Resurrection formed the pivot of his teaching, and with these he joined the thought of the Communion of Saints as realized in the Church, and the expectation of future Judgement. When he spoke of the love of Christ as manifested in the Incarnation or the Atonement, his words became full of a fire and a passion which were lacking in his treatment of some parts of the Christian faith. The

[1] *In Memory of Doctor Donne: By Mr. R. B.* (Grierson, i. 387).

[2] *The Progresse of the Soule* sets forth the one heresy, and *Juvenilia* the other.

[3] For a further discussion of this point see Husain, *The Dogmatic and Mystical Theology of John Donne.*

Whitsuntide sermons are noticeably inferior to the Christmas and Easter series, and several of the Trinity sermons do not handle the doctrine of the Trinity at all, but are rhapsodies on the love of Christ.

His attitude towards the Christian faith is not that of the professed theologian carefully building up an edifice in which every dogma has its place and which may be endangered by the removal of a single article of belief. He is rather the poet who grasps certain great ideas by intuition, not by logical reasoning, though in the framework with which he surrounds them he may call in the aid of the discursive intellect. In conveying these ideas to his hearers he displays an imagination more intense and profound than that of any other English preacher. Jeremy Taylor, his only serious rival, is dwarfed not only by the greatness of Donne's style but also by the fervour of his passion. Coleridge marked this distinction between the two men in regard to the central Christian doctrine. 'The cross of Christ is dimly seen in Taylor's works. Compare him in this respect with Donne, and you will feel the difference in a moment.'[1] One passage may be quoted to illustrate this point. It is taken from one of Donne's Trinity Sunday sermons:

'Love him then, as he is presented to thee here; Love the *Lord*, love *Christ*, love *Iesus*. If when thou lookest upon him as the *Lord*, thou findest frowns and wrinkles in his face, apprehensions of him, as of a Judge, and occasions of feare, doe not run away from him, in that apprehension; look upon him in that angle, in that line awhile, and that feare shall bring thee to love; and as he is *Lord*, thou shalt see him in the beauty and lovelinesse of his creatures, in the order and succession of causes, and effects, and in that harmony and musique of the peace between him, and thy soule: As he is *the Lord*, thou wilt feare him, but no man feares God truly, but that that feare ends in love.

'Love him as he is the *Lord*, that would have nothing perish, that he hath made; And love him as he is *Christ*, that hath made himselfe man too, that thou mightest not perish: Love him as the *Lord* that could shew mercy; and love him as *Christ*, who is that way of mercy, which the Lord hath chosen. Returne againe, and againe, to that mysterious person, *Christ*. . . .

[1] *Table Talk* (1835), i. 168.

'I love my Saviour as he is *The Lord*, He that studies my salvation; And as *Christ*, made a person able to work my salvation; but when I see him in the third notion, *Iesus*, accomplishing my salvation, by an actuall death, I see those hands stretched out, that stretched out the heavens,[1] and those feet racked, to which they that racked them are foot-stooles; I heare him, from whom his nearest friends fled, pray for his enemies, and him, whom his Father forsooke, not forsake his brethren; I see him that cloathes this body with his creatures, or else it would wither, and cloathes this soule with his Righteousnesse, or else it would perish, hang naked upon the Crosse; And him that hath, him that is, *the Fountaine of the water of life*, cry out, *He thirsts*, when that voyce overtakes me, in my crosse wayes in the world, *Is it nothing to you, all you that passe by? Behold, and see, if there be any sorrow, like unto my sorrow, which is done unto me, wherewith the Lord hath afflicted me, in the day of his fierce anger;* When I conceit, when I contemplate my Saviour thus, I love the *Lord*, and there is a reverent adoration in that love, I love *Christ*, and there is a mysterious admiration in that love, but I love *Iesus*, and there is a tender compassion in that love, and I am content to suffer with him, and to suffer for him, rather then see any diminution of his glory, by my prevarication.'[2]

The impression of vitality and unconventionality given by much of Donne's teaching is due largely to his freedom from ordinary ecclesiastical prejudices. Though his theology is orthodox, his standard of moral values is not that which is often ascribed, rightly or wrongly, to orthodox theologians. The faith seemed to him to be in less danger from its foes than from its over-zealous defenders who were excommunicating one another right and left. He described the zeal of such controversialists as 'God's sword in the devil's

[1] This passage on the Crucifixion should be compared with Donne's poem *Goodfriday*, 1613 (Grierson, i. 336), which treats the same subject, especially ll. 21–9:

> Could I behold those hands which span the Poles,
> And turne all spheares at once, peirc'd with those holes?
> Could I behold that endlesse height which is
> Zenith to us, and our Antipodes,
> Humbled below us? or that blood which is
> The seat of all our Soules, if not of his,
> Made durt of dust, or that fleshe which was worne
> By God, for his apparell, rag'd, and torne?

[2] *LXXX Sermons*, pp. 400–1.

hand'. Right belief was to him of little avail without right conduct, and right conduct meant not mere abstinence from sin but positive well-doing, a life spent in the active service of God and man. He denounced, with a bitterness born of his own experience, the ruin wrought in the soul by specific sins such as lust, pride, or worldly ambition, but though he condemned the sins, he showed a profound sympathy with the sinner. The sins which moved his contempt most were those of the selfish indolent man, who goes through life unmoved by the sufferings of others, untouched by any noble purpose, wasting his time in sloth or idle amusement, and leaves the world without having accomplished any useful work to justify his existence. The sin of 'the unlit lamp and the ungirt loin' was to Donne more heinous than any single crime committed in the heat of passion under sudden temptation, for it was the symptom of alienation from the life of God, which is endless creative activity. 'God considered primarily and in himself so, is *actus purus*, all action, all doing.'

'Is the world a great and harmonious Organ, where all parts are play'd and all play parts; and must thou only sit idle and hear it? Is every body else made to be a *Member*, and to do some real office for the sustentation of this great Body, this World; and wilt thou only be no member of this Body? Thinkest thou that thou wast made to be *Cos Amoris*, a Mole in the Face for Ornament, a Man of delight in the World? Because thy *wit*, thy *fashion*, and some such *nothing* as that, made thee a delightful and acceptable companion, wilt thou therefore pass in jeast, and be nothing? If thou wilt be no link of Gods Chain, thou must have no part in the influence and providence, derived by that, successively to us. Since it is for thy fault that God hath cursed the Earth, and that therefore it must bring forth *Thorns* and *Thistles*, wilt not thou stoop down, nor endanger the pricking of thy hand, to weed them up? Thinkest thou to eat bread, and not sweat? Hast thou a prerogative above the common Law of Nature? Or must God insert a particular clause of exemption for thy sake?'[1]

Almost on a level with Donne's hatred of sloth is his hatred of a purely formal religion, which honours God by outward observances without a corresponding spirit of love

[1] *XXVI Sermons*, 24. 343.

in the heart. As in his youth he had scornfully rejected the conventional woman-worship of the sonneteers and had substituted a fashion of almost brutal plain-speaking, so in religion he denounced the insincerity of many who thought that a zealous attendance at church on Sunday would atone for the greed and sharp practice in which they indulged on week-days. 'Sermons unpractised are threepiled sins',[1] he said on one occasion, and on another, 'Humiliation is the beginning of sanctification; and as without this, without holinesse, no man shall see God, though he pore whole nights upon the Bible; so without that, without humility, no man shall heare God speake to his soule, though hee heare three two-houres Sermons every day.'[2]

He spoke yet more scathingly to some members of his congregation:

'*Gods House is the house of Prayer*; It is his Court of Requests; There he receives petitions, there he gives Order upon them. And you come to God in his House, as though you came to keepe him company, to sit downe, and talke with him halfe an houre; or you come as Ambassadors, covered in his presence, as though ye came from as great a Prince as he. You meet below, and there make your bargaines, for biting, for devouring Usury, and then you come up hither to prayers, and so make God your Broker. You rob, and spoile, and eat his people as bread, by Extortion, and bribery, and deceitfull waights and measures, and deluding oathes in buying and selling, and then come hither, and so make God your Receiver, and his house a den of Thieves. His house is *Sanctum Sanctorum*, The holiest of holies, and you make it onely *Sanctuarium*; It should be a place sanctified by your devotions, and you make it onely a Sanctuary to priviledge Malefactors, A place that may redeeme you from the ill opinion of men, who must in charity be bound to thinke well of you, because they see you here.'[3]

This passage shows, however, clearly enough that while Donne detested formalism in religion he demanded reverence and orderliness in church worship. Many of the sermons afford curious evidence of the slovenly behaviour which was then common during divine service. Thus, preaching at

[1] *LXXX Sermons*, 45. 455.
[2] Ibid. 7. 73 (wrongly numbered in the Folio as 75).
[3] Ibid. 68. 692.

St. Dunstan's, he rebukes those who wear their hats during the reading of the Lessons.

'Are they in the Kings house at so much liberty as in their own? and is not this the King of Kings house? Or have they seene the King in his owne house, use that liberty to cover himselfe in his ordinary manner of covering, at any part of Divine Service? Every Preacher will look, and justly, to have the Congregation uncovered at the reading of his Text: and is not the reading of the Lesson, at time of Prayer, the same Word of the same God, to be received with the same reverence? . . . And therefore I must humbly intreat them, who make this Quire the place of their Devotion, to testifie their devotion by more outward reverence there; wee know our parts in this place, and we doe them; why any stranger should think himself more priviledged in this part of Gods House, then we, I know not. I presume no man will mis-interpret this that I say here now; nor, if this may not prevaile, mis-interpret the service of our Officers, if their continuing in that unreverent manner give our Officers occasion to warn them of that personally in the place, whensoever they see them stray into that uncomely negligence. They should not blame me now, they must not blame them then, when they call upon them for this reverence in this Quire; neither truly can there be any greater injustice, then when they who will not do their duties, blame others for doing theirs.'[1]

He has the same tone of dignified rebuke for those persons, some of them of high station, who refuse to kneel in church:

'Now, and here, within these wals, and at this houre, comes Christ unto you, in the offer of this abundance; and with what penuriousnesse, penuriousnesse of devotion, penuriousnesse of reverence do you meet him here? *Deus stetit*, saies *David*, *God standeth in the Congregation*; does God stand there, and wilt thou sit? sit, and never kneele? I would speake so, as the congregation should not know whom I meane; but so, as that they whom it concernes, might know I meane them; I would speake: for, I must say, that there come some persons to this Church, and persons of example to many that come with them, of whom, (excepting some few, who must therefore have their praise from us, as, no doubt, they have their thanks and blessings from God)

[1] *L Sermons*, 50. 470, 471. With this compare Walton's remark about George Herbert, that 'if he were at any time too zealous in his sermons, it was in reproving the indecencies of the people's behaviour in the time of Divine Service'.

I never saw Master nor servant kneele, at his comming into this Church, or at any part of divine service . . . kneeling is the sinners posture; if thou come hither in the quality of a sinner, (and, if thou do not so, what doest thou here, the whole need not the Physitian) put thy selfe into the posture of a sinner, kneele.'[1]

Many other passages in the *Sermons* show very clearly Donne's high ideal of his office. Preaching at the Spital in 1622 he set forth his own view of the necessary equipment of those who would be 'ministers of God's Word and Sacraments'. They must have a true sense of vocation, must be indeed called of God and also ordained by lawful authority, and in addition they must have a due equipment of learning, follow holiness of life, and preach zealously and frequently.

What was Donne's teaching with regard to the spiritual life and what was the experience which lay behind that teaching? For him it began at the very entrance to bodily life.

'*God* wrapt mee up in his Couenant, and deriu'd mee from *Christian Parents*; I suck'd *Christian* bloud, in my Mothers wombe, and *Christian* milke at my Nurses breast. The first sound that I heard, in the world, was the voice of *Christians*; and the first *Character*, that I was taught to know, was the *Crosse* of CHRIST IESVS. How many children that are borne so, borne within the *Couenant*, borne of *Christian Parents*, doe yet die before they bee *baptiz'd*, though they were borne *heires* to *Baptisme*? But *God* hath afforded me the seale of that *Sacrament*.'[2]

Yet though he had been made a member of the Christian Church in baptism, and had grown up in a Christian home, he had sinned repeatedly, and the burden of his sins lay heavy on his soul. His sense of guilt was very strong, and finds expression in the *Holy Sonnets* and in some of the sermons:

> I dare not move my dimme eyes any way,
> Despaire behind, and death before doth cast
> Such terrour, and my feeble flesh doth waste
> By sinne in it, which it t'wards hell doth weigh;

[1] *LXXX Sermons*, no. 7, preached upon Christmas Day, pp. 72, 73 (misnumbered as 75 in the Folio).

[2] *Sermon of Commemoration of the Lady Danvers*, pp. 79, 80.

Onely thou art above, and when towards thee
By thy leave I can looke, I rise againe;
But our old subtle foe so tempteth me,
That not one houre my selfe I can sustaine;
Thy Grace may wing me to prevent his art,
And thou like Adamant draw mine iron heart.[1]

Thus for Donne, as for other Christian theologians, conversion is the first stage in the soul's pilgrimage towards God. In his own words, it is a turning away from our sin and a returning towards God.[2] Conversion is with some men, as with St. Paul, a crisis of startling abruptness; in others it is the culmination of a long gradual process. Whatever uncertainty there may be about the exact date of Donne's conversion, there can be none about the fact that the cynical, sensual man of the world became the divine whose 'contemplative, harmless, humble, and holy life and conversation' made him, according to his earliest biographer, 'a shining light among his old friends'.

The prayers which form part of the *Essays in Divinity* give us a picture of Donne's mind at the time of his conversion. He is weary of sin, weary of the misery of a self-centred, self-indulgent life. He cries to God, 'Though this soul of mine, by which I partake thee, begin not now, yet let this minute, O God, this happy minute of thy visitation, be the beginning of her conversion, and shaking away confusion, darknesse and barrennesse; and let her now produce Creatures, thoughts, words, and deeds agreeable to thee.'[3] He determines to devote himself entirely to the service of God, and in so doing he gives up any reliance on his own abilities or merits of any kind. He renounces all confidence even in his own repentance, for he admits that he has found 'by many lamentable experiences' that he cannot perform his promises to God by his own efforts, and that he relapses again and again into those sins of which again and again he has repented.[4] He makes the venture of faith, and flings himself upon the mercy of God in Christ: 'Let me, in despite of Me, be of so much use to thy glory, that by thy

[1] Grierson, i. 322.
[2] *XXVI Sermons*, 8. 119.
[3] *Essays in Divinity* (1651), p. 77.
[4] Ibid., p. 221.

mercy to my sin, other sinners may see how much sin thou canst pardon.'[1]

If Donne had chosen to leave us a record of the experiences which led up to and followed his conversion, he might have written a spiritual autobiography of surpassing interest. But he never attempted the task, and later writers must be content to try and piece together some of the fragments of personal experience which are scattered throughout the mass of the poems, sermons, and letters. We are left with many gaps and obscurities, and it is difficult to mark out clearly the various stages through which he passed. The world around noted the change in him, and friends like Walton observed his growth in holiness and detachment from earthly things. Such a transformation does not take place without many agonies of heart and soul. The process of purgation is painful to even the holiest of Christians, and to Donne, with his strong passions and vivid memories of his earlier sins, it must have caused the keenest suffering. In the nineteenth *Holy Sonnet* he describes the fluctuations of his spiritual life:

> Oh, to vex me, contraryes meet in one;
> Inconstancy unnaturally hath begott
> A constant habit; that when I would not
> I change in vowes, and in devotione.
> As humorous is my contritione
> As my prophane Love, and as soone forgott:
> As ridlingly distemper'd, cold and hott,
> As praying, as mute; as infinite, as none.
> I durst not view heaven yesterday; and today
> In prayers, and flattering speaches I court God:
> Tomorrow I quake with true feare of his rod.
> So my devout fitts come and go away
> Like a fantastique Ague: save that here
> Those are my best dayes, when I shake with feare.[2]

There are similar passages in one or two of the sermons, where Donne is evidently recounting to his hearers some of his own past experiences:

'I throw my selfe downe in my Chamber, and I call in, and invite

[1] Ibid., p. 217.

[2] *Holy Sonnets*, xix (Grierson, i. 331).

God, and his Angels thither, and when they are there, I neglect God and his Angels, for the noise of a Flie, for the ratling of a Coach, for the whining of a doore; I talke on, in the same posture of praying; Eyes lifted up; knees bowed downe; as though I prayed to God; and, if God, or his Angels should aske me, when I thought last of God in that prayer, I cannot tell: Sometimes I finde that I had forgot what I was about, but when I began to forget it, I cannot tell. A memory of yesterdays pleasures, a feare of to morrows dangers, a straw under my knee, a noise in mine eare, a light in mine eye, an anything, a nothing, a fancy, a Chimera in my braine, troubles me in my prayer. So certainely is there nothing, nothing in spirituall things, perfect in this world.'[1]

'None of us hath got the victory over flesh and blood, and yet we have greater enemies then flesh and blood are. Some disciplines, some mortifications we have against flesh and blood . . . but for these powers and principalities, I know not where to watch them, how to encounter them. I passe my time sociably and merrily in cheerful conversation, in musique, in feasting, in Comedies, in wantonnesse; and I never heare all this while of any power or principality, my Conscience spies no such enemy in all this. And then alone, between God and me at midnight, some beam of his grace shines out upon me, and by that light I see this Prince of darknesse, and then I finde that I have been the subject, the slave of these powers and principalities, when I thought not of them. Well, I see them, and I try then to dispossesse my selfe of them, and I make my recourse to the powerfullest exorcisme that is, I turne to hearty and earnest prayer to God, and I fix my thoughts strongly (as I thinke) upon him, and before I have perfected one petition, one period of my prayer, a power and principality is got into me againe. *Spiritus soporis*, The spirit of slumber closes mine eyes, and I pray drousily; Or *spiritus vertiginis*, the spirit of deviation, and vaine repetition, and I pray giddily, and circularly, and returne againe and againe to that I have said before, and perceive not that I do so; and *nescio cujus spiritus sim*, (as our Saviour said, rebuking his Disciples, who were so vehement for the burning of the Samaritans, *you know not of what spirit you are*) I pray, and know not of what spirit I am, I consider not mine own purpose in prayer; And by this advantage, this doore of inconsideration, enters *spiritus erroris*, The seducing spirit, the spirit of error, and I pray not onely negligently, but erroniously, dangerously, for such things as disconduce to the glory of God, and my true happinesse, if they were granted. Nay, even the Prophet *Hosea's spiritus fornicationum*, enters into me, *The spirit of fornication*,

[1] *LXXX Sermons*, 80. 820.

that is, some remembrance of the wantonnesse of my youth, some misinterpretation of a word in my prayer, that may beare an ill sense, some unclean spirit, some power or principality hath depraved my prayer, and slackned my zeale. And this is my greatest misery of all, that when that which fights for me, and fights against me too, sicknesse, hath laid me upon my last bed, then in my weakest estate, these powers and principalities shall be in their full practise against me.'[1]

A careful study of Donne's works shows that the particular sins for which he felt the deepest repentance were those sins of the flesh committed in his youth. Again and again he laments the ruin wrought in his soul by wantonness and lust:

In mine Idolatry what showres of raine
Mine eyes did waste? what griefs my heart did rent?
That sufferance was my sinne; now I repent;
'Cause I did suffer I must suffer paine.[2]

I am a little world made cunningly
Of Elements, and an Angelike spright,
But black sinne hath betraid to endlesse night
My worlds both parts, and (oh) both parts must die.
. . . But oh it must be burnt! alas the fire
Of lust and envie have burnt it heretofore,
And made it fouler; Let their flames retire,
And burne me O Lord, with a fiery zeale
Of thee and thy house, which doth in eating heale.[3]

Donne felt that the guilt of these past sins was aggravated by the fact that he had alluded to them and even glorified them in some of his early poems. True, these poems were never published during his life-time, and according to Walton and Ben Jonson, he repented deeply of them and sought to destroy all available copies.[4] But his reputation as a poet was considerable, and his verses had enjoyed a wide

[1] *LXXX Sermons*, 45. 452, 453.

[2] *Holy Sonnets*, iii. 5–8.

[3] Ibid. v. 1–4, 10–14 (Grierson, i. 324).

[4] Walton, *Life* (1675), p. 53. 'It is a truth, that in his penitential years, viewing some of those pieces that had been loosely (God knows, too loosely) scattered in his youth, he wish't they had been abortive, or, so short liv'd that his own eyes had witnessed their funerals.' Ben Jonson, *Conversations with William Drummond*, 'and now, since he was made Doctor, repenteth highlie, and seeketh to destroy all his poems'.

circulation in manuscript which made this attempt unsuccessful. Doubtless it was the thought of these poems which gave a sting to the idea, expressed in several of his sermons, that in hell the authors of licentious books or pictures may suffer additional tortures for the sins which others have committed at their instigation.[1]

Donne was, however, sufficiently convinced of the truth of the Christian doctrine of the Atonement to believe that his repentance for these sins had been accepted in virtue of his faith in the blood of Christ. In the *Holy Sonnets* he communes thus with his own soul:

> Yet grace, if thou repent, thou canst not lacke;
> But who shall give thee that grace to beginne?
> Oh make thy selfe with holy mourning blacke,
> And red with blushing, as thou art with sinne;
> Or wash thee in Christs blood, which hath this might
> That being red, it dyes red soules to white.[2]

But though he believed that his past sins had been pardoned he often expressed his fear of a relapse. And it is clear that, however spotless Donne's outer life became, he had to wrestle through many years with thoughts and desires which he regarded as sinful. It is this conflict of the lower with the higher self, of the spirit with the flesh, that gives a strange intensity to all Donne's devotional work, whether in poetry or prose.

The conflict in Donne's soul was evidently a protracted one, and was of the same kind as that endured by Augustine and many other of the saints. It finds a parallel in St. Paul's words, 'I delight in the law of God after the inward man; but I see another law in my members, warring against the law of my mind, and bringing me into captivity to the law of sin which is in my members';[3] and Donne could have repeated the Apostle's outburst, 'O wretched man that I am! Who shall deliver me from the body of this death?'

There was another sin—that of despair—into which Donne regarded himself as especially likely to fall. At times

[1] *L Sermons*, 47. 445.
[2] *Holy Sonnets*, iv. 9–14 (Grierson, i. 323).
[3] Rom. vii. 22–4.

he writhed under the thought of himself as a lost soul. He expresses this fear in his *Hymn to God the Father:*

> I have a sinne of feare, that when I have spunne
> My last thred, I shall perish on the shore;
> But sweare by thy selfe, that at my death thy sonne
> Shall shine as he shines now, and heretofore;
> And, having done that, Thou haste done,
> I feare no more.[1]

The *Devotions* give utterance to the same thought: 'But thine Apostles feare takes hold of me, *that when I have preached to others, I my selfe should bee a cast-way;* and therefore am I *cast downe*, that I might not bee *cast away*.'[2]

It is important, however, to realize that Donne regarded this morbid fear of damnation as a sin against which he had to struggle. His theology did not, like Cowper's, incite him to look on himself as irretrievably lost, but encouraged him to see in himself a sinner indeed, perhaps the chief of sinners, but still a sinner saved by the mercy of Christ. He was conscious of his own repentance, and distrust of salvation seemed to him a lack of faith. This 'diffidence', as Donne sometimes terms it, was common among religious people of the seventeenth century, and doubtless it was fostered by the gloomy tinge of the popular Calvinistic theology of the day, with its belief in predestination to damnation. Donne says in one of his sermons that he met with seven diffident and dejected souls for one presumptuous one, and that as a pastor he had much exercise in raising dejected spirits.[3] He himself refused to believe this Calvinistic doctrine of 'reprobation', and denounced it vigorously in many of his sermons.[4] It is clear, too, that he found much comfort for his own soul in this necessity of encouraging his

[1] *Hymn to God the Father*, ll. 13–18 (Grierson, i. 369).

[2] *Devotions upon Emergent Occasions*, Expostulation, p. 3.

[3] *LXXX Sermons*, 75. 764. See also pp. 671, 672, where Donne speaks of 'inordinate griefe, and diffidence of Gods mercy' and laments that 'God hath accompanied, and complicated almost all our bodily diseases of these times, with an extraordinary sadnesse, a predominant melancholy, a faintnesse of heart'.

[4] e.g. *LXXX Sermons*, 7. 67; *L Sermons*, 50. 469.

flock. Thus in speaking of his treatment of such dejected souls, he adds:

'When I have given that man comfort, that man hath given me a Sacrament, hee hath given me a seale and evidence of Gods favour upon me; I have received from him, in his receiving from me; I leave him comforted in Christ Jesus, and I goe away comforted in my selfe, that Christ Jesus hath made me an instrument of the dispensation of his mercy; And I argue to my selfe, and say, Lord, when I went, I was sure, that thou who hadst received me to mercy, wouldst also receive him, who could not be so great a sinner as I; And now, when I come away, I am sure, that thou who art returned to him, and hast re-manifested thy selfe to him, who, in the diffidence of his sad soule, thought thee gone for ever, wilt never depart from mee, nor hide thy selfe from me, who desire to dwell in thy presence.'[1]

This deep conviction of sin has led some Christians to practise austerities of every kind as a means of purification. They have tried to subdue their sinful flesh by prolonged fasting, by solitary confinement, by flagellation, and by other forms of self-torture. There is no trace of such asceticism in Donne's history, though his later life showed a rigorous self-discipline. He disapproved of 'uncommanded and inhuman flagellations and whippings' as dishonouring the body. Retirement into a cloister or a cell seemed to him generally to be a retreat from the enemy, not a victory, though he was willing to admit that some might have a vocation for such a life.[2]

Natural affections seemed to him to be implanted by God, and therefore to be honourable so long as they were wisely directed. Love to him was 'the richest mantle', 'the noblest affection, that the nature of man hath'.[3] He knew in his own experience the love of a son for his mother, of a husband for his wife, of a father for his children. In all these relations he was tender and devoted. He found in them a stepping-stone to heaven, a rung in the ladder by which he might ascend to the love of God. He was a faithful and generous friend, repaying in his prosperity the kindness which had been shown him in years of misfortune. Similarly,

[1] *LXXX Sermons*, 75. 764.
[2] *Essays in Divinity*, p. 155.
[3] *XXVI Sermons*, 24. 335.

he retained his interest in music and poetry. He did not give up the writing of verse after his ordination, though some of his acquaintances thought it levity in him to produce even so serious a poem as the *Hymne to the Saints and the Marquess Hamilton.*[1]

For Donne, as for other Christian thinkers, all virtues are summed up in love, and the process of purgation and self-discipline has no value except in so far as it is the work of love. 'God is love; and he that dwelleth in love, dwelleth in God, and God in him.' 'He therefore that hath this hope in him, purifieth himself even as He is pure.' So Donne rises from the love of the creature to that of the Creator, and finds in this love the one essential means of purification:

'*Love*, in Divinity, is such an attribute, or such a notion, as designs to us one person in the Trinity; and that person who communicates, and applies to us, the other two persons, that is, *The Holy Ghost*: So that, as there is no *power*, but with relation to the *Father*, nor *wisdom* but with relation to the *Son*, so there should be no *love* but in the *Holy Ghost*, from whom comes this pureness of heart, and consequently the love of it necessarily: For, the love of this pureness is part of this pureness it self, and no man hath it, except he love it. All love which is placed upon lower things, admits satiety; but this love of this pureness, always grows, always proceeds: It does not onely file off the rust of our hearts, in purging us of old habits, but proceeds to a daily polishing of the heart, in an exact watchfulness, and brings us to that brightness, *Ut ipse videas faciem in corde, et alii videant cor in facie* (*Augustine*). That thou maist see thy face in thy heart, and the world may see thy heart in thy face; indeed, that to both, both heart and face may be all one.... Nor can this pureness of heart, though by these means attain'd to, be preserved, but by this noble and incorruptible affection of Love, that puts a true value upon it, and therefore prefers it above all other things.'[2]

[1] Chamberlayne, in forwarding a copy of 'certain verses of our Dean of Pauls upon the death of the Marquis of Hamilton', adds 'though they be reasonable, witty, and well done, yet I could wish a man of his years and place to give over versifying' (quoted by Dr. Jessopp, *John Donne*, pp. 170, 171).

[2] *XXVI Sermons*, 24. 336–42. The whole passage from which these extracts are taken is worth studying for its recognition both of the sanctity of earthly love (marked, it must be added, by a touch of Donne's consciousness of masculine superiority) and of the relation of such love to the higher and more spiritual passion.

The mercy of God kindled in Donne an ecstasy of adoring love. 'All divinity is love or wonder.'[1] Again and again in the sermons he loses himself in the rapturous contemplation of the mercy of God.

'O glorious beauty, infinitely reverend, infinitely fresh and young, we come late to thy love, if we consider the past daies of our lives, but early if thou beest pleased to reckon with us from this houre of the shining of thy grace upon us.'[2]

The spiritual life meant for him a growing joy in the service of God. He devoted a large part of his sermons to the inculcation of joy in the Lord, and this gladness was evidently experienced by his own heart.

'He hath joy, and not a Cistern but a fountain, the fountaine of joy, that rejoyces in God.'[3] 'That which Christ shall say to thy soule then at the last Judgement, *Enter into thy Masters joy*, Hee sayes to thy conscience now, *Enter into thy Masters joy*. The everlastingnesse of the joy is the blessednesse of the next life, but the entring, the inchoation is afforded here.'[4]

'No man hath so much pleasure in this life, as he that is at peace with God. What an Organe hath that man tuned, how hath he brought all things in the world to a Consort, and what a blessed Anthem doth he sing to that Organe, that is at peace with God? His Rye-bread is *Manna*, and his Beefe is *Quailes*, his day-labours are thrustings at the narrow gate into Heaven, and his night-watchings are extasies and evocations of his soule into the presence and communion of Saints, his sweat is *Pearls*, and his bloud is *Rubies*, it is at peace with God. No man that is at suite in himselfe, no man that carrieth a *Westminster* in his bosome, and is *Plaintiffe* and *Defendant* too, no man that serveth himselfe with Process out of his owne Conscience, for every nights pleasure that he taketh, in the morning, and for every dayes pound that he getteth, in the evening, hath any of the pleasure, or profit, that may be had in this life; nor any that is not at peace with God.'[5]

Illumination has meant to many poets a new perception of the unity and life of Nature. For Wordsworth, or for Donne's disciple Vaughan, it involved the recognition of

[1] *A Valediction: of the booke* (Grierson, i. 30).
[2] *XXVI Sermons*, 18. 269.
[3] *L Sermons*, 50. 472.
[4] *LXXX Sermons*, 66. 672.
[5] *L Sermons*, 40. 370.

> a sense sublime
> Of something far more deeply interfused,
> Whose dwelling is the light of setting suns,
> And the round ocean and the living air,
> And the blue sky, and in the mind of man.

Blake and Tennyson and Francis Thompson saw the whole secret of the universe lying hid in the grain of sand or the flower in the crannied wall. And not only the mystical poets but also certain of the saints know the same experience, which transfigures for them the face of the visible world. St. Francis preaching to his sisters the birds, Rose of Lima calling the flowers in the garden to praise God with her, George Fox seeing the whole creation opened to him so that all things became new—these in their own way express one form of mystical illumination.

Donne, however, shows no sign of such an experience. He was a Londoner born and bred, and loved the town with the fervour of Dr. Johnson or Charles Lamb. He sought the divine within the soul of man, and this is what would be expected from a study of his early poetry. He, more than any other English poet, is preoccupied with intellectual conceptions. The imagery of his love-poems is drawn not from the garden or the meadow, but from the scholastic definitions of Aquinas. So in his moments of illumination he sees the work of God in the connexion of cause and effect,[1] in the endless movement of the universe as an outward efflux of creative activity and an inward return of love towards the Author of its being; while the supreme expression of this activity is to be found in the mind of man, which has always kept a spark of the divine fire, and which remains ready to burst, at a touch from its Maker, into a flame of adoration and desire.

Donne has often been described as a mystic, and it is clear from his secular poems, especially *The Ecstasie* and *Elegie V* 'His Picture', that he was acquainted with mystical writings, and could use language proper to the mystical experience.[2]

[1] *LXXX Sermons*, 15. 146; *XXVI Sermons*, 13. 181.

[2] See Grierson's analysis of *The Ecstasie* in *Poems*, ii. 42. He distinguishes the exodus of the souls, the perfect quiet, the new insight, and the contact

This does not, however, necessarily prove him to have been a mystic,[1] and in the *Sermons* and *Devotions* there is little which can be called mystical in the technical sense of the term. This is particularly evident in his treatment of prayer and meditation, for it is here that the cleavage is most evident between such writers as Hooker and Andrewes on the one hand and mystics like Richard Rolle and St. John of the Cross on the other. This is not a cleavage between Catholic and Protestant, for the majority of Catholic writers are as non-mystical as Andrewes. In a sermon of uncertain date Donne gives us one of his fullest descriptions of what prayer may and should be.

'It may be mentall, for we may thinke prayers. It may be vocall, for we may speake prayers. It may be actuall, for we do prayers. . . . So then to do the office of your vocation sincerely, is to pray. . . . Since then every rectified man, is the temple of the Holy Ghost, when he prays, it is the Holy Ghost it selfe that prays; and what can be denied, where the Asker gives? He plays with us, as children, shewes us pleasing things, that we might cry for them, and have them. Before we call, he answers, and when we speak, he heares. . . . Physicians observe some symptoms so violent, that they must neglect the disease for a time, and labour to cure the accident, as burning fevers, in Dysenteries. So in the sinfull consumption of the soule, a stupidity and indisposition to prayer, must first be cured. . . . Things absolutely good, as Remission of sinnes, we may absolutely beg: and, to escape things absolutely ill, as sinne. But mean and indifferent things, qualified by the circumstances, we must aske conditionally and referringly to the givers will.'[2]

Donne held that prayer is not a means of wresting something from an unwilling God, but a means of receiving what God has already planned to give us. In the act of prayer we place ourselves in God's hands so that He may communicate to us Himself and whatever He may please

and union of the souls, and relates these stages to the description of 'ecstasy' given by Plotinus in the *Sixth Ennead*, ix. 11. See also H. L. Gardner, 'John Donne: Note on *Elegie V*', *M.L.R.* xxxix. 333–7.

[1] In the first edition of this study I used the term 'mystic' too loosely in my account of Donne's spiritual experience. I am indebted to Miss H. L. Gardner for some helpful criticism on this subject.

[2] *L Sermons*, 34. 304–7.

to give us. This view is clearly expressed in a letter written by Donne to his friend Sir Henry Goodyer:

'. . . even that holy exercise [i.e. prayer] may not be done inopportunely, no nor importunely. . . . And, our accesses to his [God's] presence are but his descents into us; and when we get any thing by prayer, he gave us beforehand the thing and the petition. For, I scarce think any ineffectuall prayer free from both sin, and the punishment of sin: yet as God seposed a seventh of our time for his exterior worship, and as his Christian Church early presented him a type[1] of the whole year in a Lent, and after imposed the obligation of canonique hours, constituting thereby morall Sabbaths every day; I am farre from dehorting those fixed devotions: But I had rather it were bestowed upon thanksgiving then petition, upon praise then prayer; not that God is indeared by that, or wearied by this; all is one in the receiver, but not in the sender: and thanks doth both offices; for, nothing doth so innocently provoke new graces, as gratitude.'[2]

Unlike the Puritans, Donne preferred short prayers to long:

'I would also rather make short prayers then extend them, though God can neither be surprised, nor besieged: for, long prayers have more of the man, as ambition of eloquence, and a complacencie in the work, and more of the Devil by often distractions: for, after in the beginning we have well intreated God to hearken, we speak no more to him.'[3]

Donne certainly both preached and practised those forms of prayer which all Christian saints recommend—adoration, thanksgiving, confession of sin, petition for ourselves, and intercession for others, to which we may add, from the evidence of the *Devotions*, some kind of discursive meditation. Three of these are enumerated in a single sentence: 'He [God] loves to hear us tell him, even those things which he knew before; his Benefits in our Thankfulness, And our sins in our Confessions, And our necessities in our Petitions.'[4] Walton also mentions Donne's use of ejaculatory prayer. 'He did much contemplate (especially after he entred into

[1] Should we read 'a tithe', i.e. a tenth, for 'a type'?
[2] *Letters* (1651), pp. 110–11 (Gosse, i. 228–9).
[3] Ibid., pp. 111–12.
[4] *XXVI Sermons*, 3. 31.

his Sacred Calling) the *mercies* of Almighty God, the *immortality of the Soul*, and the *joyes of Heaven*; and would often say, *Blessed be God that he is God divinely like himself*.'[1] This shows Donne as a good Christian, but not necessarily as a mystic. Walter Hilton in his *Scale of Perfection* distinguishes three kinds of contemplation, and it is clear from Donne's descriptions of his own feelings when at prayer that he had not attained to the state of 'great rest of body and soul' which Hilton described as 'the higher degree of the second part of contemplation', or to 'the third part of contemplation'.[2]

There is, however, a splendid passage in one of the great Easter sermons which suggests that Donne had some experience of the ecstasy of mystical contemplation.

'If I can say, (and my conscience doe not tell me, that I belye mine owne state) if I can say, That the blood of my Saviour runs in my veines, That the breath of his Spirit quickens all my purposes, that all my deaths have their Resurrection, all my sins their remorses, all my rebellions their reconciliations, I will harken no more after this question,[3] as it is intended *de morte naturali*, of a naturall death, I know I must die that death, what care I? nor *de morte spirituali*, the death of sin, I know I doe, and shall die so; why despaire I? but I will finde out another death, *mortem raptus*, a death of rapture, and of extasie, that death which S. *Paul* died more then once, The death which S. *Gregory* speaks of, *Divina contemplatio quoddam sepulchrum animæ*, The contemplation of God, and heaven, is a kinde of buriall, and Sepulchre, and rest of the soule; and in this death of rapture, and extasie, in this death of the Contemplation of my interest in my Saviour, I shall finde my self, and all my sins enterred, and entombed in his wounds, and like a Lily in Paradise, out of red earth, I shall see my soule rise out of his blade, in a candor, and in an innocence, contracted there, acceptable in the sight of his Father.'[4]

[1] Walton, *Lives* (1670), Life of Donne, p. 80.

[2] *The Scale of Perfection*, ed. E. Underhill, pp. 6–18. Hilton insists that the 'third part of contemplation' is given by the grace of God where He will 'but it is special, not common. And also though a man which is active have the gift of it by a special grace, nevertheless the full use of it may no man have, but he be solitary and in life contemplative.'

[3] i.e. the question which formed Donne's text on this occasion, 'What man is he that liveth, and shall not see death?'

[4] *LXXX Sermons*, 27. 273–4. For the 'red earth' cf. ib. 34. 338, 'In the

Certain mystics have described the special revelations which they have enjoyed at these moments of contemplation. Donne expected no such revelations, and in his sermons he warned his hearers against the Revelations of St. Bridget,[1] and similar works. Here is a passage in which Donne definitely attacks these claims to special revelation:

'There is a Pureness, a cleanness imagin'd (rather dream't of) in the *Romane Church*, by which (as their words are) the soul is abstracted, not onely *à Passionibus*, but *à Phantasmatibus*, not onely from passions, and perturbations, but from the ordinary way of coming to know any thing; The soul (say they) of men so purified, understands no longer, *per phantasmata rerum corporalium*; not by having any thing presented by the fantasie to the senses, and so to the understanding, but altogether by a familiar conversation with God, and an immediate revelation from God . . . . This is that Pureness in the *Romane Church*, by which the founder of the Last Order amongst them, *Philip Nerius*, had not onely utterly emptied his heart of the world, but had fill'd it too full of God; for, so (say they) he was fain to cry sometimes, *Recede a me Domine*, O Lord go farther from me, and let me have a less portion of thee. But who would be loath to sink, by being over-fraited with God, or loath to over-set, by having so much of that winde, the breath of the Spirit of God? Privation of the presence of God, is Hell; a diminution of it, is a step toward it. Fruition of his presence is Heaven; and shall any Man be afraid of having too much Heaven, too much God? . . . This Pureness is not in their heart, but in their fantasie.'[2]

In thus rejecting the claim of certain mystics Donne did not wish to deny the possibility of an ecstatic union with God such as that described by St. Paul or St. Augustine. He makes this plain on several occasions. In a sermon preached on the Feast of the Conversion of St. Paul he says:

great field of clay, of red earth, that man was made of, and mankind, I am a clod.' Theodoret, *In Genesin*, ch. xxv (in Migne, *P.G.*, lxxx. 40), inferred from a false etymology that the soil of Eden, *ὅθεν καὶ ὁ Ἀδὰμ ἐπλάσθη*, was red: *Ἀδὰμ ἐκ τοῦ ἀπὸ τῆς γῆς ἐν Ἐδὲμ γεγενῆσθαι προσηγορεύθη· Ἐδὼμ γὰρ τὸ πυρρόν.*

[1] *Fifty Sermons*, 24. 202: 'A book of so much blasphemy, and impertinency, and incredibility, that if a Heathen were to be converted, he would sooner be brought to believe *Ovids Metamorphoses*, then *Brigids Revelations*, to conduce to Religion.'

[2] *XXVI Sermons*, 24. 324, 325.

'[God] gave him a Rapture, an Extasie, and in that, an appropinquation, an approximation to himselfe, and so some possession of Heaven in this life.'[1] But he distinguishes this momentary vision from that sight of the essence of God which forms the Beatific Vision of the saints in glory:

'S. *Augustine* speaking of discourses that passed between his mother, and him, not long before her death, sayes, *Perambulavimus cuncta mortalia, et ipsum cælum*, We talked ourselves above this earth, and above all the heavens; *Venimus in mentes nostras, et transcendimus eas*, We came to the consideration of our owne mindes, and our owne soules, and we got above our own soules; that is, to the consideration of that place where our soules should be for ever; and we could consider God then, but then wee could not see God in his Essence. As it may be fairely argued that Christ suffered not the very torments of very hell, because it is essentiall to the torments of hell, to be eternall, They were not torments of hell, if they received an end; So is it fairely argued too, That neither *Adam* in his extasie in Paradise, nor *Moses* in his conversation in the Mount, nor the other Apostles in the Transfiguration of Christ, nor S. *Paul* in his rapture to the third heavens, saw the Essence of God, because he that is admitted to that sight of God, can never look off, nor lose that sight againe. Only in heaven shall God proceed to this patefaction, this manifestation, this revelation of himself; And that by the light of glory.'[2]

Thus it is clear that he regarded the highest state to which a Christian could attain in this life as that of illumination—an experience which involved constant intercourse with God, and which might be raised at moments to a height of transcendental ecstasy, but was nevertheless liable to interruption. It was this lack of absolute continuity that made him, following Aquinas, differentiate mystical experience here, even at its height, from the Beatific Vision. He who has once seen that Vision cannot turn away his eyes. Moreover, there is a sense in which flesh and blood cannot inherit the kingdom of God. '*No man ever saw God and liv'd*; and yet, I shall not live till I see God; and when I have seen him I shall never dye.'[3] Yet this life and the

[1] *LXXX Sermons*, 48. 476.

[2] Ibid. 23. 230. Donne supports his opinion by an appeal to the authority of Aquinas.

[3] *L Sermons*, 14. 117.

next are not violently sundered from one another. The light of glory has its dawn here, though the noon-tide must come hereafter.[1] The joy of heaven begins on earth, in the vision which the pure in heart see, even now, of the Eternal Truth and Goodness.

'The pure in heart are blessed already, not onely comparatively, that they are in a better way of Blessednesse, then others are, but actually in a present possession of it: for this world and the next world, are not, to the pure in heart, two houses, but two roomes,[2] a Gallery to passe thorough, and a Lodging to rest in, in the same House, which are both under one roofe, Christ Jesus; The Militant and the Triumphant, are not two Churches, but this the Porch, and that the Chancell of the same Church, which are under one head, Christ Jesus; so the Joy, and the sense of Salvation, which the pure in heart have here, is not a joy severed from the Joy of heaven, but a Joy that begins in us here, and continues, and accompanies us thither, and there flowes on, and dilates it selfe to an infinite expansion.'[3]

Donne was careful to emphasize that private prayer by itself was not enough. The joy and the sense of salvation of which he spoke were to be found in the fellowship of the Church. In the prayers of the church we realize our common humanity, our common sinfulness, and offer our common thanksgivings, raised to their highest in the Holy Communion, which is the Eucharist, a sacrifice of praise and thanksgiving.

'Yet thou must heare this voice of the Archangell in the Trumpet of God. The Trumpet of God is his loudest instrument; and his loudest Instrument is his publique Ordinance in the Church; Prayer, Preaching, and Sacraments; Heare him in these; In all these; come not to heare him in the Sermon alone, but come to him in Prayer, and in the Sacrament too. For, except the voyce come in the Trumpet of God, (that is, in the publique Ordinance of his Church) thou canst not know it to be the voyce of the Archangell.'[4]

'Heaven is here; here in Gods Church, in his Word, in his Sacra-

[1] *LXXX Sermons*, 12. 122.

[2] Cf. *Second Anniversary*, ll. 85, 86:

Thinke then, my soule, that death is but a Groome,
Which brings a Taper to the outward roome.

[3] *LXXX Sermons*, 12. 119.

[4] Ibid. 26. 258.

ments, in his Ordinances; set thy heart upon them, The Promises of the Gospel, The Seals of Reconciliation, and thou hast that treasure which is thy *Viaticum*. . . .'[1]

Donne had found in his own experience this joy in the worship offered by the Church. Walton quotes him as saying:

'The words of this Hymne [i.e. the *Hymn to God the Father*] have restored to me the same thoughts of joy that possest my Soul in my sickness when I composed it. And, O the power of Church-musick! that Harmony added to it has raised the Affections of my heart, and quickened my graces of zeal and gratitude; and I observe, that I alwayes return from paying this publick duty of Prayer and Praise to God, with an unexpressible tranquillity of mind, and a willingness to leave the world.'[2]

One aspect of Donne's theology—his attitude towards the Roman Church—has perplexed some of his biographers. Walton has described him as beginning about the nineteenth year of his age seriously to survey and consider 'the body of Divinity, as it was then controverted betwixt the Reformed and the Roman Church'. The account of Donne's researches given by Walton is substantially accurate, and is supported by Donne's own statements in *Pseudo-Martyr*, but the date can hardly be right, as Dr. Jessopp has shown.[3] Walton continued, 'Being to undertake this search, he believed the *Cardinal Bellarmine* to be the best defender of the *Roman cause*, and therefore betook himself to the examination of his Reasons. The Cause was weighty, and wilful delays had been inexcusable both towards God and his own Conscience; he therefore proceeded in this search with all moderate haste, and before the twentieth year of his age, did shew the then *Dean* of *Gloucester* (whose name my memory hath now lost)[4] all the Cardinals works marked with many weighty observations under his own hand; which works were bequeathed by him at his death as a Legacy to a most dear Friend.'[5] Dr. Jessopp observes that Walton must have antedated this period of study by a year or two, and that Donne's

[1] *XXVI Sermons*, 5. 72.
[2] Walton, op. cit., p. 55.
[3] *John Donne*, p. 14.
[4] Anthony Rudd.
[5] Walton, op. cit., pp. 15, 16.

reading of Bellarmine at this time can have extended no farther than to the famous three volumes entitled *Disputationes de controversiis fidei adversus hujus temporis Haereticos*, published at Lyons in 1593.

The result of Donne's studies was to detach him from the Church of Rome and to incline him towards the Church of England, but the third *Satire*, written probably about this time, shows the perplexity of his mind and his determination not to bind himself to any particular creed till he is fully convinced of its truth. He ridicules the man who seeks true religion at Rome merely because she was to be found there a thousand years ago, as well as the man who at Geneva woos the new fashion of Calvinism, with neither dignity nor beauty to recommend it. He laughs at the Anglican's submission to civil and ecclesiastical tyranny, at the time-server who thinks all creeds equally good, and at the sceptic who thinks them all equally bad. And then he puts before us in a few remarkable lines his own position—that of the man bewildered by the clamorous and contradictory voices of the sects, who yet will not give up in despair the search for Truth, but clings to the belief that somewhere beyond these voices she dwells in peace and harmony.

74/76

Though truth and falsehood bee
Neare twins, yet truth a little elder is;
Be busie to seeke her, beleeve mee this,
Hee's not of none, nor worst, that seekes the best.
To adore, or scorne an image, or protest,
May all be bad; doubt wisely; in strange way
To stand inquiring right, is not to stray;
To sleepe, or runne wrong, is. On a huge hill,
Cragged, and steep, Truth stands, and hee that will
Reach her, about must, and about must goe;
And what the hills suddennes resists, winne so;
Yet strive so, that before age, deaths twilight,
Thy Soule rest, for none can worke in that night.[1]

For some years Donne's mind was occupied by the distractions of war, travel, politics, and love-making, but about 1603 he returned to the study of theology. The fruits of

[1] Grierson, i. 157.

this were seen in the help which he gave Morton in his controversy with the Roman Catholics, and later in his own contribution to the controversy, *Pseudo-Martyr*. Here Donne appears as an Anglican whose quarrel with the Roman Church is chiefly political. He dislikes the Papal interference in English affairs, and maintains that Elizabeth and her successor James are lawful sovereigns whose right to the throne cannot be touched by Papal Bulls. He defends the Reformation as necessary, and refuses to treat it as a complete breach with the past. He takes his stand definitely on the Anglican side, but his tone is on the whole conciliatory, though he makes some bitter attacks on the religious orders, especially the Jesuits. *Ignatius his Conclave* is much more violent, though here again the satire is chiefly directed against the Jesuits. In a passage quoted later in full from the *Essays in Divinity* Donne has defined for us quite clearly his attitude towards the Roman Church at the time of his ordination. He calls it 'that Church from which we are by Gods Mercy escaped, because upon the foundation, which we yet embrace together, Redemption in Christ, they had built so many stories high, as the foundation was, though not destroyed, yet hid and obscured'. It remains, however, part of the true Catholic Church of Christ. 'Yet though we branch out *East* and *West*, that Church concurs with us in the root, and sucks her vegetation from one and the same ground, *Christ Jesus*.'[1] For himself, however, he prefers the *via media* of the English Church, and says that in his 'poor opinion' the form of worship established in that Church is 'more convenient, and advantageous then of any other Kingdome, both to provoke and kindle devotion, and also to fix it, that it stray not into infinite expansions and Subdivisions; (into the former of which, Churches utterly despoyl'd of Ceremonies, seem to me to have fallen; and the *Roman* Church, by presenting innumerable objects, into the later').[2]

In the eighteenth *Holy Sonnet* he touches on the same theme.

[1] *Essays in Divinity* (1651), pp. 106, 107.

[2] Ibid., p. 111.

Show me deare Christ, thy spouse, so bright and clear.
What! is it She, which on the other shore
Goes richly painted? or which rob'd and tore
Laments and mournes in Germany and here?
Sleepes she a thousand, then peepes up one yeare?
Is she selfe truth and errs? now new, now outwore?
Doth she, and did she, and shall she evermore
On one, on seaven, or on no hill appeare?
Dwells she with us, or like adventuring knights
First travaile we to seeke and then make Love?
Betray kind husband thy spouse to our sights,
And let myne amorous soule court thy mild Dove,
Who is most trew, and pleasing to thee, then
When she'is embrac'd and open to most men.[1]

The sonnet may best be interpreted as a poetical expression of the thought found in the *Essays in Divinity*, and set forth earlier in Donne's life in the third *Satire*—that so long as the Church of Christ is rent into so many portions, men will have difficulty in recognizing her, and will be bewildered by the claims of different factions. Donne longed passionately for the reunion of Christendom. He readily admitted that Rome and Geneva, as well as Canterbury, were branches of the One Church, and he was troubled all through his life by the thought of 'our unhappy divisions', but this was perfectly compatible with loyalty to the Church of England.

In two sermons preached at Whitehall[2] Donne defends the Anglican position against both Romanists and Puritans. He claims that the English Church before the Reformation was a true Church, though it was, as he describes it, enwrapped and smothered in the Roman Church. The errors of that Church did not, as the more extreme Puritans held, preclude

[1] Grierson, i. 330. It might be urged that this sonnet, which was not published till its appearance in Gosse's *Life and Letters of Donne*, expressed Donne's inward searchings of heart, while in the Sermons he presented a bold front to the world. But the *Essays in Divinity*, which show him as a loyal Anglican, were also never published during his life-time and clearly represent his inner convictions at the time of his ordination. The Sonnet may well have been written earlier, or it may represent a moment of depression and doubt after his wife's death. Sonnet 17 refers definitely to that event, but the arrangement is not necessarily chronological.

[2] *L Sermons*, nos. 24, 25.

salvation, but the Reformation was necessary, because error became more and more prevalent.

'If I be content to stay with my friend in an aguish aire, will he take it ill, if I go when the plague comes? Or if I stay in town till 20 die of the plague, shall it be lookd that I should stay when there die 1000? The infection grew hotter and hotter in *Rome*; and their *may*, came to a *must*, those things which were done before *de facto*, came at last to be articles of *Faith*, and *de jure*, must be beleeved and practised upon salvation. They chide us for going away, and they drove us away; If we abstained from communicating with their poysons, (being now growen to that height) they excommunicated us; They gave us no room amongst them but the fire, and they were so forward to burne Heretiques, that they called it heresie, not to stay to be burnt.'[1]

In an undated sermon preached at St. Paul's, Donne upholds Andrewes's contention, urged some years before in the *Responsio ad Apologiam Card. Bellarmini*, that, judged by the laws of the primitive and the medieval Church, Anglican Orders are as valid as Roman:[2]

'When our adversaries do so violently, so impetuously cry out, that we have no Church, no Sacrament, no Priesthood, because none are sent, that is, none have a right calling, for *Internall calling*, who are called by the Spirit of God, they can be no Judges, and for *Externall calling*, we admit them for Judges, and are content to be tried by their own *Canons*, and their own evidences, for our Mission and vocation, o[u]r sending and our calling to the Ministery. If they require a necessity of lawfull Ministers to the constitution of a Church, we require it with as much earnestnesse as they; *Ecclesia non est quæ non habet sacerdotem*, we professe with Saint *Hierome*, It is no Church that hath no Priest. If they require, that this spirituall power be received from them, who have the same power in themselves, we professe it too, *Nemo dat quod non habet*, no man can confer other power upon another, then he hath himself. If they require *Imposition of hands*, in conferring Orders, we joyn hands with them. If they will have it a Sacrament; men may be content to let us be as liberall of that name of Sacrament, as *Calvin* is. . . . Whatsoever their own authors, their own Schools, their own Canons doe require to be essentially and necessarily requisite in this Mission in this function, we, for our parts, and as much as concerns our Church of *England*, admit it too, and professe to have it. And whatsoever they can say for their Church,

[1] *L Sermons*, 25. 214. [2] *Responsio*, cap. vii.

that from their first Conversion, they have had an orderly derivation of power from one to another, we can as justly and truly say of our Church, that ever since her first being of such a Church, to this day, she hath conserved the same order, and ever hath had, and hath now, those Ambassadours sent, with the same Commission, and by the same means, that they pretend to have in *their* Church.'[1]

This stalwart defence of Anglican Orders is followed almost immediately in the same sermon by a passage which shows that Donne considered Apostolic Succession and the episcopal constitution of the Church of England as important but not absolutely essential, as pertaining to the *bene esse* but not the *esse* of a Church.

'This I speak of this Church, in which God hath planted us, That God hath afforded us all that might serve, even for the stopping of the Adversaries mouth, and to confound them in their own way: which I speak, onely to excite us to a thankfulnesse to God, for his abundant grace in affording us so much, and not to disparage, or draw in question any other of our *neighbour Churches*, who, perchance, cannot derive, as we can, their power, and their *Mission*, by the ways required, and practised in the Romane Church, nor have had from the beginning a continuance of Consecration by Bishops, and such other concurrences, as those *Canons* require and as our *Church* hath enjoyed. They, no doubt, can justly plead for themselves, that Ecclesiasticall positive Laws admit *dispensation* in cases of necessity; They may justly challenge a Dispensation, but we need none; They did what was lawfull in a case of necessity, but Almighty God preserved us from this necessity.'[2]

Donne's preference for the *via media* of the English Church might be proved by many passages. Thus he condemns both 'the easinesse of admitting Revelations, and Visions, and Apparitions of spirits, and Purgatory souls in the Roman Church', and 'the super-exaltation of zeale, and the captivity to the private spirit, which some have fallen into, that have not beene content to consist in moderate and middle wayes in the Reformed Church', and, a few sentences later, speaks of 'the middle way, in which we should stand, and walk'.[3]

[1] *L Sermons*, no. 40, preached at St. Paul's, pp. 368, 369.

[2] Ibid., p. 369.

[3] *LXXX Sermons*, 5. 42.

Again he honours the Virgin Mary highly, but not to the extent commanded by the Roman Church. To him as to the Fathers she is the 'Mother of God',[1] blessed 'amongst women, above women; but not above any person of the Trinity, that she should command her Son'.[2] He explains this elsewhere by condemning the belief that any can 'receive appeales from God, and reverse the decrees of God, which they (i.e. the Roman Church) make the office of the Virgin *Mary*, whom no man can honour too much, that makes her not God, and they dishonour most, that make her so much more'.[3]

He thinks prayers for the dead unadvisable, though he will not condemn St. Augustine's prayer for the dead Monica, nor St. Ambrose's for Theodosius. 'God forbid wee should condemne *Augustine* or *Ambrose* of impiety in doing so; But God forbid wee should make *Augustine* or *Ambrose* his example, our rule to doe so still.'[4]

With regard to the Sacraments, Donne's position is again that of a member of the school of Andrewes.[5] He denies transubstantiation—'There cannot be a deeper Atheisme, then to impute contradictions to God; neither doth any one thing so overcharge God with contradictions, as the Transubstantiation of the Roman Church'[6]—but he sees in the Eucharist not only a memorial feast, but a real sacrifice and the Real Presence.[7] The faithful receive indeed the Body and Blood of Christ, but the Church has no revelation from God of the means by which the bread and

[1] *LXXX Sermons*, 12. 112.

[2] Ibid. 2. 18.

[3] Ibid. 5. 46.

[4] Ibid. 5. 50, 51.

[5] For Andrewes's teaching on the Eucharist, see *Responsio*, cap. viii; *Answers to Perron*, i. 5; *Two Sermons*, xcvi, p. 445.

[6] *LXXX Sermons*, 4. 36.

[7] *XXVI Sermons*, 20. 286. '. . . It is the ordinary phrase and manner of speech in the Fathers to call that a sacrifice; not only as it is a commemorative sacrifice . . . but as it is a real sacrifice, in which the Priest doth that, which none but he does; that is, really to offer up Christ Jesus crucified to Almighty God for the sins of the people.' Compare Laud's affirmation that the Church of England believes the Real Presence while denying Transubstantiation (*Works*, ii. 328–31).

wine possess this efficacy. The fact is enough; the manner in which it is accomplished is shrouded in mystery.[1]

On the other hand, Donne is equally vigorous in support of the Anglican position against the Puritan attack.

His sense of the importance of the Sacraments is expressed in a passage which contains one of those personal touches which are not too frequent in his *Sermons*.

'I should thinke I had no bowels, if they had not earn'd and melted, when I heard a *Lady*, whose child of five or sixe daies, being ready to die every minute, she being mov'd often that the *child might be christened*, answered, That, if it were Gods will, that the child should live to the Sabbath, that it might be baptized in the Congregation, she should be content, otherwise, Gods will be done upon it, for *God needs no Sacrament.* With what sorrow, with what holy indignation did I hear the Sonne of my friend, who brought me to that place, to minister the Sacrament to him, then, upon his death-bed, and almost at his last gaspe, when my service was offered him in that kinde, answer his Father, *Father, I thanke God, I have not lived so in the sight of my God, as that I need a Sacrament.*'[2]

Donne expresses this conviction of the importance of Christian Baptism in another passage, which shows, however, that he did not share the usual theological belief that unbaptized infants were condemned to hell. He speaks of 'pure, and sincere doctrine, which doctrine is, *That Baptisme is so necessary, as that God hath placed no other ordinary seale, nor conveyance of his graces in his Church, to them that have not received that, then baptisme*'.[3] He continues:

'And they, who doe not provide duly for the Baptisme of their children, if their children die, have a heavier accompt to make to God for that child, then if they had not provided a *Nurse*, and suffered the child

[1] *LXXX Sermons*, 4. 34. 'When thou commest to this seale of thy peace, the Sacrament, pray that God will give thee that light, that may direct and establish thee, in necessary and fundamentall things; that is, the light of faith to see, that the Body and Bloud of Christ, is applied to thee, in that action; But for the manner, how the Body and Bloud of Christ is there, wait his leisure, if he have not yet manifested that to thee: Grieve not at that, wonder not at that, presse not for that; for hee hath not manifested that, not the way, not the manner of his presence in the Sacrament, to the Church.'

[2] *L Sermons*, 25. 209, 210.

[3] Ibid. 7. 55. The italics are in the original edition.

to starve. God can preserve the child without *Milke*; and he can save the child without a sacrament; but as that mother that throwes out, and forsakes her child in the field, or wood, is guilty before God of the Temporall murder of that child, though the child die not, so are those parents of a spirituall murder, if their children, by their fault die unbaptized, though God preserve that child out of his abundant, and miraculous mercy, from spirituall destruction.'[1]

Against those who hastily condemn ceremonies of all kinds he quotes Calvin[2] to the effect that it is not necessary, because things good in their institution may be depraved in their practice, to deny the people all ceremonies for the assistance of their weakness, but that these helps may be 'very behoovefull for them', if moderation be observed.[3] He loves to commemorate the great saints on their festival days, and the folio of 1640 contains a number of sermons preached by him on the Conversion of St. Paul, on All Saints' Day, and on Candlemas Day. Preaching on the last-mentioned festival he defends the use of various traditional rites in the Church:

'The Church, which is the Daughter of God, and Spouse of Christ, celebrates this day, the Purification of the blessed Virgin, the Mother of God. And she celebrates this day by the name, vulgarly, of *Candlemas day*. It is *dies luminarium*, the day of lights; The Church took the occasion of doing so, from the Gentiles; At this time of the yeare, about the beginning of February, they celebrated the feast of *Februus*, which is their *Pluto*; And, because that was the God of darknesse, they solemnized it, with a multiplicity of Lights. The Church of God, in the outward and ceremoniall part of his worship, did not disdain the ceremonies of the Gentiles; Men who are so severe, as to condemne, and to remove from the Church, whatsoever was in use amongst the Gentiles before, may, before they are aware, become Surveyors, and Controllers upon Christ himself, in the institution of his greatest seales: for Baptisme, which is the Sacrament of purification by washing in water, and the very Sacrament of the Supper it self, religious eating, and drinking in the Temple, were in use amongst the Gentiles too. It is a perverse way, rather to abolish Things and Names, (for vehement zeale will work upon Names as well as Things) because they have been abused, then to reduce them to their right use.'[4]

[1] *L Sermons*, 7. 56.
[2] Calvin, *Institutes*, lib. iv, c. x, 14.
[3] *LXXX Sermons*, 8. 80.
[4] Ibid. 12. 112.

On all the above points it will be seen that Donne's views differed little from those of Andrewes and Laud.[1] Yet there is a subtle difference which arises from Donne's Catholic upbringing, and the affection which he continued to feel for certain Catholic traditions. Consciously he gave an intellectual assent to the doctrinal formularies of the Church of England, but in various ways he showed that the pull of the older associations was strong upon him. This is particularly marked in his *Catalogus Librorum*, which shows that he retained some Catholic sympathies as late as 1611.[2] Again in *The Litanie*, written probably in 1609, the heading of stanza 5 in the Dobell, S 96 group of manuscripts is '*Our Lady*', where the edition of 1633 and the D, H 49 group of manuscripts have '*The Virgin Mary*'. His letter to his mother on the death of his sister shows that he regarded his mother, who remained a member of the Roman Church till her death, as one with whom he had a real spiritual sympathy,[3] a fellow pilgrim to God's 'Haven and eternall rest'.

'As long as the Spirit of God distills and dews his cheerfulnesse upon your heart; as long as he instructs your understanding, to interpret his mercies and his judgments aright; so long your comfort must needs be as much greater than others, as your afflictions are greater then theirs.'[4]

[1] This summary has been retained from the first edition of my book. Since it appeared, Dr. I. Husain has made a more detailed analysis in his *Dogmatic and Mystical Theology of John Donne* (pp. 1–42), which supports my view.

[2] See my discussion of the date of *Catalogus* on pp. 151–3. The anti-Protestant items were probably written some years earlier, but he did not omit them in the 1611 revision.

[3] This is disputed by E. Hardy, who in her book *Donne: A Spirit in Conflict*, pp. 235–7, thinks that Elizabeth Donne's early re-marriage after the death of Donne's father set up in the childish mind of Donne 'a pronounced hostility to her and all that she stood for'. This complex was responsible for his attacks of melancholy, his sense of insecurity, and even 'his extraordinary interest, in advance of his day, in the field of science'. She regards the rather stilted phrases of Donne's consolatory letter as proof of alienation, and perverts a sentence in the letter to indicate that he no longer thought of himself as his mother's son (p. 178). I can find no warrant for Miss Hardy's description of his mother as 'bitter and aggressive', 'a woman of fiery egoism' and 'fierce fanaticism', proud of her stubborn resistance to any authority 'other than that of the Pope and God' (p. 15).

[4] Tobie Mathew collection of *Letters*, p. 324.

This sense that there was an underlying unity, deeper than the cleavages which seemed so profound, between all Christian believers accounts for the tolerance which distinguishes many of Donne's utterances. While he could be harsh and bitter in the heat of controversy, he could not forget how closely he was bound to many of those who seemed to be on the opposite side.

Again and again he insists that charity, rather than harsh criticism, should be shown to those who may be in error. 'Nothing hinders our own salvation more, then to deny salvation, to all but our selves.'[1] 'Take heed how you condemne another man for an Heretique, because he beleeves not just as you beleeve; or for a Reprobate, because he lives not just as you live, for God is no accepter of persons.'[2]

In Donne's treatment of the possibility of salvation we can discern a largeness of mind which enabled him at times to pass beyond the narrow bounds set by the controversialists of his day. He will not limit salvation to any particular branch of the Christian Church, nay, not even to the Christian Church itself.[3] 'There are an infinite number of Stars more then we can distinguish,' he says, 'and so, by Gods grace, there may be an infinite number of soules saved, more then those of whose salvation, we discerne the *ways*, and the *meanes*.'[4]

Thus in another sermon he praises the charity of those Fathers who believed that certain of the heathen philosophers might be saved:

'And as those blessed Fathers of tender bowels, enlarged them-

[1] *L Sermons*, 32. 285. [2] *LXXX Sermons*, 6. 53.

[3] *L Sermons*, 25. 214. 'God had single sheep in many nations; *Jobs*, and *Naamans*, and such; servants, and yet not in the Covenants, sheep, and yet not brought into his flock. For though God have revealed no other way of salvation *to us*, but by breeding us in his Church, yet we must be so far from straitning salvation, to any *particular Christian Church*, of any subdivided name, *Papist* or *Protestant*, as that we may not straiten it to the *whole Christian Church*, as though God *could* not, in the largenesse of his power, or *did* not, in the largenesse of his mercy, afford salvation to some, whom he never gathered into the Christian Church.'

[4] Ibid. 32. 285.

selves in this distribution, and apportioning the mercy of God, that it consisted best with the nature of his mercy, that as his Saints had suffered temporall calamities in this world, in this world they should be recompenced with temporall abundances, so did they inlarge this mercy farther, and carry it even to the Gentiles, to the Pagans that had no knowledge of Christ in any established Church. You shall not finde a *Trismegistus*, a *Numa Pompilius*, a *Plato*, a *Socrates*, for whose salvation you shall not finde some Father, or some Ancient and Reverend Author, an Advocate. . . . To me, to whom God hath revealed his Son, in a Gospel, by a Church, there can be no way of salvation, but by applying that Son of God, by that Gospel, in that Church. Nor is there any other foundation for any, nor other name by which any can be saved, but the name of Jesus. But how this foundation is presented, and how this name of Jesus is notified to them, amongst whom there is no Gospel preached, no Church established, I am not curious in inquiring. I know God can be as mercifull as those tender Fathers present him to be; and I would be as charitable as they are. And therefore humbly imbracing that manifestation of his Son, which he hath afforded me, I leave God, to his unsearchable waies of working upon others, without farther inquisition.'[1]

It was inevitable that such a mind as Donne's should find Laud's rigid ecclesiasticism distasteful, and that on the other hand Laud should regard some of Donne's utterances with suspicion. One instance of this misunderstanding is recorded in Donne's letters.

In April 1627 Donne preached a sermon before the king and Laud, which brought him for a short time into disfavour at court. The sermon seemed to Donne himself absolutely free of offence, and he expressed his surprise and dismay in

[1] *LXXX Sermons*, 26. 261, 262. This should be compared with the view of Sir Thomas Browne in *Religio Medici* (§ lii): 'There is no Salvation to those that beleeve not in Christ, that is, say some, since his Nativity, and, as Divinity affirmeth, before also; which makes me much apprehend the ends of those honest Worthies and Philosophers which died before his Incarnation. It is hard to place those soules in Hell whose worthy lives doe teach us vertue on earth; methinks amongst those many subdivisions of hell, there might have bin one Limbo left for these: What a strange vision will it be to see their poeticall fictions converted into verities, and their imagined and fancied Furies, into real Devils? . . . It will therefore, and must at last appeare, that all salvation is through Christ; which verity I feare these great examples of vertue must confirme, and make it good, how the perfectest actions of earth have no title or claim, unto Heaven.'

two letters to his intimate friend, Sir Robert Ker. In the first of these he says:

'A few hours after I had the honour of your Letter, I had another from my Lord of *Bath* and *Wells*' (i.e. Laud, who was then Bishop of Bath and Wells), 'commanding from the King a Copy of my Sermon. I am in preparations of that, with diligence, yet this morning I waited upon his Lordship, and laid up in him this truth, that of the B. of *Canterburies*' (i.e. Archbishop Abbot's)[1] 'Sermon, to this hour, I never heard syllable, nor what way, nor upon what points he went: And for mine, it was put into that very order, in which I delivered it, more then two moneths ago. Freely to you I say, I would I were a little more guilty: Onely mine innocency makes me afraid. I hoped for the Kings approbation heretofore in many of my Sermons; and I have had it. But yesterday I came very near looking for thanks; for, in my life, I was never in any one peece, so studious of his service. Therefore, exceptions being taken, and displeasure kindled at this, I am afraid, it was rather brought thither, then met there. . . .'[2]

In the second Donne says:

'I have now put into my Lord of *Bath* and *Wells* hands the Sermon faithfully exscribed. I beseech you be pleased to hearken farther after it; I am still upon my jealousie, that the King brought thither some disaffection towards me, grounded upon some other demerit of mine, and took it not from the Sermon.'[3]

When the king read the sermon, his anger disappeared. In a third letter to Sir Robert Ker, Donne thanks his friend for having used his influence in the matter.[4] Gosse remarks that it is difficult to understand the action of Laud, and suggests that 'personal pique may have had something to do with his onslaught upon the Dean of St. Paul's, for it was in the courtyard at Donne's house that the mysterious paper was picked up, containing the words, "Laud, look to

[1] See Gosse, ii. 242, 243. The Archbishop had refused to license the *Appello Caesarem* of Montague, afterwards Bishop of Chichester, who was favoured by the King and Laud. 'It appears that Archbishop Abbot had just preached a sermon of a very Low Church character, which had offended the King, and that Charles I and Laud, putting their heads together after Donne's sermon, had come to the conclusion that the Dean of St. Paul's was preparing to support the Archbishop' (Gosse).

[2] *Letters* (1651), pp. 305, 306.

[3] Ibid., p. 308.

[4] Ibid. pp. 306, 307.

thyself, be assured thy life is sought. As thou art the fountain of all wickedness, repent thee of thy monstrous sins before thou are taken out of the world." But that Donne was innocent of such silly mystifications as this must have been patent even to Laud.'[1] Gosse's discovery of a document among the Domestic State Papers proving that in 1630 Donne's promotion to a bishopric[2] was planned shows that by that time Laud's suspicion of him had disappeared. It was only his fatal illness which stopped this advancement.

It will be clear from the above survey that Donne was not a great speculative or constructive theologian. His sermons are the work of an orator and a poet, whose strength lay in the reality of his own personal religious experience and in the power of imagination by which he bodied forth things unseen and made them almost visible to his hearers. As a controversialist, his work was generally marked by moderation and restraint, but he was happiest when he could escape from the mists of theological disputes into the clearer air of faith and devotion. His loyalty to the Anglican Church has sometimes been called in question, but there is no reason to doubt his sincerity on this point. At the same time, it is true that he never showed the peculiar love for the English Church which distinguished his intimate friend and poetical disciple, George Herbert, who dwelt fondly on every detail of its order and ceremonies. Donne's eyes were fixed on a wider vision of one great united Christian Church, and the divisions of Christendom vexed his soul as they never vexed Herbert's. His devotion was given, not to any one branch of the Church, but to the ideal figure of the Bride of Christ who should one day be revealed with her torn and soiled garments replaced by the stainless robe of perfect unity.

[1] Gosse, ii. 246. [2] Ibid. 263, 264.

V

MEDIEVAL AND RENAISSANCE ELEMENTS IN DONNE'S THOUGHT

IN his prose Donne is primarily an intellectual writer who appeals to the minds rather than to the emotions of his readers. What was the source of the ideas which he expounded? Is he a medievalist or a man of the Renaissance?

During the last thirty-five years two books have appeared on Donne championing two different points of view on this subject. Both of them are learned and well documented, full of quotations from Donne's works and from the sources on which he drew. The earlier is Miss M. P. Ramsay's thesis for the Paris doctorate, *Les Doctrines médiévales chez Donne, le poète métaphysicien de l'Angleterre* (Oxford, 1916), and the second is C. M. Coffin's *John Donne and the New Philosophy* (Columbia, 1937).

Miss Ramsay asserts that Donne's thought belongs to the Middle Ages rather than to the Renaissance. 'John Donne, comme du reste la plupart de ses contemporains, est foncièrement médiéval dans sa façon d'envisager l'Univers.'[1] 'On se rend compte de deux traits essentiels de sa pensée: elle est médiévale et plotinienne. . . . Son plotinisme lui vient à travers le moyen âge, non pas par la Renaissance, bien qu'il connaisse les néoplatoniciens de cette dernière époque.'[2] She states that Donne's thought is marked by three characteristics—it is fundamentally theological, its attitude towards natural science and the knowledge of the external world is in harmony with that of the Middle Ages, and it assigns to authority a place very similar to that given to it by medieval times.[3]

Undoubtedly Donne's thought is based on a firm conviction of the existence of God, and he sees God everywhere in the Universe. In his method of expounding this great reality he followed the Schoolmen in their respect for the

[1] Ramsay, op. cit., p. 128. [2] Ibid., pp. 337, 338.
[3] Ibid., p. 128.

past, in the constant appeal to authority, and in the frequent use of the allegorical system of interpretation.[1] There are many passages in Donne's poetry which are intelligible only to those who have some knowledge of medieval thought. Such poems as *The Extasie*, the two *Anniversaries*, or the *Obsequies to the Lord Harrington* are full of allusions which represent, not a mere superficial display of learning on Donne's part, but an intimate knowledge of the philosophy of the Schoolmen and mystics of the Middle Ages.[2]

What is true of the poems applies with even more force to the prose works. Donne did not stand alone among the Anglican preachers of his time in his adherence to medieval modes of thought. The allegorical method of interpretation was in force in Reformed as well as Catholic churches. The Fathers and the Schoolmen were cited as authorities by Hooker, Andrewes, Laud, Jeremy Taylor, and other apologists of the English Church.[3] Donne's early training intensified this habit of mind. From his youth he was familiar with the Roman writers who kept unbroken the tradition of St. Thomas Aquinas. The list of authorities given at the end of the *LXXX Sermons* shows that the authors to whom he referred most frequently were the great Fathers of the Church, Augustine pre-eminently, then Jerome, Ambrose, Chrysostom, Gregory the Great, as well as others of more doubtful orthodoxy, such as Origen and Tertullian; the mystical writers, 'Dionysius Areopagiticus', Gregory Nazianzen, Gregory of Nyssa, Bernard of Clairvaux; the Schoolmen, Aquinas and his followers; the reformers, Luther and Calvin; and the Roman theologians, Bellarmine and Cajetan.

It is not necessary here to prove in detail that the doctrines held by Donne regarding the nature of God and man, and the constitution of the universe, are those which had been

[1] The above sentences are a summary of the conclusions arrived at by Miss Ramsay in her last chapter (pp. 281–94; see also pp. 337, 338).

[2] Ramsay, op. cit., p. 282. Grierson, ii. 42–5, 192, 197, 201.

[3] Miss Ramsay (op. cit., pp. 285–8) quotes the attack made on Hooker by certain Puritans for his deference to the Schoolmen, and Taine's criticism of Jeremy Taylor, 'pas logicien, pas analyste, pédant, surchargé de citations grecques et latines, de divisions, etc. . . . à demi enfoncé dans la boue du moyen âge'.

held before him by the long procession of theological writers whose thought goes back to Augustine, and therefore to St. Paul and St. John on one hand, and to Plato and Plotinus on the other. It will be sufficient to quote a few of the more striking passages in which Donne sets forth these doctrines.

'God alone is all; not onely all that is, but all that is not, all that might be, if he would have it be.'[1]

'God is not tyed to any *place*; not by essence; *Implet et continendo implet*, (Augustine), God fills every place, and fills it by containing that place in himselfe.'[2]

'This way, our Theatre, where we sit to see God, is the whole frame of nature; our *medium*, our glasse in which we see him, is the Creature; and our light by which we see him, is Naturall Reason. *Aquinas* calls this Theatre, where we sit and see God, the whole world; And *David* compasses the world, and findes God every where, and sayes at last, *Whither shall I flie from thy presence?* . . . There is not so poore a creature but may be thy glasse to see God in. The greatest flat glasse that can be made, cannot represent any thing greater then it is: If every gnat that flies were an Arch-angell, all that could but tell me, that there is a God; and the poorest worme that creeps, tells me that.'[3]

'Sometimes we represent God by Subtraction, by Negation, by saying, God is that, which is not mortall, not passible, not moveable: Sometimes we present him by Addition; by adding our bodily lineaments to him, and saying, that God hath hands, and feet, and eares, and eyes; and adding our affections, and passions to him, and saying, that God is glad, or sorry, angry, or reconciled, as we are. Some such things may be done towards the representing of God, as God; But towards the expressing of the distinction of the Persons in the Trinity, nothing.'[4]

'Now, beloved, *Ordo semper dicitur ratione principii* (Aquinas) *Order alwayes presumes a head*, it always implyes some by whom wee are to be ordered, and it implyes our conformities to him. Who is that? *God* certainly, without all question, *God*. But between *God* and *Man*, we consider a two-fold *Order*. One, as all creatures depend upon *God*, as upon their beginning, for their very *Being*; and so every creature is wrought upon immediately by God, and whether hee discerne it or no, does obey *Gods* order, that is, that which *God* hath ordained, his purpose, his providence is executed upon him, and accomplished in him. But then the other *Order* is, not as man depends

[1] *LXXX Sermons*, 7. 63.
[2] *L Sermons*, 11. 85.
[3] *LXXX Sermons*, 23. 226.
[4] Ibid. 44. 440, 441.

upon *God*, as upon his beginning, but as he is to be reduced and brought back to God, as to his end: and that is done by means in this world.'[1]

These are enough to show that Donne's philosophy is rooted in a belief in God, and in the natural order as a chain of being derived from God. God is the Creator, the efficient cause of the universe.[2] He is also the final cause, the aim and goal of all. The soul of man is not eternal; it is created by God at the moment when it is infused by Him into the body. In this Donne follows St. Augustine:[3]

'As S. *Augustin* cannot conceive any interim, any distance, between the creating of the soule, and the infusing of the soule into the body, but eases himselfe upon that, *Creando infundit*, and *infundendo creat*, The Creation is the Infusion, and the Infusion is the Creation. . . .'[4]

In a letter to Sir Henry Goodyer he writes, 'As our soul is infused when it is created, and created when it is infused, so at her going out, Gods mercy is had by asking, and that is asked by having.'[5] And in a sermon preached on Trinity Sunday, 1627, he declares: 'Our soules have a blessed perpetuity, our soules shall no more see an end, then God, that hath no Beginning; and yet our soules are very far from being eternal.'[6]

Here are two passages, one from the *Songs and Sonnets*, the other from the *Sermons*, in which Donne sets forth the medieval doctrine that everything which is composed of contrary elements, the body, for example, is liable to dissolution, whereas that which is simple, such as God or the soul, cannot be dissolved, nor can compounds, such as the heavenly bodies, between the elements of which there is no contrariety.

[1] Sermon preached at St. Paul's Cross, 15 Sept. 1622, pp. 43–4.

[2] Medieval thinkers attached great importance to the idea of causation, which was considered in the four ways pointed out by Aristotle. Thus there is the material, the formal, the efficient, and the final cause (Ramsay, op. cit., p. 137). See *Essays in Divinity* (1651), pp. 176–7: 'God is *all-efficient*: that is, hath created the beginning, ordained the way, fore-seen the end of every thing; and nothing else is any kind of cause thereof.'

[3] In this view St. Augustine differs from Plotinus, who held that the soul was eternal, and had its existence in the intelligible, or real and eternal world, before it descended into the world of sense.

[4] *LXXX Sermons*, 51. 514.

[5] *Letters* (1651), p. 53.

[6] *LXXX Sermons*, 44. 442.

What ever dyes, was not mixt equally;
If our two loves be one, or, thou and I
Love so alike, that none doe slacken, none can die.[1]

'In Heaven we doe not say, that our bodies shall devest their mortality, so as that naturally they could not dye; for they shall have a composition still; and every compounded thing may perish; but they shall be so assured, and with such a preservation, as they shall alwaies know they shall never dye.'[2]

Then there is the Aristotelian and Scholastic doctrine of the three souls, according to which plants have a vegetative soul, which can select what it can feed on and reject what it cannot. Above this is the soul of motion, possessed by beasts who can select ends and means, and thirdly, there is the rational and immortal soul, belonging to man alone. The unborn child possesses first the soul of sense, and then the soul of motion, which absorbs the soul of sense. At last, however, God infuses into the child the immortal soul, which swallows up the two preceding souls. This doctrine appears in the poems, and again in the sermons and the *Devotions*:

Wee first have soules of growth, and sense, and those,
When our last soule, our soule immortall came,
Were swallowed into it, and have no name.[3]

'First, in a naturall man wee conceive there is a soule of vegetation and of growth; and secondly, a soule of motion and of sense; and then thirdly, a soule of reason and understanding, an immortall soule. And the two first soules of vegetation, and of sense, wee conceive to arise out of the temperament, and good disposition of the substance of which that man is made, they arise out of man himselfe; But the last soule, the perfect and immortall soule, that is immediately infused by God.'[4]

'Man, before hee hath his immortall soule, hath a *soule of sense*, and a *soule of vegitation* before that. This *immortal soule* did not forbid

[1] Grierson, i. 8 (*The good-morrow*, 19–21). In his note on this passage Grierson quotes Aquinas, *Summa* I, Quaest. LXXV, Art. 6. 'Non enim invenitur corruptio nisi ubi invenitur contrarietas; generationes enim et corruptiones ex contrariis et in contraria sunt. . . .'

[2] *LXXX Sermons*, 19. 189.

[3] *To the Countesse of Salisbury*, ll. 52–4 (Grierson, i. 225). See also *To the Countesse of Bedford*, ll. 34–5 (Grierson, i. 219), and *The second Anniversary*, ll. 160–2 (Grierson, i. 256).

[4] *LXXX Sermons*, 74. 755.

other *soules*, to be in us before, but when this soule departs, it carries all with it; no more *vegetation*, no more *sense*.'[1]

These are only a few specimens of the numerous medieval doctrines which were accepted by Donne, and appear constantly in both poetry and prose. One could add to them a score of pages—indeed Miss Ramsay devotes a hundred and fifty pages to her discussion of Donne's treatment of the nature of God, of the angels, of man, and of the natural order. Yet one feels that something is amiss with this careful analysis, that a vital and important element of Donne's thought has been omitted.[2] Donne was more than a docile follower of Aquinas and the Schoolmen. He was intensely interested in the great scientific movement of thought which was initiated by Copernicus, Kepler, and Galileo. This has been worked out in great detail by C. M. Coffin in his book, to which I am indebted for a number of points made in the succeeding pages. He declares 'He (Donne) represents the effort of the late Renaissance mind to make an adjustment to its world of changing values without sacrificing its regard for the equal claims of emotion and reason.'[3] Towards the close of this book he definitely challenges Miss Ramsay's view:

'If we are to accept Miss Ramsay's thesis, first expressed . . . in 1917, and repeated in 1931, based upon an impressive accumulation of materials, we must be disposed to find Donne more thoroughly at

[1] *Devotions upon Emergent Occasions* (1624), pp. 447–8.

[2] Some mention should be made of L. I. Bredvold's interesting essay, 'The Religious Thought of Donne in relation to Mediaeval and Later Traditions', in *Studies in Shakespeare, Milton, and Donne* (University of Michigan Publications, 1925). He emphasizes Donne's debt to Montaigne, or rather to the sceptical philosophy of Sextus Empiricus, of whom Montaigne was a disciple. Donne certainly knew something of the work both of Montaigne and of Sextus, to whom he alludes in *Essays in Divinity* (1651), pp. 56–7: 'For, Omitting the quarrelsome contending of *Sextus Empiricus* the *Pyrrhonian* . . . who with his Ordinary weapon, a two-edged sword, thinks he cuts off all Arguments against production of Nothing, by this, *Non fit quod jam est, Nec quod non est; nam non patitur mutationem quod non est.*' Jessopp in his edition of the *Essays* gives a note referring to *Hypotyposes*, iii. 14, § 112. While admitting the sceptical character of some passages in Donne's early work, I feel that Bredvold has overemphasized this aspect.

[3] Coffin, op. cit., p. 6.

home with the medievalists than with his Renaissance contemporaries. But what Miss Ramsay does is to overlook the fact that the historical meaning of words is subject to change, and that though the verbal reminders of an ancient tradition may be gathered from Donne's writings, their spiritual connotation betokens the influence of a later time. For instance, the naturalism of the Renaissance in its appeal from reason to the critical perception of natural facts, involving an alteration of the conception of the nature of knowledge and the activities of the knowing mind, though not argued philosophically, is, nevertheless, reflected in Donne as it implies the freedom of the mind to seek in fact and experience the ultimate basis for the truth about the nature of things.'[1]

Perhaps it would be a mistake to describe Donne as either a medievalist or a typical man of the Renaissance. We cannot divide history into rigid periods without doing violence to the truth. The Middle Ages lingered on long after the Renaissance had started, and men kept the framework of earlier ideas of the Universe up to the end of the seventeenth century. What had changed and was still changing was the spirit in which men approached the dogmas of the Schoolmen and the Ptolemaic theory of the Universe. Thirty years after Donne's death Milton built up *Paradise Lost* on the Ptolemaic cosmogony, while allowing the Copernican theory to be stated as a possible alternative by the Archangel Raphael in Book VIII.

Donne stood almost alone among contemporary poets in his perception of the importance of the changes which scientific discovery was bringing about. 'And new Philosophy calls all in doubt', he cried despairingly, and continues

> The Element of fire is quite put out;
> The Sun is lost, and th'earth, and no mans wit
> Can well direct him where to look for it.
> And freely men confesse that this world's spent,
> When in the Planets, and the Firmament
> They seeke so many new; they see that this
> Is crumbled out againe to his Atomies.
> 'Tis all in peeces, all cohaerence gone;
> All just supply, and all Relation. . . .[2]

[1] Coffin, op. cit., p. 284.

[2] Grierson, i. 237 (*The first Anniversary*, ll. 205, 214).

Had Donne been less sensitive and discerning he would not have realized so keenly all that was involved in the discoveries of Kepler and Galileo. He saw that the new Copernican cosmogony relegated the earth, which for so many centuries had seemed to be the centre of the Universe, to a relatively unimportant position as one of many planets revolving round the sun. If so central and fundamental a doctrine could be upset by observation and experiment, where could the mind seek a sure resting-place? The new philosophy rejected the *a priori* method of thought which had been the accredited tool of the Schoolmen. The medieval philosophers had accepted the description of the natural world given by Aristotle and Ptolemy, and had been 'satisfied with the deductions which their subtlety could elaborate from the original data'.[1] Now came Copernicus, Kepler, and Galileo, who, with their startling new theories, their telescopes, and their experiments, opened the way to every sort of revolutionary hypothesis. The Middle Ages had believed passionately in the power of pure reason. The new thinkers insisted on accumulating fresh data, which they viewed with unprejudiced minds. They were ready to sit down before the facts, to examine them and learn from them without imposing any ready-made solution. Donne was no scientist, but he had caught a glimpse of what the new scientific method might mean. He had been reared in the medieval climate of thought, and the fresh winds of scientific discovery chilled him, but he had courage enough to go on reading and studying. His friend Sir Henry Wotton was so excited by Galileo's *Sidereus Nuncius* that on the very day on which it was published in 1610, he sent a copy to the Earl of Salisbury as a present for James I, promising to send by the next ship 'one of the above-named instruments [i.e. a telescope] as it is bettered by this man [Galileo]'.[2] It was probably from Wotton that Donne received a copy early enough to allude to it twice in *Ignatius his Conclave*,[3] of which the Latin edition was entered on the Stationers'

[1] Coffin, op. cit., p. 282.
[2] L. Pearsall Smith, *Life and Letters of Wotton*, i. 486–7.
[3] 1611 edition, pp. 2, 117.

Register on 24 January 1610/11, and the English edition on 18 May 1611.

Probably Donne's earliest direct reference to Kepler's work is in Problem VIII. The printed texts for long obscured this reference by printing Kepler's name as '*Re*——'. It runs thus: 'But they whose profession it is to see that nothing be done in heaven without their consent (as *Kepler* saies in himselfe of Astrologers) have bid *Mercury* to bee neerer [i.e. to the earth than Venus].'[1] There is a parallel passage in *Ignatius his Conclave*: '*Keppler, who* (as himselfe testifies of himselfe) *ever since* Tycho Braches *death, hath received it into his care, that no new thing should be done in heaven without his knowledge.*'[2] In both places Donne is referring to Kepler's words: 'Tychone iam mortuo equidem haec me cura incessit, ne quid fortasse novi existeret in caelo me inscio.'[3] The treatise from which these words were taken, *De Stella terti Honoris in Cygno*, was printed as an appendix to Kepler's *De Stella Nova in pede Serpentarii* at Prague in 1606, so that Problem VIII cannot be earlier than 1606,[4] and more probably belongs to 1607.

In *Biathanatos*, written probably in 1608, Donne alludes to *De Stella Nova*, finding in its mention of the discovery of new stars a reason for doubting the Aristotelian doctrine. 'Are not Saint *Augustines* Disciples guilty of the same pertinacy which is imputed to *Aristotles* followers, who, defending the Heavens to be inalterable, because in so many ages nothing had been observed to have been altered, his Schollers stubbornly maintain his Proposition still, though by many experiences of new Stars, the reason which moved *Aristotle* seems now to be utterly defeated?'[5]

[1] *Juvenilia* (1st edition), sig. G 4v. The reading 'Kepler' is taken from the Phillipps MS. in the Bodleian, and the Dobell MS. (Nor. 4506) in Harvard College Library. Both editions of *Juvenilia*, and the *Paradoxes, Problemes* of 1652 have '*Re*——', while *B, O'F* have *Ripler*, and Ashmole 826 has *Kepter*.

[2] 1611 edition, p. 3. There is a marginal reference '*De Stella in Cygno*'.

[3] *Kepleri Opera Omnia*, ed. Frisch, ii. 762.

[4] Gosse (ii. 301) has assigned all the Problems to a date 'before 1600'. There are several references to 'problems' in *Letters* (1651), pp. 88, 99, 108, which can be dated in 1607 or thereabouts.

[5] *Biathanatos*, p. 146. Marginal note, *Kepplerus de Stella Serpent.* cap. 23.

This reference in *Biathanatos* to 'new stars' should be compared with the lines in *A Funerall Elegie*[1] (lines 67–70):

> But, as when heaven lookes on us with new eyes,
> Those new starres every Artist[2] exercise,
> What place they should assigne to them they doubt,
> Argue, and agree not, till those starres goe out. . . .

This seems to be a definite reference to the new star in Kepler's treatise. It had first been observed in 1604 in the constellation Serpentarius, 'had shone brightly for a while, and then had faded out completely'.[3] Similarly a bright star which had appeared in 1572 in Cassiopeia had gradually faded till in 1574 it became invisible. This had been observed by Tycho Brahe, and its appearance was fully discussed by Kepler in *De Stella Nova*. There is another reference to the observations of the stars in *The first Anniversary*:[4]

> When, if a slow pac'd starre had stolne away
> From the observers marking, he might stay
> Two or three hundred yeares to see't againe,
> And then make up his observation plaine.

And a little later in the same poem, after discussing the 'various and perplexed course' of the movements of the heavenly bodies, which, 'observ'd in divers ages' had caused men to 'finde out so many Eccentrique parts, Such divers downe-right lines, such overthwarts' and to divide the stars into forty-eight constellations, Donne continues:

> And in these Constellations then arise
> New starres, and old doe vanish from our eyes.[5]

In the two *Anniversaries* there is also imagery derived from the theory of the 'magnetick vigour' of the earth, found in the *De Magnete* of William Gilbert of Colchester. This was first published in 1600, and was an important contribution to the new philosophy. It described 'in detail, with rich illustration, a great number of "laboratory" experiments

[1] Grierson, i. 247.

[2] Compare Milton's reference to Galileo as 'the Tuscan Artist', *Paradise Lost*, ii. 288.

[3] Coffin, op. cit., p. 124. [4] Grierson, i. 235. [5] Ibid. 239.

with the loadstone, all beautifully organized to establish the thesis that the earth is a great magnet'. 'To Gilbert the concrete display of magnetic energy in the earth was an inextricable part of his theory of terrestrial motion; in fact, it was the very cause of the earth's diurnal movement.'[1] Gilbert's experiments meant that the antiquated device of the *Primum Mobile* could be disproved, and he therefore gave up the Ptolemaic system, though he seems to have hesitated between the theories of Copernicus and of Tycho Brahe. This belief in the 'magnetick nature of the earth' holding everything together gave Donne the idea of the 'Magnetique force' of the world soul, symbolized in Elizabeth Drury, able 'To draw, and fasten sundred parts in one'.[2] He alludes specifically to Gilbert's work in the *Essays in Divinity*, page 69, where he gives a marginal reference 'Gilbert de Magn. l. [lib.] 6, c. 3'.

The fullest discussion of the implications of the Copernican theory occurs in Donne's prose satire, *Ignatius his Conclave*. Here come the great innovators to claim a place in Lucifer's inner room,

> 'to which, onely they had title, which had so attempted any innouation in this life, that they gaue an affront to all antiquitie, and induced doubts, and anxieties, and scruples, and after, a liberty of beleeuing what they would; at length established opinions, directly contrary to all established before.'[3]

These claimants include Copernicus, Paracelsus, Machiavelli, Christopher Columbus, and a host of others. The description of Copernicus is particularly lively:

> As soon as the doore creekt, I spied a certaine *Mathematitian*, which till then had bene busied to finde, to deride, to detrude *Ptolemy*; and now with an erect countenance, and setled pace, came to the gates, and with hands and feet (scarce respecting *Lucifer* himselfe) beat the dores, and cried: Are these shut against me, to whom all the Heauens were euer open, who was a Soule to the Earth, and gaue it motion?
>
> 'By this I knew it was *Copernicus*: For though I had neuer heard ill of his life, and therefore might wonder to find him there; yet when

[1] Coffin, op. cit., p. 85.
[2] Grierson, i. 238.
[3] *Ignatius his Conclave* (1611), p. 6.

I remembred, that the *Papists* haue extended the name, and the punishment of Heresie, almost to euery thing, and that as yet I vsed *Gregories* and *Bedes* spectacles, by which one saw *Origen*, who deserued so well of the *Christian Church*, *burning in Hell*, I doubted no longer, but assured my selfe that it was *Copernicus* which I saw.'[1]

Copernicus makes his formal claim to 'have turned the whole frame of the world', and raised the earth into the heavens as one of the planets. Lucifer is inclined to concede a place in the inner room to Copernicus, but Ignatius Loyola counsels him to reject it in a speech which reveals Donne's inclination to believe that the Copernican system 'may very well be true'. If the new theory is true, then Copernicus' right to a place of honour in hell is very much diminished. That should belong rather to 'our *Clavius*, who opposed himselfe opportunely against you, and the truth, which at that time was creeping into every man's minde'.[2] Clavius was the famous Jesuit mathematician who felt himself bound, by his adhesion to the Aristotelian and Ptolemaic theory, to attack the work of Copernicus. He it was who also undertook a more useful work, the reform of the Julian calendar. Coffin[3] shows that by 1610 Donne had read the voluminous commentary of Clavius on Sacrobosco in the 1607 edition.

There are a number of incidental references in the prose works in which Donne mentions the Copernican philosophy for the sake of illustration or metaphor. So he says in *Devotions upon Emergent Occasions* (first edition, 1624), pp. 544–5:

'I am *up*, and I seeme to *stand*, and I goe *round*; and I am a *new Argument* of the *new Philosophie*, That the *Earth* moves round; why may I not beleeve, that the *whole earth* moves in a *round motion*, though that seeme to mee to *stand*, when as I seeme to *stand* to my *Company*, and yet am carried in a giddy and circular motion, as I *stand?*'

Similarly, in one of his letters he observes: 'methinks the new Astronomie is thus appliable well, that we which are a

[1] *Ignatius his Conclave* (1611), pp. 12–13.

[2] Ibid., p. 19. For a fuller account of the speech see pp. 198–9, *infra*.

[3] Op. cit., p. 88.

little earth, should rather move towards God, then that he which is fulfilling, and can come no whither, should move towards us'.[1]

Another achievement of the new philosophy was its dismissal of the element of fire from the place which it had held in the medieval scheme. Donne takes note of this in the line already quoted from *The first Anniversary*, 'The Element of fire is quite put out', and again in *The second Anniversary*:

> Have not all soules thought
> For many ages, that our body is wrought
> Of Ayre, and Fire, and other Elements?
> And now they think of new ingredients.[2]

Here there are two separate problems to be considered—whether fire is one of the four elements, and whether there is a region of fire above the earth and air, as the upholders of the Ptolemaic system believed. Cardan in his *De Subtilitate*, first published in 1550, denied the existence of fire as an element. He held that there were only three elements, earth, air, and water, common to all things and possessed of definite qualities which entitled them to be called elements. Donne knew this book and referred to it in another connexion in *Biathanatos*.[3] It is probable, however, that it was from Kepler rather than from Cardan that Donne derived his knowledge of the subject. Cardan's arguments had been of an elementary and inconclusive kind. Tycho Brahe had produced much more conclusive evidence, and Kepler in his *Astronomiae pars optica* (also known as *Ad Vitellionem Paralipomena*) and in the preface to his *Dioptrice* summarized the arguments of Vitellio and Pena against the existence of a fiery sphere above the earth.[4] In his earlier poems Donne had accepted the doctrine of the four elements without

[1] *Letters* (1651), p. 61.

[2] Grierson, i. 259.

[3] p. 50. 'And as *Cardan* sayes it [*Mettall is planta sepulta, and that a Mole is Animal sepultum*].' The square brackets are Donne's and the marginal reference is '*De Subtil. lib.* 5'.

[4] Coffin, op. cit., pp. 167–71.

And women, whom this flower doth represent,
With this mysterious number be content;
Ten is the farthest number; if halfe ten
Belonge unto each woman, then
Each woman may take halfe us men;
But if this will not serve their turne, Since all
Numbers are odde, or even, and they fall
First into this, five, women may take us all.

This should be compared with Donne's remarks on the number five in the *Essays in Divinity*:[1] 'In which number, compos'd of the first even, and first odd, because Cabalistick learning seems to most *Occupatissima vanitas*, I will forbear the observations, both of *Picus* in his *Heptaplus* and in the Harmony of *Francis George*, that transcending Wit . . .' and his comments on the alteration of the name Sarai to Sarah: 'And from *Sarai's* Name he took a letter, which expressed the number ten, and repos'd one, which made but *five*; so that she contributed that five which man wanted before, to show a mutuall indigence and Supplement.'[2]

Again, he examines the number 70 in the *Essays in Divinity*:

'But because any overcurious and Mysterious consideration of this Number 70, though it be composed of the two greatest Numbers (for *Ten* cannot be exceeded, but that to express any further Number you must take a part of it again; and *Seven* is ever used to express infinite), be too Cabalistic and Pythagorick for a vulgar Christian, . . . because I am one, and in a low degree, of the first and vulgar rank, and write but to my equals, I will forbear it as mis-interpretable. . . .'[3]

It should be noted that in this passage Donne joins together the two adjectives 'Cabalistic' and 'Pythagorick'. During the Renaissance the Greek belief in the philosophical importance of mathematical conceptions had an important revival. Two of the authors whom Donne quotes in the *Essays in Divinity*, Nicholas de Cusa (whom he calls Cusanus) and Pico della Mirandola, were leaders in this movement. 'De Cusa regarded God as the same as "mathematical infinity", and the world as "an infinite harmony in which all

[1] p. 14. [2] Ibid., p. 98. [3] Ibid., pp. 129, 130.

things have their mathematical proportions".' 'Pico's mathematical accomplishments, though directed towards occultism and cabalistic subtleties, enabled him to give a thoroughgoing mathematical interpretation of the world.'[1] Thus the Pythagorean doctrine that number lies at the base of the real world was handed on through Plato, the Neo-platonic tradition, and the Christian Renaissance philosophers, in whose minds it was sometimes associated with the cabalistic belief in the mystical value of numbers. Since Copernicus 'indicated that the historical basis of his work was to be found in the doctrine of the Pythagoreans', this revival of the belief in the ultimate importance of mathematics is linked with the rise of the new philosophy. When Copernicus dedicated his great book to Pope Paul the Third he explained that what first led him to seek for a new theory of the motions of the heavenly bodies was the fact that 'the Mathematicians do not agree among themselves' on the problem of the motions of the spheres.[2] He defended his new scheme by showing that it was simpler and more commodious (*paucioribus et multo convenientioribus rebus*), in fact that it was a mathematical reduction of the extremely complicated geometry of the planetary Ptolemaic system.

From the great majority of Donne's contemporaries the questions asked by the new philosophy would have received much the same reply as that given by Sir Andrew Aguecheek when Sir Toby Belch asked him 'Does not our life consist of the four elements?' 'Faith, so they say—but I think it rather consists of eating and drinking.' Donne was exceptional in that, at least for a number of years in his life, he was really interested in considering whether there were three elements or four, whether the sun moved round the earth or the earth round the sun. He was neither a scientist nor a philosopher, but a poet who could see the philosophical implications of the new scientific discoveries. Living in an age of transition he could feel the shocks which were threatening the security of the old edifice of thought. This is

[1] C. M. Coffin, op. cit., p. 73 n.

[2] Address to the Pope in the *De revolutionibus orbium coelestium* of Copernicus, quoted by Coffin, op. cit., p. 66. See also pp. 68, 69.

expressed more clearly than anywhere else in the two *Anniversaries*, but these poems are much more than a mere lament over the decay of the earlier system. They express also Donne's conviction of the ultimate realities of God and the soul. Behind the appearances of sense there is an invisible order which remains unshaken. He adjures his soul to leave these outward shows, and seek the Source of all knowledge:

> In this low forme, poore soule, what wilt thou doe?
> When wilt thou shake off this Pedantery,
> Of being taught by sense, and Fantasie?
> Thou look'st through spectacles; small things seem great
> Below; But up unto the watch-towre get,
> And see all things despoyl'd of fallacies:
> Thou shalt not peepe through lattices of eyes,
> Nor heare through Labyrinths of eares, nor learne
> By circuit, or collections to discerne.
> In heaven thou straight know'st all, concerning it,
> And what concernes it not, shalt straight forget.[1]

[1] Grierson, i. 259–60.

VI

(i) JUVENILIA

THE contents of *Juvenilia* or *Paradoxes and Problems* belong to the early part of Donne's life. We do not know the exact date of their composition, but John Donne, the younger, in his preface to the 1652 edition, described them as 'the entertainment of the Author's Youth', and compared them to 'the Primroses and violets of the Spring' which 'entertain us with more Delight than the Fruits of the Autumn'. They are clever trifles, often scurrilous in tone, and were certainly the first of Donne's prose compositions. They were never printed in his lifetime, but soon after his death a limited number of them were licensed for publication by Sir Henry Herbert. The licences were granted on 25th October 1632, but on 14th November Sir Henry was called upon by the Bishop of London, at the King's command, to explain before the Board of the Star Chamber 'why hee warranted the book of D. Duns paradoxes to bee printed'.[1] The book, however, was issued in 1633 by Henry Seyle, who had apparently obtained the manuscript in some unauthorized way. It contained eleven paradoxes and ten problems, arranged in two sections, each with a separate imprimatur dated 25 October 1632. The title runs thus:

Iuuenilia: or certaine Paradoxes, and Problemes, written by I. Donne. London, Printed by E. P. for Henry Seyle, and are to be sold at the signe of the Tygers head, in Saint Pauls Churchyard, Anno Dom. 1633.

Seyle republished the work later in 1633, but by this time the licences had been withdrawn and he omitted the imprimatur. He also added to the first problem twenty-three lines which had not appeared in the first edition. On the title-page the volume is described as 'the second Edition, corrected'.

In 1637 the younger John Donne presented a petition to Archbishop Laud in which he stated that since the death of

[1] *Calendar of Domestic State Papers, Charles I*, ccxxv. 20.

his father, lately Dean of St. Paul's, there had been many scandalous pamphlets published under his name, which were none of his. Among them the younger Donne instanced *Juvenilia*, printed for Henry Seale; another by John Marriot and William Sheares, entitled *Ignatius his Conclave*; and also certain poems, by the said Marriot. Of the abuses they had been often warned by the petitioner, but they continued to publish new impressions. He prayed the Archbishop to stop their further proceedings, and accordingly Laud issued an injunction dated 16 December 1637 requiring the parties concerned not to meddle any further with the printing or selling of any pretended works of the late Dean of St. Paul's, 'save only such as shall be licensed by public authority and approved by the petitioner'.[1]

The injunction had little effect, for Marriot issued a new edition of the *Poems* in 1639, and John Donne later admitted the genuineness of *Juvenilia* and *Ignatius his Conclave* by publishing a new edition of both in 1652.

The title of the edition runs thus: 'Paradoxes, Problemes, Essayes, Characters, Written by Dr Donne Dean of Pauls: To which is added a Book of Epigrams: Written in Latin by the same Author; translated into English by J: Maine, D.D. As also Ignatius his Conclave, A Satyr, Translated out of the Originall Copy written in Latin by the same Author; found lately amongst his own Papers. De Jesuitarum dissidiis. Quos pugnare, Scholis, clamāt, hi, (discite Regna) Non sunt Unanimes, conveniuntq; nimis. London, Printed by T: N: for Humphrey Moseley at the Prince's Armes in St Pauls Churchyard, 1652.'[2] *Ignatius his Conclave* has a separate title-page dated 1653.

The Stationers' Register contains several entries referring to this volume. On 7th March 1652–3 the rights of Richard, son of John Marriot, in *Ignatius* and the *Essays in Divinity* were transferred to Moseley, and on 10th July 1653 the following entry was made: 'Master Mosely. Entred . . . a

[1] *Calendar of Domestic State Papers, Charles I*, ccclxxiv. 4. The document was printed in full by Dr. Grosart (*Fuller Worthies' Library*, 1873, vol. ii, p. lii) and was reprinted by Sir Herbert Grierson (*Poems*, vol. ii, p. lxvi).

[2] Thomason bought his copy 8 Nov. 1652.

small tract called, *Fasciculus poematũ & Epigramatũ miscellaneorum*, by Dr Jno Donne late Deane of St Pauls. Licensed March 15, 1650, by Master Downham & subscribed by Master Stephens then warden . . . vjd.'

This last entry indicates that in 1650 it was intended that the 'Sheaf of Miscellany Epigrams' should be issued as a separate volume. Much controversy has been aroused by these epigrams, which are mostly coarse and trivial in the usual style of seventeenth-century epigrams but which include also a small group of verses referring to wars in the Low Countries, and particularly to an investiture of Duke's Wood or Bois-le-Duc.[1] In a Latin letter to Sir Henry Goodyer (*Poems*, 1633, pp. 351–2) Donne mentions *epigrammata mea Latina*, but they can hardly be the same as these verses, which contain an allusion to Heyn, a Dutch seaman, who did not become conspicuous till 1626. 'Heyns more bold adventure' probably refers to his capture of the Spanish plate fleet in 1628, and the successful siege of Bois-le-Duc also belongs to 1628, though there were earlier attacks on the town in 1587, 1600, and 1603. It is possible that Mayne may have tricked the younger Donne into thinking that he possessed Donne's verses, or he may have conspired with that worthy, who allowed spurious pieces to be added to the editions of his father's poems,[2] and who had the

[1] Dr. Jessopp at first accepted these epigrams as genuine, and in his edition of the *Essays in Divinity* (1855) argued that they showed that Donne served in Prince Maurice's army and was present in 1587 at the fight outside Bois-le-Duc, though he admitted that it was strange that Donne should have served in the Netherlands at the age of fourteen, and on the Protestant side. Dr. Grosart in his edition of Donne's poems argued at great length against the genuineness of the epigrams, and conducted a controversy in the *Athenæum* with Dr. Jessopp, who at last admitted that they must be spurious. Sir E. K. Chambers (*Poems of John Donne*, 1896, ii. 309–10) gave an excellent summary of the evidence against them, and suggested that the younger Donne might have written them himself, or that they might have been composed as well as translated by Jasper Mayne, or, finally, that they might have been the work of the John Done who composed *Polydoron*. Gosse (op. cit., i. 16–17) inclined to the belief that they were the work of Jasper Mayne, who was a witty divine and the author of certain successful comedies, and who was celebrated for his mystifications and practical jokes.

[2] Grierson, vol. ii, p. lxx.

audacity to claim on the title-page of this edition that *Ignatius his Conclave*, which had passed through several editions, both Latin and English, was a translation of a Latin original found lately among Donne's papers.

The other additions to this volume included one new paradox and seven problems, an 'Essay of Valour', and two 'Characters'—'the Character of a Scot at the first sight' and 'the true Character of a Dunce'. Two of these items, the 'Essay of Valour' and the 'Character of a Dunce', had appeared thirty years earlier in the eleventh edition (1622) of Sir Thomas Overbury's *Wife*, to which a large number of 'Characters' and miscellaneous essays were added. The second edition (1614) of the *Wife* had begun the practice of associating Overbury's poem with 'Characters' and essays by himself and his friends. Successive editions added more and more items, until Overbury's original contributions were almost lost in the mass of material contributed by different authors, such as Sir Henry Wotton, Lady Southwell, Sir Benjamin Rudyard, John Cocke, and others whose identity was indicated only by initials. Among this latter class was Donne, whose 'Newes from the very Country' appeared first on Sig. G 2 of the second edition of the *Wife*, where it was signed I. D. It was reprinted in the numerous subsequent editions, and was finally claimed as Donne's by his son, and printed in 1650 among the *Poems*, in spite of the fact that it is entirely in prose.

This 'Newes' is well known, but no previous writer on Donne has noticed that the 'Essay of Valour' and the 'True Character of a Dunce' were also included in the Overbury volume, though in a later edition than that in which the 'Newes' first appeared.[1] The eleventh edition, in which they were included for the first time, was printed by Henry Seile

[1] My friend R. E. Bennett has drawn my attention to the fact that 'An Essay of Valour' was printed as 'Valour Anatomised in a Fancie. By Sir Philip Sidney, 1581', in a volume *Cottoni Posthuma*, published in London in 1651. Evidently Sir Robert Cotton had possessed a transcript of Donne's essay, and this was found among his papers after his death, and by some accident Sidney's name was appended to it. There was no justification for ascribing it to Sidney; its cynical, anti-chivalrous tone is characteristic of Donne, and quite foreign to Sidney.

or Seyle, the publisher who in 1633 issued Donne's *Juvenilia*. The previous editions of the Overbury volume had been issued by other printers. Apparently Seyle had access to a manuscript containing some of Donne's early prose pieces. In 1622 Donne was a dignitary of the Church, and it is unlikely that he would have wished to see these witty trifles in print. No indication of their authorship is given in the Overbury volume.

Dr. Keynes has distinguished two issues of the 1652 edition of the *Paradoxes*.[1] The differences occur only in the first quire of eight leaves (A 8), and it is clear that this has been re-set, while the other sheets have remained untouched.

This edition is generally bound up with the *Essays in Divinity*, which had been printed in 1651 for a different publisher. Dr. Keynes was the first to point out that it is clear from the preface that this juxtaposition was not accidental, but was the result of the younger Donne's desire to give the 1652 volume a fictitious respectability by tempering the secularity and occasional indecency of the *Juvenilia* with the mature gravity of the *Essays*.

In 1923 a new edition of the *Paradoxes and Problemes* was issued by the Nonesuch Press, with a prefatory note by Dr. Keynes. The text followed that of the second edition of 1633 of the *Juvenilia*, amplified from the edition of 1652, and contained also an additional problem, 'Why was Sir Walter Raleigh thought the fittest Man, to write the Historie of these Times?', which had been first printed by

[1] Keynes, op. cit., pp. 61–5. One issue contains a short passage on A 3 verso which is omitted in the other issue. Dr. Keynes treats the issue without the passage as the earlier, but would author or publisher go to the expense of re-setting the first quire merely to add a few clauses which have no particular bearing on the subject? On the other hand, if the passage was misinterpretable, as it seems to me, the author might remove it for fear of offending his patron. The sentence runs thus: '. . . if they [i.e. the essays contained in the volume] could present to your *Lordship* the *youth* and *beauty* of *Hellen*, or the *courage* and *strength of Hector*, they could not have found a more *proportionable Patron*, either to *caress* the one, or *encounter* the other, you being both *Atossa*, and *Cassius* too.' For Atossa see Clement of Alexandria, *Stromata*, I. xvi (Migne, *P.G.* viii. 132): *πρώτην ἐπιστολὰς συντάξαι Ἄτοσσαν, τὴν Περσῶν βασιλεύσασαν, φησὶν Ἑλλάνικος.*

Sir Edmund Gosse[1] in 1899 from MS. Tanner 299, f. 32, in the Bodleian Library. In 1936 the Facsimile Text Society issued a facsimile reprint of the first edition of 1633 of the *Juvenilia* with an introductory note by R. E. Bennett. This was published at New York by the Columbia University Press.

The following is a list of the paradoxes and problems contained in the first edition of 1633:

Paradoxes

I. A Defence of Womens Inconstancy.
II. That Women ought to Paint.
III. That by Discord things increase.
IV. That Good is more common than Euill.
V. That all things kill themselues.
VI. That it is possible to find some vertue in some Women.
VII. That Old men are more fantastike than Young.
VIII. That Nature is our worst guide.
IX. That only Cowards dare dye.
X. That a Wise man is known by much laughing.
XI. That the gifts of the Body are better than those of the Minde.

Problems

I. Why haue Bastards best Fortunes?
II. Why Puritans make long Sermons?
III. Why did the Diuell reserue Iesuites till these latter Dayes?
IV. Why is there more Variety of Greene, than of any other Colour?
V. Why doe Young Lay-men so much study Diuinity?
VI. Why hath the Common Opinion afforded Women Soules?
VII. Why are the Fairest falsest?
VIII. Why *Venus* Starre only doth cast a shadow?
IX. Why is *Venus* Starre Multinominous, called both *Hesperus* and *Vesper*?
X. Why are new officers least oppressing?

The substance of most of these juvenile essays is very slight, though they are witty enough in style. Some sentences

[1] Op. cit. ii. 52, 53. It is found also in ten other manuscripts, five of which omit the last sentence. The Tanner MS. alone has an introductory sentence: ''Tis one of Dr. Donne's problems (but so bitter, y^t^ his son Jack Donne LL.D. thought not fitt to print it wth ye Rest;).'

from the first Paradox, 'A Defence of Womens Inconstancy', will serve as a sample.

'That Women are *Inconstant*, I with any man confesse, but that *Inconstancy* is a bad quality, I against any man will maintaine: For euery thing as it is one better than another, so is it fuller of *change*; The *Heauens* themselues continually turne, the *Starres* moue, the *Moone* changeth; *Fire* whirleth, *Aire* flyeth, *Water* ebbs and flowes, the face of the *Earth* altereth her lookes, *time* staies not; the Colour that is most light will take most dyes; soe in Men, they that haue the most reason are the most intolerable[1] in their designes, and the darkest or most ignorant, doe seldomest change; therefore Women changing more than Men, haue also more *Reason*. . . . *Inconstancy* is a most commendable and cleanly quality, and Women in this quality are farre more absolute than the Heauens, than the Starres, Moone, or any thing beneath it; for long obseruation hath pickt certainty out of their mutability. The Learned are so well acquainted with the Starrs, Signes and Planets, that they make them but Characters, to read the meaning of the Heauen in his own forehead. Euery simple Fellow can bespeake the change of the *Moone* a great while beforehand: but I would faine haue the learnedst man so skilful, as to tell when the simplest Woman meaneth to varie. Learning affords no rules to know, much lesse knowledge to rule the mind of a Woman. . . . To conclude therefore; this name of *Inconstancy*, which hath so much beene poisoned with slaunders, ought to be changed into *variety*, for the which the world is so delightfull, and a Woman for that the most delightfull thing in this world.'[2]

It will be seen from a list of the paradoxes and problems contained in the 1633 edition that many of the subjects were such as were also occupying a large place in the poems which Donne wrote between 1590 and 1600. The inconstancy of women, the relations of body and mind, the necessity of death—these were themes always in Donne's mind, and he treated them in prose with the same mingling of levity and cynicism, of wit and melancholy, which he showed in the poems of this date. But the note of passion, which redeems much that would otherwise be repellent in the poems, is lacking in the *Paradoxes*. Two of these essays deal with the

[1] *intolerable*. The 1652 edition reads *inalterable*, which does not suit the context.

[2] *Juvenilia* (1633), sig. A 3–B 1 verso.

theme which Donne was later to elaborate in *Biathanatos*, the idea of suicide. Here, in discussing the paradox 'That all things kill themselves', he alludes to several of the arguments found there:

'To affect, yea to effect their owne *death* all *liuing* things are importun'd, not by *Nature* onely which perfects them, but by *Art* and *Education*, which perfects her. . . . And if amongst *Men* not to *defend* be to *kill*, what a haynous *selfe-murther* is it, not to *defend it selfe*. This *defence* because *Beasts* neglect, they kill themselues, because they exceed vs in *number*, *strength*, and a *lawlesse liberty*: yea, of *Horses* and other beasts, they that inherit *most courage* by being bred of *gallantest parents*, and by *Artificiall nursing* are bettered, will runne to their owne *deaths*, neither sollicited by *spurres* which they need not, nor by *honour* which they apprehend not. If then the *valiant* kill himselfe, who can excuse the coward?'[1]

Paradox IX.—'That only Cowards dare Dye', regards suicide from a less favourable standpoint.

'*Extreames* are equally remooued from the *meane*; so that headlong *desperatenesse* asmuch offends true *valour*, as backward *Cowardice*: of which sort I reckon iustly all *vn-inforced deaths*. When will your *valiant* man dye of necessity? so *Cowards* suffer what cannot be auoided: and to runne into *death vnimportun'd*, is to runne into the first condemned desperatenesse. Will he dye when hee is *rich* and *happy*? then by liuing hee may doe more good: and in *Afflictions* and *miseries*, *death* is the chosen refuge of *Cowards*.

Fortiter ille facit, qui miser esse potest.

But it is taught and practised among our *Gallants*, that rather than our reputations suffer any *maime*, or wee any *misery*, wee shall offer our *brests* to the *Cannons* mouth, yea to our swords points: And this seemes a very *braue* and a very *climbing* (which is a *Cowardly*, earthly, and indeed a very *groueling*) *spirit*. Why doe they *chaine* these slaues to the *Gallyes*, but that they thrust[2] their *deaths*, and would at euery loose leape into the *sea*? Why doe they take weapons from *condemned* men, but to barre them of that ease which *Cowards* affect, *a speedy death*. Truly this *life* is a *Tempest* and a *warfare*, and he which *dares dye*, to escape the *Anguish* of it, seemes to me, but so *valiant*, as he which dares *hang* himselfe, lest he bee *prest* to the *wars*. I haue seene

[1] Ibid., sig. C 2 verso–C 3.

[2] *thrust*, an old form of 'thirst'.

one in that extremity of *Melancholy*, which was then become *Madnesse*, to make his owne *breath* an *Instrument* to stay his breath, and labour to choake himselfe; but alas, hee was *mad*. And we knew another that languished vnder the *oppression* of a poore *disgrace* so much, that he tooke more paines to *dye*, than would haue serued to haue nourished *life* and *spirit* enough to haue out-liued his *disgrace*. What *Foole* will call this *Cowardlinesse*, *valour*? Or this *Basenesse*, *Humility*?'[1]

This paradox shows that even in Donne's early days he felt the force of the moral objection to suicide. In asserting that 'only Cowards dare Dye' he condemns the faint-heartedness of those who refuse to face the troubles of life. There is nothing original in what he says—the doctrine is at least as old as Plato—but the interesting point is that even in these paradoxes in which he strives to be witty and startling, he finds himself obliged to state the case against suicide, and uses the traditional arguments. As these trifles were not intended for publication, this refutation of the case for suicide mirrors for us the strife within Donne's own mind.

Another paradox in which he anticipates his later work is that in which he asserts 'that Good is more common than Evil'. He begins with a young man's petulant outburst against the 'silly old men' who are always extolling the good old days, and denouncing the present age. If these dotards were right, they would themselves be the culprits, for if the times are changed, it is they who have changed them. But indeed good is still more plenteous than evil, as it has ever been. Good is stronger than evil; it can in truth make use of evil, and employ it, as a skilful embroiderer or lapidary makes use of dull material, to enhance the beauty of the finished work. '*Good* . . . refuses no aid, no not of her vtter contrary *Euill*, that she may bee the more common to vs.'[2]

This is in harmony with Donne's later thought, which is fundamentally optimistic. While a dark thread runs through all his work, he expresses again and again his conviction that good must triumph, and that goodness does not simply blot

[1] *Juvenilia* (1633), sig. D 4–E 1.

[2] Ibid., sig. C 1 verso. I have adopted the reading of the best manuscripts in this sentence, as the meaning is obscured by the corruption of the printed text, which has *end* for *aid*.

out evil, but makes use of it and incorporates it in the finished design.

'As poisons conduce to Physick, and discord to Musick, so those two kinds of evill, into which we contract all others, are of good use, that is, *malum pœnæ*, the evill of punishment, affliction, adversity, and *malum culpæ*, even sin it selfe, from which the punishment flowes.'[1]

And again:

'*Gods work is perfect*; How appeares that? *For all his ways are Iudgement*, sayes *Moses* in his victorious song. This is Perfection, That he hath established an order, a judgement. . . . That even disorders are done in order, that even our sins some way or other fall within the providence of God.'[2]

The Problems, like the Paradoxes, contain a mixture of cynical levity, bitter satire, coarse jokes, and underlying seriousness. The sixth problem, 'Why hath the Common Opinion afforded Women Soules?', deals with a question which was much debated in the latter half of the sixteenth century. The disputants generally referred to a passage in St. Ambrose's Commentaries on St. Paul, in which he declares that man was certainly created in God's image, but questions whether woman shared this privilege. In 1595 there appeared 'Disputatio Nova contra Mulieres qua probatur eas Homines non esse', which was answered in the same year by another thesis, 'Simonis Gedicii Defensio Sexus Muliebris, Opposita disputationi: Mulieres Homines non esse.'[3] Ben Jonson apparently refers to the first of these in his *Masque of Beautie*:

> Had those, that dwell in error foule,
> And hold that women haue no soule,
> But seen these moue; they would haue, then
> Said, *Women were the soules of men.*

To this Ben appends a note: 'There hath beene such a profane *paradoxe* published.'[4] A much earlier reference to the doctrine itself may be found in *Mary Magdalene*[5] (1567),

[1] *LXXX Sermons*, 17. 170. [2] Ibid. 37. 369.

[3] This was printed at Leipzig, where the first thesis had probably appeared, though no place or name is given.

[4] From the text of the 1616 folio, p. 910. [5] Sig. E 3.

where Infidelity argues with Mary, 'He speaketh of men, but no woman at all, Women have no souls.'

Donne's 'problem' assumes that souls have been ascribed to women only by man's folly:

'It is agreed that wee haue not so much from them as any *part* of either our *mortall soules* of *sense*, or *growth*; and wee deny *soules* to others equal to them in all but in *speech* for which they are beholding to their *bodily instruments*: For perchance an *Oxes* heart, or a *Goates*, or a *Foxes*, or a *Serpents* would speake iust so, if it were in the *breast*, and could moue that *tongue* and *Iawes*? Haue they so many *advantages* and *meanes* to hurt vs (for, euer their *louing* destroyed vs) that we dare not *displease* them, but giue them what they will? And so when some call them *Angells*, some *Goddesses*, and the *Palpulian Heretikes* make them *Bishops*, wee descend so much with the streame, to allow them soules.'[1]

In later years Donne changed his mind on this subject. In the sermon which he preached on Easter Day, 1630, he renounced the heresy:

'For, howsoever some men out of a petulancy and wantonnesse of wit, and out of the extravagancy of Paradoxes, and such singularities, have called the faculties, and abilities of women in question, even in the roote thereof, in the reasonable and immortall soul, yet that one thing alone hath been enough to create a doubt, (almost an assurance in the negative) whether S. *Ambroses* Commentaries upon the Epistles of S. *Paul*, be truly his or no, that in that book there is a doubt made, whether the woman were created according to Gods Image; Therefore, because that doubt is made in that book, the book it self is suspected not to have had so great, so grave, so constant an author as S. *Ambrose* was; No author of gravity, of piety, of conversation in the Scriptures could admit that doubt, whether woman were created in the Image of God, that is, in possession of a reasonable and immortall soul.'[2]

In writing paradoxes, an essay, and two 'characters' Donne was using forms of prose which had only just been introduced

[1] *Juvenilia*, sig. G 2 verso–G 3. 'Palpulian' is meaningless. Professor C. C. J. Webb points out that it should be 'Peputian', i.e. Montanist. Pepuza in Western Phrygia was one of their centres. Epiphanius says of them *ἐπίσκοποί τε παρ' αὐτοῖς γυναῖκες, καὶ πρεσβύτεροι γυναῖκες καὶ τὰ ἄλλα* (*Adversus Haereticos*, 49; in Migne, *P.G.* xli. 881).

[2] *LXXX Sermons*, 25. 242.

that two passages from Paradox 10 were quoted, or rather paraphrased, in the Diary of John Manningham, barrister of the Middle Temple, under the date 15 February 1603. We have no reason to think that Manningham was one of the intimate friends to whom Donne sent copies of his paradoxes soon after their composition. It seems likely, therefore, that these ten paradoxes had been circulating in manuscript for some time before Manningham saw them,[1] and 1599 to 1600 remains a likely date for them, especially as the tone of Donne's covering letter is similar to that of several others written between the beginning of Donne's employment as Egerton's secretary in 1598 and his marriage in 1601 and subsequent disgrace.

Gosse expressed his belief that all the Paradoxes and Problems were written before 1600.[2] I have shown,[3] however, that Problem 8 must be at least as late as 1606, since it contains a reference to Kepler's *De Stella in Cygno*, published at Prague in 1606. The problem about Raleigh's imprisonment and his *History* must be later than 1603, the date of the trial, and might be as late as 1609.[4] There are several references to 'problems' in Donne's letters written about 1607, such as: 'I pray reade these two problems: for such light flashes as these have been my hawkings in my Surry journies.'[5] This letter is assigned by Gosse himself to 1607, and it clearly belongs to the period of Donne's life at Mitcham in

[1] In Manningham's Diary there is a fragment of another paradox, 'Hee that weepeth is most wise', sandwiched between the two fragments from Donne's known paradoxes. R. E. Bennett (op. cit., p. 310) has argued that this represents a lost paradox by Donne, upholding the wisdom of weeping as a pendant to Paradox 10 which declares 'That a Wise Man is knowne by much Laughing'. This is possible, as Donne had already produced two Paradoxes (nos. 5 and 9) arguing the case for and against suicide. Since Manningham does not quote *verbatim*, and the piece is only a fragment, it is difficult to argue the matter on the evidence of style.

[2] Gosse, ii. 301.

[3] See p. 120 *supra*, and *Review of English Studies*, iii. 143.

[4] The reference to Raleigh as writing the 'history of his own times' instead of the *History of the World* which he really undertook shows that the 'problem' belongs to the period before the publication of the book.

[5] *Poems* (1633), p. 361. In the *Letters* of 1651 (p. 88) *Surry* [Surrey] is misprinted as *sorry*.

Surrey. Another letter to Sir Henry Goodyer, belonging to the same period, contains these words:

'I end with a probleme, whose errand is, to aske for his fellowes. I pray before you ingulfe your selfe in the Progresse, leave them for mee, and such other of my papers as you will lend mee till your returne.'[1]

There is yet another letter in which Donne sends his friend a problem:

'Else let this probleme supply, which was occasioned by you, of women wearing stones. . . . Though their unworthinesse, and your own ease be advocates for me with you, yet I must adde my entreaty, that you let goe no copy of my Problems, till I review them. If it be too late, at least be able to tell me who hath them.'[2]

Thus the Paradoxes and Problems with the two 'Characters' cover a period of eight or nine years in Donne's life and bridge the interval between the composition of the verse *Satires* and that of *Biathanatos*, which Donne himself described on the title-page of the manuscript as a 'Paradoxe'. During the first part of the time Donne was Egerton's secretary and later he was busy with hard controversial work for Thomas Morton, afterwards Bishop of Durham. He composed these trifles at odd moments in a busy life, and they were of the nature of a literary experiment. Hitherto he had been, and he still was, a poet, but poetry offered him no career. He turned to prose, and strove to polish a prose style which was as yet immature. There is little in these early pieces to anticipate the magnificence of the *Sermons*, but they are the work of a mind which was alive and sensitive to all impressions. Their satiric quality links them with the verse *Satires* and also with that later prose satire, *Ignatius his Conclave*, and the undated *Catalogus Librorum Aulicorum*.

[1] *Poems* (1633), p. 358. Also printed in *Letters* (1651), p. 99.

[2] *Letters* (1651), p. 108. R. E. Bennett shows that we should read 'by yours' for 'by you'.

(ii) CATALOGUS LIBRORUM AULICORUM

AMONG the few leaves of miscellaneous verse and prose which John Donne the younger added in 1650 to the edition of his father's poems, there was a Latin *jeu d'esprit* entitled *Catalogus Librorum*. In 1929 I identified a manuscript version of it in the Library of Trinity College, Cambridge, and found that this threw fresh light on some of the obscurities of the printed text. In 1930 the Nonesuch Press published a critical edition based on my collation of the manuscript with the edition of 1650.

The *Catalogue* is an elaborate jest in the manner of Rabelais, who had given a mock catalogue of books in the Library of Saint Victor (*Pantagruel*, II. vii). Donne gives us the titles of thirty-four imaginary books which he ascribes to real authors, whose behaviour or whose actual works might give some point to the satire. Thus Topcliffe, the notorious informer and cruel persecutor of the Catholics, is credited by Donne with a book called 'A Rival of Moses. The art of keeping clothes for more than forty years'. Sir John Harington, whose treatise *The Metamorphosis of Ajax* was a satire on the Elizabethan sewerage system, appears in Donne's *Catalogus* as the author of *Hercules*, a discussion of the sanitary arrangements of Noah's Ark. Sometimes the jest is of a different type. That Tarlton, the famous clown of the Elizabethan stage, should be assigned a book on 'The Privileges of Parliament' is a gibe at the Parliamentarians rather than at Tarlton.

In this list we have a fresh proof of Donne's familiarity with Rabelais's great work, to which he refers in his *Satires*,[1] his letters,[2] and his lines on Coryat's *Crudities*.[3] Rabelais's catalogue was inordinately long (it had 140 items) and was full of gross jests. Donne's is much shorter, and contains

[1] Grierson, *Poems*, i. 161; see ii. 121 n.

[2] Letters to Sir Henry Wotton from the Burley MS. will be found *infra*, pp. 310, 319.

[3] Verses headed 'Incipit Ioannes Dones' prefixed to Coryat's *Crudities* (1611), sig. f 5 verso (ll. 11–13).

many contemporary allusions, some of which have hitherto been obscured by the corruptions of the printed text.

The 1650 edition of Donne's *Poems* was the first edition published by the authority of his son, John Donne, Doctor of the Civil Law, who added a few pieces of miscellaneous verse and prose to justify his claim on the title-page that the volume contained 'divers Copies under his [Donne's] own hand, never before in Print'.

In one of his Latin letters to Sir Henry Goodyer Donne mentions his 'satirical catalogue of books' along with his Latin epigrams, and asks Goodyer to return them all, if he has them, that they may undergo a final revision.[1] The date of the letter seems to be 1611, as in it Donne speaks of a projected visit to the Continent, probably the visit to France with Sir Robert and Lady Drury which occupied part of 1611 and 1612.[2]

The 1650 edition of the *Catalogue* contains some elementary blunders in Latin, e.g. *excriptus* for *exscriptus*, and a few more serious errors which obscure the meaning of the text. For example, it reads *Io: Florio Stalo-Anglum*, which became, in the edition of 1719, 'Jo. Florio Stalo, *Anglum*'. The Trinity College manuscript gives us the right reading, 'Iohannem Florio *Italo-Anglum*'. Again, the allusion in Item 11 is obscured in 1650 and the editions which follow it by the reading *Iohan: Povy*, for which the manuscript has the correct form *Jo: Pory*. Here, as in the 1652 edition of *Paradoxes*, *Problemes*, *Essayes*, *Characters*, John Donne the younger showed himself a careless editor of his father's work. He took no pains to correct even the most obvious blunders of the printer, and it is no wonder that the *Catalogue*, even more than the *Paradoxes*, remained for so long neglected by Donne's editors. It was reprinted in the editions of 1654, 1669, and 1719, but it was not included in Alford's *Works of*

[1] *Poems* (1633), p. 352: 'Interim seponas oro chartulas meas, quas cum sponsione citae redhibitionis (ut barbarè, sed cum ingeniosissimo Appollinari loquar) accepisti. Inter quas, si epigrammata mea Latina, et Catalogus librorum satyricus non sunt, non sunt; extremum juditium, hoc est, manum ultimam jamjam subiturae sunt. Earum nonnullae Purgatorium suum passurae, ut correctiores emanent.'

[2] Sir E. K. Chambers, *Poems of Donne* (ii. 310).

Donne (1839), and Sir Edmund Gosse made no allusion to it in his *Life and Letters of John Donne*. Dr. Grosart dismissed it airily as 'a quaint fantastique' (*Poems of Donne*, II. liv). It was catalogued by Dr. G. L. Keynes in his *Bibliography* as one of the new items added by the younger Donne to the *Poems* of 1650, but the introductory Latin paragraph, giving Donne's ironical reasons for writing the *Catalogue*, was mentioned by Dr. Keynes as a separate contribution, and he gave no hint of the satirical nature of the piece. Sir E. K. Chambers in his *Poems of Donne* (ii. 311) made a passing reference to it. Yet when properly interpreted it throws a brilliant light on Donne's opinion of many of his contemporaries, and it is the most complete example extant of his skill in that kind of Latin improvisation which was highly esteemed in the seventeenth century.[1] Among learned men Latin was still, to some extent, a living tongue. Francis Bacon, Ben Jonson, and Milton all showed their skill in writing it. Latin was the recognized vehicle for satire among the learned, as Milton proved in his disputes with Salmasius. By such a *jeu d'esprit* as the *Catalogue* Donne showed that he could hold his own in the scholarly amusements of a brilliant literary circle. His Latin was vigorous and pointed, and though he sometimes used semi-barbarous terms, for which he apologized to Goodyer, this was a licence which was generally allowed in satirical composition. For us the interest of the *Catalogue* lies not in its Latinity but in its view of Jacobean literary society and its reflection of Donne's personal tastes. The *Catalogue* probably belongs to the period 1603–11, that is, to the years between Donne's marriage and his visit to France with Sir Robert Drury. The reference to the Royal hounds in the introductory paragraph implies that James I was on the throne, and that his inordinate fondness for his dogs was well known. The references to Bacon and Barlow show that Donne felt bitter resentment for the part which both had played in the final tragedy of the trial and execution of Essex. Thus it seems likely that the *Catalogue*, as we have it in the 1650 edition, belongs to the earlier part of the period mentioned. It would thus be contemporary

[1] *Conclaue Ignati* is Donne's longest Latin work, but it is of a different type.

with many of Donne's *Problems*, and it would precede *Biathanatos* (about 1608), *Pseudo-Martyr* (1610), and *Ignatius his Conclave* (1611).

Even if the *Catalogue* had not been vouched for by Donne's own letter and by the authority of his son, we should have guessed its authorship from the acrid flavour which marks all Donne's prose of this period. His romantic marriage in 1601 had checked his promising career and had plunged him into poverty. With a delicate wife and a rapidly growing family he had to work hard at uncongenial tasks in order to make a living. He had seen enough of the Court to be disgusted with its intrigues, and yet he hated his exile in 'the insipid dulnesse of the country'. He read omnivorously, but criticized bitterly much of what he read. From time to time he visited London and found relief from his work in meeting his friends and acquaintances in the circle of wits which included Ben Jonson, John Hoskyns, Inigo Jones, Sir Henry Goodyer, Sir Robert Cotton, and Christopher Brooke.

Several items in the *Catalogue* recall passages in Donne's *Satires*. Thus the attack on the informer Topcliffe reminds us that three manuscripts read 'Topcliffe' for 'Pursevant' in line 216 of Satire IV.[1] The item referring to Luther and the Lord's Prayer sums up the lines on the same subject in Satire II.[2] The tone of the list is more anti-Protestant than that of any of Donne's works except the *Satires*. Two possibilities suggest themselves—first, that the *Catalogue* may have been written originally between 1594 and 1600, and that it may have been brought up to date at a later period by the inclusion of some new items satirizing books recently published, such as those of Sutcliffe or Barlow. Or secondly, we may admit that Donne's sympathies remained Catholic for a number of years after he had ceased to be a member of the Roman Church. This seems to be the more probable supposition. The introduction to the *Catalogue* was clearly written after James I had come to the throne,[3] and the first item in the list refers to a book by Nicholas Hill

[1] Grierson, i. 166, and ii. 125. [2] Ibid., i. 153; see ii. 112 n.

[3] See the suggestion that one of the chief uses of learning for a courtier is to enable him to 'praise with point and grace your fellow-menials, the royal

which was published in 1601, so that even if the satire had been planned earlier we should have to admit that Donne had completely rearranged it. The evidence available suggests a date about 1604 or 1605 for the *Catalogue* as printed in 1650, and one of 1610 or 1611 for the revised form as found in the Trinity manuscript. The extremely bitter attack on Bacon in Items 27 and 28 was probably written when the memory of Bacon's ingratitude to Essex and his behaviour at the trial were still fresh in Donne's mind. In the Trinity manuscript Donne removed no. 27, which mentioned Bacon by name, and also no. 26, but retained no. 28. Egerton's name was omitted in no. 25, which thus immediately precedes no. 28 in the manuscript. Donne failed to notice that the omission of nos. 26 and 27 left no. 28 unintelligible. No. 28 is 'Cæpe advocatorum, sive ars plorandi in Iudiciis, per eundem. . . .' Thus in the manuscript *per eundem* no longer refers to Bacon, but to the author of the book mentioned in no. 25, which is 'Ars Spiritualis inescandi mulieres', a gibe against Stephen Egerton, a Puritan divine. The reason for the omission of no. 27 in the revised *Catalogue* is probably to be found in the fact that Lady Drury, the wife of Donne's new patron, was Bacon's sister. From the letter to Goodyer which has been already quoted, we see that Donne proposed to revise the *Catalogue* shortly before his visit to France in 1611 with Sir Robert and Lady Drury. There is no reason to think that the Drurys were friends with Donne before 1610, but in that year their only daughter Elizabeth died, and Donne wrote his elaborate poem, *The Anatomy of the World* (published in 1611), in her honour. The Drurys proved kind and generous patrons, and however much Donne may have disliked Bacon's behaviour to Essex he could hardly in common decency attack the Solicitor-General while enjoying the hospitality of his sister. There seems to be no particular reason for the omission of no. 26, an attack on the physician William Butler. I suggest that Donne may have intended to omit nos. 27 and 28, the two attacks on Bacon, and marked

hounds', *The Courtier's Library*, pp. 29, 41. The King's excessive fondness for hunting and for his hounds was the subject of much unfavourable comment.

his autograph manuscript to that effect. The scribe who copied the Trinity manuscript misunderstood the instructions and omitted nos. 26 and 27, instead of 27 and 28, thus leaving no. 28 pointless and '*per eundem*' unintelligible, since the scribe left out the name of the author in no. 25.

In his introductory sentences to the *Catalogue* Donne remarks that in the present age, while 'open illiteracy is supremely disgraceful, full knowledge is supremely rare'. 'Every one has a smattering of letters, no one a complete mastery of them.' Most men therefore choose a middle way, and use the epitomes or abridgements compiled by such writers as 'Lullius, Gemma, Sebundus, Empiricus, Trithemius, Agrippa, Erasmus, Ramus'. But this pinchbeck knowledge soon betrays itself, and therefore Donne slyly advises his imaginary courtier to try a route 'which is less exposed to the literary detective'. The engagements of Court life leave no leisure for literature, since the man of fashion must not rise, as a rule, till after ten o'clock, and then how long he must spend in putting on the dress appropriate to the day, to the place, and to his humour, and in composing his features in the looking-glass, deciding whether to greet so-and-so with a laugh outright or with a raised eye-brow. Meals and amusements take up most of the rest of the day, so that only a fraction is left for the cultivation of the mind. However,

'though it will be impossible for you to know what others know, you can at least find means to know what they fail to know. . . . Leaving the so-called classics for dons and school-masters to thumb, struggle with the help of all to whom you can safely confess your ignorance, to hunt out books difficult to discover. . . . I have therefore jotted down for your use the following catalogue, so that with these books at your elbow, you may in almost every branch of knowledge suddenly emerge as an authority, if not with deeper learning than the rest, at least with a learning differing from theirs.'[1]

[1] These quotations are from the English translation by my husband Percy Simpson appended to the Latin in *The Courtier's Library*, pp. 39–43. The Latin of the longer passage quoted runs thus: '. . . et quamvis scire, quæ alii sciunt, non poteris, saltem scire valeas quæ illi nesciunt. . . . Relictis authoribus, quos vocant Classicos, Academicis et pædagogis terendis, enitere per omnes,

VII

BIATHANATOS

THE date of the composition of *Biathanatos* is uncertain. It cannot be earlier than 1606, for it contains a reference to Kepler's *De Stella Nova*, which was published at Prague in that year, and its affinity to *Pseudo-Martyr* in style and in the authorities quoted inclines us to think that there can have been only a short interval between the two works.[1]

The title is a curious one. The word should be *Biaiothanatos*, which means 'dying a violent death', but it is often found in the corrupt form *Biothanatos*.[2] In *Pseudo-Martyr*, p. 208, Donne uses a latinized form in the accusative, quoting Cassianus: '. . . as *Cassianus* saies, *Biothanatum*, a selfe Murderer'. In *XXVI Sermons*, II. 157 he uses the form found in this title: 'It is *peccatum Biathanaton*, a sin that murders it self'.

Biathanatos is an exercise in casuistry on the subject of suicide, and Donne handled this difficult subject with great caution and delicacy. We know from his letters that cases of conscience interested him profoundly. This particular problem 'whether Selfe-Homicide is so naturally sinne that it may never be otherwise' had an attraction for him which he explains in his preface. From his earliest youth he had himself felt a 'sickely inclination' to suicide,[3] and this had led him to a charitable judgement of those men who died by their own hand, and to an examination of the reasons by which suicide was condemned as necessarily mortal sin. He set himself to examine and refute the arguments drawn from civil and canon law and from scripture, on which this condemnation was generally based, and in this task he showed

[1] *Pseudo-Martyr* was entered on the Stationers' Register on 2 Dec. 1609.

[2] See Ducange, under *Biothanati* and *Biothanatos*.

[3] For a discussion of the death-wish, as exemplified in Paradox 5 (see p. 139 *supra*) and throughout *Biathanatos*, see D. R. Roberts, 'The Death-Wish of John Donne', *PMLA*. lxii. 958–76, an article which unfortunately appeared after this book had been set up in type.

much curious learning. The book, however, has but little grace of style, save in a purple passage here and there.

Biathanatos was not printed during Donne's lifetime. In 1619, before his visit to Germany, he sent a manuscript copy to his friend, Sir Robert Ker. The letter which accompanied this copy was printed in the *Letters* of 1651, and is interesting as giving the reasons which prevented Donne from publishing the book, while it also indicates the lingering tenderness which he felt, even after his ordination, for this daring piece of speculation.

'*To* Sr Robert Carre *now Earle of* Ankerum, *with my Book* Biathanatos *at my going into* Germany.[1]

SIR,

I had need do somewhat towards you above my promises; How weak are my performances, when even my promises are defective? I cannot promise, no not in mine own hopes, equally to your merit towards me. But besides the Poems, of which you took a promise, I send you another Book to which there belongs this History. It was written by me many years since; and because it is upon a misinterpretable subject, I have always gone so near suppressing it, as that it is onely not burnt: no hand hath passed upon it to copy it, nor many eyes to read it: onely to some particular friends in both Universities, then when I writ it, I did communicate it: And I remember, I had this answer, That certainly, there was a false thread in it, but not easily found: Keep it, I pray, with the same jealousie; let any that your discretion admits to the sight of it, know the date of it; and that it is a Book written by *Jack Donne*, and not by D. *Donne*: Reserve it for me, if I live, and if I die, I only forbid it the Presse, and the Fire: publish it not, but yet burn it not; and between those, do what you will with it. Love me still, thus farre, for your own sake, that when you withdraw your love from me, you will finde so many unworthinesses in me, as you grow ashamed of having had so long, and so much, such a thing as

Your poor servant in Chr. Jes.
J. Donne.'

At some period of his career Donne also sent a manuscript copy to Sir Edward Herbert, afterwards Lord Herbert of

[1] *Letters* (1651), p. 21.

Cherbury. This copy[1] was presented by Lord Herbert to the Bodleian Library in 1642, and as this is the only work of any length by Donne of which we possess an authoritative manuscript, the book has a particular interest for us. It bears on its fly-leaf an autograph letter from Donne to Herbert, which I reprint here, first from the manuscript, and secondly from the *Letters* of 1651, in order that the reader may judge from this—the solitary example of an autograph letter of Donne's which is also found in the 1651 collection—of the trustworthiness or otherwise of the printed collections of letters made by the younger Donne. This is the autograph:

'To the Noblest knight
Sr Edward Herbert.

'Sr

I make account that thys Booke hath inough perform'd yt wch yt undertooke, both by Argument and Example. Itt shall therfore the lesse neede to bee yttselfe another Example of ye Doctrine. Itt shall not therfore kyll yttselfe; that ys, not bury itselfe. for if ytt should do so, those reasons by wch that Act should bee defended or excus'd, were also lost wt ytt. Since ytt ys content to liue, ytt cannot chuse a wholsomer ayre then yor Library, where Autors of all complexions are preserud. If any of them grudge thys Booke a roome, and suspect ytt of new, or dangerous Doctrine, you, who know us all, can best Moderate. To those Reasons, wch I know yor Loue to mee wyll make in my fauor, and dischardge, you may add thys, That though thys Doctrine hath not beene tought nor defended by writers, yet they, most of any sorte of Men in the world, haue practisd ytt.

yor uery true and earnest frinde, and
Seruant and Louer

J: Donne.'

The printed text is:

'*To the Noblest Knight Sr.* Edward Herbert *L. of* Cherbury; *sent to him with his Book* Biathanatos.[2]

SIR,

I make accompt that this book hath enough performed that which it undertook, both by argument and example. It shall therefore the lesse need to be it self another example of the Doctrine. It shall not

[1] Bodleian Library, MS. e Musaeo 131.
[2] *Letters* (1651), p. 20.

therefore kill it self; that is, not bury it self; for if it should do so, those reasons, by which that act should be defended or excused, were also lost with it. Since it is content to live, it cannot chuse a wholesomer aire then your Library, where Authors of all complexions are presented (*sic*). If any of them grudge this book a room, and suspect it of new or dangerous doctrine, you who know us all, can best moderate. To those reasons which I know your love to me will make in my favour and discharge, you may adde this, that though this doctrine hath not been taught nor defended by writers, yet they, most of any sort of men in the world, have practised it.

Your very true and earnest friend and servant and lover
J. Donne.'

The hand in which the Bodleian manuscript is written has a resemblance to that of Ben Jonson, though it is certainly not his. The numerous marginal notes are in Donne's own hand, and the manuscript thus annotated by Donne and sent by him with an autograph letter to Lord Herbert possesses no less authority than if it were in his autograph throughout. It is pleasant to find that, except in one or two passages mentioned below, the quarto edition published by Donne's son has reproduced the manuscript faithfully.

As we have seen, Donne wrote in 1619 to Ker 'No hand hath passed upon it to copy it', and as he added 'Reserve it for me, if I live', the copy sent to Ker was apparently his only one at that date. There would be great difficulty in believing that after his return from Germany in 1621 Donne retained sufficient interest in his old studies to cause a new copy of the book to be made, and annotated it carefully. This would be inconsistent with the tone in which he writes of *Biathanatos* to Ker, and I am therefore inclined to believe that the Bodleian copy had been made several years before 1619, and that Donne had forgotten it.

Collation with the quarto reveals a few differences, mostly unimportant, though there are a few points of interest. On p. 155 the quarto reads, 'they think they have the light and authority of Scripture, when, God knowes, truth, which is the light of Scriptures, is Divine truely under them, and removed in the farthest distance that can bee.' Here 'Divine truely' represents the manuscript 'Diametrally', i.e. diametrically, which makes the passage intelligible at once. Again on p. 214 the quarto reads, 'If then reasons', instead of the true reading, 'If theyr reasons', found in the manuscript.

On the other hand, the manuscript has several errors which do not appear in the quarto. On p. 17 the quarto reads, 'the way, and the end of the Author', where the manuscript has 'the way and of y[e] Author'. On p. 20, ll. 14–15, the quarto reading 'having been so long enlightned' is superior to the manuscript 'have bene . . .', since the construction of the sentence requires a participle. On p. 74, l. 11, the quarto reads 'interpretable' where the manuscript has the inferior reading 'interpreted'. On p. 117, l. 3, the quarto keeps the antithesis, 'this Medecine . . . this Poyson', which is lost in the manuscript, 'his Medicine . . . this poyson'. On p. 128, ll. 7–8, the quarto reads, 'for the spirituall good of another, a man should expose'. The construction of the sentence is spoilt in the manuscript by the reading 'for the spirituall good of another Man should expose'. On p. 143, l. 25, the context shows that the quarto reading, 'intermit', is the correct one as opposed to the manuscript 'admit'. Again on p. 154, l. 12, the quarto reading, 'be bold withall', is clearly superior to the manuscript, 'behold w[t]hall'.

In the extracts from *Biathanatos* given later in this chapter I have followed the text of the quarto, except in one or two passages recorded in the footnotes, where the quarto text is corrupt and the manuscript reading is clearly the right one. I have also recorded in the footnotes all important variations found in the manuscript, but as this is not a critical edition I have not attempted to give a full collation of minor differences.

Donne's son did not observe the injunction to refrain from publication which his father had laid on his friends. The book was licensed for the press on 20 September 1644 —about thirty-six years after its original composition—but it was not entered on the Register of the Stationers' Company till 25 September 1646.[1] George Thomason records

[1] The entry runs thus: 'Master War. Seale. Entred for his copie under the hands of Master Rushworth and Master Whitaker warden a tract called, *Biothonatos a declaracon of that paradox or thesis that selfe homicide is not,*

that he bought his copy of *Biathanatos* on 2 December 1647 (*Catalogue of the Thomason tracts, 1640–1661*).[1] The title-page runs thus: 'ΒΙΑΘΑΝΑΤΟΣ. A Declaration of that Paradoxe, or Thesis, that Selfe-homicide is not so Naturally Sinne, that it may never be otherwise. Wherein The Nature, and the extent of all those Lawes, which seeme to be violated by this Act, are diligently surveyed. Written by Iohn Donne, who afterwards received Orders from the Church of England, and dyed Deane of Saint Pauls, London. Jo: Saresb. de nugis Curial. Prolog. Non omnia vera esse profiteor. Sed legentium usibus inservire. Published by Authoritie. London, Printed by John Dawson,' (*sic*). This title is evidently incomplete, the name of the publisher and the date being omitted.

The younger Donne contributed an epistle dedicatory to Lord Philip Herbert, in which he defended his action in thus publishing a book which his father had withheld from the press. '. . . It was writ, long since, by my Father, and by him, forbid both the Presse, and the Fire; neither had I subjected it now, to the publique view, but that, I could finde no certaine way to defend it from the one, but by committing it to the other; For, since the beginning of this War, my Study having been often searched, all my Books (and al-most my braines) by their continuall allarums sequestred, for the use of the Committee; two dangers appeared more eminently to hover over this, being then a Manuscript; a danger of being utterly lost, and a danger of being utterly found; and fathered, by some of those wild Atheists, who, as if they came into the World by conquest, owne all other mens Wits, and are resolved to be learned, in despite of their Starres, that would fairely have enclined them, to a more modest, and honest course of life.'[2]

One of the copies of the first edition in the University

etc. . . . vjd.' 'Master War. Seale' is Henry Seale or Seyle, who was a Warden of the Stationers' Company, 1646–7, and who had previously printed Donne's *Juvenilia*.

[1] In Sept. 1938 Messrs. Maggs offered for sale a presentation copy of *Biathanatos* with an autograph letter on the fly-leaf from the younger Donne to the Earl of Denbigh, dated 16 Nov. 1647.

[2] *Biathanatos*, ¶ 3 verso–¶ 4.

Library, Cambridge (H. 6. 46 (E)), contains an autograph letter of some interest from the younger Donne:

'For ye Rt wll Edward Carter, Esqr

Sr,

I haue, here, sent you a Booke, that may, per aduenture, giue you some entertainement out of the noueltie of the subiect, but that is not all my reason for presentinge it to you, at the time: For, since I liued in this Parish I haue published a Volume of 80. Sermons preached by my Father, and haue prepared 60 more, which are licensed, and entered in the Printers halle, which is, as farr as I can driue them vntill the times allter; I was encouradged to vndertake this worke, by the learnedest men in the kingdome, of all professions, and was often told that I shoud deserue better by doinge soe, then by keepinge them to my owne vse, for by this meanes, I did not only preach to the present adge, but to our childrens children; Sr, I write this to you, that you may iudg what a sad condition a Scholler is in, when at a publicke Vestry, in this Parish, I was told by a pittifull ignorant Baker, I was an idle man and neuer preached./

your humble seruant,

Jo: Donne.'

In 1648 the sheets of *Biathanatos* were re-issued by another publisher, Humphrey Moseley, with a new title-page.[1] In 1653 there appeared anonymously a book called *Pelecanicidium: or the Christian Adviser against Self-Murder*, which also dealt with the subject of suicide. In the 'Proeme' the author (Sir William Denny) mentioned 'some late-publisht paradoxes, That self-homicide was Lawfull', and he divided his work, like Donne's, into three parts, though his treatment of the subject differed widely from that to be found in *Biathanatos*.[2] In 1700 another edition of *Biathanatos* was

[1] According to the Stationers' Register, Seale's rights in the book were transferred to Moseley on 13 June 1649.

[2] *Pelecanicidium* contains a curious mixture of prose and verse. The first book opens thus: 'Stay, Desperate Souls! Let 's have a word or two! Examine Well, what you but Once can do!' It then exhorts lovers, 'great spirits', the melancholy, the jealous, 'the bloody murtherer', 'the curious zealot', and other would-be suicides, to pause and consider their ways. After this we have a verse narrative—'A horrid, yet true Story of one that hang'd himself, upon his Knees, with a Bible on a Stool open before him, and a Paper to signifie that he had repented.' The author proceeds to argue, also

produced by an anonymous publisher, and in the same year a serious attempt to answer Donne's arguments was made by John Adams, afterwards Provost of King's, who produced a book called *An Essay Concerning Self-Murther*. Chapter V of this work is headed: 'Who they are Chiefly that maintain this Act, to be Lawful: The Stoicks: The Author of Biathanatos.'[1] According to Dr. Keynes, an examination and refutation of Donne's book is to be found in *A full enquiry into the subject of Suicide* (1790), by the Rev. Charles Moore (vol. i, pp. 83–103, and vol. ii, pp. 1–41). Alford did not include *Biathanatos* in his *Works of Donne* (1839). In 1930 it was reproduced in facsimile by the Columbia University Press for the Facsimile Text Society.

The book hardly needed elaborate refutation. Donne was right in thinking that it was not likely to do harm to weak consciences, as its method of treatment was such as to prevent it from becoming a popular book, while the learned, who alone would study it, were already familiar with many of its arguments and examples. He was prudent, however, in deciding to refrain from publication, as the sharp-eyed ecclesiastical censors of the day would almost certainly have regarded the book as heretical and dangerous. Donne himself lived to modify the opinions expressed in it. In a sermon preached on Easter Day, 1624, he used these words:

'If thou desire this first Resurrection in the third acceptation, as S. *Paul* did, To be dissolved, and to be with Christ, go Christs way to that also. He desired that glory that thou doest; and he could have laid down his soul when he would; but he staid his houre, sayes the Gospel. . . . Thou hast no such power of thine own soul and life, not for the time, not for the means of comming to this first Resurrection

in verse, that self-homicide is against Nature, Reason, and Religion. In the second and third books he unfolds a verse allegory, the cantos of which are divided from one another by prose essays, moral and consolatory.

[1] P. 41: 'This has been pretended to more particularly by a Gentleman* of our own Country, with much shew of Learning and Reason, in a Treatise intitled, *Βιαθάνατος*. Which, by the great Character of the Author, rais'd afterwards upon *better* Grounds, by the Agreeableness of the Argument to the present Age, and by its having passed some Years unanswer'd (as far as I can understand) has been highly esteem'd by *some People*.'

* Dr. *Donne*, afterwards Dean of *Paul's*.

by death; Stay therefore patiently, stay chearfully Gods leasure till he call; but not so over-chearfully as to be loath to go when he cals.'[1]

He did not, however, entirely reverse his charitable opinion of some of the examples recorded in *Biathanatos*. In his last sermon, *Deaths Duell*, he referred again to the story of Samson:

'Stil pray wee for a peaceable life against violent death, and for time of repentance against sudden death, and for sober and modest assurance against distempered and diffident death, but neuer make ill conclusions vpon persons ouertaken with such deaths; *Domini Domini sunt exitus mortis*, to God the Lord belong the issues of death. And he received *Sampson*, who went out of this world in such a manner (consider it actiuely, consider it passiuely in his owne death, and in those whom he slew with himselfe) as was subiect to interpretation hard enough. Yet the *holy Ghost* hath moued S. *Paul* to celebrate *Sampson* in his great Catalogue, and so doth all the Church.'[2]

The most interesting passages in *Biathanatos* are those in which Donne strikes the personal note. The opening sentences of the preface run thus:

'*Beza*, a man as eminent and illustrious, in the full glory and Noone of Learning, as others were in the dawning, and Morning, when any, the least sparkle was notorious, [a]confesseth of himself, that only for the anguish of a Scurffe, which over-ranne his head, he had once drown'd himselfe from the Millers bridge in *Paris*, if his Uncle by chance had not then come that way; I have often such a sickely inclination. And, whether it be, because I had my first breeding and conversation with men of a suppressed and afflicted Religion, accustomed to the despite of death, and hungry of an imagin'd Martyrdome; Or that the common Enemie find that doore worst locked against him in mee; Or that there bee a perplexitie and flexibility in the doctrine it selfe; Or because my Conscience ever assures me, that no rebellious grudging at Gods gifts, nor other sinfull concurrence accompanies these thoughts in me, or that a brave scorn, or that a faint cowardlinesse beget it, whensoever any affliction assailes me, mee thinks I have the keyes of my prison in mine owne hand, and no remedy presents it selfe so soone to my heart, as mine own sword. Often Meditation of

[a] *Epist. ante confessionem.*[3]

[1] *LXXX Sermons*, 19. 191–2.

[2] *Deaths Duell* (1632), p. 27.

[3] The marginal notes are those supplied in the quarto.

this hath wonne me to a charitable interpretation of their action, who dy so: and provoked me a little to watch and exagitate their reasons, which pronounce so peremptory judgements upon them. [a] A devout and godly man, hath guided us well, and rectified our uncharitablenesse in such cases, by this remembrance, [*Scis lapsum, etc. Thou knowest this mans fall, but thou knowest not his wrastling; which perchance was such, that almost his very fall is justified and accepted of God.*] For, to this end, saith one[b], [*God hath appointed us tentations, that we might have some excuses*[2] *for our sinnes, when he calles us to account.*][3]

[a] *B. Dorotheus doctrin.* 6.
[b] *Bosq. conc.* 2.[1]

A little later Donne shows clearly enough that his intention at the time of writing the preface was to publish the book, though he was aware that it might scandalize some.

'If therefore after a Christian protestation of an innocent purpose herein, And after a submission of all which is said, not only to every Christian Church, but to every Christian man, and after an entreaty, that the Reader will follow this advice of *Tabæus*, [c][*Qui litigant, sint ambo in conspectu tuo mali et rei*] and trust neither me, nor the adverse part, but the Reasons, there be any scandall in this enterprise of mine, it is Taken, not Given. And though I know, that the malitious prejudged man, and the lazy affectors of ignorance, will use the same calumnies and obtrectations toward me, (for the voyce and sound of the Snake and Goose is all one) yet because I thought, that as in the poole of *Bethsaida*, [d]there was no health till the water was troubled, so the best way to finde the truth in this matter, was to debate and vexe it, (for [e] [*We must as well dispute* de veritate, *as* pro veritate,]) I abstained not for fear of mis-interpretation from this undertaking. Our stomachs are not now so tender, and queasie, after so long feeding upon solid Divinity, nor we so umbragious and startling, having been so long enlightened in Gods path, that wee should thinke any truth strange to us, or relapse into that childish age, in which [f] a Councell in *France* forbad *Aristotles Metaphysiques*, and punished with Excommunication the excribing, reading, or having that booke.'[4]

[c] *Serar. Tribæres. l.* 2, *cap.* 17.
[d] *Io.* 5. 2.
[e] *Athenag. de resur.*
[f] *Filesacus de authorit. Epis. cap.* 1. § 7.

Donne goes on to explain his reasons for loading his book with a vast number of quotations which affright a modern

[1] MS. Bosquier.Monomach. Conc. 2.

[2] MS. reads 'excuse'.

[3] *Biathanatos*, pp. 17–18. The use of square brackets, as well as italics, for quotations is a feature of the printed editions and of the Bodleian MS.

[4] *Biathanatos*, pp. 19–20.

reader, and which even in Jacobean times might have been regarded as excessive.

'Every branch which is excerpted from other authors, and engrafted here, is not written for the readers faith, but for illustration and comparison. Because I undertooke the declaration of such a proposition as was controverted by many, and therefore was drawne to the citation of many authorities, I was willing to goe all the way with company, and to take light from others, as well in the journey as at the journeys end. If therefore in multiplicity of not necessary citations there appeare vanity, or ostentation, or digression my honesty must make my excuse and compensation, who acknowledge as [a] *Pliny* doth, [*That to chuse rather to be taken in a theft, then to give every man his*[1] *due, is* obnoxii animi, et infelicis ingenii.] I did it the rather because scholastique and artificiall men use this way of instructing; and I made account that I was to deale with such, because I presume that naturall men are at least enough inclinable of themselves to this doctrine.'[2]

[a] *Epist. Tit. Vesp.*

Donne closes the preface with a protestation that his aim is not to cause scandal, but to remove it.

'This is[3] my way; and my end is to remove scandall. For certainly God often punisheth a sinner much more severely, because others have taken occasion of sinning by his fact. If therefore wee did correct in ourselves this easines of being scandalized, how much easier and lighter might we make the punishment of many transgressors? for God in his judgements[4] hath almost made us his assistants, and counsellers, how far he shall punish; and our interpretation of anothers sinne doth often give the measure to Gods Justice or Mercy.

If therefore, since [b] [*disorderly long haire which was pride and wantonnesse in* Absolon, *and squallor and horridnes in* Nebuchodonozor, *was vertue and strength in* Samson, *and sanctification in* Samuel,] these severe men will not allow to indifferent things the best construction they are capable of, nor pardon my inclination to do so, they shall pardon this opinion,[5] that their severity proceeds from a self-guiltines, and give me leave to apply that[6] of *Ennodius*,[c] [*That it is the nature of stiffe wickednesse, to thinke that of others, which themselves deserve, and it is all the comfort which the guilty have, not to find any innocent.*]'[7]

[b] *Paulin. Ep.* 4, *Severo.*

[c] *Epist. ad Astyrium.*

[1] This is the reading of the manuscript. The quarto omits 'his'.

[2] *Biathanatos*, p. 23.

[3] The quarto omits 'is'.

[4] MS.: 'iudgement'.

[5] MS.: 'pardon me this opinion'.

[6] MS.: 'apply them that'.

[7] *Biathanatos*, pp. 23–4.

The book itself is divided into three parts, dealing with the three main lines of argument which have been employed to prove that suicide is necessarily sin. Donne's object is not to defend suicide in itself. He is ready to agree with politicians and divines that suicide, like other forms of manslaughter, should be condemned by the law. His main contention is, however, that as there are certain cases in which ordinary homicide is accounted lawful, so there are similar exceptions in which self-homicide may be justified. His book is indeed an exercise in casuistry, that is, an examination of particular cases of conscience which cannot be decided by general principles, but must be considered each on its own merits. Casuistry was a favourite branch of study with medieval divines, and its popularity lasted well into the seventeenth century. Jeremy Taylor's *Ductor Dubitantium* is an exhaustive examination of such cases, and Walton states that Donne himself was in the habit of keeping 'copies of divers Letters and cases of Conscience that had concerned his friends, with his observations and solutions of them'.[1] In more recent times casuistry has fallen into disrepute with the learned, and has had to take refuge with the novelists and the writers of problem plays. It may be conjectured that if Donne had lived three centuries later his interest in the problem of suicide would have taken the form, not of an elaborate discussion of the law of nature and the arguments of the Fathers, but of a narrative in which the mind of a hero who committed suicide would have been analysed with morbid but relentless skill.

In Part I Donne argues that self-homicide cannot be said to be against the law of nature, except in the general sense by which most actions of a reasonable being may be described as against nature. It is true that self-preservation may be described as part of the law of nature, but this law may be broken, by beasts as well as men, for the sake of some higher law, as in the case of the pelican which sacrifices itself to feed its young. The example of Jewish and Christian martyrs shows that the desire of life is not so natural to man, but that it may easily be conquered by the desire of a greater

[1] Walton, *Life* (1670), p. 62.

good.[1] Moreover, in certain commonwealths, both real and utopian, suicide has sometimes been not only permitted but enjoined.

'Amongst the *Athenians* condemned men were their own executioners by poyson. And amongst the *Romans* often by bloodlettings . . . . [a]*Sir Thomas Moore* (a man of the most tender and delicate conscience, that the world saw since Saint *Augustine*) not likely to write anything in jest mischieuously interpretable,[2] sayes, That in *Vtopia*, the Priests and Magistrates did use to exhort men afflicted with incurable diseases, to kill themselves, and that they were obeyed as the interpreters of Gods will; But that they who killed themselves without giving an account of their reasons to them, were cast out unburied.'[3]

[a] *Vtop. l. 2. c. de servis.*

In Part II 'Of the Law of Reason' Donne deals with the treatment of suicide by the civil and the canon law. He exhibits a vast amount of curious learning, and propounds many strange theories, e.g. that the harsh condemnation of suicide by English law is due to the inordinate desire of death in our nation.[4] He discusses the arguments of Augustine, Jerome, Peter Martyr, Clement, Thomas Aquinas, Josephus, and Aristotle, and examines the different kinds of homicide, as distinguished by Tolet.

'Homicide is one of those crying sins, and hath ever been reckoned *in Atrocibus* . . . And this *Homicide*,[b] saies *Tolet*, may bee done five wayes, by 1. Commandement, by 2. Advise, by 3. Permission, by 4. Helpe, or by the fact it selfe.'[5]

[b] *Precepto 5.*

Donne admits that it is difficult to see how self-homicide can be committed under the first two heads, though he suggests that a desire for death, which is sometimes lawful, may be interpreted as advice to oneself. Homicide by permission is interpreted as the refusal or rejection of the means of life.

'He which to himselfe denies necessarie things, or exposes himselfe

[1] Don Cameron Allen in 'Donne's Suicides', *M.L.N.* lvi. 129–33, traces Donne's list of classical suicides to Valerius Maximus for the most famous instances, and for the rest to Renaissance compendia like those of Textor and Fulgosius.

[2] MS.: 'interpreted'.

[3] *Biathanatos*, pp. 73–4.

[4] Ibid., p. 91.

[5] Ibid., pp. 117–18. MS.: 'by [1] commandement, by [3] Permission, by [2] Aduise, by [4] Helpe, or by y[e] Act it selfe'.

inordinatly to such dangers as men use not to escape, kills himselfe. He that is as sure that this[1] Medicine will recover him, as that this Poyson will destroy him, is as guilty if he forbeare the Physicke, as if he swallow the Poyson. . . . They which compare Omissions, and Committings, require no more to make them equall, but that we omit something which we could, and should doe.'[2]

Donne declares that this form of self-homicide has been generally held to be lawful in certain cases. Thus a man who is attacked by a thief may defend himself, but it is lawful also for him to refuse to defend himself and to allow himself to be killed by the thief rather than to kill his assailant in mortal sin. Again, for the spiritual good of another a man may lawfully expose himself to danger. Again, we may lawfully dispossess ourselves of food for the sake of others.

[a] *Aquin.* 22. *q.* 32. *ar.* 6.

'[a] As in a persecution, a private man, having food left sufficient only to sustaine one man, may give it to a publicke person, and so perish. And only *Sotus* denyes, that in a shipwrack, if after wee have both beene in equall danger, I catch and possesse my selfe of any thing to sustaine me, I may give this to my Father, or to a Magistrate: against the strength of *Navar*, *Tolet*, *Fra. Victor.* and many others.'[3]

Thus by easy stages Donne arrives at the consideration of those who have starved themselves to death for some spiritual reason. In this section he considers many curious cases, such as that of the friar who, 'having vowed in his journey, to eat nothing except God gave him meat immediately, refused to eat, when theeves accustomed to kill passengers by that place, came and presented him bread.' Donne adds that Cassianus, who relates the story, calls the friar 'a Selfe-Homicide', 'And yet, though he saies he killed himselfe, he imputes nothing to him but Indiscretion.'[4] He adduces also examples of extraordinary fasts—among them 'the Monkes in Prester John[5] his Dominions', who 'fast strictly fifty dayes, and stand all that time to the chinne in water'.[6] Finally,

[1] MS.: 'his'.
[2] *Biathanatos*, pp. 116–17.
[3] Ibid., p. 128.
[4] Ibid., p. 129.
[5] MS.: 'Prete Jan'.
[6] *Biathanatos*, p. 130. Donne quotes *Middendorpius*, *de Academiis*, fol. 298, as his authority for this statement.

'by the [a]Apostolicall constitutions, (which *Turrianus* extols so much, that by them he confutes much of the Reformed Churches doctrine) [*A man must fast to death, rather then receive any meat, from an Excommunicate person.*]'[1]

[a] *Clem. Apostol. Constit. l. 4. cap. 7.*

Self-homicide 'by actual helping' provides Donne with a section full of quaint examples, e.g. the story of the 'holy old man', who 'seeing his servant mistake poyson for honey, and put it into his broth, eate it neverthelesse without chiding; and when the servant perceived it, and exclaimed, Sir, I have kill'd you, answered, it is all one, for if God would have had mee eate honey, he would have directed thy hand to honey.'[2] Donne declares that it was still the custom in his time for women who despaired of a sick person to take the pillow from under him so that he might die the sooner, and that this was 'ordinarily done, and esteemed a pious office'.[3]

It is, however, the last species of homicide—the performance of the act itself—which furnishes Donne with his strongest examples.[4] Few readers were likely to have much respect for the 'holy old man' mentioned above, but the Christian virgin martyrs were in a different category. Donne celebrates their deaths in a way which shows how diligent a student of ecclesiastical history he was:

'The Church whose dignity and constancy it becomes well, that that Rule of her owne Law, be ever justly said of her self,[b] [*Quod semel placuit amplius displicere non potest*], where new reasons do not inter-

[b] *Sextus Reg. Iur: quod semel.* MS: Reg: Iur: q[d] Semel. in 6o.

[1] *Biathanatos*, p. 131.

[2] Ibid., p. 139. Donne gives as his authority B. Dorothaeus, *Doctrine* 7. *de accus. sui ipsius.*

[3] *Biathanatos*, pp. 136, 137.

[4] It is in discussing St. Augustine's objections to self-homicide that Donne introduces the argument about Aristotle's followers and the new astronomy which has already been mentioned in chap. v., p. 120 *supra*. 'But to speak a little in passing of Saint *Augustines* second reason [i.e. *None of the faithfull ever did this act*] . . . now when the Church hath thus long persevered, in not only justifying but solemnizing many examples hereof, are not Saint *Augustines* Disciples guilty of the same pertinacy which is imputed to *Aristotles* followers, who defending the Heavens to be inalterable, because in so many ages nothing had been observed to have been altered, his Schollers stubbornly maintain his Proposition still, though by many experiences of new Stars, the reason which moved *Aristotle* seems now to be utterly defeated?' [marginal references *Kepplerus de Stella Serpent.* cap. 23]. Ibid., pp. 145–6.

pose,[a] celebrates upon the 9. of *February* the Birth, (that is the death) of the Virgin and Martyr *Appollonia*;[1] who, after the persecutors had beat out her teeth, and vexed her with many other tortures, when she was presented to the fire, being inflamed with a more burning fire of the Holy Ghost, broke from the Officers hands, and leapt into the fire.

'For this act of hers many Advocates rise up for her, and say, that either the History is not certain, (yet the Authors are *Beda*, *Usuardus*, *Ado*, and (as *Barronius*[2] sayes) *Latinorum cæteri*) Or else, says *Sayr* [b], you must answer that she was brought very neer the fire, and as good as thrown in: Or else that she was provoked to it by divine inspiration. But, but that another divine inspiration, which is true Charity, moved the beholders then to beleeve, and the Church ever since to acknowledge, that she did therein a Noble and Christian act, to the speciall glory of God, this act of hers, as well as any other, might have been calumniated to have been done, out of wearinesse of life, or fear of relapse, or hast to Heaven, or ambition of Martyrdome.

'The memory of *Pelagia*,[c] as of a virgin and Martyr, is celebrated the ninth of *June*. And though the History of this woman suffer some perplexity, and giue occasion of doubting the truth thereof, (for *Ambrose* says, That she and her Mother drownd themselves; and *Chrysostome* that they flung themselves downe from a house top. And *Baronius* saw this knot to be so hard to unentangle, that he says, [*Quid ad haec dicamus, non habemus*]), yet the Church, as I said, celebrates the Act, as though it were glad to take any occasion of approving such a courage in such a cause, which was but preservation of Chastity. [d] [*Their Martyrdome saith Saint* Augustine *was ever in the Catholique Church frequented* Veneratione Celeberrima.]

'And Saint *Ambrose*,[e] when his sister *Marcellina*, consulted him directly upon the point, what might be thought of them who kill themselves in such cases, (and then it is agreed by all that the opinions of the Fathers are especially to be valued, when they speake of a matter, not incidently or casually, but directly and deliberately) answers thus, [*We have an example of such a Martyrdome in* Pelagia]. And then he presents her in this religious meditation, [*Let us die, if we may have leave, or if we be denied leave, yet let us die. God cannot be offended with this, when we use it but for a remedy;*] and our faith takes away all offence. Here is no difficulty: for who is willing to dye, and cannot, since there are so many waies to death? I will not trust my hand least it strike not home: nor my breast, least it withdraw it selfe: I will leave no escape to my flesh, for we can dye with our own weapons, and without the benefit of an Executioner.

a *Baron. Martyrolog.*

b *Sayr. Thesaur. Cas. Cons. l.* 9. *c.* 7. *num.* 11. MS. Thesaur. l. 9. c. 7. n. ii.

c *Baron. Mart.* 16. MS: Baron: Martyrolo:

d *August. de Civitate Dei, l.* 1. *cap.* 26.

e *De Virg. l.* 3.

1 MS.: Apollonia.

2 MS.: Baronius.

'And then having drest her selfe as a Bride, and going to the water, Here, sayes she, let us be baptized; this is the Baptisme where sinnes are forgiven, and where a kingdome is purchased: and this is the baptisme after which none sinnes. This water regenerates; this makes us virgines, this opens heaven, defends the feeble, delivers from death, and makes us Martyrs. Onely we pray to God, that this water scatter us not, but reserve us to one funerall. Then entred they as in a dance, hand in hand, where the torrent was deepest, and most violent. And thus dyed, (as their mother upon the bank called them) [*These Prelates of virginitie, Captaines of Chastitie, and companions in Martyrdome.*]'[1]

Thus Donne arrived at Part III, 'Of the Law of God.' In this he examines *seriatim* the texts which have been quoted against suicide and exposes the 'wretched poverty and feeblenesse' of many of the arguments professedly deduced from them. He decides that only one text, *Thou shalt not kill*, can rightly be urged against self-homicide, and he acknowledges that this is in fact a general prohibition of the act. But he urges that as exceptions are admitted by which one man may lawfully kill another, so there are similar exceptions in which for similar reasons suicide may be lawful. He gives an instance of the kind of exception which is in his mind.

'If perchance a publique exemplary person, which had a just assurance that his example would governe the people, should be forced by a Tyrant, to doe an act of Idolatry, (although by circumstances he might satisfie his owne conscience, that he sinned not in doing it,) and so scandalize and endanger them, if the matter were so carried and disguised, that by no way he could let them know, that he did it by constraint, but voluntarily, I say, perchance he were better kill himselfe.'[2]

He then proceeds to show that according to Scripture we should use charity in our judgement of others, and devotes one section to the praise of charity, 'the mother, and forme[3] of all vertue; which shall not onely lead us to heaven, (for faith opens us the doore) but shall continue with us when we are there, when both Faith, and Hope, are spent and uselesse.'[4] He examines the instances of self-homicide in

[1] *Biathanatos*, pp. 147–9.
[2] Ibid., p. 166.
[3] MS.: 'and the forme'.
[4] *Biathanatos*, p. 182.

Scripture, and points out that Samson's death, which was self-inflicted, for he killed himself with the Philistines, is celebrated by the Church as a martyrdom. This is because Samson's motive was the glory of God, but no such motive is apparent in the history of two other suicides, Saul and Achitophel. Achitophel is probably to be condemned, but the case of Saul is doubtful, for some think that he died repentant, obeying the sentence of death which had been pronounced on him by Samuel's apparition, and thinking it dishonourable to die by the hand of God's enemies. The sin of Judas was his betrayal of Christ, and 'that act of killing himselfe, is not added to his faults in any place of Scripture', nay, Origen suggests that it was a sign of repentance. '[*For it may be*, *saith* Origen, *that Satan which had entred into him*, *staid with him till Christ was betray'd*, *and then left him*, *and thereupon repentance followed*.] And perchance, sayes he, he went to prevent, and goe before his Master, who was to dye, and so to meet him with his naked soule, that he might gaine Mercy by his confession and prayers.'[1] In the books of Maccabees Eleazar, who exposed himself to certain death for his people, is honoured as a hero, and Rasis is not condemned by the text, though St. Thomas Aquinas speaks of his death as cowardly. Donne admits that Aristotle and St. Augustine also regarded suicide as a form of cowardice, but he points out that Augustine acknowledged a certain greatness of mind in Cleombrotus and Cato, who both slew themselves.

This third part has an introductory and a concluding chapter, in which Donne leaves the consideration of particular arguments and instances, and discusses more general principles. These two chapters are perhaps the finest in the book, which throughout most of its course lacks the usual magnificence of Donne's style.

I quote one passage from the final chapter:

'And this is as farre as I allowed my discourse to progresse in this way: forbidding it earnestly all darke and dangerous Secessions[2] and divertings[3] into points of our Free-will, and of Gods Destiny: though

[1] *Biathanatos*, p. 207.
[2] MS.: 'successions'.
[3] MS.: 'diuerting'.

allowing many ordinary contingencies, to be under our Election, it may yet seem reasonable, that our maine periods, of Birth, of Death, and of chief alterations in this life be more immediately wrought upon by Gods determination. It is usefully said, and appliable to good purpose (though [a] by a wicked man, and with intention to crosse *Moses*,) [*That man was made of shaddow, and the Devil of fire.*] For as shaddow is not darknes, but grosser light, so is mans understanding in these mysteries, not blind but clouded. And as fire doth not always give light[1] (for that is accidentall, and it must have aire to work upon,) but it burneth naturally, so that desire of knowledge which the Devill kindles in us, (as he doth as willingly bring bellows to inflame a heart curious of knowledge, as he doth more ashes to stupifie and bury deeper, a slumbering understanding) doth not alwaies give us light, but it always burnes us, and imprints upon our judgment stigmaticall marks, and at last seares up our conscience.

[a] *Alcor. Azo.* 65. MS. Alcoran 65.

'If theyr[2] reasons which differ from me, and my reasons be otherwise equall, yet theirs have this disadvantage that they fight with themselves and suffer a Civill Warre of contradiction. For many of their reasons incline us to a love of this life, and a horror of death, and yet they say often, that wee are too much addicted to that naturally. But it is well noted by [b]*Alcuinus* (and I thinke from Saint *Augustine*) [*That though there bee foure things which wee must love, yet there is no precept given upon any more then two, God and our neighbour.*] So that the other which concerne our selves, may be pretermitted in some occasions.

[b] *Alcuin. Ep.* 23.

'But because of the benefits of death, enough hath beene occasionally interserted before, having presented [b]*Cyprians* encouragement to it, who out of a contemplation that the whole frame of the world decayed and languished, cries to us, [Nutant parietes, *The walls and the roofe shake, and would'st not thou goe out? Thou art tyred in a pilgrimage, and wouldst thou not goe home?*] I will end with applying [c]*Ausonius* thanks to the Emperour, to death, which deserveth it better, [*Thou providest that thy benefits, and the good which thou bringest shall not be transitory; and that the ills from which thou deliverest us, shall never returne.*][3]

[b] *Cypr. Serm. de mortalitate.*

[c] *Gratiar. act. de cons.*

[1] Cf. *LXXX Sermons*, 36. 355: 'Hell is presented to us by fire, but fire without light.'

[2] This is the reading of the manuscript. The quarto has 'then', which is clearly a misprint.

[3] *Biathanatos*, pp. 213–15.

VIII

PSEUDO-MARTYR AND IGNATIUS HIS CONCLAVE

DONNE AS A CONTROVERSIALIST

THERE is a close connexion between *Biathanatos* and *Pseudo-Martyr*, though at first sight there would appear to be little in common between a treatise on the justification of suicide and another on the Oath of Allegiance. But in fact the argument of the two books is complementary, and the idea of self-inflicted death forms the link. In *Biathanatos* Donne argues that the general prohibition, *Thou shalt not kill*, covers the case of self-murder, and condemns it in general, but he dwells particularly on the point that this general law admits of certain exceptions. These exceptions do not, however, depend on individual caprice, but must be justified by the requirements of the general good and the glory of God. Thus Samson, who slew himself in company with the Philistines, was a suicide but also a hero, and the Church honours his example. The chaste Lucretia preferred death to dishonour, and many Christian virgins in times of persecution killed themselves to escape from their licentious persecutors. In all such cases it must be the motive and the attendant circumstances, not the bare act, argues Donne, by which our praise or condemnation is determined.

In *Pseudo-Martyr* he lays stress on the other side of the argument. The Jesuits are urging the English Roman Catholics to refuse their allegiance to the king, on the ground that he is a heretic and has been dethroned by the Pope. They promise their followers a martyr's crown if insubordination is punished with death by the civil power. Donne argues that such a death is not martyrdom but suicide. God has given to lawful princes an authority of which no Pope can dispossess them. Englishmen are bound to own the King as their rightful sovereign, and in the apostle's words, 'those who resist shall receive to themselves condemnation'. To die for sedition is not to die for the glory of God nor for the general good. Those who persist in such courses after their error has been pointed out to them are practically self-murderers. The line between suicide and martyrdom is a narrow one—let them beware lest in their blind zeal they overstep it. The passage which opens Chapter I of *Pseudo-Martyr* gives the key to the whole book, and its tone is strikingly similar to that of many sentences in *Biathanatos*.

The two books have much in common in style and manner. They are the most carefully reasoned, the most overloaded with learning, and also, it must be added, the dullest of Donne's works. They are the typical product of those 'middle years' which were the most dreary part of his life, when he was overworked and underpaid, the victim of unceasing anxiety for his family and his future. It is not wonderful, therefore, that they lack some of those qualities which have made famous his earlier and his later works. There is no passion and very little wit or eloquence in these elaborate treatises. The reader is impressed by Donne's learning and ingenuity, but he soon feels himself lost in a desert of scholastic reasoning and his interest quickly evaporates.[1] Of the two *Biathanatos* has proved the more attractive to modern critics, but this is perhaps due to its subject, a problem of more permanent interest than that treated of in *Pseudo-Martyr*.

Pseudo-Martyr, which appeared in 1610,[2] was the first of Donne's prose works to be published. Some years were yet to elapse before Donne took orders in the Church of England, but he had already done a considerable amount of controversial work in defence of the Anglican against the Roman position. Between 1605 and 1607 he had helped Morton in the series of books which that Anglican divine produced in quick succession.[3] Dr. Jessopp points out that even if we had

[1] The late Dr. Jessopp, himself an ardent student and admirer of Donne's prose works, wrote to me in a private letter in 1910: 'Who but a monomaniac would read *Pseudo-Martyr* through?'

[2] It was entered on the Stationers' Register on 2 Dec. 1609.

[3] These were the *Apologia Catholica* (1605); *An exact Discoverie of Romish Doctrine in the Case of Conspiracy and Rebellion* (1605); *Apologiae Catholicae*

not been told by Walton that Donne gave Morton constant and valuable assistance, a comparison of the authorities quoted in Morton's *Catholic Appeal* with those quoted in *Pseudo-Martyr* would have convinced a careful reader of the fact.[1]

Walton ascribes the composition of *Pseudo-Martyr* to a command received by Donne from the king.

'About this time, there grew many disputes, that concerned the *Oath of Supremacy* and *Allegiance*, in which, the King had appeared, and engaged himself by his publick writings now extant: and, his Majesty discoursing with Mr. *Donne*, concerning many of the reasons which are usually urged against the taking of those Oaths; apprehended such a validity and clearness in his stating the Questions, and his Answers to them, that his Majesty commanded him to bestow some time in drawing the Arguments into a method, and then to write his Answers to them: and, having done that, not to send, but be his own messenger and bring them to him. To this he presently and diligently applied himself, and within six weeks brought them to him under his own handwriting, as they be now printed; the Book bearing the name of *Pseudo-martyr*, printed *anno* 1610.'[2]

The scope of the book is clearly indicated in its sub-title, 'wherein out of certaine Propositions and Gradations, This Conclusion is euicted. That those which are of the Romane Religion in this Kingdome, may and ought to take the Oath of Allegeance.' It is not a general defence of the Church of England; it confines the argument to one definite point of controversy, the question of the king's supremacy. Donne writes as a layman, and is careful not to enter upon a discussion of purely theological subjects. His argument is that the sufferings which the Catholic recusants have brought

secunda pars (1606); *A full satisfaction concerning a double Romish Iniquitie* (1606). Within the next few years Morton produced *A Preamble unto an Incounter with P. R.* (1608); *The Encounter against Mr. Parsons* (1609); *A Catholick Appeal* (1609); *A Direct Answer unto the Scandalous Exceptions of Theophilus Higgons* (1609).

[1] Jessopp, *John Donne*, p. 57.

[2] Walton, *Life* (1675, p. 35). This differs in one or two details from the original draft of the *Life* as prefixed to the *LXXX Sermons*, and it is not altogether consistent with the statement made by Donne in his dedication of *Pseudo-Martyr* to the king. It is most unlikely that Donne could have written so long and so well-documented a book in so short a time as six weeks.

upon themselves are the just punishment of rebellion against their lawful sovereign. The recusants are therefore 'pseudo-martyrs', and have no right to the honour which is ascribed to those who suffer in the cause of religion.

The tone which Donne adopts throughout the book is calm and reasonable. He alludes in his *Advertisement to the Reader* to the Roman Catholic traditions of his own family, and the sufferings which many of his relatives had borne. He writes as one whose convictions are definitely on the side of the Anglican Church, but his position is essentially that of the patriotic Englishman who refuses to allow any alien domination in the land, and who wishes to convince his opponents not of errors of faith but of a mistaken ecclesiastical policy. He fortifies his arguments with innumerable quotations from the Fathers and from the writings of well-known Roman controversialists, such as Bellarmine, Baronius, and Serarius. The moderation and learning shown in the book commended it to many, and on 17 April 1610 the University of Oxford conferred on Donne the honorary degree of Master of Arts, Convocation permitting him to receive the degree without exercises and without taking the preliminary degree of B.A.[1] The grace which conferred this honour stated that it was to the credit of the university that such men as he, who had deserved so well of Church and State, should be distinguished by academic honours.[2]

The king also approved of Donne's labours, and according to Walton, 'descended to a persuasion, almost to a solicitation, of him to enter into sacred Orders'. Donne, however, was still unwilling, and we can see from his letters that he continued to hope for secular preferment.

Pseudo-Martyr is a quarto volume with the collation A^4 ¶^{2} B–Z Aa–Zz Aaa–Ggg^4 Hhh^2. The title (on A 1) runs thus:

Pseudo-Martyr. Wherein out of certaine Propositions and Grada-

[1] It will be remembered that Donne had studied for three years at Hart Hall, Oxford, but had left the university without taking a degree.

[2] 'Causa est quod huic Academiae maxime ornamento sit ut eiusmodi viri, optime de republica et ecclesia meriti, gradibus Academicis insigniantur.' Gosse, i. 252; Jessopp, p. 72.

tions, This Conclusion is euicted. That those which are of the Romane Religion in this Kingdome, may and ought to take the Oath of Allegeance.

Deut. 32. 15.

But he that should haue beene vpright, when he waxed fatte, spurned with his heele: Thou art fat, thou art grosse, thou art laden with fatnesse.

Iob. 11. 5.

But oh that God would speake and open his lips against thee, that he might shew thee the secrets of wisedome, how thou hast deserued double according to right.

2. Chro. 28. 22.

In the time of his tribulation, did he yet trespasse more against the Lord, for he sacrificed vnto the gods of Damascus, which plagued him.

London
Printed by *W. Stansby* for *Walter Burre.*
1610.

This is followed by a dedicatory epistle to King James I, which occupies four pages. In it Donne ascribes the composition of his book to the influence of the king's example, rather than, as Walton would have us believe, to the express command of James.

'The influence of those your Maiesties Bookes, as the Sunne, which penetrates all corners, hath wrought vppon me, and drawen vp, and exhaled from my poore Meditations, these discourses: Which, with all reuerence and deuotion, I present to your Maiestie, who in this also haue the power and office of the Sunne, that those things which you exhale, you may at your pleasure dissipate, and annull; or suffer them to fall downe again, as a wholesome and fruitfull dew, vpon your Church and Commonwealth. Of my boldnesse in this addresse, I most humbly beseech your Maiestie, to admit this excuse, that hauing obserued, how much your Maiestie had vouchsafed to descend to a conuersation with your Subiects, by way of your Bookes, I also conceiu'd an ambition, of ascending to your presence, by the same way, and of participating, by this meanes, their happinesse, of whome, that saying of the Queene of *Sheba*, may bee vsurp'd: Happie are thy men, and happie are those thy Seruants, which stand before thee alwayes, and heare thy wisdome. For, in this, I make account, that I haue performed a duetie, by expressing in an exterior, and (by your Maiesties permission) a publicke Act, the same desire, which God heares in my daily prayers, That your Maiestie may very long gouerne vs in your Person, and euer, in your Race and Progenie.'[1]

The next two pages are occupied by *A Table of the Chapters*. This table contains the headings of fourteen chapters, but only twelve of these are to be found in the book. Donne explains his reasons for the omission of the two last chapters in his *Advertisement to the Reader*, which immediately follows, and which occupies three pages. This *Advertisement* throws much light on Donne's method of composition, and is perhaps the most interesting part of the book.

'Though I purposed not to speake any thing to the Reader, otherwise then by way of Epilogue in the end of the Booke, both because I esteemed that to be the fittest place, to giue my Reasons, why I respited the handling of the two last Chapters, till another time, and also, because I thought not that any man might well and properly be called a Reader, till he were come to the end of the Booke: yet, because both he, and I, may suffer some disaduantages, if he should not be fore-possessed, and warned in some things, I haue changed my purpose in that point.

'For his owne good therefore (in which I am also interessed) I must first intreat him, that he will be pleased, before hee reade, to amend with his pen, some of the most important errors, which are hereafter noted to haue passed in the printing. Because in the Reading, he will not perchance suspect nor spy them, and so he may runne a danger, of being either deceiued, or scandalized.

'And for my selfe, (because I haue already receiued some light, that some of the Romane profession, hauing onely seene the Heads and Grounds handled in this Booke, haue traduced me, as an impious and profane vnder-valewer of Martyrdome), I most humbly beseech him, (till the reading of the Booke, may guide his Reason) to beleeue, that I haue a iust and Christianly estimation, and reuerence, of that deuout and acceptable Sacrifice of our lifes, for the glory of our blessed Sauiour. For, as my fortune hath neuer beene so flattering nor abundant, as should make this present life sweet and precious to me, as I am a Moral man: so, as I am a Christian I haue beene euer kept awake in a meditation of Martyrdome, by being deriued from such a stocke and race, as, I beleeue, no family, (which is not of farre larger extent, and greater branches,) hath endured and suffered more in their persons and fortunes, for obeying the Teachers of Romane Doctrine,

[1] *Pseudo-Martyr*, sig. A 3.

then it hath done. I did not therefore enter into this, as a carnall or ouer-indulgent fauourer of this life, but out of such reasons, as may arise to his knowledge, who shall be pleased to read the whole worke.

'In which, I haue abstained from handling the two last Chapters vpon diuers reasons; whereof one is, that these Heads hauing beene caried about, many moneths, and thereby quarrelled by some, and desired by others, I was willing to giue the Booke a hasty dispatch, that it might cost no man much time, either in expecting before it came, or in reading, when it was come.

'But a more principall reason was, that since the two last Chapters depend vpon one another, and haue a mutuall Relation, I was not willing to vndertake one, till I might perseuere through both. And from the last chapter it became me to abstaine, till I might vnderstand their purposes, who were formerly engaged in the same businesse. For the first Discouerie giues some title to the place, and secludes others, without the Discouerers permission; And in men tender and iealous of their Honour, it is sometimes accounted as much iniurie to assist, as to assault.

'When therefore I considered, that the most Reuerend and learned Sir *Edward Coke*, Lord chiefe Iustice of the common Pleas (whom, they which are too narrow to comprehend him, may finde arguments enow to loue, and admire, out of the measure and proportion of his malice who hath written against him, (since wee ought to loue him so much, as such men hate him) had in this point of Iurisdiction, laid so solid foundations, raised so strong walls, and perfited his house vpon so sure a Rocke, as the lawes of this Kingdome are. And when I saw, that as the diuell himselfe is busiest to attempt them, who abound in strength of Grace, (not forbearing our Sauiour himselfe) so an ordinary Instrument of his, (whose continuall libels, and Incitatorie bookes, haue occasioned more afflictions, and drawne more of that bloud, which they call Catholique, in this Kingdome, then all our Acts of Parliament haue done,) had oppugned his Lordships Booke, and iterated and inconculcated those his oppositions, I could not know whether his Lordship reserued any farther consideration of that matter to his owne leasures, or had honoured any other man, with his commandement, or allowance to pursue it. Till therefore I might know, whether any such were embarqued therein, as would either accept my Notes, and dignifie them with their stile, or submit their Notes to my method, and the poore apparell of my language, or vndertake it entirely, or quit it absolutely, as a body perfit already, by that forme which his Lordship hath giuen it, I chose to forbeare the handling thereof at this time.

'One thing more I was willing the Reader should be forewarned of; which is, that when he findes in the printing of this Booke oftentimes a change of the Character, hee must not thinke that all those words or sentences so distinguished, are cited from other Authors; for I haue done it sometimes, onely to draw his eye, and vnderstanding more intensly vpon that place, and so make deeper impressions thereof.

'And in those places which are cited from other Authors (which hee shall know by the Margine) I doe not alwayes precisely and superstitiously binde my selfe to the words of the Authors; which was impossible to me, both because sometimes I collect their sense, and express their Arguments or their opinions, and the Resultance of a whole leafe, in two or three lines, and some few times, I cite some of their Catholique Authors, out of their owne fellowes, who had vsed the same fashion of collecting their sense, without precise binding themselues to All, or onely their words. This is the comfort which my conscience hath, and the assurance which I can giue the Reader, that I haue no where made any Author, speake more or lesse, in sense, then hee intended, to that purpose, for which I cite him. If any of their owne fellowes from whom I cite them, haue dealt otherwise, I cannot be wounded but through their sides. So that I hope either mine Innocence, or their own fellowes guiltinesse, shall defend me, from the curious malice of those men, who in this sickly decay, and declining of their cause, can spy out falsifyings in euery citation: as in a iealous, and obnoxious state, a Decipherer can pick out Plots, and Treason, in any familiar letter which is intercepted.

'And thus much it seemed necessary to mee, to let the Reader know, to whose charitable and fauourable opinion I commit the booke, and my selfe to his Christianly and deuout Prayers.'[1]

The reference is to Sir Edward Coke's handling of the question of ecclesiastical jurisdiction in his *Reports* and to the attacks which Robert Parsons, the Jesuit, made upon him.[2] One of Parsons's books made Morton as well as Coke an object of attack.

[1] *Pseudo-Martyr*, sig. ¶ 1 and 2.

[2] Parsons wrote two books on this subject:

(1) *An Ansvvere to the fifth part of Reportes Lately set forth by Syr Edward Cooke Knight, the Kinges Attorney General. Concerning The ancient and moderne Municipall lawes of England, which do apperteyne to Spirituall Power and Iurisdiction. . . . By a Catholicke Deuyne. Matth. 22. v. 21 Reddite quæ sunt Cæsaris Cæsari; et quæ sunt Dei Deo. . . . Imprinted with licence, Anno Domini* 1606.

(2) *A Quiet and Sober Reckoning with M. Thomas Morton . . . concerning*

The headings of the two chapters which were omitted are given as follows in the *Table*:

'Chap. xiii. *That all which his Maiesty requires by this Oath, is exhibited to the Kings of Fraunce, And not by vertue of any Indult, or Concordate, but by the inhærent right of the Crowne.*

'Chap. xiiii. *Lastly, That no pretence, eyther of Conuersion at first, Assistance in the Conquest, or Acceptation of any Surrender from any of our Kings, can giue the Pope any more right ouer the Kingdome of England, then ouer any other free State whatsoeuer.*'

One page is occupied by a list of the errata, which are numerous. There are also a number of errors in the text which are not corrected here.[1] Donne alludes to these in a note which he prefixes to the list: 'Those literall and punctuall Errors, which doe not much endanger the sense, I haue left to the discretion and fauour of the Reader, as he shall meete with them. The rest he may be pleased to mend thus.'

This is followed by 'A Preface to the Priestes, and Iesuits, and to their Disciples in this Kingdome', which occupies twenty-seven pages. In it Donne speaks modestly of his own mental equipment for the task, and alludes also to his early training in the Roman faith, and the period of theological inquiry through which he had passed. He also defends himself for writing, though a layman, on a subject of a theological nature, and points out that the matter in dispute is the supremacy of the king. Some paragraphs early in the preface give a fuller account of Donne's mental struggles before joining the Church of England than he has left us anywhere else, and they also express his desire for a certain degree of mutual toleration:

'And if they' [i.e. the writers on the Roman side] 'will be content to

certaine imputations of wilfull falsities objected to. . . . T. M. in a Treatise of P. R. intituled of Mitigation. . . . There is also adjoyned a peece of a Reckoning with Syr E. Cooke, . . . about a Nihil dicit, and some other points uttered by him in the late Preambles to his sixt and Seaventh Partes of Reports. 1609.

[1] Keynes (op. cit., p. 5) points out also that the pagination of sheets Y and Aa is faulty, pp. 133, 136, 137, 140, 154 being numbered as 121, 124, 125, 128, 156. Collation of the three copies in Trinity College Library, Cambridge, shows that a number of errors were corrected while the book was passing through the press, e.g. I have noted corrections on Nn 3^{r}, Oo 1^{r}, and Oo 4^{v}.

impute to me all humane infirmities, they shall neede to faine nothing: I am, I confesse, obnoxious enough. My naturall impatience not to digge painefully in deepe, and stony, and sullen learnings: My Indulgence to my freedome and libertie, as in all other indifferent things, so in my studies also, not to betroth or enthral my selfe, to any one science, which should possesse or denominate me: My easines, to affoord a sweete and gentle Interpretation, to all professors of Christian Religion, if they shake not the Foundation,[1] wherein I haue in my ordinary Communication and familiar writings, often expressed and declared my selfe: hath opened me enough to their malice, and put me into their danger, and giuen them aduantage to impute to me, whatsoeuer such degrees of lazines, of liberty, of irresolution, can produce.

'But if either they will transferre my personall weaknesses vpon the cause, or extend the faults of my person to my minde, or to her purest part, my conscience: If they will calumniate this poore and innocent worke of mine, as if it were written, either for *Ostentation* of any ability or faculty in my selfe; or for *Prouocation*, to draw them to an aunswere, and so continue a Booke-warre; or for *Flattery* to the present State; which, though my seruices be by many iust titles due to it, needs it not; or for *exasperation*, to draw out the ciuill sword in causes, which haue some pretence and colour of being spirituall; or to get *Occasion* hereby to vncouer the nakednes, and lay open the incommodious and vndefensible sentences and opinions, of diuers seuerall Authors in that Church; or to maintaine and further a scisme and diuision amongst you, in this point of the Popes pretence to temporall iurisdiction: I haue no other shelter against these imputations, but an appeale to our blessed Sauiour, and a protestation before his face, that my principall and direct scope and purpose herein, is the vnity and peace of his Church. For as when the roofe of the Temple rent asunder, not long after followed the ruine of the foundation it selfe: So if these two principall beames and Toppe-rafters, *the Prince* and *the Priest*, rent asunder, the whole frame and Foundation of Christian Religion will be shaked. And if we distinguish not between Articles of faith and iurisdiction, but account all those super-edifications and furnitures, and ornaments which God hath affoorded to his Church, for exteriour gouernment, to be equally the Foundation it selfe, there can bee no Church: as there could be no body of a man, if it were all eye.

'They who haue descended so lowe, as to take knowledge of me,

[1] Donne expressed the same desire several years later in *Essays in Divinity*. See the passage quoted on p. 230.

and to admit me into their consideration, know well that I vsed no inordinate hast, nor precipitation in binding my conscience to any locall Religion. I had a longer worke to doe then many other men; for I was first to blot out, certaine impressions of the Romane religion, and to wrastle both against the examples and against the reasons, by which some hold was taken; and some anticipations early layde vpon my conscience, both by Persons who by nature had a power and superiority ouer my will, and others who by their learning and good life, seem'd to me iustly to claime an interest for the guiding, and rectifying of mine vnderstanding in these matters. And although I apprehended well enough, that this irresolution not onely retarded my fortune, but also bred some scandall, and endangered my spirituall reputation, by laying me open to many mis-interpretations; yet all these respects did not transport me to any violent and sudden determination, till I had, to the measure of my poore wit and iudgement, suruayed and digested the whole body of Diuinity, controuerted betweene ours and the Romane Church. In which search and disquisition, that God, which awakened me then, and hath neuer forsaken me in that industry, as he is the Authour of that purpose, so is he a witnes of this protestation; that I behaued my selfe, and proceeded therin with humility, and diffidence in my selfe; and by that, which by his grace, I tooke to be the ordinary meanes, which is frequent praier, and equall and indifferent affections.

'And this course held in rectifying and reducing mine vnderstanding and iudgment, might iustifie and excuse my forwardnes; if I shold seeme to any to haue intruded and vsurped the office of others, in writing of Diuinity and spirituall points, hauing no ordinary calling to that function. For, to haue alwaies abstained from this declaration of my selfe, had beene to betray, and to abandon, and prostitute my good name to their misconceiuings and imputations; who thinke presently, that hee hath no Religion, which dares not call his Religion by some newer name then *Christian*. And then, for my writing in Diuinity, though no professed Diuine; all Ages, all Nations, all Religions, euen yours, which is the most couetous and lothest to diuide, or communicate with the Layety, any of the honours reserued to the Clergie, affoord me abundantly examples, and authorities for such an vndertaking.

'But for this poore work of mine, I need no such *Aduocates*, nor *Apologizers*; for it is not of Diuinity, but meerely of temporall matters that I write.'[1]

The argument of the preface is directed against the Pope's

[1] *Pseudo-Martyr*, sig. B 1 verso–B 3 verso.

claim to temporal jurisdiction. 'To offer our liues for defence of the Catholique faith, hath euer beene a religious custome; but to cal euery pretence of the Pope, Catholique faith, and to bleede to death for it, is a sicknesse and a medicine, which the Primitiue Church neuer vnderstood.'[1] Donne defends the Reformation as necessary and wholesome,[2] and attacks the Papal policy of excommunicating sovereigns who have adopted the reformed faith. Those who revolt against their lawful rulers are not martyrs but rebels, and Donne closes his preface with an eloquent appeal to those who have in the past shed their blood for the Christian faith:

'I call to witnesse against you, those whose testimonie God himselfe hath accepted. Speake then and testifie, O you glorious and triumphant Army of Martyrs, who enioy now a permanent triumph in heauen, which knew the voice of your Shepheard, and staid till he cald, and went then with all alacritie: Is there any man receiued into your blessed Legion, by title of such a Death, as sedition, scandall, or any humane respect occasioned? O no, for they which are in possession of that Laurell, are such as haue washed their garments, not in their owne blood onely (for so they might still remaine redde and staind) but in the *blood of the Lambe which changes them to white*. . . .

'Thus much I was willing to premit, to awaken you, if it please you to heare it, to a iust loue of your owne safetie, of the peace of your Countrey, of the honour and reputation of your Countreymen, and of the integritie of that, which you call the Catholicke cause; and to acquaint you so farre, with my disposition and temper, as that you neede not be afraid to reade my poore writings, who ioyne you with mine owne Soule in my Prayers, that your Obedience here, may prepare your admission into the heauenly *Hierusalem*, and that by the same Obedience, *Your dayes may bee long in the land, which the Lord your God hath given you*. Amen.'[3]

The main argument of the book occupies 392 pages. Donne reasons learnedly and temperately with his opponents, but the subject has lost its interest for modern readers, and there are very few 'purple patches' of eloquence and imagination, though here and there a fine passage rewards the attentive reader.

[1] Ibid. sig. C 3.
[2] Ibid. sig. C 4–D 1.
[3] Ibid. sig. E 1–2.

Such a passage occurs at the beginning of Chapter I, and may be quoted here.

'As a *Depositarie* to whose trust some pretious thing were committed, is not onely encombred and anxious, to defend it from the violencies and subtleties of outward attempters, but feeles within himselfe some interruptions of his peace, and some inuasions vpon his honesty, by a corrupt desire, and temptation to possesse it, and to employ vpon his owne pleasure or profit, that of which he is no *Proprietary*: and neuer returnes to his security, out of these watchfulnesses against other, and reluctations with himselfe; till he who deliuered this Iewell, resume it againe: So, till it please the Lord, and owner of our life to take home into his treasurie, this rich *Carbuncle* our soule, which giues vs light in our night of ignorance, and our darke body of earth, we are still anguished and trauelled, as well with a continuall defensiue warre, to preserue our life from sickenesses, and other offensiue violences; as with a diuers and contrary couetousnes, sometimes to enlarge our State and terme therein, sometimes to make it so much our owne, that we may vnthriftily spend it vpon surfets, or licentiousnes, or reputation.'[1]

The tone of *Pseudo-Martyr* is one of studied moderation, and it hardly deserved the abuse heaped on it by Thomas Fitzherbert, one of the spokesmen of the Catholic party, who criticized it in his 'Supplement to the Discussion of M. D. Barlowes Answere To the Iudgment of a Catholike Englishman' which appeared in 1613.

'But to tell thee, good reader, my opinion briefly of his [Donne's] *Pseudo-Martyr* (wherein he hath disgorged all the venym of his Satyricall veyne against Catholicke religion) I assure thee, that hauing taken a view of the whole worke, and some paynes to examine particulerly some parts thereof I haue discouered so many impertinent, and weake arguments, such misconstruction, and sometimes flat corruption of authors, such wresting of places to his purpose, mistaking, or changing the state of the question, such slender satisfaction to obiections (though made sometimes by himselfe) such dissembling, and hudling vp of points of importance, such sleights and shifts, such contradictions, strang paradoxes, profane, idle, and impertinent matter (prouing nothing against vs, though it were granted) and finally so little substance, and solyd learning in the whole; that howsoeuer some may perhaps be pleased with his gibing vein, or abused with the shew and

[1] *Pseudo-Martyr*, pp. 1–2.

pretense of diligence in reading and cyting our Catholicke writers: yet I verily think, that there is no man of iudgement (especially if he take paines to examine his citations, and marke well the applications of them) but he will rather take his Treatise for a tale of some Mountebanke, cunningly framed to set forth and sell some Sophisticate and counterfait ware, then for such a learned discourse as might deserue to be dedicated to his Maiesty, especially concerning a matter of such importance, as is the Oath.'[1]

Fitzherbert also objects to 'M. Dunns Lucianicall and Atheisticall' humour (p. 106), and hopes some further critic will

'display M. *Dunns* ignorance to the world, yea and make him vnderstand, that it had byn much more for his reputation to haue kept himselfe within his compasse, and not to haue passed *vltra crepidam*, that is to say, beyond his old occupation of making Satyres (wherein he hath some talent, and may play the foole without controle) then to presume to write bookes of matters in cōtrouersy, which are to be scanned and sifted by learned men, and require much more substance, then his skambling studyes, and superficiall knowledge can affoard.'

'So that you see into what a quicksand (as I may say) or quagmire of absurdityes M. *Dunne* hath plunged himselfe ouer head and eares, whiles he hath ouer hoatly and hastily followed the chase of his owne idle conceiptes, insomuch that now he hath need of some good help to draw Dunne out of the mire.'[2]

Conclaue Ignati, or *Ignatius his Conclave*, the next of Donne's prose works to be published, is very different in style and subject from *Pseudo-Martyr*, though it continues Donne's controversy with the Roman Church. It is a lively satire, written with much vigour of imagination, though scurrilous in places. It appeared anonymously in two forms —Latin and English—the title-page of the English edition stating that it was 'translated out of Latin'. The seventeenth-century controversialists allowed themselves great licence of abuse when writing in Latin, and Donne availed himself of this privilege in the bitter attacks on the Jesuits which form so large a part of *Conclaue Ignati*. These attacks were occasioned by the alarm which was felt in England over

[1] Fitzherbert, *Supplement to the Discussion*, p. 106.
[2] Ibid., pp. 107, 105.

the assassination of Henri IV in May 1610. Numerous pamphlets were published both in France and England attacking the Jesuits as the authors of the doctrine that violence might be used against kings who resisted the temporal sovereignty of the papacy. The Spanish Jesuit Mariana had affirmed this doctrine in the sixth chapter of his *De Rege*, first published in 1598, and his book was proscribed by the Faculty of Divines of the University of Paris in June 1610, and was ordered to be burnt by a decree of the Parliament of Paris.[1]

Ignatius his Conclave is a satire of the Lucianic kind, but it is not necessary to suppose that Donne went directly to Lucian for his model. It is more likely that he was inspired by the famous *Satyre Ménippée*, published anonymously in 1594, and by its supplement, published in 1595, *Le Supplément du Catholicon, ou nouvelles des régions de la lune*.[2]

It is not, however, for its attack on the Jesuits that the book now interests readers, but for its references to the 'new astronomy' and the discoveries of Galileo and Kepler. Gosse showed[3] that it must have been written later than *Pseudo-Martyr*, and that the date of its composition cannot be earlier than the close of 1610, since it contains references to the *Sidereus Nuncius* of Galileo, published in Venice early in 1610.[4] There are also references to the work of Kepler,[5]

[1] C. M. Coffin, op. cit., pp. 198–200.

[2] The points of resemblance between *Ignatius his Conclave* and these two French works are enumerated in detail by Coffin, op. cit., pp. 201–3.

[3] Gosse, i. 257, 258.

[4] The preface is dated from Padua, 12 Mar. The work concludes with a record of the original configurations of Jupiter's satellites observed by Galileo from 1 Jan. to 2 Mar.

[5] Gosse in his attempt to date *Conclaue Ignati* assigned the Kepler quotation on p. 196 to the *Dissertatio cum Nuncio Sidereo*, which he dated 1611. But the quotation is from the earlier *De Stella in Cygno*; and the *Dissertatio* was published in 1610, the preface being dated from Prague, 19 Apr., 1610.

It is interesting to find that Donne's book came to the notice of Kepler himself, who called it 'an impudent satire', because the author 'pricks me by name in the very beginning', and later 'brings up poor Copernicus to the judgment seat of Pluto' (note 8 of 'notae in Somnium Astronomicum', *Kepleri Opera Omnia*, ed. Frisch, viii. 41, 42). This was pointed out by Professor Marjorie Nicholson, whose translation I have used, in 'Kepler, who was still a young man, just rising to fame, and the whole book affords evidence of the extraordinary interest taken by Donne in the scientific discoveries of his time.

Internal evidence of another kind also shows that *Ignatius his Conclave* must have followed *Pseudo-Martyr*, and could not have been written as early as 1608, the year to which Dr. Jessopp assigned it.[1] There is a reference to his 'other Book' (i.e. *Pseudo-Martyr*) in the epistle, 'The Printer to the Reader'.

> 'Doest thou seeke after the Author? It is in vaine; for hee is harder to be found then the parents of Popes were in the old times: yet if thou haue an itch of gessing, receiue from me so much, as a friend of his, to whom he sent his booke to bee read, writ to me. "The Author "was vnwilling to haue this booke published, thinking it vnfit both for "the matter, which in it selfe is weighty and serious, and for that "grauity which himselfe had proposed and obserued in an other booke "formerly published, to descend to this kinde of writing. But I on the "other side, mustred my forces against him, and produced reasons "and examples.
>
> " . . . At last he yeelded, and made mee owner of his booke, which "I send to you to be deliuered over to forraine nations, farre from the "father: and (as his desire is) his last in this kinde. Hee chooses and "desires, that his other book should testifie his ingenuity, and candor, "and his disposition to labour for the reconciling of all parts. This "Booke must teach what humane infirmity is, and how hard a matter "it is for a man much conuersant in the bookes and Acts of *Iesuites*, so "throughly to cast off the *Iesuits*, as that he contract nothing of their "naturall drosses, which are *Petulancy*, and *Lightnesse*. Vale.'

Dr. Keynes has identified two Latin editions which he ascribes to the year 1611. One of these, a duodecimo volume, has no imprint, while he suggests that the other, which is in quarto,[2] may have been printed at Hanau, since both the two copies known are bound up with other tracts printed there, and the typography suggests that they were issued from the same press.[3]

'The Somnium, and John Donne', *Journal of the History of Ideas*, i. 3 (1940), 259–80, and by C. M. Coffin in his introduction to the Facsimile Society's reprint (1941) of *Ignatius his Conclave*.

[1] Jessopp, *John Donne*, p. 68.

[2] The only copies known are in the University Library, Cambridge (Acton Collection).

[3] Keynes, op. cit., pp. 8–12.

The edition, however, can be exactly dated. We find that the book was entered on the Stationers' Register on 24 January 1610/11 to the publisher, Walter Burre.

'Walter Burre. Entred for his Copy vnder thandes of Doctor Moreton, Doctor Mokett and master Adames warden, A booke in Latyne called, *Conclaue Ignatij, siue eius in nuperis Inferni Comitij Inthronisatio vbi varia de Jesuitarum indole, de novo Inferno creando, de Ecclesia Lunatica instituenda, per Satyram congesta sunt, Accessit et Apologia pro Jesuiticis* . . . vj^d.'

The English edition was entered on 18 May 1611 to another publisher, Richard Moore or More:

'Richard Moore. Entred for his Copy vnder th'andes of Doctor Mokett, and Th'wardens, A booke called, *Ignatius his Conclaue, or his inthronizacon in a late eleccon in Hell etc.* . . . vj^d.'

The title is the same, though differently spaced, in the two Latin editions:

'Conclaue Ignati: Siue eius in nuperis inferni comitiis Inthronisatio. Vbi varia

De Iesuitarum Indole,
De nouo inferno creando,
De Ecclesia Lunatica instituenda,

per Satyram congesta sunt. Accessit & Apologia pro Iesuitis. Omnia Duobus Angelis Aduersariis, qui Consistorio Papali, & Collegio Sorbonae praesident, dedicata.'

The first English edition is a small duodecimo volume with the collation A–G^{12}. The title runs thus:

'Ignatius his Conclaue: or His Inthronisation in a late Election in Hell: Wherein many things are mingled by way of Satyr; Concerning The Disposition of Iesuits, The Creation of a new Hell, The establishing of a Church in the Moone. There is also added an Apology for Iesuites. All dedicated to the two Aduersary Angels, which are Protectors of the Papall Consistory, and of the Colledge of Sorbon. Translated out of Latine. London, Printed by N. O. for Richard More, and are to be sold at his shop in S. Dunstones Churchyard 1611.'

Dr. Keynes distinguishes another issue of this edition, with the misprint 'suits' for 'Iesuits' on the title-page, and with the words 'Translated out of Latine' omitted.[1]

The edition of 1626 follows that of 1611 closely. The title is the same, except that the printer is 'M. F.' instead of 'N. O.', and the date is altered.

Another edition appeared in 1634, giving the author's name for the first time. It describes him as 'Iohn Donne, Doctor of Divinitie, and late Deane of Saint Pauls'. Dr. Keynes has identified another issue with the same sheets, but with the date on the title-page altered to 1635.

In 1652 *Ignatius his Conclave* was included by John Donne the younger in his edition of his father's *Paradoxes and Problems*. It was stated by him to be 'Translated out of the Originall Copy written in Latin by the same Author; found lately amongst his own Papers'. In addition to this mention of *Ignatius* on the general title-page of the volume, which is dated 1652, there is a separate title-page which gives the date as 1653. The Latin version was reprinted in 1680, without Donne's name, and in company with a Latin work by 'Lucius Cornelius Europaeus'.[2] The title runs thus: 'Lucii Cornelii Europaei Monarchia Solipsorum. Et Conclave Ignatii: Sive Ejus in Nuperis Inferni Comitiis Inthronisatio. Londini, Prostat venalis apud Jacobum Collins, in Vico vulgo vocato Essex Street. 1680.'

In 1929 John Hayward reprinted *Ignatius his Conclave* from the edition of 1611, in *John Donne: Complete Poetry and Selected Prose*, published by the Nonesuch Press. A second edition appeared in 1930. In 1941 the Facsimile Text Society issued a reproduction of the 1611 edition, with an introduction by C. M. Coffin, printed by the Columbia University Press.

Ignatius his Conclave opens with a reference to the traditional dispute between the Sorbonne and the Papal Consistory. Donne then throws his story into the form of a

[1] Keynes (op. cit., p. 13) explains that he knows of no copy in which this actually forms the title; but that the British Museum copy of the ordinary issue has such a title-page on its last leaf. I have found a copy in the Chapter Library of St. George's Chapel, Windsor, with a similar cancel title-page as the last leaf, but it has 'ofesuits', not 'of suits'.

[2] i.e Giulio Clemente Scotti.

vision of hell, and begins with an interesting reference to the astronomical discoveries of Galileo and Kepler, which helps us to date the composition of the book.

'I was in an *Extasie*, and

> *My little wandring sportful Soule*
> *Ghest, and Companion of my body*[1]

had liberty to wander through all places, and to suruey and reckon all the roomes, and all the volumes of the heauens, and to comprehend the situation, the dimensions, the nature, the people, and the policy, both of the swimming Ilands, the *Planets*, and of all those which are fixed in the firmament. Of which, I thinke it an honester part as yet to be silent, then to do *Galilæo* wrong by speaking of it, who of late hath summoned the other worlds, the Stars to come neerer to him, and giue him an account of themselues. Or to *Keppler*,[2] who (as himselfe testifies of himselfe) *euer since* Tycho Braches *death, hath receiued it into his care, that no new thing should be done in heauen without his knowledge.* For by the law, *Preuention* must take place; and therefore what they haue found and discoured first, I am content they speake and vtter first. Yet this they may vouchsafe to take from me, that they shall hardly find *Enoch*, or *Elias* any where in their circuit. When I had surueid al the Heauens, then as

Nuncius Sydereus.

De stella in Cygno.

> *The Larke by busie and laborious wayes,*
> *Hauing climb'd vp th'etheriall hill, doth raise*
> *His Hymnes to* Phoebus *Harpe, And striking then*
> *His sailes, his wings, doth fall downe backe agen*
> *So suddenly, that one may safely say*
> *A stone came lazily, that came that way,*

In the twinckling of an eye, I saw all the roomes in Hell open to my sight. . . . As for the *Suburbs* of Hel (I meane both *Limbo* and *Purgatory*) I must confesse I passed them ouer so negligently, that I saw them not: and I was hungerly caried, to find new places, never discouered before.

[1] This must be the earliest English rendering of Hadrian's famous lines:

> Animula vagula, blandula
> hospes comesque corporis
> quae nunc abibis in loca?

[2] From *Joannis Kepleri de Stella tertii Honoris in Cygno, quae usque ad annum MDC fuit incognita, necdum exstinguitur, Narratio Astronomica*, Prague, 1606. 'Tychone iam mortuo equidem haec me cura incessit, ne quid fortasse novi existeret in caelo me inscio' (*Kepleri Opera Omnia*, ed. Frisch, ii. 762).

. . . Proceeding therefore to more inward places, I saw a secret place, where there were not many, beside *Lucifer* himselfe; to which, onely they had title, which had so attempted any innouation in this life, that they gaue an affront to all antiquitie, and induced doubts, and anxieties, and scruples, and after, a liberty of beleeuing what they would; at length established opinions, directly contrary to all established before. . . . And here Pope *Boniface* 3, and *Mahomet*, seemed to contend about the highest roome. Hee gloried of hauing expelled an old Religion, and *Mahomet* of hauing brought in a new: each of them a great deluge to the world.'[1]

To this inner room come various claimants, who urge the great innovations which they have wrought in the world, and of these the first is Copernicus.

'Now to this place, not onely such endeauour to come, as haue innouated in matters, directly concerning the soule, but they also which haue done so, either in the Arts, or in conuersation, or in any thing which exerciseth the faculties of the soule, and may so prouoke to quarrelsome and brawling controuersies: For so the truth is lost, it is no matter how. But the gates are seldome opened, nor scarce oftner then once in an Age. But my destiny fauoured mee so much, that I was present then, and saw all the pretenders, and all that affected an entrance, and *Lucifer* himselfe, who then came out into the outward chamber, to heare them pleade their owne Causes. As soon as the doore creekt, I spied a certaine *Mathematitian*, which till then had bene busied to finde, to deride, to detrude *Ptolomey*; and now with an erect countenance, and setled pace, came to the gates, and with hands and feet (scarce respecting *Lucifer* himselfe) beat the dores, and cried: Are these shut against me, to whom all the Heauens were euer open, who was a Soule to the Earth, and gaue it motion?

'By this I knew it was *Copernicus*: For though I had neuer heard ill of his life, and therefore might wonder to find him there; yet when I remembred, that the *Papists* haue extended the name, and the punishment of Heresie, almost to euery thing, and that as yet I vsed *Gregories* and *Bedes* spectacles, by which one saw *Origen*, who deserued so well of the *Christian Church*, *burning in Hell*, I doubted no longer, but assured my selfe that it was *Copernicus* which I saw.'[2]

Bellar. de purgat. l. 2. *cap*. 8.

A dialogue then follows between Lucifer and Copernicus, in which the latter urges the great innovation which he has

[1] *Ignatius his Conclave* (1611 edition), pp. 2–7.
[2] Ibid., pp. 11–13.

made in the scheme of the universe. Lucifer is puzzled whether to grant or deny the astronomer's claim, but Ignatius Loyola, who is near the Devil's chair, is determined to oppose all claimants except those of his own Order. He therefore challenges Copernicus' claim on the ground that Lucifer has profited nothing by the introduction of the new astronomy, and that, worst of all, the Copernican theory *may very well be true*. The Devil should surely give more honour to the labours of Clavius,[1] who had opposed the theories of Copernicus and had moreover a large share in the establishment of the new Gregorian Calendar, an innovation which had caused endless disturbance in heaven and earth.

'But for you,' says Ignatius to Copernicus, 'what new thing haue you inuented, by which our *Lucifer* gets any thing? What cares hee whether the earth trauell, or stand still? Hath your raising vp of the earth into heauen, brought men to that confidence, that they build new towers or threaten God againe? Or do they out of this motion of the earth conclude, that there is no hell, or deny the punishment of sin? Do not men beleeue? do they not liue iust, as they did before? Besides, this detracts from the dignity of your learning, and derogates from your right and title of comming to this place, that those opinions of yours may very well be true. If therfore any man haue honour or title to this place in this matter, it belongs wholly to our *Clauius*, who opposed himselfe opportunely against you, and the truth, which at that time was creeping into euery mans minde. Hee onely can be called the Author of all contentions, and schoole-combats in this cause; and no greater profit can bee hoped for heerein, but that for such brabbles, more necessarie matters bee neglected. And yet not onely for this is our *Clauius* to bee honoured, but for the great paines also which hee tooke in the *Gregorian Calender*, by which both the peace of the Church, and Ciuill businesses haue beene egregiously troubled: nor hath heauen it selfe escaped his violence, but hath euer since obeied his apointments: so that S. *Stephen*, *Iohn Baptist*, and all the rest, which haue bin commanded to worke miracles at certain appointed daies, where their Reliques are preserued, do not now attend till the day come, as they were accustomed, but are awaked ten daies

[1] Christopher Clavius was entrusted by Pope Gregory XIII with the charge of verifying the calculations and expounding the principles of the new Gregorian Calendar. His great work was the *Romani Calendarii a Gregorio XIII. P.M. restituti Explicatio*, published at Rome in 1603.

IX
ESSAYS IN DIVINITY

THE *Essays in Divinity* have perhaps less literary value than the *Devotions* or the *Sermons*, but they are of great importance for those who wish to study the development of Donne's thought. They are linked with *Biathanatos*, *Ignatius his Conclave*, and the verse *Anniversaries*, which preceded them, and with the *Sermons* which followed them. They are vital for the understanding of Donne's position during the difficult years which preceded his entry into Holy Orders, when he was hesitating on the threshold. The exact date of their composition is uncertain, but from the address 'To the Reader' prefixed by Donne's son to the edition of 1651 it has generally been deduced that they were written at the end of 1614 or the beginning of 1615.[1] The address runs thus:

'It is thought fit to let thee know, that these *Essayes* were printed from an exact Copy, under the Authors own hand: and, that they were the voluntary sacrifices of severall hours, when he had many debates betwixt God and himself, whether he were worthy, and competently learned to enter into Holy Orders. They are now publish'd both to testifie his modest Valuation of himself and to shew his great abilities; and they may serve to inform thee in many Holy Curiosities. *Fare-well.*'

This, however, is less conclusive than Gosse imagined. Donne had had 'many debates . . . whether he were worthy, and competently learned to enter into Holy Orders' for a number of years before he actually took the final step. Several dates between 1611 and January 1615 might fit this statement, but the general tone of the *Essays* makes it clear that they were written later than *Ignatius his Conclave*, and that Donne's interests were beginning to be predominantly theological. His concern with the 'new philosophy' is still

[1] Gosse, ii. 321: 'This narrows the date of their composition to December 1614 and January 1615.' Ramsay, op. cit., p. 118: 'Son ordination eut lieu en janvier 1615. C'est pendant les mois qui la précédèrent qu'il se donna pour tâche d'écrire les *Essais de Théologie*.'

there, but it is much less urgent than in the two *Anniversaries* and *Ignatius his Conclave*. He is still reading the works of Raymond of Sebund, Francis George (F. G. Zorgi), Pico Mirandola, Reuchlin, and Petrus Galatinus, all of whom are satirized in *Catalogus Librorum*. He shows himself interested in the Jewish Cabbalists, in Hermes Trismegistus, Zoroaster, and the Koran, but Augustine and Aquinas are beginning to assert their authority over these extremely unorthodox thinkers. He is beginning to think of himself as a preacher, and can write 'Though these lack thus much of Sermons, that they have no Auditory, yet as Saint *Bernard* did almost glory, that Okes and Beeches were his Masters, I shall be content that Okes and Beeches be my schollers, and witnesses of my solitary Meditations.'[1]

The Essays in Divinity have never been as popular with readers as the *Devotions*. This is partly due to their fragmentary character, and also to the fact that their style is much less polished. They are essentially private meditations, whereas the *Devotions* were carefully prepared for the press. They have some eloquent passages, notably the prayers and the long dissertation on the unity of the Church, but in many places the style is dry and crabbed. Coffin has emphasized their importance in the history of Donne's thought, but other writers on Donne have been much less sympathetic.[2] Many have neglected any discussion of the book. Gosse called it 'a dull little book', and his suggestion that it was written to be laid before Archbishop Abbot

[1] *Essays in Divinity* (1651), pp. 87–8.

[2] Coffin, op. cit., p. 249. 'Whether or not we accept the younger Donne's statement that they [the *Essays*] were written for his father's own satisfaction on the threshold of his going into the ministry, we must believe that they were "private" rather than public discourses, in which he wished to clear up in his mind certain fundamental religious problems. In this respect they are more fitting as a companion piece to the *Anniversaries* than as a prelude to his assumption of holy orders. Donne has been confronted, through a study of the new philosophy rendering the old conception of a unified world scheme entirely hopeless, with the necessity of discovering other means whereby the natural world may be significantly related to a new universal order. . . . Donne looks to pagan and Christian alike, occultist and orthodox Christian, for means to help him; hence, the generous attitude toward Catholic and Protestant, cabalist and occult mystic, and Greek philosopher.'

before Donne's ordination as a proof of his orthodoxy,[1] is a most infelicitous one. Abbot was a narrow-minded man, bitterly hostile to the Church of Rome,[2] and his suspicions of Donne, if he had any, would have been increased rather than allayed by a treatise in which the author wrote: 'So Synagogue and Church is the same thing, and of the Church, *Roman* and *Reformed*, and all other distinctions of place, Discipline, or Person, but one Church, journying to one *Hierusalem*, and directed by one guide, Christ Jesus.'[3] Misled by his own unwarranted assumption that Donne needed to clear himself in Abbot's eyes of complicity in the Somerset divorce, Gosse was prepared to judge the *Essays* harshly. He remarked: 'When we examine the *Essays in Divinity*, however, for evidence of Donne's state of soul at this juncture, we meet with considerable disappointment. There is no revelation here of the writer's personal experience; nothing is for edification. These short homilies are more like the notes of a theological professor who is lecturing on Genesis and the early chapters of Exodus, than the outpourings of a man who is trembling on the threshold of the Holy of Holies. There is a total absence of unction, even of spiritual enthusiasm; the essays are scholastic exercises and no more.'[4]

The book itself, if studied attentively, refutes this last

[1] Gosse, ii. 63. On the previous page Gosse states: 'It is more than probable that Abbot, who was very well informed, was aware, as Donne feared that he might be, of Donne's activity for Somerset in the business of the nullity. Very possibly the documents which Donne drew up for the favourite, and which still exist, had passed under the eyes of Abbot.' As we have already seen, these documents were written by Sir Daniel Dunne and not by Donne (see p. 29 *supra*) and the mere composition of an epithalamium for a marriage which had been graced by the King's presence could hardly have been a valid reason for refusing ordination to Donne. Incidentally we may notice that Abbot had nothing to do with Donne's ordination. The right of conferring Orders is vested in the diocesan bishop, and Donne was duly ordained by John King, Bishop of London, the diocese in which he was to serve.

[2] Abbot had the temerity to write a protest in 1622 to King James against the latter's proposed decree of toleration for Catholics, in which he inveighed against 'that most *Damnable* and *Heretical Doctrine* of the *Church* of *Rome*, the Whore of *Babylon*'.

[3] *Essays in Divinity*, p. 110.

[4] Gosse, ii.63.

charge. It is the kindest, the happiest, the least controversial of Donne's prose works. The melancholy which pervaded his mind during the writing of the *Anniversaries* has vanished. His subject during the first half of the book is the creation of the world, and he looks upon the world with admiring eyes. He speaks of the Book of Creatures,[1] in which man may see God the Creator. 'Certainly, every Creature shewes God, as a glass, but glimmeringly and transitorily, by the frailty both of the receiver, and beholder: Our selves have his Image, as Medals, permanently and preciously delivered.'[2]

There is a gentleness which is very pleasant in such a passage as this:

> 'Let no smalnesse retard thee: if thou beest not a Cedar to help towards a palace . . . yet thou art a shrub to shelter a lambe, or to feed a bird; or thou art a plantane, to ease a childs smart; or a grasse to cure a sick dog.'[3]

Death is hardly mentioned,[4] and there is no morbid discussion of disease or corruption. Gosse himself excepted the prayers contained in the volume from his general censure of its supposed dullness. He considered one of them so fine an expression of Donne's feelings that he wished to detach it from the rest of the book, and ascribed it to a period three years later, when he believed that Donne, in his agony of grief over his wife's death, passed through the crisis of conversion.[5] He failed, however, to see that this prayer and its companions are intimately connected with the whole

[1] *Essays*, p. 7.

[2] Ibid., pp. 37–8.

[3] Ibid., p. 145. This should be compared with Donne's remark that 'the Indian priests expressed an excellent charity, by building Hospitalls and providing chirurgery for birds and beasts lamed by mischance, or age, or labour' (*Letters*, 1651, p. 47). He was certainly an animal-lover in an age when cruelty to animals was fashionable.

[4] On p. 168 Donne says 'the slumber of death shall overtake us'.

[5] Gosse, ii. 102–3. Gosse quoted in particular the sentence, 'And as, though thy self hadst no beginning, thou gavest a beginning to all things in which thou wouldst be served and glorified; so, though this soul of mine, by which I partake thee, begin not now, yet let this minute, O God, this happy minute of thy visitation, be the beginning of her conversion, and shaking away confusion, darknesse, and barrennesse; and let her now produce Creatures, thoughts, words, and deeds agreeable to thee.'

argument of the book. The first prayer sums up Donne's meditations on the Name of God, and on the creation of heaven and earth out of nothing. The second and third apply his meditations on Exodus to his own experience, and have an intensely personal note. Here is a passage from the second prayer which shows how a piece of intimate self-revelation can flower out of the dry wood of a discussion of the first verse of the Book of Exodus.

'Thou hast delivered me, O God, from the Egypt of confidence and presumption, by interrupting my fortunes, and intercepting my hopes; And from the Egypt of despair by contemplation of thine abundant treasures, and my portion therein; from the Egypt of lust, by confining my affections; and from the monstrous and unnaturall Egypt of painfull and wearisome idleness, by the necessities of domestick and familiar cares and duties. Yet as an Eagle, though she enjoy her wing and beak, is wholly prisoner, if she be held by but one talon; so are we, though we could be delivered of all habit of sin, in bondage still, if Vanity hold us but by a silken thred. But, O God, as mine inward corruptions have made me mine own *Pharaoh*, and mine own *Egypt*; so thou, by the inhabitation of thy Spirit, and application of thy merit, hast made me mine own Christ; and contenting thy self with being my Medicine, allowest me to be my Physician.'[1]

The central position occupied by the *Essays* is shown by their intimate connexion with the verse *Anniversaries* and certain of the *Divine Poems* on the one hand, and with the early *Sermons* on the other.

The verbal links with the two *Anniversaries* are worth enumeration. In *The first Anniversary* Donne had written:

> Vouchsafe to call to minde that God did make
> A last, and lasting'st peece, a song. He spake
> To *Moses* to deliver unto all,
> That song, because hee knew they would let fall
> The Law, the Prophets, and the History,
> But keepe the song still in their memory.[2]

In the *Essays in Divinity* he writes:

'And God himself in that last peice of his, which he commanded *Moses* to record, that Heavenly song which onely himself compos'd . . . this which himself cals a Song, was made immediately by himself,

[1] *Essays in Divinity*, pp. 166–7.
[2] Grierson, i. 245.

and *Moses* was commanded to deliver it to the Children; God choosing this way and conveyance of a Song . . . because he knew that they would ever be repeating this Song. . . .'[1]

In *The second Anniversary*, 425–8, we find:

> But as the Heathen made them severall gods,
> Of all Gods Benefits, and all his Rods,
> (For as the Wine, and Corne, and Onions are
> Gods unto them, so Agues bee, and Warre).[2]

This is expanded in the *Essays* thus:

'Have they furthered, or eased thee any more, who not able to consider whole and infinit God, have made a particular God, not only of every power of God, but of every benefit? . . . Out of this proceeded *Dea febris*, and *Dea fraus*, and *Tenebrae*, and *Onions*, and *Garlike*. For the *Egyptians*, most abundant in Idolatry, were from thence said to have Gods grow in their gardens.'[3]

The same thought is expressed in the *Sermons*:

'The Gentiles were not able to consider God so; not so entirely, not altogether; but broke God in pieces, and changed God into single money, and made a fragmentarie God of every Power, and Attribute in God, of every blessing from God, nay of every malediction and judgment of God. . . . *Feare* came to be a God, and a *Fever* came to be a God.'[4]

More important than these parallels[5] is the likeness in theme between the *Anniversaries* and some passages of the *Essays*. In the poems Donne takes a view of the universe, through which the soul ascends to heaven. 'This slow-pac'd soule, which late did cleave To a body, and went but by the bodies leave' stays not in the air, and knows not whether she has passed through the element of fire.

> She baits not at the Moone, nor cares to trie
> Whether in that new world, men live, and die. . . .
> But ere she can consider how she went,
> At once is at, and through the Firmament.

[1] *Essays*, pp. 204–5.

[2] Grierson, i. 263.

[3] *Essays*, p. 41. Jessopp points out the reference to Juvenal, *Sat.* xv. 10. 'O sanctas gentes quibus haec nascuntur in hortis Numina.'

[4] *LXXX Sermons*, 50. 502.

[5] A smaller example may be found in *The second Anniversary*, 281–2, and *Essays in Divinity*, p. 23, on the 'hundred differences . . . concerning an Ant'.

And as these starres were but so many beads
Strung on one string, speed undistinguish'd leads
Her through those Spheares, as through the beads, a string,
Whose quick succession makes it still one thing:
As doth the pith, which, lest our bodies slacke,
Strings fast the little bones of necke, and backe;
So by the Soule doth death string Heaven and Earth . . . .'[1]

The whole passage with its mention of the planets Venus, Mercury, Mars, Jupiter, and Saturn, and finally of the firmament and the fixed stars, gives a wonderful impression of the immensities of outer stellar space. Again and again in these two poems, and in the *Funerall Elegie*, attached to *The second Anniversary*, Donne makes mention of the 'new Starres' which Kepler and Galileo had revealed to the world.

But, as when heaven lookes on us with new eyes,
Those new starres every Artist exercise,
What place they should assign to them they doubt,
Argue, and agree not till those starres goe out.[2]

By the time that Donne wrote *Essays in Divinity* the excitement produced in him by the discoveries of the new astronomy had largely disappeared. He no longer appended marginal notes, referring to the works of Kepler and Galileo, as he had done in *Biathanatos* and *Ignatius his Conclave*. But the wide cosmic view still persists in the first book of the *Essays*—that which is devoted to the creation of the world. In one of the most eloquent passages in the book he returns to the contemplation of the universe, the fixed stars, the planets, and finally the earth itself:

'So that this *Heaven* and *Earth*,[3] being themselves and all between them, is this World; the common house and City of Gods and men, in *Cicero*'s words;[4] and the corporeal and visible image and son of the invisible God, in the description of the *Academicks*: which being but one, (for *Universum est omnia versa in unum*) hath been the subject of Gods labor, and providence, and delight, perchance almost six thousand

[1] Grierson, i. 256–7.
[2] Ibid. 247 (*A Funerall Elegie*, 67–70).
[3] A reference to the text on which Donne is meditating, Genesis 1. 1: 'In the beginning God created Heaven and Earth.'
[4] Cicero, *De Natura Deorum*, lib. ii. c. 6.

years; whose uppermost first moving Orbe is too swift for our thoughts to overtake, if it dispatch in every hour three thousand times the compass of the Earth [marginal reference 'Gilbert de Magn' l. 6. c. 3.], and this exceeds fifteen thousand miles.[1] In whose firmament are scattered more *Eyes* (for our use, not their owne) then any cyphers can esteeme or expresse. For, how weake a stomack to digest knowledge, or how strong and misgovern'd faith against common sense hath he, that is content to rest in their number of 1022 Stars?[2] whose nearer regions are illustrated with the Planets, which work so effectually upon man, that they have often stop'd his further search, and been themselves by him deified. . . . Of the glory of which (i.e. the world), and the inhabitants of it, we shall best end in the words of *Sirach*'s Son,[3] *When we have spoken much, we cannot attain unto them; but the sum of all is, that God is all.*'[4]

Donne goes on to claim that the true possessor of the earth is not the King of Spain, though it is said that 'the Sun cannot hide himself from his Eye, nor shine out of his Dominions', nor the Sultan of Turkey, nor any other potentate, however wide his sway, but it is the wise man, who uses the world without setting his heart upon it, and sees himself as the tenant who holds it in trust from God, the true owner.

'What are these [i.e. kings and princes] our fellow-ants, our fellow-durt, our fellow-nothings, compared to that God whom they make but their pattern? And how little have any of these, compared to the whole Earth? whose hills, though they erect their heads beyond the Country of Meteors, and set their foot, in one land, and cast their shadow into another, are but as warts upon our [*read*, her] face: And

[1] Coffin, op. cit., p. 84, n. 54, comments on this passage and translates the words of Gilbert in his *De Magnete* (VI. iii. 218) thus: 'Leaving out the ninth sphaere, if the convexity of the *Primum Mobile* be duly estimated in proportion to the rest of the sphaeres, the vault of the *Primum Mobile* must in one hour run through as much space as is comprised in 3000 great circles of the Earth, for in the vault of the firmament it would complete more than 1800.'

[2] Dr. Jessopp was the first to point out that here also Donne is following Gilbert. The Ptolemaic catalogue of stars gave 1,022 as the total number. This passage should be compared with Donne's attack in *Biathanatos*, p. 146, on '*Aristotles* Schollers' who go on maintaining that the heavens are inalterable, in spite of the discovery of new stars.

[3] Ecclesiasticus xliii. 27.

[4] *Essays in Divinity*, pp. 69–71.

her vaults, and caverns, the bed of the winds, and the secret streets and passages of al rivers, and Hel it self, though they [marg. ref. Munster l. 1. c. 16.] afford it three thousand great miles, are but as so many wrinkles, and pock-holes.'[1]

This passage is closely linked with a great passage in *The first Anniversary*, 286–301, in which we have the same reflection that in comparison with the whole extent of the earth, the highest hills and the deepest caverns are but 'warts' and 'pock-holes':

> But keepes the earth her round proportion still?
> Doth not a Tenarif, or higher Hill
> Rise so high like a Rocke, that one might thinke
> The floating Moone would shipwracke there, and sinke? . . .
> If under all, a Vault infernall bee,
> (Which sure is spacious, except that we
> Invent another torment, that there must
> Millions into a straight hot roome be thrust)
> Then solidnesse, and roundnesse have no place.
> Are these but warts, and pock-holes in the face
> Of th' earth?[2]

In the body of the *Essays in Divinity*, as distinct from the prayers, there is very little affinity with *La Corona* and the *Holy Sonnets*. The *Essays* are for the most part impersonal, while the *Divine Poems* are intensely personal, the record of Donne's inner strife. There is, however, one link which may be mentioned. The *Holy Sonnets* draw on the apocalyptic imagery of the Book of Revelation for their background of 'the round earth's imagin'd corners',[3] the angels' trumpets,[4] the rising of the dead from earth and sea,[5] the dyeing of souls in Christ's blood which makes them white,[6] the description of Christ as 'the Lamb slain from the foundation

[1] Ibid., p. 74. See also *LXXX Sermons*, 73. 747, where there is a reference to the same passage in Sebastian Munster's *Cosmographia* which inspired the conjectures about hell in *The first Anniversary*.

[2] Grierson, i. 240.

[3] *Holy Sonnets*, vii. 1, see Rev. vii. 1: 'I saw four Angels standing on the four corners of the Earth.'

[4] Ibid. 1, 2, and Rev. viii. 2, 6–12.

[5] Ibid. 2–7, and Rev. xx. 13, 14.

[6] Ibid. iv. 13, 14, and Rev. vii. 14.

of the world'.[1] Similarly the *Essays in Divinity* open with a reference to Rev. iii. 7, and continue with references on page 31 to Rev. i. 8, on page 61 to 'the last great fire' (Rev. xx. 9, 10, 14, 15), on page 63, 'some have prayed to have *Hils fall upon them*' (Rev. vi. 16), on page 113 to the '*Multitude in white before the Lamb, which none could number*', and the '*number of them which were sealed 144,000*' (Rev. vii. 4, 9), and on page 168 to the Last Judgement (Rev. xx. 11–13). Donne had a special affection for the Book of Revelation, and preached a number of sermons on texts taken from it (e.g. *LXXX Sermons*, nos. 19 and 44; *Fifty Sermons*, nos. 4 and 32).

In the prayers found in the *Essays*, on the other hand, there is a kinship of spirit with the *Holy Sonnets*. Here, in prosaic language,[2] is that plea to God for an overpowering access of grace which shall overcome the stubbornness of Donne's will—a plea which reaches its finest expression in the intensity of *Holy Sonnet* XIV: 'Batter my heart, three-person'd God.'

While the book has many links with Donne's previous works, it marks at the same time a new departure. It is the first of the definitely theological works, the precursor of the *Sermons* and the *Devotions*. It lays down, though somewhat tentatively, the lines of Donne's later thought. The universe is to be seen in relation to God, otherwise the perspective will be distorted. The world is God's world, and is therefore no longer 'this rotten world', as Donne had called it in *The first Anniversary*, but 'this glorious world', as he now terms it. We hear nothing in the *Essays* of the decay and disillusionment which occupy so much of the *Anniversaries*. Donne is absorbed in studying the eternal purpose of God in the world, and in contemplating the mercy, power, and justice of God. As yet we have no discussion of those distinctively Christian doctrines of the Incarnation and the Atonement, which were to occupy so large a place in the Sermons. These are implicit in much of the argument, but

[1] *Holy Sonnets*, xvi. 5, 6, and Rev. xiii. 8.

[2] *Essays*, p. 217. See also the parallel between *Holy Sonnets*, ii. 7, 8 and *Essays*, p. 219, and between *Holy Sonnets*, xix. 1–11 and *Essays*, p. 221.

for the moment Donne is concerned with God as the Creator of the Universe.

There are a number of close verbal parallels between the *Essays* and some undated sermons, which probably belong to the early years of Donne's ministry. Thus the discussion of God's revelation of Himself by name, which occupies pages 44–5 of the *Essays*, is reproduced fairly closely in a sermon on one of the penitential Psalms. The passage in the *Essays* begins with a quotation from Aquinas (marginal reference 'Aq. 1. q. 13. Ar. 1'):

'So that it is truly said, there is no name given by man to God, *Ejus essentiam adaequatè representans*. And *Hermes*[1] says humbly and reverently, *Non spero*, I cannot hope, that the maker of all Majesty, can be call'd by any one name, though compounded of many. I have therefore sometimes suspected, that there was some degree of pride, and overboldness, in the first naming of God; the rather, because I marke, that the first which ever pronounced the name, *God*, was the Divell; and presently the woman; who in the next chapter proceeded further, and first durst pronounce that sacred and mystick name of foure letters. For when an Angell did but Ministerially represent God wrestling with *Jacob*, he reproves *Jacob*, for asking his name; *Cur quaeris nomen meum?* And so also to *Manoah*, *Why askest thou my Name*, *quod est mirabile?* And God, to dignify that Angell which he promises to lead his people, says *Fear him*, *provoke him not*, etc. *For my Name is in him*; but he tels them not what it is. But since, necessity hath enforced, and Gods will hath revealed some names. For in truth, we could not say this, God cannot be named, except God could be named.'

'God is come nearer to us then to others, when we know his Name. For though it be truly said in the Schoole, that no name can be given to God, *Ejus essentiam adaequatè repraesentans*, No one name can reach to the expressing of all that God is; And though *Trismegistus* doe humbly, and modestly, and reverently say, *Non spero*, it never fell into my thought, nor into my hope, that the maker and founder of all Majesty, could be circumscribed, or imprisoned by any one name, though a name compounded and complicated of many names, as the Rabbins have made one name of God, of all his names in the Scriptures; Though *Iacob* seeme to have been rebuked *for asking Gods*

[1] The marginal reference is '*Dial. Asclep.*' It was probably from the works of Patricius (Fran. Patrizzi, 1529–97) that Donne derived his knowledge of the works attributed to the fabled Hermes Trismegistus.

name, when he wrestled with him; And so also the Angel which was to do a miraculous worke . . . would not permit *Manoah* to enquire after his name, *Because*, as he sayes there, *that name was secret and wonderfull*; And though God himselfe, to dignifie and authorize that *Angel*, which he made his Commissioner, and the Tutelar and Nationall Guide of his people, sayes of that *Angel*, to that people, *Feare him, provoke him not, for my Name is in him*, and yet did not tell them, what that name was; Yet certainly, we could not so much as say, God cannot be named, except we could name God by some name; we could not say, God hath no name, except God had a name; for that very word, *God*, is his name.'[1]

In the same sermon there is another passage in which the argument of the *Essays* is reproduced in almost identical words. It is too long to quote in full, but it begins in the *Essays* with the words, 'This is the Name, which the *Jews* stubbornly deny ever to have been attributed to the *Messias* in the Scriptures',[2] and in the sermon, 'This is that name which the Jews falsly, but peremptorily . . . deny ever to have been attributed to the *Messias*, in the Scriptures.'[3]

An undated sermon preached at Lincoln's Inn, and therefore belonging to the earlier part of Donne's ministry, contains a passage in which a verse of Canticles is applied, as it had been in the *Essays*, to the divisions of the Christian Church, and Donne's longing for unity.[4] The earliest of Donne's sermons which we possess, that preached at Greenwich on 30 April 1615, has a passage which is closely parallel to a passage in the *Essays in Divinity*. In the *Essays* we read:

'In the first constitution of the *Roman* Empire . . . they easily foresaw, that men would soon decline and stray into a chargeable and sumptuous worship of their Gods; And therefore they resisted it with this law, *Deos frugi colunto*. This moderated their sacrifices. . . .'[5]

In the *XXVI Sermons* we read:

'And whereas the Heathens needed laws to restrain them, from an

[1] *LXXX Sermons*, 50. 501. The marginal references are to Gen. 32. 29, Judges 13. 18, and Exodus 23. 20, references which are also found in the margin of the parallel passage of the *Essays*.

[2] *Essays in Divinity*, pp. 47–9.

[3] *LXXX Sermons*, 50. 502.

[4] *Essays in Divinity*, p. 112, and *Fifty Sermons*, 21. 183.

[5] *Essays in Divinity*, p. 143.

expensive, and wastful worship of their Gods, every man was so apt to exceed in sacrifices and such other religious duties, til that law, *Deus* (read, *Deos*) *frugi Colunto* Let men be thrifty and moderate in religious expenses, was enacted. . . .'[1]

These are merely samples of the continuity of thought and expression between the *Essays* and the *Sermons*, and they could be multiplied almost indefinitely.

The *Essays in Divinity* form a duodecimo volume with the collation A^8, B–K^{12}, L^4. Signature A 1 is blank, and remains intact in the Bodleian copy. A 2 is occupied by the title, which runs thus:

> 'Essayes in Divinity; By the late Dr Donne, Dean of St Paul's. Being Several Disquisitions, Interwoven with Meditations and Prayers: Before he entred into Holy Orders. Now made publick by his son J. D. D^r of the Civil Law. London, Printed by T. M. for Richard Marriot, and are to be sold at his Shop in St Dunstan's Church-yard Fleet-street. 1651.'

Signatures A 3–A 7 originally contained the dedication 'To the Great Example of Honour and Devotion, Sir H. Vane, Junior'. The address, 'To the Reader', follows on A 8.

In this form the book was published early in 1651/2, for Thomason bought his copy on 11 January.[2] John Donne the younger evidently thought it politic to cancel the dedication to Vane and reissue the book later in 1652 in company with the *Paradoxes, Problemes*, which he dedicated to Francis Lord Newport. In this issue the leaves containing the original dedication are omitted, and the 'Address to the Reader' follows the title-page, being pasted on the edge of a cancelled leaf. The text begins with pagination on B 1, and occupies 213 pages. It is followed by four prayers, which occupy eleven pages.

The juxtaposition of the *Essays* and the *Paradoxes* is sufficiently startling, and in reality they are separate publications, the *Essays* having been issued by Richard Marriott,

[1] *XXVI Sermons*, II. 160.

[2] The Thomason copy in the British Museum (shelf-mark E. 1362) lacks signatures A 3 and A 6. Dr. Jessopp used a perfect copy for his reprint of 1855. Worcester College, Oxford, possesses a perfect copy.

and the *Paradoxes* by Humphrey Moseley; but it is plain from the dedication to Lord Newport that the younger Donne intended them to form one volume. He stated that the book contained 'the *Essays* of *two Ages*, where you may see the *quicknesse* of the *first*, and the *firmness* of the latter. . . . Here then you have the *entertainment* of the Authors *Youth*; and the *Assumption* of his *Wit* when it was employed in more *Heavenly* things.'

In 1855 Dr. Augustus Jessopp produced an edition of the *Essays* with introduction and notes. It was published in London by John Tupling.

The *Essays* take the first verses of Genesis and Exodus respectively as their two chief topics for meditation, but Donne could never confine himself to exposition of particular texts of Scripture without considering the wider questions of philosophy and theology which might be raised. Thus he begins the book by meditating on the first verse of Genesis, 'In the Beginning God created Heaven and Earth', and his first reflection is that true humility does not preclude a reverent inquiry into the ways of God:

'I do not therefore sit at the door, and meditate upon the threshold, because I may not enter further; For he which is *holy and true, and hath the key of David, and openeth and no man shutteth, and shutteth and no man openeth;* hath said to all the humble in one person, *I have set before thee an open door, and no man can shut it, for thou hast a little strength.* And the holy Scriptures, signified in that place, as they have these properties of a well provided Castle, that they are easily defensible, and safely defend others. So they have also this, that to strangers they open but a litle wicket, and he that will enter, must stoop and humble himselfe. To reverend Divines, who by an ordinary calling are Officers and Commissioners from God, the great Doors are open. Let me with *Lazarus* lie at the threshold, and beg their crums. *Discite à me*, sayes our blessed Saviour, *Learn of me*, as Saint *Augustine* enlarges it well, not to do Miracles, nor works exceeding humanity; but, *quia mitis sum*; learn to be humble. His humility, to be like us, was a Dejection; but ours, to be like him, is our chiefest exaltation; and yet none other is required at our hands. Where this Humility is, *ibi Sapientia.* Therfore it is not such a groveling, frozen, and stupid Humility, as should quench the activity of our understanding, or make us neglect the Search of those Secrets of God, which are accessible. For, Humility, and Studiousnesse, (as it is opposed to curiosity, and transgresses not her bounds) are so near of kin, that they are both agreed to be limbes and members of one vertue, *Temperance*.'[1]

After a further meditation in this strain, Donne divides his subject thus:

'Before we consider each stone of this threshold, which are 1. The *time*, *In the beginning*: 2. The *person*, *God*: 3. The *Action*, *He created*: And 4. the *Work*, *Heaven and Earth*; we will speak of two or three other things, so many words. Of the *Whole Book*; Of the *Author* of those first 5 Books; And of this *first book*.'[2]

In the first of these subdivisions, which Donne entitles '*Of the Bible*', he compares the Bible with God's other books, the Book of Life, the knowledge of which is sealed from man, and the Book of Creatures, or Nature, of which he quotes the opinion of Raymond of Sabund (or Sebund, as Donne calls him) that there is enough in it 'to teach us all particularities of Christian Religion', and that it 'in this, is safer then the Bible it self, that it cannot be falsified by Hereticks'.[3] Donne qualifies this estimate of the Book of Creatures by admitting that Sebund may be 'too abundant' in his praise, and by remarking that while philosophy may teach us the Unity of the Godhead, only the Bible can show us the Trinity. After a comparison of the Bible with the books of philosophers, and with the Koran and the Talmud, he decides that it is 'the only legible book of life'.

In the next subdivision, '*Of Moses*', Donne gives a curious display of learning in discussing whether Moses can be considered the earliest author whose works we possess, or whether Zoroaster or Hermes Trismegistus must be reckoned before him. Donne says of Zoroaster that Epiphanius places

[1] *Essays in Divinity* (1651), pp. 1–3.

[2] Ibid., p. 4.

[3] Ibid., pp. 7, 8. Donne gives only a qualified approval to these opinions of Sebund, who was a Spanish philosopher of the late fourteenth and early fifteenth century. He was born at Barcelona and lectured in theology and medicine at Toulouse. His great work was the *Liber naturae sive creaturarum*, in which he declared that the book of nature and the Bible were both divine revelations, the one general, the other specific. He is now best known by Montaigne's 'Apologie' for him in book ii, chap. xii of the *Essais*.

him in Nembrot's (i.e. Nimrod's) time, and Eusebius in Abraham's, 'since his language is *Chaldaick*, his works miraculously great, (for his Oracles are twenty hundred thousand verses) and his phrase more express, and clear, and liquid, in the Doctrine of the Trinity, then *Moses*. For where sayes this, as the other, [*Toto mundo lucet Trias, cujus Monas est princeps?*]'[1] Donne also shows his intimate acquaintance with the Trismegistic literature, and with the critical questions which had already been raised in connexion with it:

> 'From whence shall we say that *Hermes Trismegistus* sucked his not only Divinity, but Christianity? in which no Evangelist, no Father, no Councell is more literall and certain. Of the fall of Angels, Renovation of the world by fire, eternity of punishments, his *Asclepius* is plaine. Of Regeneration who sayes more then [*Nemo servari potest ante regenerationem, & regenerationis generator est Dei filius, homo unus?*] Of imputed Justice, with what Autor would he change this sentence, [*Justificati sumus in Justitia absente?*] Of our corrupt will, and Gods providence he says, [*Anima nostra relicta à Deo, eligit corpoream naturam; at electio ejus est secundùm providentiam Dei.*] To say with *Goropius*, that there was no such man, because the publick pillars and statues in which were engraved morall Institutions were called *Hermæ*, is improbable, to one who hath read *Patricius* his answers to him. And if it be true which *Buntingus* in his Chronology undisputably assumes, that he was the Patriarch *Joseph*, as also that *Goropius* confounds *Zoroaster* and *Japhet*, then *Moses* was not the first Author. But *Hermes* his naming of Italy, and the 12. Constellations in the Zodiaque, are Arguments and impressions of a later time. To unentangle our selvs in this perplexity, is more labour then profit, or perchance possibility.'[2]

Donne decides that in the face of so disputed a question it is best merely to affirm that God was the author of the Decalogue, and that Moses was the earliest of the sacred writers, and to give a later place to 'the Divine and learned book of *Job*', which 'hath somwhat a Greek taste', and to end this inquiry by remembering that as 'it was God which hid *Moses*'s body, And the Divell which laboured to reveal it', so there are some things 'which the Author of light hides from us, and the prince of darkness strives to shew to us;

[1] *Essays in Divinity* (1651), pp. 17, 18. The square brackets are Donne's.
[2] Ibid., pp. 18, 19.

but with no other light, then his firebrands of Contention, and curiosity'.[1]

In the next essay, '*Of Genesis*', Donne refers to Pico Mirandola,[2] 'happier in no one thing in this [? his] life, then in the Author which writ it to us', i.e. Sir Thomas More, Donne's famous kinsman. Pico, by following the rules of the Cabbalists, had wrung a summary of the Christian religion out of the first verse of Genesis. Though the ingenuity of such an interpretation interested Donne, his sound sense obliged him to reject it.

> 'But since our merciful God hath afforded us the whole and intire book, why should wee tear it into rags, or rent the seamless garment? ... To put him (Moses) in a wine-presse, and squeeze out Philosophy and particular Christianitie, is a degree of that injustice, which all laws forbid, to torture a man, *sine indiciis aut sine probationibus*.'[3]

In the next essay, Donne begins his meditation on the substance of the text (Genesis i. 1) by a prayer based on the first four chapters of the *Confessions* of his favourite author, St. Augustine:

> 'In the Beginning whereof, O onely Eternall God, of whose being, beginning, or lasting, this beginning is no period, nor measure; which art no Circle, for thou hast no ends to close up; which art not within this *All*, for it cannot comprehend thee; nor without it, for thou fillest it; nor art it thy self, for thou madest it; which having decreed from all eternity, to do thy great work of Mercy, our Redemption in the fulnesse of time, didst now create *time* it selfe to conduce to it; and madest thy glory and thy mercy equal thus, that though thy glorious work of Creation were first, thy mercifull work of Redemption was greatest. Let me in thy beloved Servant *Augustine's* own words, when with an humble boldnesse he begg'd the understanding of this passage, say, *Moses writ this, but is gon from me to thee; if he were here, I would hold him, and beseech him for thy sake, to tell me what he meant. If he spake Hebrew, he would frustrate my hope; but if Latine, I should comprehend him. But from whence should I know that he said true? Or when*

[1] Ibid., pp. 20, 21.

[2] Pico Mirandola (1463–94) was the pupil and friend of Ficino, the translator of Plato and Plotinus, and was also an oriental scholar who took a deep interest in the occult teaching of the Cabbala. Walton in his *Life of Donne* compares Donne and Pico as prodigies of youthful learning.

[3] *Essays*, pp. 22–4. I follow Jessopp in reading *sine* for *semi*.

I knew it, came that knowledge from him? No, for within me, within me there is a truth, not Hebrew, nor Greek, nor Latin, nor barbarous; which without organs, without noyse of Syllables, tels me true, and would enable me to say confidently to Moses, Thou say'st true.'[1]

He then turns to St. Thomas Aquinas, whom he calls 'another instrument and engine of thine, whom thou hadst so enabled, that nothing was too minerall nor centrick for the search and reach of his wit', and quotes the decision of the *Summa Theologiæ*: '*That it is an Article of our Belief, that the world began.*'[2] He also compares this use of the phrase 'In the beginning', in this first verse of the first book of the Bible, with the different use made of it in the first verse of the Gospel of St. John, 'which we know to be last written of all',[3] where the reference is not to time but to eternity.

He next discusses the date of the Creation, and comes to no certain conclusion.

'That then this Beginning *was*, is matter of *faith*, and so, infallible. *When* it was, is matter of *reason*, and therefore various and perplex'd. In the Epistle of *Alexander the Great* to his Mother, remembred by *Cyprian* and *Augustin*, there is mention of 8000. years. The *Caldeans* have delivered observations of 470000 years. And the *Egyptians* of 100000. The *Chineses* vex us at this day, with irreconciliable accounts.'[4]

He ends the essay with a noble passage which anticipates some of the harmonies of Sir Thomas Browne's meditations on the age of the world in *Urn Burial*:

'Truly, the *Creation* and the *last Judgement*, are the *Diluculum* and *Crepusculum*, the *Morning* and the *Evening* twi-lights of the long day of this world. Which times, though they be not utterly dark, yet they are but of uncertain, doubtfull, and conjecturall light. Yet not equally; for the break of the day, because it hath a succession of more and more light, is clearer then the shutting in, which is overtaken with more and more darknesse; so is the birth of the world more discernable then the death, because upon this God hath cast more clouds: yet

[1] *Essays*, pp. 26, 27.

[2] *Summa Theol.*, pt. i, Quaest. xlvi, art. ii. 'Utrum mundum incoepisse sit ar ticulusfidei (Affirm.).' In the margin of the *Essays* the reference is wrongly given as part ii.

[3] *Essays*, p. 29.

[4] Ibid., p. 33.

since the world in her first infancy did not speak to us at all (by any Authors;) and when she began to speak by *Moses*, she spake not plain, but diversly to divers understandings; we must return again to our strong hold, *faith*, and end with this, *That this Beginning was, and before it, Nothing*. It is elder then darknesse, which is elder then light; And was before Confusion, which is elder then Order, by how much the universall Chaos preceded forms and distinctions. A beginning so near *Eternity*, that there was no *Then*, nor a minite of *Time* between them. Of which, Eternity could never say, *To morrow*, nor speak as of a future thing, because this *Beginning* was the first point of time, before which, whatsoever God did, he did it uncessantly and unintermittingly; which was but the *generation of the Son*, and *procession of the Spirit*, and *enjoying one another*; Things, which if ever they had ended, had begun; And those be terms incompatible with Eternity. And therefore Saint Augustin says religiously and exemplarily,[1] *If one ask me what God did before this beginning, I will not answer, as another did merrily, He made Hell for such busie inquirers: But I will sooner say, I know not, when I know not, then answer that, by which he shall be deluded which asked too high a Mystery, and he be praysed, which answered a lie.*'[2]

In the next essay, '*Of God*', Donne compares the knowledge of God derived from reason and natural religion with the immediate knowledge of Him derived from faith. He deals tenderly with those who seek God in nature, though he maintains that faith is the surer guide:

'Men which seek God by reason, and naturall strength, (though we do not deny common notions and generall impressions of a soveraign power) are like Mariners which voyaged before the invention of the Compass, which were but Costers,[3] and unwillingly left the sight of the land. Such are they which would arrive at God by this world, and contemplate him onely in his Creatures, and seeming Demonstration. Certainly, every Creature shewes God, as a glass, but glimeringly and transitorily, by the frailty both of the receiver, and beholder: Our selves have his Image, as Medals, permanently and preciously delivered. But by these meditations we get no further, then to know what he *doth*, not what he *is*. But as by the use of the Compass, men safely

[1] *Confessions*, xi. 12. [2] *Essays*, pp. 34–6.

[3] i.e. coasters, sailors who keep near the coast. The word occurs in the form 'Coasters' in *Pseudo-Martyr*, p. 133, where the same metaphor of the improvement in navigation made by the invention of the compass is given a different application.

dispatch *Vlysses* dangerous ten years travell in so many dayes, and have found out a new world richer then the old; so doth Faith, as soon as our hearts are touched with it, direct and inform it in that great search of the discovery of Gods Essence, and the new *Hierusalem*, which Reason durst not attempt. And though the faithfullest heart is not ever directly, & constantly upon God, but that it somtimes descends also to Reason; yet it is [not] thereby so departed from him, but that it still looks towards him, though not fully to him: as the Compass is ever Northward, though it decline, and have often variations towards East, and West. By this faith, as by reason, I know, that God is all that which all men can say of all Good; I beleeve he is somewhat which no man can say nor know. For, *si scirem quid Deus esset, Deus essem*. For all acquired knowledg is by degrees, and successive; but God is impartible, and only faith which can receive it all at once, can comprehend him.'[1]

Donne then considers the imperfection of all definitions of the nature of God, whether by negations, such as that 'God is that which cannot be named, cannot be comprehended', or by concrete terms which admit of comparison, such as that He is Good, Just, Wise, by superlatives as that He is the best, or by abstractions, such as that He is Goodness. He shows that the heathen were in error in exalting every attribute of God into a separate deity, and that the anthropomorphism of the Scriptures does not fully express Him—'too particular and restrain'd are all those descents of God in his word, when he speaks of a body, and of passions, like ours'—and that the same objection applies to 'their reverend silence, who have expressed God in Hieroglyphicks, ever determining in some one power of God, without larger extent',[2] while the practice of the Roman Church, which exalts the saints into intermediaries between man and God, does not satisfy the craving of the human soul. He concludes with a passage which admirably expresses his own attitude of mind towards so great a subject—an attitude which is devout, tolerant, and essentially that of a mystic.

'Thou shalt not then, O my faithfull soul, despise any of these erroneous pictures, thou shalt not destroy, nor demolish their buildings; but thou shalt not make them thy foundation. For thou beleevest more then they pretend to teach, and art assur'd of more

[1] *Essays*, pp. 37–9. [2] Ibid., p. 42.

then thou canst utter. For if thou couldest express all which thou seest of God, there would be somthing presently beyond that. Not that God growes, but faith doth. For, God himself is so unutterable, that he hath a name which we cannot pronounce.'[1]

The next two or three essays have less general interest, though they show Donne's knowledge of Hebrew and his stores of unfamiliar learning. He discusses the pronunciation of the Name of God—the Tetragrammaton—and decides against the form Jehovah, which is used in the Authorized Version. He rejects the argument which deduces a proof of the Trinity from the employment of the plural form *Elohim* with a singular verb in this verse of Genesis, calling it an 'extortion and beggarly wresting of Scriptures', and deciding that he is convinced 'by collation of many places in the Scriptures, that it is a meer Idiotism',[2] i.e. idiom. In discussing whether the world was created out of nothing, Donne follows the arguments of St. Augustine and St. Thomas Aquinas, and the influence of Plato's *Timaeus* is also perceptible.[3]

'To make our approches nearer, and batter effectually, let him that will not confess this Nothing, assign somthing of which the world was made. If it be of itself, it is God: and it is God, if it be of God; who is also so simple, that it is impossible to imagine any thing before him of which he should be compounded, or any workman to do it. For to say, as one doth,[4] that the world might be eternall, and yet not be God, because Gods eternity is all at once, and the worlds successive, will not reconcile it; for yet, some part of the world must be as old as God, and infinite things are equall, and equalls to God are God. The greatest Dignity which we can give this world, is, that the *Idœa* of it is eternall, and was ever in God. . . .'[5]

The last section of these meditations on Genesis deals with 'Heaven and Earth', the work which God created. After enumerating the interpretations of the words given by various schools of commentators, Donne contemplates the

[1] Ibid., p. 43. [2] Ibid., p. 52.

[3] Miss Ramsay (op. cit., pp. 140–8) summarizes the chief medieval theories on this subject, and discusses Donne's indebtedness to earlier thinkers.

[4] Here Donne adds a marginal reference to Boethius, *De Consolatione*, 5, pros. 6.

[5] *Essays*, pp. 57–8.

glory of the visible world in a passage which has already been quoted on page 209.

Yet this glorious world is to be loved in due measure, and with a first regard to God its Creator.

'To love it too much, is to love it too little; as overpraysing is a kind of libelling. . . . Ambassadours in their first accesses to Princes, use not to apply themselves, nor divert their eye upon any, untill they have made their first Dispatch, and find themselves next the Prince; and after acknowledg and respect the beams of his Majesty in the beauties and dignities of the rest. So should our soul do, between God, and his Creatures; for what is there in this world immediately and primarily worthy our love, which (by acceptation) is worthy the love of God? *Earth* and *Heaven* are but the foot-stool of God: But *Earth it self* is but the foot-ball of wise men.'[1]

Donne ends this first division of the book with a prayer which sums up the meditations in which he has been engaged. As Gosse quoted only certain passages, which seemed to him to support his theory, I subjoin the whole prayer, so that the reader may be able to see for himself how closely its thought is connected with the argument of the preceding sections of the book:

'O Eternall and Almighty power, which being infinite, hast enabled a limited creature, Faith, to comprehend thee; And being, even to Angels but a passive Mirror and looking-glasse, art to us an Active guest and domestick, (for thou hast said, *I stand at the door and knock, if any man hear me, and open the doore, I will come in unto him, and sup with him, and he with me*), and so thou dwellest in our hearts; And not there only, but even in our mouths; for though thou beest greater, and more remov'd, yet humbler and more communicable then the Kings of *Egypt*, or *Roman* Emperours, which disdain'd their particular distinguishing Names, for *Pharaoh* and *Caesar*, names of confusion; hast contracted thine immensity, and shut thy selfe within Syllables, and accepted a Name from us; O keep and defend my tongue from misusing that Name in lightnesse, passion, or falshood; and my heart, from mistaking thy Nature, by an inordinate preferring thy Justice before thy Mercy, or advancing this before that. And as, though thy self hadst no beginning thou gavest a beginning to all things in which thou wouldst be served and glorified; so, though this soul of mine, by which I partake thee, begin not now, yet let this minute, O God, this

[1] *Essays*, pp. 71–2.

happy minute of thy visitation, be the beginning of her conversion, and shaking away confusion, darknesse, and barrennesse; and let her now produce Creatures, thoughts, words, and deeds agreeable to thee. And let her not produce them, O God, out of any contemplation, or (I cannot say, *Idæa*, but) *Chimera* of my worthinesse, either because I am a man and no worme, and within the pale of thy Church, and not in the wild forrest, and enlightned with some glimerings of Naturall knowledge; but meerely out of Nothing: Nothing pre[e]xistent in her selfe, but by power of thy Divine will and word. By which, as thou didst so make Heaven, as thou didst not neglect Earth, and madest them answerable and agreeable to one another, so let my Soul's Creatures have that temper and Harmony, that they be not by a misdevout consideration of the next life, stupidly and trecherously negligent of the offices and duties which thou enjoynest amongst us in this life; nor so anxious in these, that the other (which is our better business, though this also must be attended) be the less endeavoured. Thou hast, O God, denyed even to Angells, the ability of arriving from one Extreme to another, without passing the mean way between. Nor can we pass from the prison of our Mothers womb, to thy palace, but we must walk (in that pace whereto thou hast enabled us) through the street of this life, and not sleep at the first corner, nor in the midst. Yet since my soul is sent immediately from thee, (let me for her return) rely, not principally, but wholly upon thee and thy word: and for this body, made of preordained matter, and instruments, let me so use the materiall means of her sustaining, that I neither neglect the seeking, nor grudge the missing of the Conveniencies of this life: And that for fame, which is a mean Nature between them, I so esteem opinion, that I despise not others thoughts of me, since most men are such, as most men think they be: nor so reverence it, that I make it alwayes the rule of my Actions. And because in this world my Body was first made, and then my Soul, but in the next my soul shall be first, and then my body, In my Exterior and morall conversation let my first and presentest care be to give them satisfaction with whom I am mingled, because they may be scandaliz'd, but thou, which seest hearts, canst not: But for my faith, let my first relation be to thee, because of that thou art justly jealous, which they cannot be. Grant these requests, O God, if I have asked fit things fitly, and as many more, under the same limitations, as are within that prayer which (As thy *Manna*, which was meat for all tasts, and served to the appetite of him which took it, and was that which every man would) includes all which all can aske, *Our Father which art, etc.*'[1]

[1] Ibid., pp. 76–80.

The second part of the book deals with the first verse of the first chapter of Exodus: 'Now these are the Names of the Children of Israel which came into Egypt.' Donne sees in this verse an epitome of the whole book of Exodus. He opens with a characteristic use of his favourite image of the circle:

> 'In this book our entrance is a *going out*: for *Exodus* is *Exitus*.[1] The Meditation upon Gods works is infinite; and whatsoever is so, is Circular, and returns into it selfe, and is every where beginning and ending, and yet no where either: Which the Jews (the children of God by his first spouse the *Law*, as we are by *Grace*, his second) express'd in their round Temples; for God himselfe is so much a Circle, as being every where without any corner, (that is, never hid from our Inquisition;) yet he is no where any part of a straight line, (that is, may not be directly and presently beheld and contemplated) but either we must seek his Image in his works, or his will in his words; which, whether they be plain or darke, are ever true, and guide us aright. For, as well the Pillar of *Cloud*, as that of *Fire*, did the Office of directing. Yea, oftentimes, where fewest Expositors contribute their helpes, the Spirit of God alone enlightens us best; for many lights cast many shadows, and since controverted Divinity became an occupation, the Distortions and violencing of Scriptures, by Christians themselves, have wounded the Scriptures more, then the old Philosophy or *Turcism*.'[2]

Donne feels that in thus meditating at length upon one short sentence he may seem to fall into the error of those over-subtle commentators 'who for ostentation and magnifying their wits, excerpt and tear shapeless and unsignificant rags of a word or two, from whole sentences, and make them obey their purpose in discoursing'. He condemns 'the curious refinings of the Allegoricall Fathers, which have made the Scriptures, which are stronge toyles, to catch and destroy the bore and bear which devast our Lords vineyard, fine cobwebs to catch flies',[3] and the practice of certain modern preachers who 'will attempt to feed miraculously great Congregations with a loafe or two, and a few fishes; that is, with two or three incoherent words of a sentence'. In his own choice of a text he seems to come dangerously near this

[1] The text has *Excitus*, clearly a misprint.

[2] *Essays*, pp. 81–2.

[3] Ibid., pp. 84–5.

practice, but he defends himself on the ground that he is pursuing a fixed plan, that of taking the beginning of each book in the Bible for the subject of a meditation, and also on the ground that this verse virtually comprehends the whole book of Exodus, which being a history of God's miraculous mercy to His own people, is summarized in the statement that from so small a number He propagated so great a nation. Donne describes his meditations as sermons, though they are written and not spoken. He quotes the words of Gerson, *Scriptor manu praedicat*, and continues:

'Though these lack thus much of Sermons, that they have no Auditory, yet as Saint *Bernard* did almost glory, that Okes and Beeches were his Masters, I shall be content that Okes and Beeches be my schollers, and witnesses of my solitary Meditations.'[1]

After a few general reflections on the book of Exodus as a whole, Donne proceeds to a consideration of the reasons why God is willing that those through whom He prepares His miracles should be named, and why they are differently named in different places. In his meditation on the transitory nature of human fame, Donne almost anticipates some sentences of Sir Thomas Browne's famous chapter in *Urn Burial*.

'Amongst men, all Depositaries of our Memories, all means which we have trusted with the preserving of our Names, putrifie and perish. Of the infinite numbers of the Medals of the Emperors, some one happy Antiquary, with much pain, travell, cost, and most faith, beleeves he hath recovered some one rusty piece, which deformity makes reverend to him, and yet is indeed the fresh work of an Impostor.

'The very places of the *Obeliscs*,[2] and *Pyramides* are forgotten, and the purpose why they were erected. Books themselves are subject to the mercy of the Magistrate: and as though the ignorant had not been enemie enough for them, the Learned unnaturally and treacherously contribute to their destruction, by rasure and mis-interpretation. . . . But Names honour'd with a place in this book, cannot perish, because the Book cannot. Next to the glory of having his name entred into the *Book of Life*, this is the second, to have been matriculated in this Register, for an example or instrument of good. *Lazarus* his name is enrolled, but the wicked rich mans omitted.'[3]

[1] Ibid., pp. 87–8. [2] '*Obelises*' in the text. [3] *Essays*, pp. 92–4.

In his meditation on the reasons for the different forms of the names here given to the Israelite patriarchs, Donne strays from the consideration of the particular point at issue to a question which always occupied an important place in his thoughts, the divisions of the Church of Christ. The passage gives a clearer and fuller exposition of Donne's own point of view than can be found elsewhere in his writings:

'I encline to think, that another usefull document arises from this admitting of variety; which seems to me to be this, that God in his eternall & ever-present omniscience, foreseeing that his universal, Christian, Catholick Church, imaged, and conceived, and begotten by him in his eternall decree, born and brought to light when he travail'd and labored in those bitter agonies and throes of his passion, nourced ever more delicately and preciously then any natural children . . . fore-seeing, I say, that this his dearly beloved Spouse, and Sister, and Daughter, the Church, should in her latter Age suffer many convulsions, distractions, rents, schisms, and wounds, by the severe and unrectified Zeal of many, who should impose necessity upon indifferent things, and oblige all the World to one precise forme of exterior worship, and Ecclesiastick policie; averring that every degree, and minute and scruple of all circumstances which may be admitted in either beleif or practice, is certainly, constantly, expressly, and obligatorily exhibited in the Scriptures; and that Grace, and Salvation is in this unity and no where else; his Wisdome was mercifully pleas'd, that those particular Churches, devout parts of the Universall, which, in our Age, keeping still the foundation and corner stone Christ Jesus, should piously abandon the spacious and specious super-edifications which the Church of *Rome* had built therupon, should from this variety of Names in the Bible it selfe, be provided of an argument, *That an unity and consonance in things not essentiall, is not so necessarily requisite as is imagined.* Certainly, when the Gentils were assum'd into the Church, they entred into the same fundamentall faith and religion with the Jews, as *Musculus* truly notes; and this conjunction in the roote and foundation, fulfill'd that which was said, *Fiet unum Ovile, & unus Pastor*, One fold, and one shepherd. For, by that before, you may see that all Christs sheep are not alwayes in one fold, *Other sheep have I also, which are not of this fold.* So, all his sheep are of one fold, that is, *under one Shepherd, Christ*; yet not of one fold, that is, not *in one place*, nor form. For, that which was strayed and alone, was his sheep; much more any flock which hearken together to his voice, his Word, and feed together upon his Sacraments. Therefore that Church from which we are by Gods Mercy escaped, because upon the foundation, which we yet embrace together, Redemption in Christ, they had built so many stories high, as the foundation was, though not destroyed, yet hid and obscured; And their Additions were of so dangerous a construction, and appearance, and misapplyableness, that to tender consciences they seem'd Idolatrous, and are certainly scandalous and very slippery, and declinable into Idolatry, though the Church be not in circumstantiall and deduced points, at unity with us, nor it self; (for, with what tragick rage do the Sectaries of *Thomas* and *Scotus* prosecute their differences? and how impetuously doth *Molinas* and his Disciples at this day, impugne the common doctrine of grace and freewill? And though these points be not immediately fundamentall points of faith, yet radically they are, and as neer the root as most of those things wherein we and they differ;) yet though we branch out *East* and *West*, that Church concurs with us in the root, and sucks her vegetation from one and the same ground, *Christ Jesus*; who, as it is in the *Canticle*, lies between the brests of his Church, and gives suck on both sides.[1] And of that Church which is departed from us, disunited by an opinion of a necessity that all should be united in one form, and that theirs is it, since they keep their right foot fast upon the Rock Christ, I dare not pronounce that she is not our Sister; but rather as in the same *Song of Solomon's*, *We have a little sister, and she hath no brests: if she be a wall, we will build upon her a silver palace.*[2] If therefore she be a wall, That is, *Because* she is a wall; for so *Lyra* expounds those words, as on her part, she shall be safer from ruine, if she apply her self to receive a *silver palace* of Order, and that Hierarchy which is most convenient and proportionall to that ground and state wherein God hath planted her; and she may not transplant her self: So shall we best conserve the integrity of our own body, of which she is a member, if we laboriously build upon her, and not tempestuously and ruinously demolish and annull her; but rather cherish and foment her vitall and wholsome parts, then either cut, or suffer them to rot or moulder off. As naturall, so politick bodies have *Cutem, & Cuticulam.* The little thin skin which covers al our body, may be broken without pain or danger, and may reunite it selfe, because it consists not of the chief and principiant parts. But if in the skin it self, there be any solution or division, which is seldome without drawing of blood, no art nor good disposition of Nature, can ever bring the parts together again, and restore the same substance, though it seem to the ey to have sodder'd it self. It will ever seem so much as a deforming Scar, but is in truth a breach. Outward Worship is this *Cuticula*: and integrity of

[1] Cant. i. 13.

[2] Cant. viii. 8, 9.

faith the skin it self. And if the first be touched with anything too corrosive, it will quickly pierce the other; and so Schism, which is a departure from obedience, will quickly become Heresie, which is a wilfull deflexion from the way of faith. Which is not yet, so long as the main skin is inviolate: for so long that Church which despises another Church, is it self no other then that of which the *Psalm* speakes, *Ecclesia Malignantium.* Thus much was to my understanding naturally occasioned and presented by this variety of Names in the Scriptures; For, if *Esau*, *Edom*, and *Seir* were but one man; *Jethro* and *Revel*, &c. but one man, which have no consonance with one another, and might thereby discredit and enervate any History but this, which is the fountain of truth; so Synagogue and Church is the same thing, and of the Church, *Roman* and *Reformed*, and all other distinctions of place, Discipline, or Person, but one Church, journying to one *Hierusalem*, and directed by one guide, Christ Jesus; In which, though this Unity of things not fundamentall, be not absolutely necesary, yet it were so comely and proportionall with the foundation it self, if it were at Unity in these things also, that though in my poor opinion, the form of Gods worship, established in the Church of *England* be more convenient, and advantageous then of any other Kingdome, both to provoke and kindle devotion, and also to fix it, that it stray not into infinite expansions and Subdivisions; (into the former of which, Churches utterly despoyl'd of Ceremonies, seem to me to have fallen; and the *Roman* Church, by presenting innumerable objects, into the later.) And though to all my thanksgivings to God, I ever humbly acknowledg, as one of his greatest Mercies to me, that he gave me my Pasture in this Park, and my milk from the brests of this Church, yet out of a fervent, and (I hope) not inordinate affection, even to such an Unity, I do zealously wish, that the whole catholick Church, were reduced to such Unity and agreement, in the form and profession Established, in any one of these Churches (though ours were principally to be wished) which have not by any additions destroyed the foundation and possibility of salvation in Christ Jesus; That then the Church, discharged of disputations, and misapprehensions, and this defensive warr, might contemplate Christ clearly and uniformely. For now he appears to her, as in *Cant.* 2. 9. *He standeth behind a wall, looking forth of the window, shewing himself through the grate.* But then, when all had one appetite, and one food, one nostrill and one purfume, the Church had obtained that which she then asked, *Arise ô North, and come ô South, and blow on my garden, that the spices thereof may flow out.*[1] For then, that *savour of life unto life* might allure

[1] Cant. iv. 16.

and draw those to us, whom our dissentions, more then their own stubborness with-hold from us.'[1]

The next section deals with the numbers of the Israelites who came into Egypt, and here Donne shows much ingenuity and a store of curious learning in reconciling the statements made here with those in Genesis and Acts. The mystical significance of various numbers always attracted his attention, and the number here mentioned, seventy, provides him with an opportunity of which he makes use, though he is careful not to dwell too long on this subject as being 'too Cabalistick and Pythagorick for a vulgar Christian', under which denomination he ranks himself, in contrast to those learned theologians who require 'a Meta-theology and super-divinity'[2] in order to dispute with philosophers and Jews.

From this Donne proceeds to a consideration of the Mercy, Power, Justice, and Judgement of God, 'of which, if nothing can be said new, nothing can be said too often'. By far the greater part of this last division of the book is occupied by Donne's meditation on the first of these attributes, the Mercy of God, which was to be the subject of many of the finest passages in the *Sermons*. His style does not rise here to the height of the great Christmas sermon of 1624, but he anticipates something of the delight expressed there in emphasizing the mercy of God as contrasted with His justice.

'Of all these four Elements *Mercy* is the uppermost and most Embracing. *Miserationes ejus super omnia opera ejus.* . . . His Mercy is infinite in Extent: for it is in all places; yea, where there is no place: And it is infinite in Duration; For as it never begun, (for the Ideating of this world, which was from everlasting, was a work of mercy) and as the interruptions which by acts of Justice it seemes to suffer here, discontinue it not, (for though God say, *For a moment in mine anger I hid my face from thee*; yet he adds there, *yet with everlasting Mercy have I had compassion on thee;*) so also is it reasonable to think, that it shall never have end.'[3]

This Mercy of God, so richly shown to man, must incline man to mercy towards his fellows.

[1] *Essays*, pp. 104–12. [2] Ibid., p. 129.
[3] Ibid., pp. 137–9.

'Now that we have removed the expensive dignifying[1] of images, and relicks, what other exercise is there left for our charity, then those nearer images both of God, and of our selves, the poore? *Be mercifull then, as your Father in heaven is mercifull.* . . . Let no greatness retard thee from giving, as though thou wert above want. . . . Let no smalnesse retard thee: if thou beest not a Cedar to help towards a palace, if thou beest not Amber, Bezoar, nor liquid gold, to restore Princes; yet thou art a shrub to shelter a lambe, or to feed a bird; or thou art a plantane, to ease a childs smart; or a grasse to cure a sick dog.'[2]

In this history of the Exodus God's mercy was shown towards the Israelites in bringing them into Egypt, in propagating them there, and in delivering them from Egypt. In considering the rapid growth of the Jewish nation in Egypt, Donne touches on the encouragement which great states have thought it advisable to give to the fathers of families in order that the population may not diminish, but he also defends those who have taken up a monastic life from the charge of neglecting their duty to the state.

'Of these men . . . I dare not conceive any hard opinion: For though we be all Gods tenants in this world, and freeholders for life, and are so bound amongst other duties, to keep the world in reparation, and leave it as well as we found it, (for, *ut gignamus geniti*) yet since we have here two employments, one to conserve this world, another to increase Gods Kingdome, none is to be accused, that every one doth not all, so all do all. . . . So, though every one should watch his own steps, and serve God in his vocation; yet there should be some, whose Vocation it should be to serve God; as all should do it, so some should do nothing else.'[3]

In considering the deliverance from Egypt, Donne turns for a few pages from the literal meaning of the story to the allegorical and spiritual interpretation.

'Only to paraphrase the History of this Delivery, without amplifying, were furniture and food enough for a meditation of the best perseverence, and appetite, and digestion; yea, the least word in the History would serve a long rumination. If this be in the bark, what is in the tree? If in the superficiall grass, the letter; what treasure is there in the hearty and inward Mine, the Mistick and retired sense?

[1] 'Dignising' in the text.
[2] *Essays*, pp. 144–5.
[3] Ibid., pp. 154–5.

Dig a little deeper, O my poor lazy soul, and thou shalt see that thou, and all mankind are delivered from an Egypt; and more miraculously then these.'[1]

We lay in bondage to the Devil, 'that great *Pharaoh*, whose Egypt all the world is by usurpation.' 'And then, camest thou, O Christ, thine own *Moses*, and deliveredst us; not by doing, but suffering; not by killing, but dying.' Then comes one of the few passages of intimate self-revelation on Donne's part to be found in these *Essays*: the prayer which has already been quoted on page 207.

God's mercy was also shown in the preservation of the Israelites in the desert, and here Donne makes use of the doctrine, to which reference is made in his poems and sermons,[2] that the soul of man is not immortal in itself, but only by preservation through the will of God.

'God hath made nothing which needs him not, or which would not instantly return again to nothing without his special conservation: Angels and our Souls are not delivered from this dependancy upon him. And therefore Conservation is as great a work of Power as Creation.'[3]

Donne then turns to a consideration of the Power of God, and here he sees clearly the many theological and philosophical difficulties involved in the idea of omnipotence. He takes up a position which is nearly that of many modern liberal theologians. God's omnipotence must be understood in a limited sense, and He delights not so much in the exercise of His power, as in that of His mercy and justice.

'Of all the wayes in which God hath expressed himselfe towards us, we have made no word which doth lesse signifie what we mean, then *Power*: for *Power*, which is but an ability to do, ever relates to some future thing: and God is ever a present, simple, and pure Act. But we think we have done much, and gone far, when we have made up the word *Omnipotence*, which is both wayes improper; for it is much too short, because *Omnipotence* supposes and confesses a matter and subject to work upon, and yet God was the same, when there was nothing. And then it over-reaches, and goes down-wards beyond God:

[1] Ibid., p. 164.
[2] e.g. *LXXX Sermons*, 27. 269; *Poems*, Grierson, i. 197 (note, ii. 160).
[3] *Essays*, pp. 168–9.

for God hath not, or is not such an Omnipotence, as can do all things; for though squeamish and tenderer men think it more mannerly to say, *This thing cannot be done*, then, *God cannot do this thing*; yet it is all one: And if that be an Omnipotence, which is limited with the nature of the worker, or with the congruity of the subject, other things may incroach upon the word *Omnipotent*; that is, they can do all things which are not against their nature, or the nature of the matter upon which they work. *Beza* therefore might well enough say, That God could not make a body without place; And *Prateolus* might truly enough infer upon that, that the *Bezanites* (as he calls them) deny omnipotence in God; for both are true. And therefore I doubt not, but it hath some mysterie, that the word *Omnipotence* is not found in all the Bible; nor *Omnipotent* in the New Testament.[1] And where it is in the Old, it would rather be interpreted *All-sufficient*, then *Almighty*; between which there is much difference. . . . So that, as yet our understanding hath found no word, which is well proportioned to that which we mean by *power of God*.'[2]

Donne proceeds to consider the question of miracles and here again, though he believes firmly in the truth of the miracles recorded in Exodus, his philosophical attitude is almost that of many modern thinkers. He analyses the difficulty inherent in the conception of a miracle as something contrary to the course of nature:

'*Nature* is the *Common law* by which God governs us, and *Miracle* is his *Prerogative*. For Miracles are but so many *Non-obstantes* upon Nature. And Miracle is not like prerogative in any thing more then in this, that no body can tell what it is. For first, Creation and such as that, are not Miracles, because they are not (to speak in that language) *Nata fieri per alium modum*.[3] And so, only that is Miracle, which might be done naturally, and is not so done. And then, lest we allow the Divell a power to do Miracles, we must say, that Miracle is *contra totam Naturam*, against the whole order and disposition of Nature. . . . I can change some naturall things (as I can make a stone fly upward) a Physician more, and the Divell more then he; but only God can change all. And after that is out of necessity established,[4] that

[1] Donne had evidently overlooked the use of the word in Rev. xix. 6.

[2] *Essays*, pp. 174–8.

[3] This and the following sentences are taken from St. Thomas Aquinas, *Summa Theol.*, i, qu. cv. 7–8 (Jessopp).

[4] Dr. Jessopp compares Hooker's treatment of this subject in the *Laws of Ecclesiastical Polity*, Bk. I, iii. 5.

Miracle is against the whole *Order* of Nature, I see not how there is left in God a power of Miracles. For, the Miracles which are produced to day, were determined and inserted into the body of the whole History of Nature (though they seem to us to be but interlineary and Marginall) at the beginning, and are as infallible and certain, as the most Ordinary and customary things. Which is evicted and approved by that which *Lactantius* says, and particularly proves, that all Christs Miracles were long before prophecied. So that truly nothing can be done against the Order of Nature. For, Saint *Augustine* says truly, That is Naturall to each thing, which God doth, from whom proceeds all Fashion, Number and Order of Nature: for that God, whose Decree is the Nature of every thing, should do against his own Decree, if he should do against Nature. As therefore if we understood all created Nature, nothing would be *Mirum* to us; so if we knew Gods purpose, nothing would be *Miraculum*.'[1]

Donne attaches but a slight value to miracles as evidence for faith.

'To discountenance then their (i.e. the Magicians') deceits, and withall to afflict the Land of *Egypt*, was the principall purpose of God in these Miracles: not to declare himself, or beget faith; for he doth not alwayes bind miracles to faith, nor faith to miracles. He will somtimes be believed without them; and somtimes spend them upon unbelievers; lest men should think their faith gave strength to his power. For though it be said, *Christ could do no great works in his own countrey, for their unbeliefe*: yet he did some there; which Saint *Hierom* sayes, was done, lest they should be excusable, having seen no Miracle: And he did not *many*, least, as *Theophylact* sayes, he should after many Miracles resisted, have been forced in justice to a severer punishment of them. But because the danger of beleeving false miracles is extreamly great, and the essentiall differences of false and true, very few, and very obscure . . . I encline to think, that God for the most part, works his miracles rather to shew his Power, then Mercy, and to terrifie enemies, rather then comfort his children. For miracles lessen the merit of faith.'[2]

He admits the possibility of a continuance of miracles in the Christian Church, but thinks that many of the stories of such miracles are merely pious frauds, which should be denounced.

[1] *Essays*, pp. 179–81.

[2] Ibid., pp. 184–6. Dr. Jessopp compares Sir Thos. Browne's *Religio Medici*, pt. i, sections ix and xxvii.

'God forbid I should discredit or diminish the great works that he hath done at the tombs of his Martyrs, or at the pious and devout commemoration of the sanctity and compassion of his most Blessed Mother. But to set her up a Banke almost in every good Town, and make her keep a shop of Miracles greater then her Sons, (for is it not so, to raise a childe, which was born dead, and had been buried seventeen days, to so small end?) (for it died again as soon as it was carried from her sight[1]) is fearfull and dangerous to admit. . . . And no hardnesse of heart is enough to justifie a toleration of these *devout deceits* and *holy lyes*, as they are often called amongst themselves. The Power of God, which we cannot name, needs not our help. And this very History (in expounding of which *Pererius* inculcates so often, *Non multiplicanda miracula*) which seems the principallest record of Gods Miracles, though literally it seem to be directed to his enemies, by often expressing his power; yet to his children it insinuates an Admonition, to beware of Miracles, since it tels them how great things the Divel did. . . . For God delights not so much in the exercise of his *Power*, as of his *Mercy* and *Justice*, which partakes of both the other: For *Mercy* is his *Paradise* and garden, in which he descends to walk and converse with man: *Power* his *Army* and *Arsenel*, by which he protects and overthrows: *Justice* his *Exchequer*, where he preserves his own Dignity, and exacts our Forfeitures.'[2]

Donne proceeds to consider the Justice of God, but here again he finds occasion to exalt Mercy above Justice:

'Even at first God intimated how unwillingly he is drawn to execute *Justice* upon transgressors; for he first exercised all the rest: *Mercy*, in purposing our Creation: *Power*, in doing it; and *Judgment*, in giving us a Law. . . . So that almost all Gods Justice is but Mercy: as all our Mercy is but Justice; for we are all mutuall debtors to one another; but he to none. Yea, both his *Nature*, and his *will* are so condition'd, as he cannot do Justice so much as man can. For, for his *will*, though he neither will nor can do any thing *against* Justice, he doth many things *beside* it. Nothing unjustly, but many things not justly: for he rewards beyond our Merits, and our sins are beyond his punishments. And then, we have exercise as well of Commutative Justice as Distributive; God only of the later, since he can receive nothing from us. And indeed, Distributive Justice in God, is nothing but Mercy. So that there is but one limb of Justice left to God, which is Punishment;

[1] In the margin Donne gives the reference: '*Miracula B. Virg. ab Anno* 1581 *ad* 1605. fo. 150.'

[2] *Essays*, pp. 187–90.

And of that, all the degrees on this side finall condemnation, are acts of Mercy. So that the *Vulture*, by which some of the Ancients figured *Justice*, was a just symbole of this Justice; for as that bird prayes onely upon Carcasses, and upon nothing which lives; so this Justice apprehends none but such as are dead and putrified in sin and impenitence.'[1]

'Our justification now consists not in a pacification of God, . . . but in the application of the merits of Christ to us.' 'We are bound at Gods tribunall to plead our pardon, and to pay the fees of contrition and penance.'[2] To inquire further into the manner of our justification is but a stumbling-block and a temptation. 'Almost all the ruptures in the Christian Church have been occasioned by such bold disputations *De Modo*.'[3] Leaving aside such over-curious inquiries we should rest on the contemplation of God's mingled justice and mercy, of which the rainbow after the Deluge was a symbol. Even the judgements on the Israelites and on the Egyptians recorded in Exodus had generally a merciful purpose. With one or two exceptions, 'it will scarce be found that any of the afflictions proceeded from meer Justice, but were rather as Physick, and had only a medicinall bitternesse in them.'[4]

Donne ends his meditations on the first verse of Exodus by considering the Judgements of God, first in a general sense, and then as expressed in the Law. The giving of the Law was a blessing to the Jews, since it in some measure restored them to the first light of Nature, and also prepared them for the coming of Christ. 'We are brought neerer home, and set in a fairer way then the Jews; though their and our Law differ not as diverse in species; but as a perfect and grown thing from an unperfect and growing.'[5]

The whole book concludes with four very beautiful prayers, which sum up Donne's meditations. The first of these is intensely personal, and applies the lessons of Exodus to his own case:

'O Eternall God, as thou didst admit thy faithfull servant *Abraham*, to make the granting of one petition an incouragement and rise to

[1] Ibid., pp. 190–2.
[2] Ibid., p. 193.
[3] Ibid., p. 195.
[4] Ibid., p. 199.
[5] Ibid., p. 206.

another, and gavest him leave to gather upon thee from fifty to ten; so I beseech thee, that since by thy grace, I have thus long meditated upon thee, and spoken of thee, I may now speak to thee. As thou hast enlightned and enlarged me to contemplate thy greatness, so, O God, descend thou and stoop down to see my infirmities and the Egypt in which I live; and (If thy good pleasure be such) hasten mine *Exodus* and deliverance, for I desire to be disolved, and be with thee. O Lord, I most humbly acknowledg and confess thine infinite Mercy, that when thou hadst almost broke the staff of bread, and called a famine of thy word almost upon all the world, then thou broughtest me into this Egypt, where thou hadst appointed thy stewards to husband thy blessings, and to feed thy flock. Here also, O God, thou hast multiplied thy children in me, by begetting and cherishing in me reverent devotions, and pious affections towards thee, but that mine own corruption, mine own *Pharaoh* hath ever smothered and strangled them. And thou hast put me in my way towards thy land of promise, thy Heavenly *Canaan*, by removing me from the Egypt of frequented and populous, glorious places, to a more solitary and desart retiredness, where I may more safely feed upon both thy Mannaes, thy self in thy Sacrament, and that other, which is true Angells food, contemplation of thee. O Lord, I most humbly acknowledg and confess, that I feel in me so many strong effects of thy Power, as only for the Ordinariness and frequency thereof, they are not Miracles. For hourly thou rectifiest my lameness, hourly thou restorest my sight, and hourly not only deliverest me from the Egypt, but raisest me from the death of sin. My sin, O God, hath not onely caused thy descent hither, and passion here; but by it I am become that hell into which thou descendedst after thy Passion; yea, after thy glorification: for hourly thou in thy Spirit descendest into my heart, to overthrow there Legions of spirits of Disobedience, and Incredulity, and Murmuring. O Lord, I most humbly acknowledg and confesse, that by thy Mercy I have a sense of thy Justice; for not onely those afflictions with which it pleaseth thee to exercise mee, awaken me to consider how terrible thy severe justice is; but even the rest and security which thou affordest mee, puts me often into fear, that thou reservest and sparest me for a greater measure of punishment. O Lord, I most humbly acknowledg and confesse, that I have understood sin, by understanding thy laws and judgments; but have done against thy known and revealed will. Thou hast set up many candlesticks, and kindled many lamps in mee; but I have either blown them out, or carried them to guide me in by and forbidden ways. Thou hast given mee a desire of knowledg, and some meanes to it, and some possession of it; and I have arm'd my self with thy weapons against thee: Yet, O God, have mercy upon me, for thine own sake have mercy upon me. Let not sin and me be able to exceed thee, nor to defraud thee, nor to frustrate thy purposes: But let me, in despite of Me, be of so much use to thy glory, that by thy mercy to my sin, other sinners may see how much sin thou canst pardon. Thus show mercy to many in one: And shew thy power and al-mightinesse upon thy self, by casting manacles upon thine own hands, and calling back those Thunder-bolts which thou hadst thrown against me. Show thy Justice upon the common Seducer and Devourer of us all: and show to us so much of thy Judgments, as may instruct, not condemn us. Hear us, O God, hear us, for this contrition which thou hast put into us, who come to thee with that watch-word, by which thy Son hath assured us of access. *Our Father which art in Heaven, etc.*'[1]

The remaining prayers are expressed in the first person plural, and were evidently composed by Donne for the use of a small congregation, as is shown by a phrase in the second prayer:

'Behold us, O God, here gathered together in thy fear, according to thine ordinance, and in confidence of thy promise, that when two or three are gathered together in thy name, thou wilt be in the midst of them, and grant them their petitions.'[2]

The note of personal penitence, however, is heard as clearly and distinctly in these as in the first prayer. It is Donne's own experience which inspires the confession of the third prayer, for example:

'O most glorious and most gracious God, into whose presence our own consciences make us afraid to come, and from whose presence we cannot hide our selves, hide us in the wounds of thy Son, our Saviour Christ Jesus; And though our sins be as red as scarlet, give them there another redness, which may be acceptable in thy sight. We renounce, O Lord, all our confidence in this world; for this world passeth away, and the lusts thereof: Wee renounce all our confidence in our own merits for we have done nothing in respect of that which we might have done; neither could we ever have done any such thing, but that still we must have remained unprofitable servants to thee; we renounce all confidence, even in our own confessions, and accusations of our self; for our sins are above number, if we would reckon them; above weight and measure, if we would weigh and measure them; and past finding out, if we would seek them in those dark corners, in which we have

[1] *Essays*, pp. 214–18.

[2] Ibid., pp. 218–19.

multiplied them against thee: yea we renounce all confidence even in our repentances; for we have found by many lamentable experiences, that we never perform our promises to thee, never perfect our purposes in our selves, but relapse again and again into those sins which again and again we have repented. We have no confidence in this world, but in him who hath taken possession of the next world for us, by sitting down at thy right hand. We have no confidence in our merits, but in him, whose merits thou hast been pleased to accept for us, and to apply to us, we have: no confidence in our own confessions and repentances, but in that blessed Spirit, who is the Author of them, and loves to perfect his own works and build upon his own foundations, we have: Accept them therefore, O Lord, for their sakes whose they are; our poor endeavours, for thy glorious Sons sake, who gives them their root, and so they are his; our poor beginnings of sanctification, for thy blessed Spirits sake, who gives them their growth, and so they are his: and for thy Sons sake, in whom only our prayers are acceptable to thee: and for thy Spirits sake which is now in us, and must be so whensoever we do pray acceptably to Thee; accept our humble prayers. . . .'[1]

The fourth and last prayer again begins with a confession of sin, and continues with a petition for new grace.

'Begin in us here in this life an angelicall purity, an angelicall chastity, an angelicall integrity to thy service, an Angelical acknowledgment that we alwaies stand in thy presence, and should direct al our actions to thy glory. Rebuke us not, O Lord, in thine anger, that we have not done so till now; but enable us now to begin that great work; and imprint in us an assurance that thou receivest us now graciously, as reconciled, though enemies; and fatherly, as children, though prodigals; and powerfully, as the God of our salvation, though our own consciences testifie against us.'[2]

[1] *Essays*, pp. 220–2. [2] Ibid., pp. 223–4.

X

DEVOTIONS UPON EMERGENT OCCASIONS

IT was during Donne's dangerous illness in the winter of 1623 that he composed the curious *Devotions upon Emergent Occasions*, which proved one of the most popular of his works and ran through several editions. Walton thus describes its composition:

'He was made Dean the fiftieth year of his age; and in his fifty fourth year a dangerous sickness seized him, which inclined him to a Consumption.[1] But God, as *Job* thankfully acknowledged, *preserved his spirit*, and kept his intellectuals as clear and perfect, as when that sickness first seized his body: but it continued long and threatned him with death; which he dreaded not. . . . Within a few days' [after a visit from Henry King, described at length by Walton] 'his distempers abated; and as his strength increased, so did his thankfulness to Almighty God, testified in his most excellent Book of *Devotions*, which he published at his Recovery. In which the Reader may see, the most secret thoughts that then possest his Soul, Paraphrased and made publick: a book that may not unfitly be called a *Sacred picture of Spiritual Extasies*, occasioned and applyable to the emergencies of that sickness; which book being a composition of *Meditations*, *Disquisitions* and *Prayers*, he writ on his sick-bed; herein imitating the Holy Patriarchs, who were wont to build their Altars in that place, where they had received their blessings.'[2]

Walton's description of Donne's sickness as 'a Consumption' is likely to mislead modern readers. It was certainly not tuberculosis, and Walton uses the term to denote any wasting disease. Gosse is yet more misleading, for he tries to

[1] The 1640 edition of Walton's *Life* describes this illness more fully as 'a dangerous sicknesse, which turned to a spotted Feaver, and ended in a Cough, that inclined him to a Consumption'. The spots are mentioned in Section 13 of the *Devotions*.

[2] Walton, *Life* (1670), pp. 49–52. During this illness Donne also composed the *Hymn to God the Father*, 'Wilt thou forgive that sinne where I begunne', which Walton describes as a 'heavenly *Hymne*, expressing the great joy that then possest his soul in the Assurance of Gods favour to him'. After his recovery Donne caused the poem to be set 'to a most grave and solemn Tune, and to be often sung to the *Organ* by the *Choristers* of St. *Pauls* Church, in his own hearing, especially at the Evening Service'.

connect it with the fatal illness which finally killed Donne. According to Dr. Norman Moore, whom Gosse consulted, the cause of Donne's death in 1631 was almost certainly 'an abdominal new growth, which was first distinctly developed in August 1630', and which was probably cancer of the stomach.[1] In spite of this Gosse writes of the violent sickness which attacked Donne in the autumn of 1623: 'We have no distinct knowledge of what his chronic disease was, but it was attended with violent internal pain, its crises were apt to be brought on by anxiety or excess of intellectual work, as well as by cold, and it was supposed to be "a consumption". . . . It was aggravated by his neurotic temperament. . . . We are tempted to suppose that Donne had suffered from what we now call typhoid fever in his youth, and that it had left behind a chronic tendency to gastritis. Whatever medical name we call it by, it was evidently a burning away of the internal organs, which gradually consumed, and at last destroyed him.'[2] This is quite at variance with the information given us by Donne himself in the *Devotions*. Here he states that the onset of the disease was sudden. In Meditation 1 he writes, 'this minute I was well, and am ill, this minute. I am surpriz'd with a sodaine change, and alteration to worse, and can impute it to no cause, nor call it any name.' In Meditation 2 he analyses his symptoms further. He has lost his appetite, and everything tastes insipid; his knees are weak, and give way under him; he sweats from his forehead to the soles of his feet, and he finds himself unable to sleep. A message is sent to the physician, and meanwhile Donne is left alone by his friends, for they fear infection (Meditation 5). When the physician arrives he takes a grave view of the case, and Donne detects this, in spite of the physician's attempt to disguise it. 'I feare the more, because he disguises his fear, and I see it with the more sharpnesse, because hee would not have me see it' (Meditation 6). He turns to God, and prays that he may submit everything to the will of God. The king hears of Donne's illness, and sends his own physician to consult with Donne's doctor (Meditation 8). They prescribe physic, and Donne accepts

[1] Gosse, ii. 374–5.

[2] Ibid., p. 181.

it gladly (Meditation 9), but the disease grows worse, so that the physicians prescribe the fashionable remedy of applying pigeons cut in half[1] 'to draw the vapors from the Head' (Meditation 12). In Meditation 13 we are told that the sickness 'declares the infection and malignity thereof by spots'. Donne cannot sleep by day or night, and the bells of the neighbouring church seem by their tolling to summon him to prepare for death (Meditations 15–18). At last, however, the crisis is over, and he begins to recover, but the physicians immediately apply their favourite purgatives. He is told by them that he may get out of bed, but he finds that he can hardly stand (Meditation 21). Finally he is convalescent, and he employs his leisure in arranging his devotions during his sickness into a little volume to be published immediately.

This evidence shows that Donne suffered from a violent fever, which ran its course in about three weeks. It left him extremely weak, but after a protracted convalescence he was able to resume his usual duties, and on Easter Day 1624 he preached at St. Paul's, and followed this up by a number of other sermons. During the next six years he was able to live an active energetic life, preaching frequently at St. Paul's and St. Dunstan's, and paying visits in the summer to Sevenoaks and Keyston. Thus there is nothing about this particular sickness to justify Gosse's hypothesis of a chronic disease aggravated by a neurotic temperament. What is noteworthy is the sane and commonsense view which Donne took of his sickness. He recognized that he was acutely ill, summoned the doctor and obeyed his instructions, prepared himself for the possibility of death but hoped for recovery, and rejoiced when he found that the sickness had abated. It is true that the *Devotions* show a morbid delight in analysing his own conflicting emotions, and that some of their appeal is due to the minuteness of his introspection, but this should not blind us to the practical good sense of his behaviour.

[1] Pepys in his Diary for 19 Oct. 1663 records that 'the Queene . . . was so ill as to be shaved, and pidgeons put to her feet, and to have the extreme unction given her by the priests'.

The book was printed early in 1624,[1] and Donne wrote to his friend, Sir Robert Ker, asking him to read the sheets and give advice on the subject of the proposed dedication to the Prince of Wales.

'*Sir*, Though I have left my bed, I have not left my bed-side; I sit there still, and as a Prisoner discharged, sits at the Prison doore, to beg Fees, so sit I here, to gather crummes. I have used this leisure, to put the meditations had in my sicknesse, into some such order, as may minister some holy delight. They arise to so many sheetes (perchance 20.) as that without staying for that furniture of an Epistle, That my Friends importun'd me to Print them, I importune my Friends to receive them Printed. That, being in hand, through this long Trunke, that reaches from Saint *Pauls*, to Saint *James*, I whisper into your eare this question, whether there be any uncomlinessse, or unseasonableness, in presenting matter of Devotion, or Mortification, to that Prince, whom I pray God nothing may ever Mortifie, but Holinesse. If you allow my purposes in generall, I pray cast your eye upon the Title and the Epistle, and rectifie me in them: I submit substance, and circumstance to you, and the poore Author of both,

Your very humble and very thankfull Servant in Christ Jesus

J. Donne.'[2]

Donne sent a copy of the *Devotions* to the unfortunate Queen of Bohemia, with the following letter:

'Your Majesty hath had the patience heretofore to hear me deliver the messages of God to your self. In the hearing of me deliver my messages to God, I can hope for the continuance of your Majestie's patience. He is a very diffident man, that can doubt of that vertue in your Majestie; for of your great measure of that vertue, the World hath had more proofe than it needed. But I consider alwayes, that it had been in me a disloyall thing (I afford no milder a word to that fault) to have any way conjured to the exercising of your Majestie's patience; Therefore I have forborn, to thrust into your Majestie's presence my name, or any thing which hath proceeded from me, though alwayes the dignity of the subject, and sometimes the expresse commandment, sometimes the gracious alarum of your most royall Father, might have gon far in my excuse, in such a boldnesse to your

[1] It was entered on the Stationers' Register on 9 Jan. 1623/4 to the publisher Thomas Jones.

[2] *Letters* (1651), pp. 249–50.

Majestie. Now (for since I am doing a bold action, I may speak words that sound of boldnesse too) I surprise your Majestie, I take you at an advantage, I lay an obligation upon you, because that which your Brother's Highnesse hath received, your Majestie cannot refuse. By your own example you can suffer, by his example you may be pleased to accept this testimony of the zeal of your, etc.'[1]

To this letter Elizabeth returned a very gracious answer, also reprinted in the Tobie Mathew collection:

'*Good Doctor.*

None should have cause to pitty me, nor my selfe to complain, had I met with no other exercise of my patience, than the hearing of you deliver (as you call them) the messages of God, unto me: which truly I never did, but with delight, and I hope some measure of edification. No doubt then but I shall read yours to him with pleasure, and I trust by his assistance, to whom they are directed, not without profit. For what I have already read, I give you hearty thanks; and if my better fortunes make progression with my reading (whereof I now begin to have good hope) I will not faile upon any good occasion to acknowledge this courtesie at your hands; and in the meantime I remaine yours, etc.'[2]

The first edition of the *Devotions* is in duodecimo, with the collation A^{8}, B–Z, Aa–Dd^{12}, Ee^{4}. The title-page runs thus:

'Deuotions vpon Emergent Occasions, and seuerall steps in my Sicknes:
Digested into
1. Meditations vpon our Humane Condition.
2. Expostulations, and Debatements with God.
3. Prayers, vpon the seuerall Occasions, to him.
By Iohn Donne, Deane of S. Pauls, London.
London, Printed by A. M. for Thomas Iones. 1624.'[3]

There is a dedicatory epistle 'To the Most Excellent Prince, Prince Charles', followed by a list of the twenty-three 'steps' in Donne's 'sickness', each of which has a meditation, 'expostulation', and prayer allotted to it—'Stationes, siue Periodi in Morbo, ad quas referuntur Meditationes

[1] *Letters*, Tobie Mathew Collection, pp. 296–7.

[2] Ibid., pp. 297–8.

[3] Keynes has identified another issue of this edition with a different imprint, 'London, Printed for Thomas Iones. 1624.'

sequentes.' This is followed by a short list of errata. The text begins on B 1, where the pagination also begins, and occupies 630 pages.

A second edition appeared later in the same year. Its title-page is a reproduction of that of the earlier edition, except that the words 'The second Edition' appear on it. The errata of the previous edition have been corrected. The text is printed more closely, so that it occupies only 589 pages instead of 630. A colophon has been added, which runs thus:

'London Printed for Thomas Iones, and are to be sold at the black Rauen, in the Strand. 1624.'

Other editions followed in 1626–7, 1634, and 1638.[1] Of these the two last contained a frontispiece depicting the effigy of Donne wrapped in his shroud. Above his head is a skull wreathed with laurel, on either side are two biblical scenes with texts inscribed above and below.

The *Devotions* were included in Alford's *Works of Donne* (1839), and were reprinted separately in 1840 by William Pickering, and in 1841 by D. A. Talboys. An edition by John Sparrow with a bibliographical note by Dr. Keynes was issued at Cambridge in 1923. In 1925 another edition, with an introduction by the Rev. W. H. Draper, Master of the Temple, was produced in London in the Abbey Classics series.

According to Morhof, *Polyhistor* (1714), the *Devotions* were translated into Dutch in 1655.[2] No copy of this is known, but the statement 'is sufficiently definite to make it probable that such a translation does exist; if so, it is probably by Sir Constantine Huyghens, who had already translated some of Donne's poems.'[3]

The book is divided into twenty-three portions, each

[1] Keynes (op. cit., pp. 50, 51) has identified two separate issues of the third (1626–7) edition.

[2] *Polyhistor*, lib. vi, cap. iv, § 18: 'Scripsit et *Meditationes* super morbo suo *sacras*, quae in Linguam Belgicam conversae et Amstelodami 1655 in 12° editae sunt.'

[3] Keynes, op. cit., p. 46. For an account of Huyghens's translation of the poems see pp. 130–1, and Grierson, *Poems*, ii, p. lxxvii.

representing a stage in the development or cure of the disease. The whole scheme is thoroughly characteristic of Donne's introspective, self-analytical mind, which noted carefully every symptom of his bodily and spiritual condition. The rich, sustained eloquence of the *Sermons* is lacking, but in other respects the prose of these *Devotions* shows the usual features of Donne's style—the brilliant display of metaphysical wit, with its far-fetched allusions and similes, the immense amount of learning of all kinds, the delight in paradox, and the passionate sincerity which gives life to even the most fantastic exercises of Donne's intellect.

The first two sections deal with the onset of Donne's sickness. The attack was sudden and violent:

> 'In the same instant that I feele the first attempt of the disease, I feele the victory; In the twinckling of an eye, I can scarse see; instantly the tast is insipid, and fatuous; instantly the appetite is dull and desirelesse: instantly the knees are sinking and strengthlesse; and in an instant, sleepe, which is the picture, the copy of death, is taken away, that the *Originall*, *Death* it selfe may succeed, and that so I might haue death to the life. . . . I sweat againe, and againe, from the brow, to the sole of the foot, but I eat no bread, I tast no sustenance.'[1]

In section 3 Donne takes to his bed, and in section 4 the physician is sent for. 'The Phisician comes' is the heading of section 5, and 'The Phisician is afraid' of section 6. In section 7 the physician desires a consultation with others, and in section 8 the king sends his own physician—a kindness which affords Donne scope for a recapitulation of James's favours towards him. Sections 9 to 12 are occupied with the measures taken by the physicians to cope with the disease. In section 13 'the Sicknes declares the infection and malignity thereof by spots'. 'The Phisicians obserue these accidents to haue fallen vpon the criticall dayes' is the heading of section 14, and 'I sleepe not day nor night' of section 15. Sections 16 to 18 contain Donne's meditations on death occasioned by the tolling of the bells of an adjoining church.

In section 19 the patient begins to recover. 'At last, the Physitians, after a long and stormie voyage, see land; They haue so good signes of the concoction of the disease, as that

[1] *Devotions* (1624, first edition), pp. 25–6.

they may safely proceed to purge.' This they perform in section 20, and in section 21 'God prospers their practise, and he, by them, calls *Lazarus* out of his tombe, mee out of my bed'. In section 22 'the Phisitians consider the root and occasion, the embers, and coales, and fuell of the disease, and seeke to purge or correct that'. The last section (23) is occupied by a warning against 'the fearefull danger of relapsing'.

Although the book follows in its arrangement the course of Donne's illness, the greater part of it is concerned with the usual subjects of his meditation, whether in sickness or in health—the power of sin, the miseries of human life, the mercy and the judgements of God, the universality of death, and the hope of resurrection. Donne's thoughts pass quickly in almost every chapter from the consideration of his own sickness to the more general topics which his symptoms might suggest, and he finds a spiritual parallel for each stage of the disease. He does not, however, content himself with allegorizing the course of his complaint, but passes on rapidly to those metaphysical conceptions which always occupied so large a part of his mind. Thus the greater part of the meditation in section 14, which is suggested by the heading, 'The Phisicians obserue these accidents to haue fallen vpon the criticall dayes', is occupied by a discussion of the ideas of time and space:

'All things are done in some *place*; but if we consider *place* to be no more, but the next hollow *Superficies* of the *Ayre*, *Alas*, how thinne, and fluid a thing is *Ayre*, and how thinne a *filme* is a *Superficies*, and a *Superficies* of *Ayre*? All things are done in *time* too; but if we consider *Tyme* to be but the *Measure of Motion*, and howsoeuer it may seeme to haue three *stations*, *past*, *present*, and *future*, yet the *first* and *last* of these *are* not (one is not, now, and the other is not yet) And that which you call *present*, is not *now* the same that it was, when you began to call it so in this *Line*, (before you sound that word, *present*, or that *Monosyllable*, *now*, the present, and the *Now* is past), if this *Imaginary halfe-nothing*, *Tyme* be of the Essence of our *Happinesses*, how can they be thought *durable*? *Tyme* is not so; How can they bee thought to be? *Tyme* is not so; not so, considered in any of the *parts* thereof. If we consider *Eternity*, into that, *Tyme* neuer Entred; *Eternity* is not an euerlasting flux of *Tyme*; but Tyme is as a short *parenthesis* in a longe *period*; and *Eternity* had bin the same, as it is, though time had neuer beene.'[1]

Again, in section 10, when the physicians 'find the Disease to steale on insensibly, and endeauour to meet with it so', Donne plunges into a metaphysical consideration of the nature of the universe and the immortality of the soul, and comes to the conclusion, expressed also in *LXXX Sermons*, p. 269, that the soul is immortal only by preservation, not by nature, so that God alone can truly be considered immortal in Himself:[2]

'This is *Natures nest of Boxes*; The *Heavens* containe the *Earth*, the *Earth*, *Cities*, *Cities*, *Men*. And all these are *Concentrique*; the common *center* to them all, is *decay*, *ruine*; onely that is *Eccentrique*, which was neuer made; only that place, or garment rather, which we can *imagine*, but not *demonstrate*, That light which is the very emanation of the light of *God*, in which the *Saints* shall dwell, with which the *Saints* shall be appareld, only that bends not to this *Center*, to *Ruine*; that which was not made of *Nothing*, is not threatned with this annihilation. All other things are; euen *Angels*, euen our *soules*; they moue vpon the same *poles*, they bend to the same *Center*; and if they were not made immortall by *preseruation*, their *Nature* could not keepe them from sinking to this *center*, *Annihilation*.'[3]

Donne's acquaintance with the medical learning of his times is shown in various places. Thus in section 9 he discusses the great number of sicknesses by which man may be attacked.

'If there were no *ruine* but *sicknes*, wee see, the Masters of that *Art*, can scarce *number*, not *name* all sicknesses; euery thing that *disorders* a faculty, and the function of that is a sicknesse: The names wil not serue them which are giuen from the *place affected*, the *Plurisie* is so; nor from the *effect* which it works, the *falling sicknes* is so; they cannot haue names ynow, from *what it does*, nor *where it is*, but they must extort names from what *it is like*, what it *resembles*, and but in some one thing, or els they would lack names; for the *Wolf*, and the *Canker*, and the *Polypus* are so.'[4]

[1] *Devotions*, pp. 333–6.

[2] See also Professor Grierson's note on ll. 57–8 of Donne's verse letter to the Countess of Bedford (Grierson, *Poems*, ii. 160–2).

[3] *Devotions*, pp. 226–8.

[4] Ibid., pp. 202–3.

In section 11 he considers the relative importance of the heart, brain, and liver, as then understood by the physicians of the time:

'And since the *Braine*, and *Liuer*, and *Heart*, hold not a *Triumuirate* in *Man*, a *Soueraigntie* equally shed vpon them all, for his *well-being*, as the foure *Elements* doe, for his very *being*, but the *Heart* alone is in the *Principalitie*, and in the *Throne*, as *King*, the rest as *Subiects*, though in eminent *Place*, and *Office*, must contribute to that . . . therefore doth the *Phisician* intermit the present care of *Braine*, or *Liuer*, because there is a possibilitie, that they may subsist, though there bee not a present and a particular care had of them, but there is no possibilitie that they can subsist, if the *Heart* perish.'[1]

There are a number of references to the medical practices of the time. Of these the most curious is to be found in section 12: 'They apply Pidgeons, to draw the vapors from the Head,

Spirante Columbâ
Suppositâ pedibus, Reuocantur ad ima vapores.'

Donne meditates on his own responsibility for the origin of these vapours:

'What haue I done, either to *breed*, or to *breath* these *vapors*? They tell me it is my *Melancholy*; Did I infuse, did I drinke in *Melancholy* into my selfe? It is my *thoughtfulnesse*; was I not made to *thinke*? It is my *study*; doth not my *Calling* call for that? I haue don nothing wilfully, peruersly toward it, yet must suffer in it, die by it.'[2]

But he soon turns to a metaphorical consideration of evils in the state:

'these *vapours* in vs, which wee consider here pestilent, and infectious fumes, are in a State *infectious rumors*, detracting and dishonourable *Calumnies*, *Libels*. The *Heart* in that *body* is the *King*; and the *Braine*, his *Councell*; and the whole *Magistracie*, that ties all together, is the *Sinewes*, which proceed from thence; and the *life* of all is *Honour*, and iust *respect*, and due *reuerence*; and therfore, when these *vapors*, these venimous *rumors*, are directed against these *Noble parts*, the whole body suffers.'[3]

[1] *Devotions*, pp. 255, 258, 259.

[2] Ibid., pp. 290–1 (I have here followed the second edition in omitting a comma between *nothing* and *wilfully*).

[3] Ibid., pp. 294–5.

He finds an allegorical interpretation for the pigeon which was to be used in his own cure:

'these libellous and licentious *Iesters*, vtter the *venim* they haue, though sometimes *vertue*, and alwaies *power*, be a good *Pigeon* to draw this *vapor* from the *Head*, and from doing any deadly harme there.'[1]

In his 'Expostulation' in this Section he proceeds further to give a spiritual meaning to the vapours and the pigeon:

'Therefore hast thou bin pleased to afford vs this remedy in *Nature*, by this application of a *Doue*, to our lower parts, to make these *vapors* in our *bodies*, to descend, and to make that a *type* to vs, that by the visitation of thy *Spirit*, the *vapors* of sin shall descend, and we tread them vnder our feet. At the baptisme of thy *Son*, the *Doue* descended, and at the exalting of thine *Apostles* to preach, the same spirit descended. Let vs draw downe the *vapors* of our own *pride*, our own *wits*, our own *wils*, our own *inuentions*, to the *simplicitie* of thy *Sacraments*, and the obedience of thy word, and these *Doues*, thus applied, shall make vs liue.'[2]

As a manual of devotion this curious book compares unfavourably with the *Devotions* of Bishop Andrewes or the *Holy Living* of Jeremy Taylor. It is too introspective, too metaphysical, too much overloaded by learning of different kinds. The ordinary reader finds it hard to believe that so elaborately planned a work could represent the natural overflow of Donne's religious feelings, and is inclined to suspect the writer of artifice and a desire to exhibit his wit and learning. But when the book is studied in connexion with Donne's other works, both prose and poetry, it is seen to be in truth the sincere expression of a mind which was always subtle and introspective to an extraordinary degree, and which habitually employed metaphors and allusions of a type which seems strangely unexpected and far-fetched to the ordinary mind. These meditations and prayers, which range so startlingly from the spots on Donne's body produced by the fever to the proportions of sea and land in the eastern and western hemispheres, are exactly what might have been expected from the author of the *Valediction forbidding Mourning* and the *Divine Poems*.

[1] Ibid., p. 297.

[2] Ibid., pp. 305–6.

Donne would not offer to his God the sacrifice of a merely conventional devotion, modelled on the language and imagery of the Fathers or the Reformers. As in the love poetry of his youth, so in the devotions of his later life he chose his own way, rejecting trite devotional expressions and pious ejaculations, and setting on all his meditations and expostulations with God the seal of his own paradoxical self-tormenting individuality. Behind all the fantastic display of metaphysical wit and learning there is a passionate sincerity which redeems Donne's worst extravagances. These *Devotions* are our nearest counterpart in prose to the *Holy Sonnets*, which were written a few years earlier, and which give expression in verse to the same intensity of spiritual conflict. Over and over again Donne pours forth his repentance for the sins of his youth and his hatred of the sinful impulses which still torment him at times. He writhes under a sense of God's infinite purity and stern justice, and then again he takes courage as he remembers the death of Christ, and entreats the mercy of God through His Son.

'I [open] my *soule* to thee, O my *God*, in an humble confession, That there is no *veine* in mee, that is not full of the bloud of thy *Son*, whom I haue crucified, and Crucified againe, by multiplying many, and often repeating the same sinnes: that there is no *Artery* in me, that hath not the *spirit of error*, *the spirit of lust*, *the spirit of giddines* in it; no *bone* in me that is not hardned with the custome of *sin*, and nourished, and soupled with the *marrow* of *sinn*; no *sinews*, no *ligaments*, that do not tie, and chain sin and sin together.'[1]

'Looke therefore upon me, *O Lord*, in this distresse, and that will recall mee from the borders of this bodily death; Look vpon me, and that wil raise me again from that *spirituall death*, in which my parents buried me, when they begot mee in *sinne*, and in which I haue pierced euen to the iawes of *hell*, by multiplying such heaps of actuall sins, vpon that foundation, that root of *originall sin.* Yet take me again, into your *Consultation*, *O blessed* and *glorious Trinitie*; and thogh the *Father* know, that I haue defaced his *Image* receiued in my *Creation*; though the *Son* know, I haue neglected mine interest in the *Redemption*, yet, *O blessed spirit*, as thou art to my *Conscience*, so be to them a witnes, that at this *minute*, I accept that which I haue so often, so often, so rebelliously refused, thy blessed inspirations; be

[1] *Devotions*, pp. 215–16.

thou my witnes to them, that at more poores then this slacke body sweates teares, this sad soule weeps blood; and more for the *displeasure* of my *God*, then for the stripes of his displeasure.'[1]

Donne implores a respite from God's anger in this sickness, and for a moment attributes his affliction to the devil, but speedily decides that it is in reality the merciful correction of God's hand, and that even should it prove fatal, he may hope for a joyful resurrection:

'And therefore how little soeuer I bee, as *God calls things that are not, as though they were*, I, who am as though I were not, may call vpon *God*, and say, *My God, my God*, why comes thine anger so fast vpon me? Why dost thou melt me, scatter me, powre me like water vpon the ground so instantly? Thou staidst for the first world, in *Noahs* time, 120 yeres; thou staidst for a rebellious generation in the wildernesse 40 yeares, wilt thou stay no minute for me? . . . *My God, my God*, thou wast not wont to come in *whirlwinds*, but in soft and gentle ayre. Thy first breath breathed a *Soule* into mee, and shall thy breath blow it out? Thy breath in the *Congregation*, thy *Word* in the *Church*, breathes *communion*, and *consolation* here, and *consummation* heereafter; shall thy breath in this Chamber breathe *dissolution*, and *destruction*, *diuorce*, and *separation*? Surely it is not thou; it is not thy hand. The deuouring sword, the consuming fire, the winds from the wildernes, the diseases of the body, all that afflicted *Iob*, were from the hand of *Satan*; it is not thou. It is thou; Thou *my God*, who hast led mee so continually with thy hand, from the hand of my Nurce, as that I know, thou wilt not correct mee, but with thine own hand. My parents would not giue mee ouer to a *Seruants* correction, nor my *God*, to *Satans*. *I am fallen into the handes of God* with *Dauid*, and with *Dauid* I see that his *Mercies are great*. For by that mercy, I consider in my present state, not the haste, and the dispatch of the disease, in dissoluing this body, so much, as the much more hast, and dispatch, which my *God* shal vse, in recollecting, and reuniting this *dust* againe at the *Resurrection*. Then I shall heare his *Angels* proclaime the *Surgite Mortui*, *Rise yee dead*. Though I be dead, I shall heare the voice; the sounding of the voice, and the working of the voice shall be all one; and all shall rise there in a lesse *Minute*, then any one dies here.'[2]

He finds in his very weakness a claim on the compassion of Christ:

'*My God*, and *my Iesus*, *my Lord*, and *my Christ*, *my Strength*, and

[1] Ibid., pp. 223–5. [2] Ibid., pp. 29–35.

my Saluation, I heare thee, and I hearken to thee, when thou rebukest thy *Disciples*, for rebuking them, who brought children to thee; *Suffer little children to come to mee*, saiest thou. Is there a verier child then I am now? I cannot say with thy seruant *Ieremy*, *Lord*, *I am a child*, *and cannot speake*; but, *O Lord*, I am a sucking childe, and cannot eate, a creeping childe, and cannot goe; how shall I come to thee?'[1]

Here is the note of devotion to the Person of Christ which can be heard in the thirteenth of the *Holy Sonnets*, and which echoes again and again through the *Sermons*.[2] The grotesqueness of much of the imagery should not blind us to the reality of the conflicting emotions in Donne's soul, revealed in the *Devotions* with a minute self-analysis which finds full play here as nowhere else in his writings.

[1] *Devotions*, pp. 47–8.

[2] See especially *LXXX Sermons*, nos. 40 and 41.

XI
THE SERMONS

IT is in the *Sermons* that Donne's powers as a prose-writer are best displayed. He was the most famous preacher of his day, in an age of great preachers, and the qualities which drew men of all classes to hear him are evident still in the printed record of his words. The value of his other prose works is largely historical and antiquarian; it is in virtue of the *Sermons* that he takes his place among the greatest masters of English prose. 'They are as unlike any other sermons as his poems are unlike any other poetry', said Charles Eliot Norton,[1] and this judgement is but the echo of earlier and greater critics, such as Coleridge, who was a lover of Donne, and once asked, 'Why is not Donne's volume of sermons reprinted at Oxford?'[2]

The *Sermons* show Donne's immense learning, his knowledge of Scripture,[3] the Fathers, the Schoolmen, the Roman and Protestant controversialists, as well as his interest in law, medicine, and science, but all this weighty material is made acceptable to his hearers by his powers of wit and imagination, and by his command of the most familiar or the most dignified prose style. In his controversial or casuistical works this is not always the case, and the reader is repelled by the numerous quotations from unfamiliar authors and by the obscurity of Donne's prose. In the pulpit, however, Donne aimed at edifying, rather than mystifying, his audience, and it was necessary for him to speak more plainly than it was his wont to write. Many of the *Sermons* are easier reading (apart from the quotations from the Fathers) than his private correspondence, as reprinted in the *Letters* of 1651. Donne clarified his thought for the benefit of his hearers, and sought to win their attention by the beauty and eloquence of his

[1] *Letters*, ii. 318.

[2] *Table Talk*, i. 168 (1835 edition).

[3] For an examination of Donne's knowledge of the Hebrew of the Old Testament, the Greek of the New Testament, the Vulgate, and other Latin versions, see D. C. Allen, 'Dean Donne sets his Text', *E.L.H.* x. 208–29.

style. He aimed at 'carrying some', as Walton says, 'to Heaven in holy raptures, and enticing others by a sacred art and courtship to amend their lives: here picturing a vice so as to make it ugly to those that practised it; and a virtue so as to make it beloved, even by those that loved it not'.

Donne's style is richer and more varied in the *Sermons* than elsewhere. He is a master of the long paragraph, cunningly marshalling his clauses for a cumulative shock effect, as in the famous description of damnation, or the almost equally famous passage on God's mercy, which occurs in one of the Christmas sermons:

> 'God made Sun and Moon to distinguish seasons, and day, and night, and we cannot have the fruits of the earth but in their seasons: But God hath made no decree to distinguish the seasons of his mercies; In paradise, the fruits were ripe, the first minute, and in heaven it is alwaies Autumne, his mercies are ever in their maturity. . . . He brought light out of darknesse, not out of a lesser light; he can bring thy Summer out of Winter, though thou have no Spring; though in the wayes of fortune, or understanding, or conscience, thou have been benighted till now, wintred and frozen, clouded and eclypsed, damped and benummed, smothered and stupified till now, now God comes to thee, not as in the dawning of the day, not as in the bud of the spring, but as the Sun at noon to illustrate all shadowes, as the sheaves in harvest, to fill all penuries, all occasions invite his mercies, and all times are his seasons.'[1]

But the long period is not his only instrument. Scattered throughout the *Sermons* are felicitous short phrases which linger in the memory. 'Certainly he that loves not the *Militant Church*, hath but a faint faith in his interest in the *Triumphant*. He that cares not though the *materiall Church* fall, I am afraid is falling from the *spirituall*.'[2] 'Nothing hinders our own salvation more, then to deny salvation, to all but our selves.'[3] 'Even humility it self is a pride, if we think it to be our own.'[4] 'God makes sometimes a plaine and simple mans good life, as powerfull, as the eloquentest Sermon.'[5]

Sometimes Donne uses the homeliest phrases and imagery to drive home his meaning.

[1] 'Preached at Pauls, upon Christmas Day, in the Evening. 1624.' *LXXX Sermons*, 2. 13. [2] *L Sermons*, 36. 330. [3] Ibid. 32. 285.
[4] *XXVI Sermons*, 12. 172. [5] *LXXX Sermons*, 5. 49.

'We have sold our selves for nothing; and however the ordinary murmuring may be true, in other things, that all things are grown dearer, our souls are still cheap enough, which at first were all sold in gross, for (perchance) an Apple, and are now retailed every day for nothing.'[1] 'God doth but call us, he does not constrain us, He does not drive us into a pound; He cals us as Birds do their young, and he would gather us as a Hen doth her Chickins.'[2] 'It is not enough for you, to rest in an imaginary faith, and easinesse in beleeving, except you know also what, and why, and how you come to that beliefe. Implicite beleevers, ignorant beleevers, the adversary may swallow; but the understanding beleever, he must chaw, and pick bones, before he come to assimilate him, and make him like himself.'[3]

A carefully balanced antithesis marks many of Donne's sentences.

'From that inglorious drop of raine, that falls into the dust, and rises no more, to those glorious Saints who shall rise from the dust, and fall no more, but, as they arise at once to the fulnesse of *Essentiall* joy, so arise daily in *accidentiall* joyes, all are the children of God, and all alike of kin to us.'[4] 'The whole life of Christ was a continuall Passion; others die Martyrs, but Christ was born a Martyr. He found a *Golgatha*, (where he was crucified) even in Bethlem, where he was born; For, to his tendernesse then, the strawes were almost as sharp as the thornes after; and the Manger as uneasie at first, as his Crosse at last.'[5]

This carefully wrought and artfully varied style, which distinguishes the prose of the *Sermons*, indicates the high ideal which Donne had formed of the duties of the ministry. 'Religious preaching', he said in one of his earlier sermons,

'is a grave exercise, but not a sordid, not a barbarous, not a negligent. There are not so eloquent books in the world, as the Scriptures. . . . The style of the Scriptures is a diligent, and an artificial style; and a great part thereof in a musical, in a metrical, in a measured composition, in verse. . . . So the Holy Ghost hath spoken in those Instruments, whom he chose for the penning of the Scriptures, and so he would in those whom he sends for the preaching thereof: he would put in them a care of delivering God[s] messages, with consideration, with meditation, with preparation; and not barbarously, not suddenly, not

[1] *XXVI Sermons*, 11. 161.
[2] Ibid. 14. 199.
[3] *LXXX Sermons*, 18. 178.
[4] *L Sermons*, 41. 376.
[5] *LXXX Sermons*, 4. 29.

occasionally, not extemporarily, which might derogate from the dignity of so great a service. That Ambassadour should open himself to a shrewd danger and surprisall, that should defer the thinking upon his Oration, till the Prince, to whom he was sent, were reading his letters of Credit: And it is a late time of meditation for a Sermon, when the Psalm is singing. *Loquere Domine*, sayes the Prophet; speak, O Lord: But it was when he was able to say, *Ecce paratus*, Behold I am prepared for thee to speak in me: If God shall be believed, to speak in us, in our ordinary Ministry, it must be, when we have, so as we can, fitted our selves, for his presence.'[1]

This passage indicates Donne's dislike of the extempore preaching affected by many of the Puritan clergy—a dislike which he expressed elsewhere in the words, 'Extemporall, unpremeditated Sermons, that serve the popular eare, vent, for the most part, doctrines that disquiet the Church.'[2] It is clear, however, from several references, as well as from Walton's express statement, that he did not read his sermons, but carefully prepared the heads of his discourse beforehand, making voluminous notes, and trusting his meditations to his memory.[3] If a copy of the sermon was afterwards required by friends, he wrote out the discourse from these notes. Thus, when Sir Henry Goodyer asked for a copy of a sermon delivered some time before, Donne replied, 'I will pretermit no time to write it, although in good faith I have half forgot it.' He 'faithfully exscribed' the sermon which he delivered at Whitehall in April 1627, when the king and Laud found fault with it, and he was commanded to furnish a copy for examination.[4] In this case the written copy would follow closely Donne's spoken words, but when there was a considerable interval before the sermon was written out in full many changes might be made. Thus Donne supplies the

[1] *XXVI Sermons*, 2. 20, 21. 'Preached at Whitehall, 12 Feb. 1618.'

[2] *L Sermons*, 25. 216.

[3] This was the practice of other Jacobean divines, as is seen in Donne's mention of another preacher in one of the *Letters*: 'I remember I heard the old King [i.e. James the First] say of a good Sermon, that he thought the Preacher never had thought of his Sermon, till he spoke it: it seemed to him negligently and extemporally spoken. And I knew that he had weighed every syllable, for halfe a year before, which made me conclude, that the King had before, some prejudice upon him.' *Letters* (1651), p. 309.

[4] Ibid., p. 305. The passage is quoted in chap. iv, p. 110.

following heading for No. 71 of the *LXXX Sermons*: 'At the *Haghe* Decemb. 19. 1619. I Preached upon this Text. Since in my sicknesse at *Abrey-hatche* in Essex, 1630, revising my short notes of that Sermon, I digested them into these two.'[1] Such a delay is probably the cause of the differences between the text of the 'Sermon of Valediction at my going into Germany', as it appears in the *XXVI Sermons* on the one hand, and in *Sapientia Clamitans* or the Bodleian manuscript on the other.[2]

Walton's account of Donne's method of preparing his sermons agrees with these references.

> 'The latter part of his life may be said to be a continued study; for as he usually preached once a week, if not oftner, so after his Sermon he never gave his eyes rest, till he had chosen out a new Text, and that night cast his Sermon into a form, and his Text into divisions; and the next day betook himself to consult the Fathers, and so commit his meditations to his memory, which was excellent.'[3]

Donne's manner in the pulpit and the effect of his eloquence on his hearers have been described by several of his audience. Walton's testimony is well known: 'preaching the Word so, as shewed his own heart was possest with those very thoughts and joyes that he laboured to distill into others: A Preacher in earnest; weeping sometimes for his Auditory, sometimes with them; alwayes preaching to himself, like an Angel from a cloud, but in none . . . and, all this with a most particular grace and an unexpressible addition of comeliness.' Sir Lucius Cary, afterwards Lord Falkland, gave a similar description in his *Elegie on Dr. Donne:*

> Nor yet forget that heavenly Eloquence,
> With which he did the bread of life dispense,
> Preacher and Orator discharg'd both parts
> With pleasure for our sense, health for our hearts,
> And the first such (Though a long studied Art
> Tell us our soule is all in every part),
> None was so marble, but whil'st him he heares,
> His Soule so long dwelt only in his eares . . .

[1] *LXXX Sermons*, 71. 717.

[2] For an account of these differences see pp. 280–6.

[3] Walton, *Life* (1670), p. 61.

Nor was there expectation to gaine grace
From forth his Sermons only, but his face;
So Primitive a looke, such gravitie
With humblenesse, and both with Pietie;
So milde was Moses countenance, when he prai'd
For them whose Satanisme his power gainsaid;
And such his gravitie, when all Gods band
Receiv'd his word (through him) at second hand,
Which joyn'd, did flames of more devotion move
Than ever Argive Hellens could of love.[1]

But while Donne was a preacher of great influence, beloved of such men as Walton, Herbert, and Sir Lucius Cary, and while his sermons drew vast crowds of the more educated Londoners, he was not popular with the extreme Puritans, who sometimes apparently showed their disapproval in church. The lines 'In memory of Doctor Donne', by R. B.,[2] affixed to the *Poems* of 1633, give a vivid picture of the differing opinions of the two sections of his audience.

Mee thinkes I see him in the pulpit standing,
Not eares, or eyes, but all mens hearts commanding,
Where wee that heard him, to our selves did faine
Golden Chrysostome was alive againe;
And never were we weari'd, till we saw
His houre (and but an houre) to end did draw.
How did he shame the doctrine-men, and use,
With helps to boot, for men to beare th'abuse
Of their tir'd patience, and endure th'expense
Of time, O spent in hearkning to non-sense,
With markes also, enough whereby to know,
The speaker is a zealous dunce, or so.
'Tis true, they quitted him, to their poore power,
They humm'd against him; And with face most sowre
Call'd him a strong lin'd man, a Macaroon,
And no way fit to speake to clouted shoone.
As fine words (truly) as you would desire,
But (verily,) but a bad edifier.
Thus did these beetles slight in him that good,
They could not see, and much lesse understood.
But we may say, when we compare the stuffe
Both brought; He was a candle, they the snuffe.[3]

[1] Grierson, i. 381, 382. [2] i.e. Richard Busby. [3] Grierson, i. 386, 387.

This difference between Donne and the 'doctrine-men' is insisted on in another elegy, that 'On Dr. Donnes death' by Jasper Mayne:

> Yet have I seene thee in the pulpit stand,
> Where wee might take notes, from thy looke, and hand;
> And from thy speaking action beare away
> More Sermon, then some teachers use to say.
> Such was thy carriage, and thy gesture such,
> As could divide the heart, and conscience touch.
> Thy motion did confute, and wee might see
> An errour vanquish'd by delivery.
> Not like our Sonnes of Zeale, who to reforme
> Their hearers, fiercely at the Pulpit storme,
> And beate the cushion into worse estate,
> Then if they did conclude it reprobate,
> Who can out pray the glasse, then lay about
> Till all Predestination be runne out.
> And from the point such tedious uses draw,
> Their repetitions would make Gospell, Law.
> No, In such temper would thy Sermons flow,
> So well did Doctrine, and thy language show,
> And had that holy feare, as, hearing thee,
> The Court would mend, and a good Christian bee.[1]

Donne's own sensations while preaching, and his consciousness of Puritan disapproval, are expressed in one of his Lincoln's Inn sermons:

'I am not all here, I am here now preaching upon this text, and I am at home in my Library considering whether *S. Gregory*, or *S. Hierome*, have said best of this text, before. I am here speaking to you, and yet I consider by the way, in the same instant, what it is likely you will say to one another, when I have done. You are not all here neither; you are here now, hearing me, and yet you are thinking that you have heard a better Sermon somewhere else, of this text before; you are here, and yet you think you could have heard some other doctrine of down-right *Predestination*, and *Reprobation* roundly delivered somewhere else with more edification to you.'[2]

As for the frequency and earnestness of his preaching, the number and nature of the printed *Sermons* prove his zeal—

[1] Ibid., p. 384. [2] *L Sermons*, 14. 116.

a zeal which apparently was too great for his strength, and helped to shorten his life.[1] In an undated Whitsunday sermon he points out the urgent need that the clergy should defend and arm their people with 'more and more instructions' against the insinuations of the Roman proselytizers, whom he compares to kites hovering over a brood of chickens, and continues:

'And if they deride us, for often preaching, and call us fooles for that, as *David* said, *He would be more vile*, he would Dance more, So let us be more fooles, in this foolishnesse of preaching, and preach more. . . . Let him that hath preached once, do it twice, and him that hath preached twice, do it thrice. But yet, not this, by comming to a negligent, and extemporall manner of preaching, but we will bee content to take so many hours from our rest, that we, with you, may rest the safelyer in *Abrahams* bosome, and so many more houres from our meat, that we, with you, may the more surely eat, and drink with the Lamb, in the kingdome of heaven.'[2]

Few preachers have impressed their personality on their sermons so vividly as Donne. He was no recluse, unable to feel for human weakness, and no hypocrite, claiming a saintliness which he did not possess; but a man of like passions with his hearers, a man whose history they all knew, whose penitence was as real as his sins had been, whose experience had taught him humility, compassion, and trust in the mercy of God.

It is this note of intense personal religious experience which gives to the *Sermons* their unique power. Behind their eloquence and elaborate rhetoric we hear the voice of a human soul, tortured at times by remorse for past sins,

[1] Two months before his death he wrote to George Gerrard, 'I have been always more sorry, when I could not preach, then any could be, that they could not hear me. It hath been my desire (and God may be pleased to grant it me), that I might die in the Pulpit; if not that, yet that I might take my death in the Pulpit, that is, die the sooner by occasion of my former labours' (*Letters*, pp. 242–3). This was in answer to a rumour that his illness was exaggerated in order that he might be free from preaching, and the truth of his assertion was proved by his last sermon, which was preached before the king when he was already a dying man, in so emaciated a condition that Charles and his Court called it 'the Doctors owne Funerall Sermon'.

[2] *LXXX Sermons*, 33. 325.

agonizing with his hearers to rescue them from temptations of which he knows the awful power, but inspired also by a great hope and a great devotion. The sermons of Andrewes or Laud or Barrow or South seem cold beside this ardour of penitence, this glowing love to the person of Christ, this yearning desire for the souls of men. Donne never glosses over the sinfulness of his past life, but in the fact that God has had mercy on his own soul, he sees encouragement and hope for the most despairing of his hearers.

Thus, speaking in joyful expectation of the resurrection of the dead, he rests all his confidence on Christ's merits.

> 'Christ shall bear witnesse for me, in ascribing his righteousnesse unto me, and in delivering me into his Fathers hands, with the same tendernesse, as he delivered up his owne soule, and in making me, who am a greater sinner, then they who crucified him on earth for me, as innocent, and as righteous as his glorious selfe, in the Kingdome of heaven.'[1]

His sense of the mercy of God shown in the person of Christ leads to some of the most passionate outbursts in the *Sermons:*

> 'Earth cannot receive, Heaven cannot give such another universall soul to all: all persons, all actions, as Mercy. And were I *the childe of this Text*,[2] that were to live *a hundred yeares*, I would ask no other marrow to my bones, no other wine to my heart, no other light to mine eyes, no other art to my understanding, no other eloquence to my tongue, then the power of apprehending for my self, and the power of deriving and conveying upon others by my Ministery, the Mercy, the early Mercy, the everlasting Mercy of yours, and my God.'[3]

> 'That soule that is washed, and thereby sees, to what a faire conformity with her Saviour she is come, is come also to a scorne, to a disdaine to compare any beauty in this world, to that face, which Angells desire to looke upon; any nearenesse to great persons in this world, to the *following of the Lambe wheresoever he goes*; any riches of this world, to that riches wherewith the poverty of Christ Jesus hath made us rich; any length of life in this world, to that union which

[1] *L Sermons*, 37. 343.
[2] Isa. lxv. 20. 'The child shall die a hundred years old.'
[3] *L Sermons*, 26. 222.

we shall have, to the *Antient of dayes*; where even the everliving God, shall not overlive us, but carry out our days to the unmeasured measure of his owne, to eternity.'[1]

This consciousness of God's mercy leads Donne to a fervent love for the souls of men, and to a desire to welcome other sinners to the fellowship of Christ's compassion:

'Shall we wonder that Christ would live with sinners, who was content to die for sinners? Wonder that he would eat the bread and Wine of sinners, that gave sinners his own flesh to eat, and his own blood to drink? Or if we do wonder at this, (as, indeed, nothing is more wonderful) yet let us not calumniate, let us not mis-interpret any way, that he shall be pleased to take, to derive his mercy to any man: but, (to use *Clement* of *Alexandria*'s comparison) as we tread upon many herbs negligently in the field, but when we see them in an Apothecaries shop, we begin to think that there is some vertue in them; so howsoever we have a perfect hatred, and a religious despite against a sinner, as a sinner; yet if Christ Jesus shall have been pleased to have come to his door, and to have stood, and knock'd, and enter'd, and sup'd, and brought his dish, and made himself that dish, and seal'd a reconciliation to that sinner, in admitting him to that Table, to that Communion, let us forget the Name of Publican, the Vices of any particular profession; and forget the name of sinner, the history of any mans former life; and be glad to meet that man now in the arms, and to grow up with that man now in the bowels of Christ Jesus; since Christ doth [not][2] now begin to make that man his, but now declares to us, that he hath been his, from all eternity: For in the Book of Life, the name of *Mary Magdalen* was as soon recorded, for all her incontinency, as the name of the blessed Virgin, for all her integrity; and the name of St. *Paul*, who drew his sword against Christ, as soon as St. *Peter*, who drew his in defence of him: for the Book of life was not written successively, word after word, line after line, but delivered as a Print, all together. There the greatest sinners were as soon recorded, as the most righteous; and here Christ comes *to call*, *not the righteous* at all, *but* onely *sinners to repentance*.'[3]

Yet the passages of directly personal allusion are not numerous. The witness of the *Sermons* to the arresting force of Donne's personality is all the more powerful because the personal element is so seldom consciously and deliberately

[1] *L Sermons*, 8. 65–6. [2] The sense requires this insertion.
[3] *XXVI Sermons*, 8. 111.

introduced. Such passages of direct self-revelation as occur are chiefly to be found, not in the sermons preached at St. Paul's as Dean, but in those delivered at Lincoln's Inn, where Donne had himself been a student and where the Benchers were, many of them, his intimate friends. Thus it was at Lincoln's Inn that Donne gave his reasons for preaching so often from the Psalms and St. Paul's Epistles:

'Almost every man hath his *Appetite*, and his *tast* disposed to some kind of *meates* rather then others; He knows what dish he would choose, for his first, and for his second course. We have often the same disposition in our *spirituall Diet*; a man may have a particular love towards such or such a book of Scripture, and in such an affection, I acknowledge, that my spirituall appetite carries me still, upon the *Psalms of David*, for a first course, for the Scriptures of the Old Testament: and upon the *Epistles of Saint Paul*, for a second course, for the New, and my meditations even for these *publike exercises* to Gods Church, returne oftnest to these two. For, as a hearty entertainer offers to others, the meat which he loves best himself, so doe I oftnest present to Gods people, in these Congregations, the meditations which I feed upon at home, in those two Scriptures. If a man be asked a reason why he loves one meat better then another, where all are equally good, (as the books of Scripture are) he will at least, finde a reason in some good example, that he sees some man of good tast, and temperate withall, so do: And for my Diet, I have *Saint Augustines* protestation, that he loved the *Book of Psalms*, and Saint *Chrysostomes*, that he loved Saint *Pauls Epistles*, with a particular devotion. I may have another more particular reason, because they are Scriptures, written in such forms, as I have been most accustomed to; Saint *Pauls* being Letters, and *Davids* being Poems: for, God gives us, not onely that which is meerly necessary, but that which is convenient too; He does not onely feed us, but *feed us with marrow, and with fatnesse*; he gives us our instruction in cheerfull forms, not in a sowre, and sullen, and angry, and unacceptable way, but cheerfully, in *Psalms*, which is also a limited, and a restrained form; Not in an *Oration*, not in *Prose*, but in *Psalms*; which is such a form as is both curious, and requires diligence in the making, and then when it is made, can have nothing, no syllable taken from it, nor added to it.'[1]

Elsewhere Donne gives a very characteristic reason for considering Ezekiel the greatest of the major prophets.

[1] *L Sermons*, 19. 151 (wrongly numbered in the folio as 159), 152.

'Amongst the four great ones, our Prophet *Ezekiel* is the *greatest*. I compare not their extraction and race; for, though *Ezekiel* were *de genere sacerdotali*, of the Leviticall and Priestly race. . . . *Esay* was of a higher, for he was of the extraction of their Kings, of the bloud royall. But the extraordinary greatnesse of *Ezekiel*, is in his extraordinary depth, and mysteriousnesse. . . .'[1]

In another sermon preached at Lincoln's Inn Donne refers to an incident in his visit to Aix.

'Lying at *Aix*, at *Aquisgrane*, a well known Town in *Germany*, and fixing there some time, for the benefit of those *Baths*, I found my self in a house, which was divided into many families, and indeed so large as it might have been a little Parish, or, at least, a great lim of a great one; But it was of no Parish: for when I ask'd who lay over my head, they told me a family of *Anabaptists*; And who over theirs? Another family of *Anabaptists*; and another family of *Anabaptists* over theirs; and the whole house, was a nest of these boxes; severall artificers; all *Anabaptists*; I ask'd in what room they met, for the exercise of their Religion; I was told they never met: for, though they were all *Anabaptists*, yet for some collaterall differences, they detested one another, and, though many of them, were near in bloud and alliance to one another, yet the son would excommunicate the father, in the room above him, and the Nephew the Uncle. As *S. John* is said to have quitted that *Bath*, into which *Cerinthus* the Heretique came, so did I this house; I remembred that *Hezekiah* in his sicknesse, turn'd himself in his bed, to pray *towards that wall*, that look'd to *Ierusalem*; And that *Daniel* in *Babylon*, when he pray'd in his chamber, opened those windows that look'd *towards Ierusalem*; for, in the first dedication of the Temple, at *Ierusalem*, there is a promise annext to the prayers made *towards the Temple*: And I began to think, how many roofs, how many floores of separation, were made between God and my prayers in that house.'[2]

To read the sermons side by side with a good life of Donne is to obtain a new and vivid light on the working of Donne's mind. It becomes clear that the sermons were no mere academic treatises, compiled by Donne in his study from a careful comparison of the works of the Fathers. They represent, it is true, the result of his wide and industrious reading, but they are far more than this—they reflect the varied course

[1] *L Sermons*, 24. 199.
[2] Ibid., no. 21, 'Preached at Lincolns Inne', p. 183.

of his life, and the cares and emotions which possessed him. After the great sorrow of his wife's death, his sermon on the text 'I am the man, that hath seen affliction, by the rod of his wrath' is said by Walton to have so worked upon the affections of his hearers that it 'melted and moulded them into a companionable sadness'. After another heavy blow, the death of his daughter Lucy, at the age of eighteen, his Easter sermon dealt with the women who 'received their dead raised to life again', and with the hope of a better resurrection. The father's grief and resignation find their expression in the words:

'He was but a Heathen that said, If God love a man, *Iuvenis tollitur*, He takes him young out of this world; And they were but Heathens, that observed that custome, To put on mourning when their sons were born, and to feast and triumph when they dyed. But thus much we may learne from these Heathens, That if the dead, and we, be not upon one floore, nor under one story, yet we are under one roofe. We think not a friend lost, because he is gone into another roome, nor because he is gone into another Land; And into another world, no man is gone; for that Heaven, which God created, and this world, is all one world. If I had fixt a Son in Court, or married a daughter into a plentifull Fortune, I were satisfied for that son and that daughter. Shall I not be so, when the King of Heaven hath taken that son to himselfe, and married himselfe to that daughter, for ever? . . . This is the faith that sustaines me, when I lose by the death of others, or when I suffer by living in misery my selfe, That the dead, and we, are now all in one Church, and at the resurrection, shall be all in one Quire.'[1]

When Donne was preparing for his visit to Bohemia as a member of Lord Hay's embassage, his sense of the dangers of the journey found expression not only in the 'Hymn to Christ' but also in the 'Sermon of Valediction at my going into Germany', with its urgent appeal for the thoughts and prayers of his friends.

'As we remember God, so for his sake, let us remember one another. In my long absence, and far distance from hence, remember me, as I shall do you in the ears of that God, to whom the farthest East, and the farthest West are but as the right and left ear in one of us; we

[1] *LXXX Sermons*, no. 22, 'Preached at S. *Pauls*, upon Easter-day. 1627', p. 220.

hear with both at once, and he hears in both at once; . . . And so as your eyes that stay here, and mine that must be far of, for all that distance shall meet every morning, in looking upon that same Sun, and meet every night, in looking upon the same Moon; so our hearts may meet morning and evening in that God, which sees and hears every where.'[1]

The plague which devastated London in the summer and autumn of 1625, and which led to his seclusion for three months in Sir John Danvers's house at Chelsea, is described in a sermon preached by Donne at St. Dunstan's on 15 January 1625/6, on the text, 'For there was not a house in which there was not one dead.' In it he gives a vivid picture of the horrors just past, of the 'men whose rapine and covetousness broke into houses, and seeking the wardrobes of others found their own winding-sheet, in the infection of that house where they stole their own death', of the rioting and drunkenness in which some, driven desperate, had indulged, and so met their death. And again his friendship for Lady Danvers, the mother of George Herbert, finds expression in the sermon 'preached at Chelsea, where she was buried, 1 July 1627'—a sermon which gives so fresh and beautiful a description of the home life of the Herberts that it is worthy to rank with Walton's picture in the *Lives*.

Donne's interest in the history of his times is also reflected in his sermons. There are few references to the internal politics of the day, except in so far as these had reference to religious matters, but Donne shows a lively interest in the events which led up to the Thirty Years War. This was natural, since he had known the luckless Queen of Bohemia, first as Princess Elizabeth and then as Electress Palatine, and had written an Epithalamium for her marriage and had preached before her at Heidelberg. An undated sermon preached at St. Paul's exhorts to sympathy and help for all in distress, 'whether Princes be dispossest of their naturall patrimony, and inheritance, or private persons afflicted with sicknesse, or penury, or banishment, let us goe Gods way, all the way. . . . Let us, us, with all the power we have, remove or slacken those calamities that lie upon them.'[2] The same

[1] *XXVI Sermons*, 19. 280.

[2] *LXXX Sermons*, 79. 808.

sermon speaks of ways of deliverance which are not God's ways, and takes as an example 'he may strengthen our Armies by calling in the Turke'.[1]

Another undated sermon may perhaps have been preached when the conflicting rumours of Frederick's defeat at Prague were perplexing men's minds, and there was a popular demand that England should join in the struggle. Donne rebukes the man whose faith is weakened by rumours of defeat.

> 'Hee stays not to give God his leasure, whether God will succour his cause to morrow, though not to day. Hee stays not to give men their Law, to give Princes, and States time to consider, whether it may not be fit for them to come to leagues, and alliances, and declarations for the assistance of the Cause of Religion next year, though not this. But *continuò scandalizatur*, as soon as a *Catholique army* hath given a blow, and got a victory of any of our forces, or friends, or as soon as a *crafty Jesuit* hath forged a Relation, that that Army hath given such a blow, or that such an Army there is, (for many times they intimidate weake men, when they shoote nothing but Paper, when they are onely *Paper-Armies*, and *Pamphlet-Victories*, and no such in truth) *Illico scandalizatur*, yet with these forged rumours, presently hee is scandalized.'[2]

King James's suppression of religious controversy during the negotiations for the Spanish marriage, and the revival of controversy when war broke out with Spain, are referred to in a sermon preached at St. Paul's, 21 May 1626, in which Donne, hearing 'that Drums beat in every field abroad', considers that it behoves him and his fellow clergy 'to returne to the brasing and beating of our Drums in the Pulpit too', and accordingly, after a loyal mention of James as 'he who was in his desire and intention, the Peace-maker of all the Christian world' and of Charles as 'he, who was then our hope, and is now the breath of our nostrils, and the Anointed of the Lord',[3] he proceeds to a slashing attack on the doctrine of prayers for the dead, purgatory, and indulgences.

There are also two interesting passages referring, one to the death of Elizabeth,[4] and the other to the death of

[1] Ibid. 79. 806.
[2] *L Sermons*, 18. 147.
[3] *LXXX Sermons*, 77. 778, 779.
[4] *XXVI Sermons*, 24. 351–2.

James.[1] The latter forms part of a funeral sermon in which Donne's eulogies of his dead master, though they would sound fulsome to modern ears, are yet moderate in tone when compared with the extravagant utterances of certain other divines on the same occasion. The passage on the death of Elizabeth and the accession of James is contained in a sermon on 24 March 1616/17. It was of this sermon that John Chamberlain wrote to Sir Dudley Carleton:

'I had almost forgotten that on Monday . . . the archbishop of Canterbury, the lord keeper . . . with divers other great men, were at Pauls Cross, and heard Donne, who made there a dainty sermon upon the 11th verse of the 22d of Proverbs, and was exceedingly well liked generally, the rather for that he did Queen Elizabeth great right, and held himself close to the text, without flattering the time too much.'[2]

In his interpretation of Scripture in the *Sermons* Donne made large use of the allegorical method which medieval divines had inherited from Clement of Alexandria and the early Christian Platonists. This method, which saw a symbolical meaning as well as the literal one in all the history of the Old Testament, was beginning to go out of fashion in Donne's time. It was being superseded by the plain historical exegesis which Colet had introduced into his treatment of St. Paul's epistles early in the sixteenth century. The allegorical interpretation had been pressed so hard in the later Middle Ages that the literal meaning of the text had been obscured and almost forgotten, and the new common-sense method was hailed as a way from darkness into the light of day. Donne himself in several passages declares that the allegorical method had been pressed too far. In the *Essays in Divinity* he condemns the 'curious refinings of the Allegoricall Fathers', and expresses his conviction that the word of God must be understood in its literal sense, although 'that also is not the literall, which the letter seems to present, for so to diverse understandings there might be diverse literall senses; but it is called literall, to distinguish it from

[1] *L Sermons*, 33. 303. Both this and the preceding passage are quoted by Mr. Pearsall Smith, op. cit., pp. 47, 57.

[2] *Court and Times of James I*, ii. 4.

the Morall, Allegoricall, and the other senses; and is that which the Holy Ghost doth in that place principally intend'.[1]

Yet Donne himself saw all material things as symbols of an inner reality. Thus, in spite of his intellectual conviction of the superiority of the plain historical interpretation of Scripture, he fell back constantly in his sermons, as in the *Essays*, into the use of the allegorical method. Though he abuses it in some places, it is one source of the perennial interest of his sermons. The comments of divines who used the newer methods are now out of date. The historical exegesis of Colet and those who followed him did its work and has been superseded by the later discoveries of more modern critics. But Donne's half-fantastic and poetical interpretations of Scripture have lost little by the passage of time. They are the result, not of scientific investigation of dates and sources, but of an insight into the heart of man, which is older than all philosophies, and yet is renewed in every child. Thus the Fall of Man which really concerns him is the fall, not of Adam, but of John Donne and his hearers from the innocence of childhood to the depravity of manhood. The wanderings of the Israelites in the wilderness are the wanderings of the Church of God through the desert of this world. Every detail is allegorized—even the quails, of which 'it is not said that every man had an equall number: some might have more, some lesse', and which are therefore interpreted to mean the knowledge, not of simple truths (the manna given to all), but of difficult points in religion.[2]

This method sometimes brings Donne curiously close to the modernists of to-day, but it would be a mistake to think that he held modernist views of the Bible. If he treated Jonah's whale as a symbol, it was because to him all whales, like all things else on earth, were symbols of a higher reality. He did not use allegory as a means of escaping from difficulties in the Bible story. The symbolic meaning did not replace the literal one—rather, it interpreted and enriched the poor obscure fragments of historical truth till they became a glowing whole in the crucible of the preacher's eloquence.

[1] *Essays in Divinity* (1651), p. 84.

[2] *LXXX Sermons*, 79. 807.

Among so large a collection of sermons as that contained in the folios it is natural that there should be a certain amount of repetition. The same quotations from the Fathers reappear in different contexts, and Donne uses his favourite images over and over again. There are also certain long paragraphs which are repeated with various minor alterations in such a way as to suggest that Donne sometimes used his old notes and wrote up passages which could be suitably transferred to a new context. The longest example I have discovered is to be found in two sermons separated from one another by nearly six years. Here the wording is so similar, though the context is a different one, that mere reminiscence would not explain the resemblance.

[1] How farre then is that wretched and sinfull man, from giving any testimony or glory to Christ in his life, who never comes to the knowledge, and consideration, *why* he was sent into this life? who is so farre from doing his errand, that he knowes not what his errand was; not whether he received any errand or no. But, as though that God, who for infinite millions of ages, delighted himself in himself, and was sufficient in himself, and yet at last did bestow *six dayes labour* for the creation, and provision of *man*, as though that God, who when man was sowr'd in the lumpe, poysoned in the fountaine, withered in the roote, in the loins of *Adam*, would then ingage *his Sonne*, his beloved Sonne, his onely Sonne, to be *man*, by a temporary life,

[2] How far is he from doing so, that never so much as considers why he was sent into this world; who is so far from having done his errand here, that he knows not, considers not what his errand was; nay knows not, considers not, whether he had any errand hither or no. But as though that God, who for infinite millions of millions of generations, before any creation, any world, contented himself with himself, satisfied, delighted himself with himself in heaven, without any creatures, yet at last did bestow six daies labor upon the Creation and accommodation of men, as though that God who when man was sour'd in the whole lump, poysoned in the fountain, perished at the chore, withered in the root, in the fall of *Adam*, would then in that dejection, that exinanition, that evacuation of the dignity of man, and not in his

[1] *L Sermons*, 37. 336, 'Preached at *St. Pauls* on Midsommer day. 1622.'

[2] *XXVI Sermons*, 15. 206, 'A Sermon Preached at *White-hall. February* 29. 1627', i.e. 1627/8.

and to be *no man*, by a violent and a shamefull death, as though that God, who when he was pleased to come to a creation, might have left out *thee*, amongst *privations*, amongst *nothings*, or might have shut thee up, in the close prison, of a bare *being* and no more, (as he hath done *earth* and *stones*) or, if he would have given thee life, might have left thee a *Toad*, or, if he would have given thee a *humane soule*, might have left thee a *heathen*, without any knowledge of God, or, if he had afforded thee a Religion, might have left thee a *Jew*, or though he had made thee a Christian, might have left thee a *Papist*; as though that God that hath done so much more, in breeding thee in his true Church, had done all this for *nothing*, thou passest thorough this world, like a *flash*, like a *lightning*, whose beginning or end nobody knowes, like an *Ignis fatuus* in the aire, which does not onely not give light for any use, but not so much as portend or signifie any thing; and thou passest out of the world, as thy hand passes out of a basin of water, which may bee somewhat the fouler for thy washing in it, but retaines no other impression of thy having been there; and so does the world for thy life in it. When God placed *Adam* in the *world*, he bad him *fill it*, and *subdue* it, and *rule* it; and when he placed him in *para-*

former better estate, engage his own Son, his only, his beloved Son, to become man by a temporary life, and then to become no man by a violent, and yet a voluntary death; as though that God who he was pleased to come to a creation, might yet have left thee where thou wast before, amongst privations, a nothing; or if he would have made thee something, a creature, yet he might have shut thee up in the closs prison of a bare being and no more, without life or sense, as he hath done earth and stones; or if he would have given thee life and sense, he might have left thee a toad, without the comeliness of shape, without that reasonable and immortal Soul, which makes thee a man; or if he had made thee a man, yet he might have lost thee upon the common amongst the Heathen, and not have taken thee into his inclosures, by giving thee a particular form of religion; or if he would have given thee a religion, He might have left thee a Jew; or if he would have given thee Christianity, He might have left thee a Papist, as though this God who had done so much more for thee, by breeding thee in a true Church, had done all this for nothing; thou passest through this world as a flash, as a lightning of which no man knows the beginning or the ending, as an *ignis fatuus* in the air, which does not only not give light for any use, but does not so much as portend or signifie anything; and thou passest *dise*, he bad him *dresse*, and *keepe paradise*; and when he sent his children into the overflowing *Land of promise*, he bad them *fight*, and *destroy* the Idolaters; to every body some task, some errand for his glory; And thou comest from him, into this world, as though he had said nothing unto thee, but *Go and do as you see cause, Go, and do as you see other men do.*

out of the world, as a hand passes out of a bason, or a body out of a bath, where the water may be the fouler for thy having washed in it, else the water retains no impression of thy hand or body, so the world may be the worse for thy having liv'd in it, else the world retains no marks of thy having been there. When God plac'd *Adam* in the world, God enjoyned *Adam* to fill the world, to subdue the world, and to rule the world; when God plac'd him in Paradise, He commanded him to dress Paradise, and to keep Paradise; when God plac'd his children in the land of promise, he enjoyned them to fight his battails against Idolatry, and to destroy Idolators; to every body some errand, some task for his glory; and thou commest from him into this world, as though he had said nothing to thee at parting, but go and do as thou shalt see cause, go and do as thou seest other men do, and serve me so far, and save thine own Soul so far, as the times, and the places, and the persons, with whom thou doest converse, will conveniently admit.

Very few of Donne's sermons were published during his lifetime. Of the six[1] which appeared in print before his

[1] These six were published as follows: (1) A Sermon . . . Preached at the Crosse the 15th of September. 1622. . . . Printed by William Stansby for Thomas Iones . . . 1622; (2) A Sermon . . . Preach'd To the Honourable Company of the Virginian Plantation. 13°. Nouemb. 1622. . . . Printed by A. Mat: for Thomas Iones . . . 1622; (3) Encaenia. The Feast of Dedication. Celebrated At Lincolns Inne, in a Sermon there vpon Ascension day, 1623. . . . Printed by Aug. Mat. for Thomas Iones . . . 1623; (4) The first sermon preached to King Charles, At Saint Iames: 3°. April. 1625. . . . Printed by A. M. for Thomas Iones . . . 1625; (5) A sermon, preached to the Kings Mtie. at

death, the most interesting are the *Sermon . . . Preach'd to the Honourable Company of the Virginian Plantation* and the *Sermon of Commemoration of the Lady Danuers*, i.e. Magdalen Herbert. Soon after his death his last sermon was printed as *Deaths Duell* (1632), which ran into a second edition the next year. In 1634 the University of Cambridge published six more of Donne's sermons, and these were afterwards included in the *Fifty Sermons* of 1649. The chief collections of Donne's sermons, however, are those which his son prepared for the press and issued in 1640, 1649, and 1660/1. These are known respectively as the *LXXX*, *Fifty*, and *XXVI Sermons*.

The *LXXX Sermons* of 1640 is a magnificent folio, beautifully printed, containing an engraving by Merian of a bust of Donne, a dedicatory epistle to King Charles from the younger Donne, the first draft of Izaak Walton's *Life and Death of Dr. Donne*, a copy of the epitaph on Donne's monument in St. Paul's, and a table of the sermons with their texts. These are followed by the *Imprimatur* dated 'Novemb. 29. 1639'. The sermons themselves occupy 826 pages, and are grouped according to the festivals on which they were delivered. They are followed by an elaborate index, containing first 'The Table of such places of Scripture, as are illustrated and expounded in this Booke', then 'The Table of such Authors, as are either cited, illustrated, or refelled in this Booke', and finally 'An Alphabeticall Table of the Principall Contents in this Book'.

The *Fifty Sermons* appeared in 1649, also in folio. They were prefaced by a dedicatory epistle from the younger Donne to Basil, Earl of Denbigh, and by a shorter epistle to Whitlock, Keeble, and Leile, the Lords Commissioners of the Great Seal, in which Donne states that the reward which had been promised him 'many yeares since' for the publication of these sermons had been lately conferred upon him 'under the authority of the Great Seale'. Though there is an intro-

Whitehall, 24 Febr. 1625. . . . Printed for Thomas Iones . . . 1626; (6) A sermon of commemoration of the Lady Danuers . . . 1. July 1627. . . . Printed by I. H. for Philemon Stephens, and Christopher Meredith . . . 1627. The earlier of these were collected in successive volumes as *Three Sermons* (1623), *Foure Sermons* (1625), and *Fiue Sermons* (1626).

ductory table of the texts, there is no index. The sermons occupy 464 pages, and are grouped according to the occasions on which they were delivered (e.g. Sermons preached at Marriages, Christenings, Churchings) or the place of their delivery—Lincoln's Inn, Whitehall, St. Paul's, St. Dunstan's.

The *Fifty Sermons* are well printed on the whole. There are a few errors in pagination, for example, page 150 is numbered as 158, page 151 as 159, page 212 as 312. In all these cases the subsequent pagination is not affected by the mistake (e.g. after the wrongly numbered 159, really 151, follows page 152). But page 290 is wrongly numbered as 300, and from this the numbering goes on as 301, 302, &c., 290–9 being omitted.

The textual errors are not numerous. Occasionally two or three misprints occur on one page (for example, page 265 has *wordly* for *worldly*, *to ever* for *so ever*, and *anothet* for *another*). But on the other hand, we find stretches of ten or twelve pages without a single error. Such mistakes as occur are generally obvious misprints which can easily be corrected, such as '*Corrasive*' (page 3, line 19) for '*Corrosive*', '*Induere*' (page 52, line 37) for '*Induere*', '*them them*' (page 75, line 39) for '*them*'.

Six of the sermons in this volume (Nos. 3, 12, 13, 28, 29, 35) had been published in 1634 by the University of Cambridge. A collation of the two editions does not reveal any considerable differences. There are certain obvious errors in the *Six Sermons* which have been corrected in the *Fifty Sermons*, for example, the latter reads 'I leave' (page 20, line 25) for the earlier 'I have'; 'low' (page 241, line 15) for 'law'; 'Vulgat' (page 245, line 50) for 'vulgar'. On the other hand, there are some passages in which the text of the *Six Sermons* is to be preferred.

The *LXXX* and the *Fifty Sermons* were prepared for the press at the same time by John Donne the younger, though an interval of nine years elapsed between the publication of the two volumes. Three entries in the Stationers' Register make this clear:

3 Jan. 1639/40

Master ffesher and Master Marriott	Entred for their Copie vnder the hands of Master Browne and Master Bourne warden a booke called *ffowerscore sermons* penned and preached by

the reverend John Donne Doctor in divinity late Deane of Saint Pauls vj[d]

19 Feb. 1639/40

Richard Roiston. Assigned ouer vnto him by vertue of a note vnder the hands and seales of Master ffesher and Master Marriott and subscribed by master Bourne warden a full third parte or share in the booke called *ffourscore sermons* penned and preached by the reuerend John Dunne doctor [of] D[ivinity]: late deane of Saint Pauls vj[d]

eodem die

Master ffesher
Master Marriott
and
Richard: Roiston. Entred for their Copie vnder the hands of A: ffrewen, vice-chancellor of the vniuersity of Oxford and master Bourne warden a booke called *ffifty Sermons* penned and preached by the reverend John Dunne doctor: [of] D[ivinity]: and late deane of Saint Pauls vj[d]

with his picture and the tables and all the six score and ten *sermons*.

The *XXVI Sermons* of 1660/1 are much less carefully printed. There are in reality only twenty-four sermons included, for No. 16 is a repetition of No. 5, with an alteration in the date as given in the title (February 22 for February 12), and No. 17 is a repetition of No. 3 without the title.

The pagination is faulty, numbers 121–8 being omitted, and 177–83 being used twice. Page 209 is wrongly numbered as 109, and pages 244, 245 as 236, 237. Numbers 285–96 are used twice. Page 349 is numbered as 333, and page 363 as 361. Numbers 393–6 are omitted.

The collation also is most irregular, as will be seen from its formula, A^2, B^4, B^4–Q^4, S^4–Mm^4, Nn^6–Oo^6, Pp^4–Ccc^4,[1] Ddd^6, Fff^4–Ggg^4. It will be noticed that the absence of R^4 corresponds with the omission of 121–8 in the pagination. Since *Sermon* 8 ends on page 120, and the sermon which follows it immediately on the page numbered as 129 is called *Sermon* 10 both in the title and in the margin, it may be surmised that another sermon numbered as 9 should have

[1] There are irregularities in the Pp–Tt sheets. Pp 1 appears in some copies as Ppp, followed by Pp 2. Qq 1 and 2 are marked as Qqq and Qqq 2. The Rr sheet begins correctly with Rr, followed, however, by Rrr 2. Ss 1 and 2 appear as Sss and Sss 2, and Tt 2 as Ttt 2.

occupied pages 121–8 (R4), but that while the volume was passing through the press, it was for some reason omitted. The requisite number of sermons is made up by dividing *Sermon* 10 into two, with separate headings, though both parts are numbered as 10.

Misprints are fairly numerous.[1] The most interesting sermons from a textual point of view are numbers 3 (or 17), 5 (or 16), 19, and 26. There are a considerable number of slight differences in reading and punctuation between the two forms of *Sermons* 3 and 5. The text of *Sermon* 3 is on the whole to be preferred to that of 17, though it has some errors which are corrected in the latter. Similarly the text of 5 is to be preferred to that of 16. The chaotic state of the collation shows that John Donne the younger was obliged for some reason or other to change his plan of the sermons which he meant to include. He may have intended to reprint the Virginia Company sermon and some of the other sermons published by Thomas Jones, but if the publisher interfered and claimed his right, Donne would find himself in a difficulty, since he had already printed 130 of his father's sermons in the two previous folios, and his stock of manuscript was evidently running low. He had promised the world a volume of twenty-six sermons, but in order to make up the number he was forced to print two sermons twice over, to cut a long sermon into two short ones, and to reprint the famous *Deaths Duell* without any mention of the occasion on which it had been preached or any acknowledgement that it had already passed through two editions. In fact his Preface 'to the Reader' is full of the grossest misrepresentation. He laments the scanty recompense which he has hitherto received for the publication of his father's sermons, and adds a postscript which runs thus: 'By the Dates of these *Sermons*, the Reader may easily collect, that although they are the last that are published, they were the first that were Preached;

[1] A collation of the copies found in the British Museum, the Bodleian, the Cambridge University Library, and St. Paul's Cathedral Library, shows that a number of corrections were made while the volume was passing through the press. The St. Paul's (large-paper) copy has many corrections of mistakes found in the other copies mentioned.

and I did purposely select these from amongst all the rest, for, being to finish this Monument, which I was to erect to his Memory, I ought to reserve those materials that were set forth with the best Polish.' One glance at the headings will show that among the dated sermons three belong to the last three years of Donne's life, and one of the undated ones (*Deaths Duell*) is his very last.

A collation of *Deaths Duell* with the sermon here printed as No. 26 reveals very few important changes. The spelling, punctuation, and use of italics in *Deaths Duell* are more archaic, and probably nearer to Donne's manuscript. A number of errors in *Deaths Duell* are corrected in the *XXVI Sermons*, for example, on page 397, l. 8 the latter reads '*ad salutes*' for 'and *salutes*'. But it adds a few fresh printer's errors, for example, on page 397, l. 15 it reads '*belongs*' for '*belong*', and later in the same line, 'it is his power' for 'it is in his power'.

An interesting problem is raised by the sermon numbered as 19 in the *XXVI Sermons*, and headed 'A Sermon of Valediction at my going into *Germany*, at *Loncolns-Inne* [*sic*], April. 18. 1619'. Dr. Keynes[1] showed that this sermon was published, without Donne's name, as early as 1638, in a volume bearing the title, 'Sapientia Clamitans, Wisdome Crying out to Sinners to returne from their evill wayes: Contained in three pious and learned Treatises . . . Heretofore communicated to some friends in written copies: but now published for the generall good, By William Milbourne[2] Priest . . . . London, Printed by I. Haviland, for R. Milbourne at the Unicorne neere Fleet-bridge. 1638.'

The first two treatises have been identified by Dr. Keynes as sermons by Thomas Jackson, Dean of Peterborough. The third sermon, which is Donne's *Sermon of Valediction*, has a sub-title: 'Mans timely remembring of his Creator; or An exposition delivered in a Sermon upon Ecclesiastes 12. 1. Remember now thy Creator in the dayes of thy youth. London, Printed by John Haviland, for Robert Milbourne. 1638.'

[1] Op. cit., pp. 35–6.

[2] R. C. Bald has drawn attention to a letter from Milbourne in *The Correspondence of John Cosin* (Surtees Society, vol. 52, pp. 221–2) in which he expresses annoyance at the appearance of his name on the title-page.

The book was reissued in 1639 by another printer.[1] The title-page is slightly altered, and runs thus: 'Wisdome crying out to Sinners to returne from their evill wayes. . . . London, Printed by M. P. for Iohn Stafford, dwelling in Blackhorse Alley neere Fleetstreet. 1639.'

This sermon is also found in three seventeenth-century manuscripts—the Lothian MS. (*L*) belonging to the Marquess of Lothian, the Ashmole (*A*), MS. Ash. 781 in the Bodleian Library, and the Dobell (*Do*), MS. Nor. 4506 in Harvard College Library. These three contain a large number of trivial scribal variants, but their text is substantially the same as that found in *Sapientia Clamitans*, and differs widely from that in *XXVI Sermons*. Collation makes it clear that the text found in the manuscripts and *Sapientia Clamitans* represents Donne's original version preached at Lincoln's Inn, while the *XXVI Sermons* contains a carefully revised text, in which alterations have been made in almost every sentence.[2] The two versions were printed in 1932 in my edition, *Donne's Sermon of Valediction*, by the Nonesuch Press, and a comparison shows that in the *XXVI Sermons* there is a certain amount of compression, and here and there whole sentences have been omitted. The phrasing is less vivid and dramatic, and this is natural, for an eloquent preacher like Donne would inevitably introduce rhetorical questions and repetitions which would be effective enough in the pulpit, though he would omit them from his written copy. Compare, for example, *XXVI*, 19. 270: 'Now, *in this day*, and *in these dayes* Remember first the Creator,' with *Sapientia Clamitans*, 256: '*Now in thy day*, and, *Now in these dayes*, Remember. But *whom*? First, *The Creator*.' Notice also the dramatic close of the sermon as reported in *Sapientia*

[1] There is a copy of this issue in the Cambridge University Library. Emmanuel College, Cambridge, has a copy, in which the date on the title-page is given as 1640.

[2] In the first edition of this *Study* I suggested that the version found in the Ashmole MS. and *Sapientia Clamitans* might have been written out from notes taken by one of Donne's hearers. The discovery of the sermon in almost exactly the same form in the Lothian MS. has disproved this theory, for the Lothian MS. contains seven other sermons by Donne, all written out in the summer of 1624, and evidently copied from another manuscript.

Clamitans and the manuscripts as compared with the end in the *XXVI Sermons* (quoted *infra*, p. 286). Or again, compare *XXVI*, 19. 273: 'God did not make the fire for us; but much less did he make us for that fire; that is, make us to damn us' with the forcible reading of *Sapientia Clamitans* 274 (supported by the manuscripts), 'God did not make that fire for us, much lesse did hee make us for that fire: (make us to damne us? God forbid:).'

In several places *Sapientia Clamitans* and the manuscripts enable us to correct evident errors in the folio. Thus in *XXVI*, 19. 272, we read, 'every man hath a pocket picture about him, *Emanuel*, a bosome book,' while *Sapientia Clamitans* offers the correct reading, 'every man hath a *pocket-picture* about him, a *manuall*, a *bosome booke*', and this is supported by the manuscripts. Again, 'Remember thy Creator, and remember thy Creator' (*XXVI*, 19. 270) is a meaningless repetition, to which the reading of *Sapientia Clamitans*, 257 gives point, '*Remember the Creator:* and *Remember thy Creator.*' *XXVI*, 19. 274 reads: 'This is then our first day the true passion of Christ Jesus', a phrase which seems entirely out of place in the context, where no mention has been made of the Passion. *Sapientia Clamitans* (page 278) reads: 'This is then our first day, The *Light*, the *knowledge* the profession of the Gospell of *Christ Jesus*', and the manuscripts, which agree with the latter, enable us to see how the reading of *XXVI* arose from the contraction of 'profession'.

The folio text, however, is superior to that in *Sapientia Clamitans* and the manuscripts in point of style. When Donne revised the sermon he rewrote many loose and shambling sentences, omitted some digressions, and made the main argument clearer. Now and then he adjusted the rhythm of the sentences, as in his alteration of the original phrase 'in the Fall, about September' to 'at the fall of the leaf, in the end of the year', where instead of compressing, he has lengthened the sentence so as to make its modulation more pleasing to the ear.[1]

A series of parallel passages will show some of the more important changes. As the text of the Lothian MS. has been

[1] See *Donne's Sermon of Valediction*, pp. 5–8.

reprinted in full in my Nonesuch edition, the passages here are printed from the Ashmole MS.

MS. Ashmole, p. 3.

Consider ye other faculty ye will of Man and thereby ye bitternesse wch haue passed between y^{e} *Iesuits* & y^{e} *Dominicans in* y^{e} *Roman Church.* even to ye imputac̃ons of the crime of heresie vpon one annother in questions concerning ye will of Mann, and how y^{t} concernes wth ye grace of *God* ꝑticularly whether ye same ꝑporc̃on of grace being offered by *God* to two men equallie disposed towards him must not necessarily worke equally in those 2, *And* by those bitternesses amongest *Persones* neerest even to ye drawing of swordes in questions of ye same kind, ꝑticularly, whether y^{t} ꝑporc̃on of grace, wch doth effectually convert a ꝑticular Man might not haue bin resisted, by y^{e} ꝑversness of that Mannes will whether y^{t} grace were irresistable or no, By all theis & infinite such difficulties wee may see vntractable & vntamable a facultie of ye will of Mann is: But leaue ye vnderstanding & ye will and come to ye memory. Come not wth ye matter of law but matter of fact. Let *God* make his wonderfull works to be had

Sap. Clam. 260–2.

Consider the other facultie, the *will* of man; and thereby those bitternesses between the *Jesuites* and the *Dominicans* in the *Romane* Church, even to the imputation of the crime of heresie upon one another, in questions concerning the *Will* of man, and how that concurres with the *Grace of God*; particularly, *Whether the same proportion of Grace being offered by God to two men equally disposed towards him before, must not necessarily worke equally in those two?* And by those bitternesses amongst persons nearest us, even to the drawing of swords, in questions of the same kinde; particularly, *Whether that proportion of Grace, which doth effectually convert a particular man, might not have been resisted by the perversenesse of that mans will? Whether that grace were irresistible or no?* By all these and infinite such difficulties wee may see how untractable and untameable a facultie *the will* of man is. But leave the *Vnderstanding* and the *Will*, and come to the *Memorie*, not with matter of *Law*, but with

XXVI. 19. 271.

Consider the other faculty, the will of man, by those bitternesses which have passed between the Jesuits and the Dominicans, (amongst other things belonging to the will) whether the same proportion of grace, offered to men alike disposed, must necessarily work alike upon both their wills? And amongst persons neerer to us, whether that proportion of grace, which doth convert a man, might not have been resisted by perversness of his will? By all these difficulties we way [*sic*] see, how untractable, and untameable a faculty the wil of man is. But come not with matter of law, but matter of fact, *Let God make his wonderful works to be had in remembrance*: present the history of Gods protection of his children, from the beginning, in the ark, in both captivities, in infinite dangers . . .'

MS. *A*, p. 3 *contd.*	*Sap. Clam.* 260–2 *contd.*	
in remēbrance, *as David saies Present* the historie of *Gods* ꝑtec̃on of his Children in *ye Arke* in y^{e} *wilderness in ye Captivitie* in infinite other daingers . . .'	matter of *Fact*; Let *God make his wonderful works to be had in remembrance* (as *David* speaketh;) present the histories of Gods protection of his children in the Arke, in the wildernesse, in the Captivities, in infinite other dangers . . .'	

MS. *A*, p. 3.	*Sap. Clam.*	*XXVI.* 19. 271.
Present many of y^{e} ꝓphecies of the revelac̃on Concerninge *Antichrist*, and a *Papist* vnderstandinge will take them of a single, and a sodaine & a transitorie man, that must last but 3 yeares and a halfe, but *Protestants* vnderstandinge will take it of a succession & continuance of men. y^{t} haue lasted a 1000 yeares at least already.	Omitted altogether.	present any of the prophecies of the Revelation concerning Antichrist, and a Papist will understand it of a single, and momentane, and transitory man, that must last but three yeer and a half; and a Protestant may understand it of a succession of men, that have lasted so 1000. yeers already.

MS. *A*, p. 4.	*Sap. Clam.* 263.	*XXVI.* 19. 271.
And so in deliveringe y^{e} *Ghospell* in one principall seale thereof the ꝑticipiation of his body and blood in the Sacrament. He ꝓceeds so to ye recommende it to their *memory Doe this in remembrance of me.* This is ye faculty y^{t} *God* desires to worke vppon, and therfore if thy vnderstanding be to narrow to comp^{r}hend or reconcile all differences in Churches (as what vnderstanding is	And so in delivering the *Gospell*, one principall *Seale* thereof, the participation of his *Bodie* and *Blood* in the Sacrament, hee proceeds so too, hee recommends it to their *Memorie*; *Doe this in remembrance of mee.* This is the facultie that God desires to worke upon. And therefore, if thine *understanding* be too narrow to comprehend or reconcile all differences in all Churches, as what *understanding* is	And so in delivering the Gospel in one principal seal thereof, the sacrament of his body, he recommended it only to their memory, *Do this in remembrance of me.* This is the faculty that God desires to work upon; And therefore if thine understanding cannot reconcile differences in all Churches, if thy will cannot submit it self to the ordinances of thine own Church, go to thine own memory . . .

MS. *A*, p. 4 *contd.*

large enoughe to do so.) if thy will be too scrupulous to submitt it selfe, to the ordinance of thy owne Church as somtymes a Zeale. thoe not ꝑverse. yet vndigested may worke that, Yet haue a reconverse to thy *memorie*.

Sap. Clam. 263 *contd.*

large enough to doe so? If thy *will* bee too scrupulous to submit it selfe to the *Ordinances* of thine owne *Church*, which sometimes a *Zeale*, though not *perverse*, yet *indigested*, may worke: yet have recourse to thine owne m*emorie*.

MS. *A*, pp. 9, 10.

and sinc God hath giuen vs this day ye light of the *Ghospell* to those vses to try, o^{r} owne p^{u}pos^{s} by, in o^{r} selues. & to shew & Iustifie o^{r} actiones by, to ye world since wee see this religion to be good y^{t} is ꝑfest advisedly not implicitly, but he y^{t} is able to abide any triall that ye aduersarie will put vs to of *Antiquitie & Fathers & Councells*, Since it is so severed from darkness, as y^{t} no corrupt ꝑtes ar mingled wth it, and so severed as y^{t} there be sufficient lawes & meanes for ye abolishinge vtterly, *Since God* hath giuen vs this day. *Qui non humiliavit anima in die hac*, *as Moses saith*, of other dayes of Gods institution, he y^{t} will not throw downe himselfe before God in this day. in humble thankes. that wee haue it in humble prayers, that we may still haue it; He doth not remember *God* in

Sap. Clam. 283, 284.

And since God hath given us *This day*, *The light of the Gospell*, to these uses, to trie our owne purposes by, in our selves, and to shew and justifie our actions by, to the world; since wee see this *Religion* to bee good, and that it is professed advisedly, and not implicitly; but so that it is able to abide any triall that the adversarie will put us to, *of antiquities*, *Fathers and Councels*; since it is so severed, as that there are sufficient lawes and meanes for the abolition of superstition utterly: since God hath given us *this day: Qui non humiliabit animam in die hac*, *etc*. (as *Moses* speakes of other dayes of Gods institution) hee that will not throw downe himselfe before God *on this day*, in humble thanks that wee have it, and in humble prayer that wee may still have it: hee does not *remember God in his first*

XXVI. 19. 274, 275.

And since God hath given us this day, the brightness of his Gospel, that this light is first presented, that is, all great actions begun with this consideration of the Gospel; since all other things are made by this light, that is, all have relation to the continuance of the Gospel, since God hath given us such a head, as is sharp-sighted in seeing the several lights, wise in discerning the true light, powerful in resisting forraign darkness; since God hath given us this day, *qui non humiliabit animam suam in die hac*, as *Moses* speaks of the dayes of Gods institution, he that will not remember God now in this day, is impious to him, and unthankful to that great instrument of his, by whom this day spring from an [*sic*] high hath visited us.

MS. *A*, pp. 9, 10 *contd.*	*Sap. Clam.* 283, 284 *contd.*	
his first day, he doth not Consider how great a the pfession of y^{e} *Ghospell* is.	*day*; he doth not consider how great a blessing *the light*, *the profession of the Gospell* is.	

MS. *A*, p. 16.	*Sap. Clam.* 306, 307.	*XXVI.* 19. 279.
that so neither heyght. nor dep[t]h nor any other Creature. may sepate thee from God, not only sepate finally; but not returned thee any other wayes, but as the loue of the Creature, may lead thee to the Creator, Wee see fair shipps in the River, but all their vse were gon if y^{t} river lead not out into ye sea. Wee see men fraught. wth honor and riches, but all their vse is gon, if that lead them. not to the honor & glory of the Creator; And therfore saies the *Apostle*. let them that suffer Comitt their soules to *God*, as to a faithfull Creator, He had gratious p^{u}pos^{s} vppon vs in o^{r} Creation, and if he bringe vs back againe to as good estate as wee had in o^{r} Creation. wee enioy ye very redemption too.	that so *neither height*, *nor depth*, *nor any other Creature may separate* thee from God; not onely *separate* thee finally, but not *retard* thee any other wayes; but as the love of the *Creature* may lead thee to *the Creator*. Wee see faire shipping in the River: but all their use were gone, if the River led not into the Sea. Wee see men fraughted with honour and riches: but all their use is gone, if they lead them not to the honour and glory of the *Creator*. And therefore saies the *Apostle*, *Let them that suffer commit their soules to God as to a faithfull Creator*. Hee had gracious purposes upon us in our *Creation*; and if hee bring us back againe to as good a state as wee had in our *Creation*, wee enjoy the very *Redemption* too.	That so neither *height nor depth*, *nor any other creature may separate thee from God*; not only not separate thee finally, but not separate so, as to stop upon the creature, but to make the best of them, thy way to the Creator; We see ships in the river; but all their use is gone, if they go not to sea; we see men fraighted with honor, and riches, but all their use is gone, if their respect be not upon the honor and glory of the Creator; and therefore sayes the Apostle, *Let them that suffer*, *commit their souls to God*, *as to a faithful Creator*; that is, He made them, and therefore will have care of them.

MS. *A*, p. 18.	*Sap. Clam.* 316, 317.	*XXVI.* 19. 280, 281.
& Christ Iesus remēber vs all in his kingdome. to wch thoe wee must saile through a sea yet it is a sea of his blood in wch soule never	And *Christ Jesus remember* us all in his kingdome, to which though wee must saile through a sea, yet it is the sea of his bloud,	and Christ Jesus remember us all in his Kingdome, to which, though we must sail through a sea, it is the sea of his blood, where

MS. *A*, p. 18 *contd.*	*Sap. Clam.* 316, 317 *contd.*	*XXVI.* 19. 280, 281 *contd.*
suffered shipwracke Though wee must be blowne wth strong winds. wth vehement sighs & groanes for or siñes, yet is the spirritt of *God.* that blowes all that winde in vs, and shall blow away all Contrarie windes of difference in his mercy.	in which never soule suffered shipwrack. Though we must bee blowne with strong windes, with vehement sighes and groans for our sinnes: yet it is the Spirit of God that blowes all that winde in us, and shall blow away all contrarie windes of diffidence in his mercy.	no soul suffers shipwrack; though we must be blown with strange winds, with sighs and groans for our sins, yet it is the Spirit of God that blows all this wind, and shall blow away all contrary winds of diffidence or distrust in Gods mercy.
MS. *A*, p. 19.	*Sap. Clam.* 318, 319.	*XXVI.* 19. 281.
where wee shall haue more strength & no enemies, wee shall liue & never dye, where wee shall meete & never ꝑte, but here wee must.	where wee shall have more strength, and no enemie; where wee shall live, and never die; where we shall meet, and never part; but here we must.	(last words of sermon): where we shall be stronger to resist, and yet have no enemy; where we shall live and never die, where we shall meet and never part.

The sermons as a whole were reprinted by Dean Alford in 1839 in a six-volume edition described as *The Works of John Donne*. This was a most misleading title, for the edition omitted *Juvenilia*, *Biathanatos*, *Pseudo-Martyr*, *Ignatius his Conclave*, *Catalogus Librorum*, *Essays in Divinity*, and many of the letters and poems, but as far as the sermons are concerned, it is fairly complete, for it contains all the sermons found in the three folios, with the addition of the sermons preached to the Virginia Company, and at the funeral of Lady Danvers. Alford modernized the text in spelling, punctuation, and the use of capitals, but when allowance is made for this, his text is more accurate than one would expect from Gosse's criticism.[1] His text of the poems is worthless,

[1] Gosse, i, p. x. 'But, worse than all this, Alford was so little acquainted with the difficulties of press-reading and collation, that his text absolutely swarms with errors. His notes are few, but they are almost always glaringly inaccurate. In short, this edition of the works of Donne, which is the only one which has ever been attempted, is (it is distressing to have to say) no better than so much waste paper.'

but his reprint of the sermons compares favourably in point of accuracy with Gosse's own reprint of Donne's letters.

Four sermons (*LXXX Sermons*, Nos. 18, 19, 20, 21) were reprinted in *The Sacred Classics, or Cabinet Library of Divinity* in London in 1835. In 1921 Mr. Wilfred Merton produced a privately printed facsimile of Donne's sermon on Psalm 38. 9, from the Dowden MS. in his possession. The same sermon was printed from the Harvard MS., Nor. 4506 (the Dobell MS.), with an introduction and notes by G. R. Potter, by the Stanford University Press, California, in 1945. A reprint of *LXXX Sermons*, Nos. 15 and 66, was published in 1921, by the Cambridge University Press. In 1923 the Nonesuch Press issued *X Sermons preached by . . . John Donne*, with a bibliographical note by G. L. Keynes. In 1932 the Nonesuch Press issued *Donne's Sermon of Valediction . . . Printed from the Original Version in the Lothian and Ashmole Manuscripts and from XXVI Sermons*, with an introduction and notes by Evelyn M. Simpson.

This list of editions shows the fluctuations of Donne's fame. Between 1661 and 1835 no edition of the sermons or of the *Devotions* was published. There was then a short revival of his popularity, followed by another seventy years of neglect. Since 1919 there has been another revival, and his position as one of our great prose-writers is now well established.

Two causes combined to cause the revival in the first half of the nineteenth century. One was the enthusiastic praise of Coleridge, the other was the rise of the Oxford Movement in the Church of England. Coleridge is by far the greatest critic who has ever undertaken a careful examination of Donne's sermons. His notes on the *LXXX Sermons*, printed by his son Derwent Coleridge in *Notes on the English Divines* (1853), show his attitude towards Donne's theology, with which he was not always in sympathy.

As examples of his praise we may instance his commendation of No. 6 of the *LXXX Sermons* as 'A noble sermon in thought and diction',[1] or of the passage on death beginning 'The ashes of an Oak in the Chimney, are no Epitaph of that

[1] *Notes on the English Divines*, i. 85.

Oak, to tell me how high or how large that was; It tels me not what flocks it sheltered while it stood, nor what men it hurt when it fell. The dust of great persons graves is speechlesse too, it sayes nothing, it distinguishes nothing. . . .'[1] On this Coleridge remarks briefly 'Very beautiful indeed'.[2] Donne's comment on the story of the young ruler 'He was no ignorant man, and yet he acknowledged that he had somewhat more to learn of Christ, than he knew yet. Blessed are they that inanimate all their knowledge, consummate all in Christ Jesus . . .'[3] excites the remark, 'The whole paragraph is pure gold. Without being aware of this passage in Donne I expressed the same conviction, or rather declared the same experience, in the Appendix to the Statesman's Manual.'[4] When Donne declares that nothing is essentially good but God, and that there is nothing in the world which does not in some measure partake of that goodness,[5] Coleridge finds himself in entire agreement, and observes

> 'All excellent, and [paragraph] D. most so. Thus, thus our old divines showed the depth of their love and appreciation of the Scriptures, and thus led their congregations to feel and see the same. Here is Donne's authority (*Deus non est ens, etc.*) for what I have so earnestly endeavoured to show, that *Deus est ens super ens*, the ground of all being, but therein likewise absolute Being, in that he is the eternal self-affirmant, the I Am in that I Am; and that the key of this mystery is given to us in the pure idea of the will, as the alone *Causa Sui*. O! compare this manhood of our Church divinity with the feeble dotage of the Paleyan school, the "natural" theology, or watchmaking scheme, that knows nothing of the maker but what can be proved out of the watch.'[6]

On a comparison of God's mercy with His judgements Coleridge comments 'A just sentiment beautifully expressed',[7] and a little lower on the page, when Donne quotes Gregory Nazianzen to show that the Christian religion is *simplex et nuda, nisi pravè in artem difficillimam converteretur*, the comment is

> 'A religion of ideas, spiritual truths, or truth-powers,—not of notions

[1] *LXXX*. 15. 148. [2] *Notes*, i. 97. [3] *LXXX*. 17. 165.
[4] *Notes*, i. 105. [5] *LXXX*. 17. 167, paragraphs B, C, D.
[6] *Notes*, i. 107–8. [7] Ibid., p. 89 on *LXXX*. 7. 71.

and conceptions, the manufacture of the understanding,—is therefore *simplex et nuda*, that is, immediate; like the clear blue heaven of Italy, deep and transparent, an ocean unfathomable in its depth, and yet ground all the way. Still as meditation soars upwards, it meets the arched firmament with all its suspended lamps of light. O, let not the *simplex et nuda* of Gregory be perverted to the Socinian "plain and easy for the meanest understandings!" The truth in Christ, like the peace of Christ, passeth all understanding.'[1]

There are, however, a number of passages in which Coleridge strongly criticizes Donne's theology or philosophy. On a paragraph in one of the Christmas sermons he observes 'A very meagre and inadequate interpretation of this sublime text'.[2] A fuller criticism is that on Donne's statement: 'and certainly our works are more ours then our faith is, and man concurres otherwise in the acting and perpetration of a good work, then he doth in the reception and admission of faith'. Coleridge pounces on this with scorn:

'Why? Because Donne confounds the act of faith with the assent of the fancy and understanding to certain words and conceptions. Indeed, with all my reverence for Dr. Donne, I must warn against the contents of this page, as scarcely tenable in logic, unsound in metaphysics, and unsafe, slippery divinity; and principally in that he confounds faith—essentially an act, the fundamental work of the Spirit—with belief, which is then only good when it is the effect and accompaniment of faith.'[3]

He has a more moderate criticism of Donne's description of the Eucharist as an epiphany of Christ:

'O! would that Donne, or rather that Luther before him, had carried out this just conception to its legitimate consequences;—that as the sacrament of the Eucharist is the epiphany for as many as receive it in faith, so the crucifixion, resurrection, and ascension of Christ himself in the flesh, were the epiphanies, the sacramental acts and *phaenomena* of the *Deus patiens*, the visible words of the invisible Word that was in the beginning, symbols in time and historic fact of the redemptive

[1] Ibid.

[2] Ibid., p. 71, on *LXXX*. 1. 9, paragraph C.

[3] Ibid., p. 92, on *LXXX*. 8. 79, paragraph D. There is another vigorous criticism on p. 77, where Coleridge remarks 'Taking the words, however, in their vulgar sense, I most deliberately protest against all the paragraphs in this page, from A to E. . . .' The reference is to *LXXX*. 3. 25.

functions, passions, and procedures of the Lamb crucified from the foundation of the world.'[1]

On Donne's statement, 'We place in the School, for the most part, the infinite merit of Christ Jesus . . . rather *in pacto* than *in persona*, etc.' Coleridge comments, 'O, this is sad misty divinity! far too scholastical for the pulpit, far too vague and unphilosophic for the study.'[2] There is another comment of the same kind on Donne's quotation from Augustine: 'So says St. Augustine, *Audeo dicere*, though it be boldly said, yet I must say it, *utile esse cadere in aliquod manifestum peccatum*, etc.' Coleridge observes:

> 'No doubt, a sound sense may be forced into these words: but why use words, into which a sound sense must be forced? Besides, the subject is too deep and too subtle for a sermon. In the two following paragraphs, especially, Dr. Donne is too deep, and not deep enough. He treads waters, and dangerous waters.'[3]

On a passage in *LXXX Sermons*, 16. 157 Coleridge writes: 'Donne was a poor metaphysician; that is, he never closely questioned himself as to the absolute meaning of his words. What did he mean by the "soul"? what by the "body"?'[4]

There is more of the same kind, but nothing quite so severe as Coleridge's comment on one of Jeremy Taylor's treatises, 'it makes my very heart as dry as the desert sands, when I read it',[5] or his exclamation at the close of another long passage by Taylor, 'Thank God! Here comes common sense.'[6] In spite of much outspoken criticism, however, Coleridge loved Donne's prose. His highest praise is given to a sentence which he describes as 'Worthy almost of Shakespeare!',[7] a noble tribute from one great poet and prose-writer to another.

[1] *Notes*, i. 79, 80, on *LXXX*. 4. 30, paragraph B.

[2] Ibid., p. 113, on *LXXX*. 18. 179.

[3] Ibid., p. 110, on *LXXX*. 17. 171.

[4] Ibid., pp. 101–2. [5] Ibid., p. 272. [6] Ibid., p. 297.

[7] Ibid., p. 103. The sentence is from *LXXX*. 17. 161, 'That world, which finds itself truly in an autumn in itself, finds itself in a spring in our imaginations.'

XII

THE LETTERS

DONNE'S letters throw a flood of light on the character of the man. They show him as he appeared to his intimate friends, with whom he had no need to be on his guard, and there are passages which give an explanation of apparent inconsistencies which might puzzle us in his life and work. We see in them that mingling of magnificence and meanness which was characteristic of the Elizabethan age. With all his revolt against the spirit of the time, Donne was a true Elizabethan in his passionate friendships, his acts of sudden generosity, and also in his fits of meanness and his moments of selfish calculating ambition. We see him repeating court gossip, making bad jokes, bewailing his poverty, criticizing his contemporaries, or at other times offering tender sympathy and meditating on the profoundest mysteries of life. In these letters he conceals nothing. Friendship was to him his 'second religion',[1] and he gave his friends his full confidence and affection, demanding from them in return an equal measure of frankness.

Most of his correspondence which has been preserved was given to the world by his son in two volumes—*Letters to Severall Persons of Honour: written by John Donne* (1651), and *A Collection of Letters, made by Sr Tobie Mathews K^t^*. (1660). The researches of I. A. Shapiro[2] and R. E. Bennett[3] have shown that the younger Donne tampered with the headings of many of the letters in an attempt to curry favour with Mistress Bridget Dunch, to whom the *Letters* of 1651 were dedicated. There are also a few prose letters contained in the early editions of the *Poems*, and in Walton's *Life of Mr. George Herbert* (1670). During the nineteenth century about thirty fresh letters came to light, and in the first edition of the present volume I was able, by the kindness of Mr.

[1] *Letters* (1651), p. 85.

[2] 'The Text of Donne's *Letters to Severall Persons*', *R.E.S.* vii. 291–301.

[3] 'Donne's *Letters to Severall Persons*', *P.M.L.A.* lvi. 120–40.

Pearsall Smith and Sir Herbert Grierson, to print from the Burley MS. a series of letters from Donne to Wotton or to friends of Wotton, which had never before been published. Thus we have in all a collection of over two hundred letters, covering the greater part of Donne's life, and addressed to more than forty different correspondents.

The letters are of primary importance for the right understanding of much of Donne's life and character, but they do not hold a high place in literature. Donne's prose style, magnificent at its best, was ill suited for familiar correspondence. There are no such delightfully intimate outpourings on every possible subject, grave or gay, as we find in the best eighteenth- or nineteenth-century letter-writers, such as Horace Walpole, Cowper, or Lamb. Donne has many profound and ingenious sayings in these letters, and he tells us also much of his daily life, but the thought seems to move in a panoply of armour which encumbers it sadly. Thus when he 'writes Consolatorily to a Lady, upon the Death of her Husband', he opens the letter in the following strain:

'*Madam*,

Those things, which God dissolves at once, as he will do the Sun, and Moon, and those Bodies, at the last Conflagration, he never intends to re-unite; but in those things, which he takes in pieces (as he doth Man and Wife, in these divorces by death; and single persons, in the divorce of Bodie, and Soul) God hath another purpose, to make them up, again. That peece, which he takes to himself, is cast into a mould, and in an instant, made fit for his use; For Heaven is not a place of proficiencie, but of present perfection; That peece, which he leaves behind in this World, by the death of a part thereof, growes fitter and fitter for him, by the good use of his corrections, and the intire conformity to his will. . . .'[1]

To his familiar friend, Sir Robert Ker, he writes thus:

'*SIR*,

Your man surprised me, as I came into my house; and loth to stay him, or defraud my self of reading your Letter, I read it in his sight, and said, though not so much as I would have written, yet, perchance, more then he hath thought necessary to remember.

[1] Tobie Mathew Collection, p. 106. Also in *Letters* (1651), p. 7. The lady addressed was Lady Kingsmell.

I had bin long in my chamber, and practised how to put out breath, almost to my last gasp; and now I had been abroad to take in aire, and as a man that hath received mony, but not yet received it; so, I had taken in breath, but not articulated it, nor, perchance, said enough, to let you know, that I shall lose the honour of waiting upon you at your time: which I feel the more, because I desired much to have been in my Lord Chancellor's sight. . . .'[1]

On occasion, however, Donne could abandon this cumbersome style, and relate news in a more readable form. Here is part of another letter to Goodyer:

'Hither came lately Letters with goodspeed from *Vienna*, in which there is no mention of any such defeat, as in rumour C. *Mansfeld* hath been said to have given to the D. of *Bavyer*:[2] but their forces were then within such distance, as may have procured something before this time. Those which watched advantages in the Court of the Emperour, have made that use of C. *Mansfelds* proceedings, as that my Lord *Digby* complains, that thereby, the forwardnesse in which his negotiation was, is somewhat retarded. He proceeds from thence into *Spain*. The D. of *Bavyer* hath presented the Emperour an account of 1200^{ml}. sterling in that warre, to be reimbursed: and finding the Palatinate to be in treaty, hath required a great part of *Austria* for his security, and they say, it is so transacted; which is a good signe of a possibility in the restitution of the Palatinate. For any thing I discern, their fears are much greater from *Hungary*, then from *Bohemia*; and the losse of Canon, in a great proportion, and other things, at the death of *Bucquoy*, was much greater, then they suffered to be published. . . .'[3]

Sometimes the news is of a more personal character, particularly in letters written to such intimate friends as Goodyer or Wotton. For some years Donne seems to have written a weekly letter to Goodyer, in which he gave a vivid picture of the poverty-stricken household at Mitcham and his own frequent ailments. We hear of the death of one child and the dangerous sickness of another, of the ague which afflicted Donne, and of the cramp which twisted his

[1] Tobie Mathew Collection, pp. 307–8.

[2] i.e. Maximilian of Bavaria. The whole letter, the date of which was misprinted in the 1651 edition as 'Aug. 30, 1611', is full of allusions to the campaign which was being waged in Germany in 1621.

[3] *Letters* (1651), pp. 156–7.

hand so that he could hardly write. He sends scraps of verse with his letters—*The Litanie* or a verse epistle written for the Countess of Bedford or for Goodyer himself. He comments on the books he has been reading, and some of his criticisms are pungent enough.

'In the mean time, I will adventure to say to you, without inserting one unnecessary word, that the Book is full of falsifications in words, and in sense, and of falshoods in matter of fact, and of inconsequent and unscholarlike arguings, and of relinquishing the King, in many points of defence, and of contradiction of himself, and of dangerous and suspected Doctrine in Divinitie, and of silly ridiculous triflings, and of extreme flatteries, and of neglecting better and more obvious answers, and of letting slip some enormous advantages which the other gave, and he spies not.'[1]

This is of a book written in defence of the cause which Donne himself was upholding, and it is possible that his extreme dissatisfaction with the author's treatment of the subject was one of the reasons which led to the composition of his own *Pseudo-Martyr*.

The letters written during Donne's visit to France in 1611 and 1612 are more cheerful and are full of news and gossip. The young King (Louis XIII) is said to have 'cruell and tyrannous' inclinations; 'when he is any way affected, his stammering is so extreme, as he can utter nothing.'[2] 'The D. of *Espernon* is come to *Paris*, with (they say) 600 horse in his train; all which company, came with him into the Court: which is an insolency remarkable here.'[3] 'The main bravery was the number of horses which were above 800 Caparazond. Before the daies, the town was full of the 5 Challengers cartells, full of Rodomontades; but in the execution, there were no personall reencounters, nor other triall of any ability, then running at the Quintain, and the Ring.'[4] In these letters Donne begins to repent of the publication of his *Anniversaries*, which had apparently offended certain great

[1] *Letters* (1651), p. 163. The reference is clearly to a book written in support of the Oath of Allegiance against the Roman objectors; it was probably Bishop Barlow's *Answer to a Catholic Englishman* (see Gosse, i. 221).

[2] *Letters* (1651), pp. 124–5.

[3] Ibid., p. 123.

[4] Ibid., p. 128.

ladies to whom he was in the habit of writing eulogistic verses. The praise of Elizabeth Drury seemed to them excessive, and Donne hastens to meet their objections.

'Of my Anniversaries, the fault that I acknowledge in my self, is to have descended to print any thing in verse, which though it have excuse even in our times, by men who professe, and practise much gravitie; yet I confesse I wonder how I declined to it, and do not pardon my self: But for the other part of the imputation of having said too much, my defence is, that my purpose was to say as well as I could: for since I never saw the Gentlewoman, I cannot be understood to have bound my self to have spoken just truths, but I would not be thought to have gone about to praise her, or any other in rime; except I took such a person, as might be capable of all that I could say. If any of those Ladies think that Mistris *Drewry* was not so, let that Lady make her self fit for all those praises in the book, and they shall be hers.'[1]

Such half-contemptuous references to his own work are not infrequent in the letters of Donne's middle period—the stormy years between his marriage and his ordination. We would gladly have learnt something of the circumstances which gave rise to the earlier *Songs and Sonets*, but no letters in the published collections can be dated before 1601, and even the earlier letters in the Burley MS. contain but one explicit reference to the poems.

The letters written soon after Donne's return from France show him still anxious about his future, seeking official preferment, and uncertain of his true vocation. After the decision was made and he had taken orders, his letters become calmer, but there is no marked change in tone. The letters written earlier from Mitcham had contained many references to theological problems and passages which showed Donne's sincerity in religious matters, and though the habit of sermonizing in familiar letters grows stronger after his ordination, he evinces plenty of interest still in mundane affairs. Just before his ordination he shows himself extremely anxious to clear off the accumulation of debt which had for some years oppressed him. He appeals to his noble patronesses with some success, though in a letter to Goodyer he com-

[1] Ibid., pp. 238–9.

ments rather ungraciously on Lady Bedford's gift of £30.[1] After his wife's death in 1617, his daughters begin to occupy a larger share of his thoughts, and he busies himself to provide suitable husbands for them. His first matrimonial scheme for Constance, the eldest girl, goes awry, as he explains at length.[2] A little later he marries her to Edward Alleyn, the old actor who became the founder of Dulwich College, and the subsequent correspondence between Donne and Alleyn gives us the story of various small misunderstandings and petty quarrels between the two men. Two of his most intimate correspondents, Goodyer and Magdalen Herbert, are lost to him by death, but new friends appear, such as Mrs. Cokain, in whose sympathy he takes much pleasure. He tells her of his cough, his deafness, his toothache, as years begin to grow heavy upon him, but his spirit is still vigorous within him, and he refuses her request to bestow a benefice on a certain Mr. Hazard, with courtesy and also with a dignified firmness.[3]

[1] *Letters* (1651), pp. 218–19: 'For her other way of expressing her favour to me, I must say, it is not with that cheerfulnesse, as heretofore she hath delivered her self towards me. I am almost sorry, that an Elegy should have been able to move her to so much compassion heretofore, as to offer to pay my debts; and my greater wants now, and for so good a purpose, as to come disingaged into that profession, being plainly laid open to her, should work no farther but that she sent me 30*l*. . . .'

[2] Ibid., pp. 185–6: 'Tell both your daughters a peece of a storie of my *Con.* which may accustome them to endure disappointments in this world: An honourable person (whose name I give you in a schedule to burn, lest this Letter should be mis-laid) had an intention to give her one of his sons, and had told it me, and would have been content to accept what I, by my friends, could have begged for her; but he intended that son to my Profession, and had provided him already 300^{l} a year, of his own gift in Church livings, and hath estated 300^{l} more of inheritance for their children: and now the youth, (who yet knows nothing of his fathers intention nor mine) flies from his resolutions for that Calling, and importunes his Father to let him travell. The girle knows not her losse, for I never told her of it: but truly, it is a great disappointment to me. More than these, Sir, we must all suffer, in our way to heaven, where, I hope you and all yours shall meet

Your poor friend, and affectionate servant

J. Donne.'

[3] *Letters* (Tobie Mathew Collection), p. 355: 'For, my noble sister, Goes there no more to the giving of a Scholler a Church in *London*: but that he

There is also to be heard in the letters that deeper note which is never absent from Donne's work for long. Again and again he turns aside from the affairs of the day to discuss with his friends such topics as the nature of prayer, or the differences between the Roman and the Anglican Churches.[1] Even in his Mitcham days he devotes three pages of a letter to a discussion of the nature of the soul.[2] In truth, Donne's meditations move so easily from time to eternity, from the court of King James to the angelic hierarchy, that it is impossible to draw a line between things sacred and profane in his letters.

The first of Donne's letters to be printed were the eleven included in the *Poems* of 1633. Two of these were addressed to the Countess of Bedford, one to Sir Robert Ker, and the remaining eight to Sir Henry Goodyer.[3] The inclusion of a few prose letters among the lyrics and verse epistles is rather surprising, and lends support to Grierson's conjecture that the nucleus of the 1633 volume was a manuscript which had belonged to Goodyer, in which Donne's poems and letters were transcribed.[4] In the 1635 edition of the *Poems* four more prose letters were added.[5] Two others[6] appeared in 1654 in a volume entitled *Cabala. Mysteries of State, in letters of the great Ministers of K. James and K. Charles.* The 1658 edition of Walton's *Life of Dr. Donne* contained five

was a young Gentleman's School-master? You know the ticklishnesse of *London*-Pulpits, and how ill it would become me, to place a man in a *London*-Church that were not both a strong and a sound man.'

[1] *Letters* (1651), pp. 29–30, 100–2. The fine passage on the nature of prayer (pp. 110–12) is particularly noteworthy.

[2] Ibid., pp. 16–18.

[3] *Poems* (1633), pp. 139, 367 (to Lady Bedford); p. 164, numbered as 148 in some copies (to Sir Robert Ker); pp. 351–66, 368–72 (to Sir Henry Goodyer). Of these the letter to Lady Bedford on p. 367 and the seven to Sir Henry Goodyer on pp. 353–66 and 368–72 were reprinted in the *Letters* of 1651. Gosse reprinted the whole correspondence, except the letter on p. 351 to Sir Henry Goodyer, which is in Latin.

[4] Grierson, ii, pp. xc, xci.

[5] *Poems* (1635), p. 283 ('to the La. G.'), pp. 285–8 (to George Gerrard). These were all reprinted in the *Letters* of 1651, and later by Gosse.

[6] Both of these were addressed to Buckingham. The second was reprinted in the Tobie Mathew Collection, and both were reprinted by Gosse.

letters which had already appeared in the *Letters* of 1651, but the third of these is in a different form from that in the 1651 volume. In the 1670 collected edition of the *Lives* Walton included the first of these and part of the third, but omitted the others, and added another letter which has been shown by R. E. Bennett[1] to be a pastiche made out of five separate letters from the *Letters* of 1651. Walton's *Life of Mr. George Herbert* (1670) contained four letters from Donne to Magdalen Herbert, which had not previously been printed. These were reproduced in the subsequent editions of the *Lives*, and are to be found also in Gosse's *Life and Letters*.

The 1651 edition of the *Letters* was prepared for the press by the younger Donne. It has the following title: *Letters to Severall Persons of Honour: Written by John Donne Sometime Deane of St Pauls London. Published by John Donne Dr. of the Civill Law. London, Printed by J. Flesher, for Richard Marriot, and are to be sold at his shop in St Dunstans Church-yard under the Dyall. 1651.*

The book contains 129 letters, of which 117 appeared here for the first time. The frontispiece is a portrait of Donne engraved by Pieter Lombart after the oil-painting now at the Deanery of St. Paul's. There is an epistle dedicatory from the younger Donne: 'To the most virtuous and excellent Lady M^ris. Bridget Dunch.' The letters themselves occupy 318 pages.

The sheets of this edition were re-issued in 1654 with a new title-page bearing the imprint: 'Printed by J. Flesher, and are to be sold by John Sweeting, at the Angel in Popeshead-Alley. 1654.'

Sir Tobie Mathew's collection of letters, containing 38 letters written by Donne or to him, was prepared for the press in 1660 by the younger Donne, as is seen from the epistle dedicatory and from the title of the reprint issued in 1692, though his name does not appear on the title-page of the original edition. The title of the first edition runs thus:

[1] *Philological Quarterly*, xvi. 30–4. Walton did not intend to deceive his readers, for he introduced it as an extract 'collected out of some few of his [Donne's] many letters'.

A Collection of Letters, made by Sr Tobie Mathews K^t. With a Character of the most Excellent Lady, Lucy, Countesse of Carleile: By the same Author. To which are Added many Letters of his own, to severall Persons of Honour, Who were Contemporary with him. London, Printed for Henry Herringman, and are to be sold at his Shop, at the sign of the Anchor in the Lower walk in the New Exchange. 1660.

There is a frontispiece, facing the title-page, with an engraving by James Gammon of a portrait of Sir Tobie, bearing the words, 'The lively Portraicture of Sr Tobias Mathewes Kn^t.' The book opens with an epistle dedicatory from the younger Donne to Lucy, Countess of Carlisle, followed by 'The Character of the Most excellent Lady, Lucy Countess of Carleile'. The collection of letters is a large one, and most of the Donne correspondence is to be found at the end of the book (pages 296–356), though there are a few letters from Donne among the earlier pages.[1]

The sheets which made up this volume were re-issued in 1692 with a new title-page inserted after the original one. The new imprint runs thus: 'Published by the Rev^d Dr. J. Donne. London, Printed for Tho. Horne, Tho. Bennet, and Francis Saunders; at the Royal Exchange, St. Paul's Churchyard, and the New Exchange in the Strand. 1692.'

During the nineteenth century certain of Donne's letters were published for the first time. Ten were printed from the Loseley MSS. in 1835 by A. J. Kempe, and nine of these were reprinted in an edition of Walton's *Life of Donne*, published in 1852 by H. K. Causton, with notes by T. E. Tomlins.[2] Two[3] were printed among the documents edited by S. R. Gardiner for the Camden Society in 1868 and 1871. Nineteen appeared in 1899 in Sir Edmund Gosse's *Life and Letters of John Donne*. Gosse also reprinted the letters contained in the earlier collections, and endeavoured

1 Three of these (on pp. 63, 64, 68) were not reprinted by Gosse.

2 These letters (except the sixth, which was strangely omitted) were reprinted by Gosse (i. 104–14; ii. 47).

3 The first of these is to Sir Dudley Carleton (Gosse, ii. 143), the second to Buckingham (ibid., p. 140).

to arrange them in order of composition and to explain the allusions to contemporary persons and events.

The *Letters to Severall Persons of Honour* of 1651 were included by Dean Alford in his edition of the *Works of John Donne* in 1839. He rearranged them into two sections, the first including those which were dated or contained some indication of date, while the second comprised those of uncertain date. A limited edition of 600 copies of the *Letters to Severall Persons of Honour* was issued in 1911 in New York, under the editorship of C. S. Merrill.

One hitherto-unprinted letter from the Loseley MSS. was printed by M. de Havilland in the *London Mercury*, xiii. 159–60, in 1925, and three additional letters from manuscript sources were printed by John Hayward in *John Donne: Complete Poems and Selected Prose*, 1929. In 1930 Theodore Spencer printed a letter from Donne to Sir Nicholas Carey [Carew] for the first time.

A larger collection was printed in 1924 in the first edition of the present volume. It consisted of thirty-two letters transcribed from the manuscript at Burley-on-the-Hill by order of the Clarendon Press, when Logan Pearsall Smith was preparing his *Life and Letters of Sir Henry Wotton* (1907). The manuscript was subsequently destroyed by fire, but it had been examined by Sir Herbert Grierson, who described it as 'a manuscript of great importance for the editor of Donne's letters'. 'Amid its varied contents are some letters, unsigned but indubitably by Donne; ten of his *Paradoxes* with a covering letter; and a few poems of Donne's with other poems.'[1]

This collection has a particular interest, for it covers an earlier period of Donne's life than that represented in the *Letters* of 1651. Walton had described the lifelong friendship which existed between Wotton and Donne, but the letters which the two were known to have exchanged were so few that Gosse doubted the accuracy of Walton's statement.[2] Now, however, we possess a number of letters which testify

[1] Grierson, ii, pp. cx, cxi. See also allusions to the letters in the same volume, pp. 2, 133.

[2] Gosse, i. 18–19; ii. 314–15.

to the close intimacy between the two men,[1] and also throw fresh light on one of the most interesting parts of Donne's life—the period from the 'Islands Voyage' in 1597 to his marriage in 1601.

Mr. Pearsall Smith gives an account of the manuscript in his *Life and Letters of Wotton* (ii. 489–90). It resembled the commonplace books of the sixteenth and seventeenth centuries which are to be found in many old libraries, and it contained several letters and documents which are usually included in such collections—e.g. Sir Philip Sidney's letter to Queen Elizabeth on the Alençon marriage, and Lord Monteagle's letter which led to the discovery of the Gunpowder Plot. These documents had already been enumerated by Mr. Alfred J. Horwood, who was sent in 1878 to examine the manuscripts at Burley-on-the-Hill, in his report printed by the Historical Manuscripts Commission (Seventh Report, page 516). It was Mr. Horwood's remark that the volume contained 'copies of letters and papers seemingly by and to Sir Henry Wotton' that led to Mr. Pearsall Smith's examination of the volume. He found copies, made by various hands, of nineteen letters and dispatches which, although unsigned, he was able to identify as Wotton's, and a large number of documents relating to Wotton's various occupations and interests during his first embassy at Venice, as well as extracts from the letters of the three other resident English ambassadors of the time, Sir Thomas Edmondes at Brussels, Sir George Carew in France, and Sir Charles Cornwallis in Spain. The volume also contained a number of poems and letters, some of which were clearly Donne's, and Mr. Pearsall

[1] It should be noted that Walton's twice-made statement (*Life of Donne*, 1670, p. 9; *Life of Wotton*, 1670, p. 19) was supported by Henry King, Bishop of Chichester, in a letter addressed by him to Walton on 17 Nov. 1664, and prefixed to the 1670 edition of the *Life of Donne*: 'I shall begin with my most dear and incomparable Friend Dr. *Donne*. . . . I am glad that the general Demonstration of his Worth was so fairly preserved, and represented to the World by your Pen in the History of his Life. . . . After the performance of this task for Dr. *Donne*, you undertook the like office for our Friend Sir *Henry Wotton*: betwixt which two there was a Friendship begun in *Oxford*, continued in their various Travels, and more confirmed in the religious Friendship of Age. . . .'

Smith at first intended to print these in a separate volume. Most of the poems, however, were satires, elegies, and epigrams which had appeared in the seventeenth-century editions or else were of doubtful authenticity. Sir Herbert Grierson, in his edition of Donne's poems, printed only one of them (the verse letter, *H. W. in Hiber: belligeranti*)[1] as a new poem which could definitely be assigned to Donne, and made a selection from the other unpublished poems in his Appendix C among 'Poems attributed to Donne in MSS.' (i. 437–43).

The letters which Mr. Pearsall Smith believed to be Donne's fall into two groups—those in a hand which he calls D 1, and those in a hand which he identifies as that of William Parkhurst, one of Wotton's secretaries. The D 1 hand is that in which most of the Donne poems appear in this volume; another hand (D 2), used for a few of the poems, does not appear among the letters which may be attributed to Donne.

The D 1 group comprises all the letters which can be assigned to Donne with absolute certainty, e.g. the prose postscript in folio 286, added to his verse letter 'To Sir H. W. going to Venice', and the letter on the back of folio 308, accompanying the *Paradoxes*. One letter, that on folio 295, beginning 'I must wonder', seems to be written by Wotton to Donne, and was printed as Wotton's by Mr. Pearsall Smith. The majority of the other letters contained in this group bear the marks of Donne's style, and I have printed all of them in the ensuing pages.[2]

The letters in Parkhurst's hand present rather more difficulty. In the transcript they are separated from the D 1 letters by a letter which from internal evidence we can prove not to be Donne's. It was evidently addressed to Wotton at Venice by an unknown Englishman who needed help. Some of the letters which follow are not at all in Donne's manner, e.g. the letter on folio 302, beginning 'Mille volte ringratio

[1] Grierson, i. 188. See also the notes on this poem (ii. 152).

[2] The fact that the letters are unsigned presents no difficulty. All the letters in the Tobie Mathew Collection lack signatures, though Sir Tobie has often supplied the name of the writer in a heading.

V. E. dell' efficacissimi pegni', but there are others which contain phrases thoroughly reminiscent of his peculiar style, and there are one or two short letters which contain no clue as to their authorship. In these circumstances I have relegated to an appendix those letters which I believe not to have been written by Donne, and have retained the others in a group distinct from the D I letters. There are certain disadvantages in this arrangement, as it prevents me from placing all the new letters in a regular chronological sequence, but it seems advisable to allow the reader to differentiate between the two sets of letters, and to exclude letters clearly not by Donne.

The transcriber was evidently not familiar with the contractions used in Elizabethan script. For example, the contraction of '-us' in 'affectib^{9}' appears as 'affectibg'. Such errors have been corrected in the text here printed, but the inconsistent use of medial *u* and *v* appears to have been in the original, and has been retained.

D I *hand*

[I]

(f. 294^{v}.) Writen frō Plymouth

The first act of y^{t} play wch I sayd I would go over ye water to see is done & yet ye people hisse. how it will end I know not ast ego vicissim risero.[1] it is true y^{t} Jonas was in a whales belly three dayes but hee came not voluntary as I did nor was troubled wth ye stinke of 150 land soldiers as wee & I was there 20 dayes of so very very bad wether y^{t} even some of ye marriners haue beene drawen to thinke it were not altogether amisse to pray & my self heard one of y^{em} say god help vs. for all our paynes wee haue seene ye land of promise spaine whether wee shall enter or no I guess not I think there is a blott in there tables but ꝑchaunce tis not on o^{r} dice to hitt it. wee are now againe at plymouth quasi ply ⸗ mouth; for wee do nothing but eate & scarce that: I think when wee came in the burghers tooke vs for ye spanish fleet for they haue either hid or convayd all there mony. never was

[1] The transcript has 'Cicero'. Dr. Paul Maas pointed out to me that the phrase is a quotation from Horace, *Epode* xv. 24. The original scribe apparently mistook the short Elizabethan 'r' for 'c', and when this initial blunder had been made, the change from 'c' to 'C' and from 's' to 'c' followed naturally. See my note in *Review of English Studies*, xx. 224–5.

extreame beggery so extreamely braue except when a company of mūmers had lost theire box. I do not think that 77 Kelleys[1] could distill 10l out of all ye towne he yt hath supt and hath 2 or 3s is a king; for none hath a crowne fayth lands ierkins knighthoods are reprobate pawnes[2] & but for ye much gay cloathes[3] (wch yet are much melted) I should thinke wee were in vtopia: all are so vtterly coyneles. in one bad bare word ye want is so generall that ye lo: generall wants & till this day wee wanted ye lo: generall: yo will ꝑdone me if I write nothing ernest. Salute all whome thou louest in my name & loue me as I would deserue.

This letter, which must have been written in August 1597, is the earliest-known prose letter of Donne's. It belongs to the same occasion which gave rise to his verse letters, *The Storme* and *The Calme*,[4] written to his friend Christopher Brooke. The islands voyage of 1597 was less successful than the Cadiz expedition of the previous year, owing chiefly to the unfortunate weather which it experienced.[5] A considerable fleet had been fitted out under the command of Essex, assisted by Howard and Raleigh, to destroy the new Spanish armada which was believed to be in preparation. Part of this fleet set out in June, but immediately encountered such tempests that it was forced to return to Plymouth, where the remainder of the expedition assembled. About

[1] 77 *Kelleys*. Edward Kelley (1555–95) was a well-known alchemist and charlatan, who was associated with John Dee in an attempt to produce the Philosophers' Stone. He worked his way into the favour of the Emperor Rudolph II by boasting that he possessed the Stone. Rudolph twice imprisoned him in order to force him to produce some definite proof of his power; on the second occasion Kelley was killed in an attempt to escape. There are numerous references to Kelley in the literature of the time, e.g. Dekker, *Gull's Hornbook* (1609), Proem: 'rich *Midasse*, that had more skill in *alchimy* then *Kelly* with the Philosophers stone'. Cf. Gabriel Harvey, *Pierces Supererogation* (1593), p. 28; Ben Jonson, *Alchemist*, Act iv, sc. 1, l. 90.

[2] *Pawne* here means something deposited as security for a debt, a pledge (*O.E.D.* pawn, sb.[2]).

[3] The gay clothes worn by the gallants on this voyage became famous. See Ben Jonson, *Silent Woman*, I. iv. 61–3: 'I had as faire a gold ierkin on that day, as any was worne in the *Iland*-voyage, or at *Caliz*.'

[4] Grierson, i. 175–80.

[5] For a full account of the expedition see *Purchas his Pilgrimes*, pt. ii, bk. x: 'The Voyage to the Iles of Azores, under the conduct of the Right Honorable Robert Earle of Essex, 1597.'

the 9th of July the whole fleet put out to sea, and after a few days of fair weather it met so fierce a storm that all the vessels were driven back to the English coast. It reassembled at Plymouth and was there refitted for sea, but owing to unfavourable weather it could not put forth again till 17 August. During this time Essex went up to court to receive fresh orders from the queen, and returned a few days before the fleet again put forth. Sir Arthur Gorges gives a vivid picture of the violence of the storms which the luckless expedition encountered, and his description of the delay at Plymouth should be compared with Donne's.

'For during the space of an whole moneth together (after wee were againe readie) the weather stood flat opposite to our course, insomuch that wee were not able to worke our selves out of the Harbour. And in this consumption of Time we lost the best season of the yeere for our purpose, and also greatly decayed our victualls and provisions; besides the number of our Souldiers and Mariners that daily diminished.'[1]

Gorges relates the desertion of some of the gaily dressed young gallants who had joined the expedition.

'But yet this violent and dangerous tempest had so cooled and battered the courages of a great many of our young Gentlemen (who seeing that the boysterous winds and mercilesse Seas, had neither affinitie with London delicacie, nor Court bravery) as that discharging their high Plumes, and imbroydered Cassockes, they secretly retired themselves home, forgetting either to bid their friends farwell, or to take leave of their Generall.'

He gives a more favourable account than Donne of the behaviour of the merchants of Plymouth.

'During all this time of our abode in Plimouth, (which was some six or seven weekes) we neither found eyther want or dearth of any manner of victualls, either in the Towne, where our Mariners were daily resident, or in the Countrey, where the Land Army was quartered; nor yet that extreame manner of inhaunsing the prices of all things used in London, and in other places of the Realme, upon the extraordinary assembling of any such great troupes.'

[1] Gorges, *A larger Relation of the said Iland Voyage.*

[2]

(f. 294.) S^{r}. In y^{r} whole fortune you haue not adventured so much, nor throwne y^{r} self into so great daungers as by descending into my frendship: there can bee none found weaker then my self; yet I haue alwayes beene either so strong or stubborne against any assault of fortune, that shee hath rather pickt quarrells wth my frends then wth my self & so in y^{t} Irel: & this Eng: & in other corners of ye world: shee hath gleaned lately many of my deerest frends as though it were fault enough to loue me: but S^{r} my frendship cannot bee accessary to any such misfortune in you. bycause fortune saw in y^{o} many vertues & worthinesses fit to bee envied by her before it pleased y^{o} to betroath y^{r} frendship to me and so hath a directer quarrell to y^{o} for being learned & valiant & otherwise vertuous then for being content to allow me a roome in y^{r} good opiniō. in wch as it hath pleased y^{o} to place me & giue me ye assurance vnder y^{r} owne hand by y^{r} kind letter from Irel: so I intreat y^{t} I may continew y^{r} tenaunt there ever or so long till I bee slack in doing the offices & loving services to such a landlord. I would bee sorry you should stay long in ye loathsomnes of Ire: for death & misery is in fashion there & much worne by the best men whome I feare least y^{o} should to much imitate & do as they do. dy. and so s^{r} before I can see you I must dy to for my ernest desyre of seing you must make more hast then naturally I should how much better cheap may you see En: y^{r} desirous frends & peace & poore me, by retorning? I dare not doubt but that at y^{r} retorne y^{o} wilbe content y^{t} I see you & to giue me some knowledg thereof if y^{o} come into o^{r} parts y^{t} I may (if in no other worthines) yet in shewing my loue to y^{o} iustyfy y^{t} conceit wch through m^{r} W. you disdaine not to embrace of me. wch I would faine y^{t} I could tell y^{o} here in Eng: for in Ir: tis against y^{r} discretions to beleeue any thinge. S^{r} amongst all y^{r} oldest frends you haue none more gladder of y^{r} loue then I & this youth of my frendship hath such strenght y^{t} I hope it shall grow to haue experience wth yours & so full of a thankfull desire to see you I rest.

This letter was probably written by Donne to a friend of Wotton in Ireland in the summer of 1599. It cannot be addressed to Wotton himself, for Donne speaks of his friendship as a new thing, and Donne and Wotton had been friends since their early days at Oxford together. The reference to 'y^{t} conceit wch through m^{r} W. you disdaine not to embrace of me', indicates that Wotton was the intermediary through whom Donne and his correspondent had become acquainted.

[3]

S^r^. but y^t^ I haue much ernest sorrow for ye losse of many deere (f. 299^v^.) frends in Ir: I could make shift to greiue for ye losse of a poore letter of mine wch sought y^o^ there after y^r^ retorne: in wch though there were nothing to bee cōmended but y^t^ it was well suted for the place & barbarous enough to go thither: yet it should haue brought ye thanks & betroathed to y^o^ the loue & services of one who had rather bee honest then fortunate: this letter hath a greater burthen & charge; for it caries not only an assuraunce of myself to you but it begs a pardon that I haue not in these weekes sought y^o^ out in Eng: by letters & acknowledged how deep roote the kindnes of y^r^ letter hath taken in me: but as in former innocent tymes estates of lands passed safly[1] in few words (for these many entangling clauses are ether intended at least to p^r^vent or breed deceit) so vnchangeable frendship being ever the same & therefore not subiect to the corruption of these tymes may now in these few & ill lines deliver me vnto y^o^ & assure y^o^ none hath better title then y^o^ in

y^r^ poore frend & lover.

This letter evidently belongs to the autumn of 1599, and was probably written a few weeks after Wotton's return from Ireland in September. It should be compared with Donne's verse letter, *H. W. in Hiber: belligeranti*, which was printed by Sir Herbert Grierson from the Burley MS. (*Poems*, i. 188–9), and also with two unsigned and undated letters in the same manuscript which Mr. Pearsall Smith printed (*Wotton*, i. 308–10) as having probably been written from Ireland by Wotton to Donne. In the verse letter Donne had complained that Wotton's friendship for him had suffered by the Irish expedition, since he had received so few letters.

> Went you to conquer? and have so much lost
> Yourself, that what in you was best and most,
> Respective friendship, should so quickly dye?

Wotton's answer indicated that he had received very few letters from Donne, and that at least one of his own must have been lost on the way.

[1] Transcript 'safty'.

[4]

(f. 295^{v}.)

They shake[1] wthout flattery that wch wthout suspitiō of flattery I cannot repeate.[2]

Omnes omnia bona dicere et laudare fortunas meas
Qui amicum haberem tali ingenio p^{r}ditū.[3] So much of y^{t} matter. yor last (if it were so) ye 25 of Ja: was but receaved this morning so y^{t} it lost ye grace in a kind of affectation of gravity. I had rather y^{o} would send y^{r} letters in ye french then in ye spanish pace[4] to me. I am now free from an ague.[5] though I am afrayd ye state bee not so: for certaynly the court hath in it much vnnaturall heate & ye courts & seats of princes are ye harts of all realms wch taking forme from theyre humors are more or lesse corrupted as they confine or enlarge theyre owne wills: when I speake of ye wills of princes I speake of verie vnlimited things: well what so ever o^{r} diseases are I must wish y^{t} wch phaps is votum melioris civis q̄ viri y^{t} is y^{t} they may be contagious: my meaning is I would have other states (or neighbours) infected wth them as well as o^{r} selus least wthin a while there be no historie so rich of great errors nor padventure of great vices as ours. it was an excellent brag of Livies[6] y^{t} ye Ro: state (whose actions he entended to deliv^{r}) was of all other in ye world most fertill of good examples. I call it a brag & so think it. for certaynly all tymes are of owne nature & all courts produce ye same effects of envie & detraction of ielousy & other humane weakneses.[7] thus it must be till we gett aboue ye moone whose motions as some haue ingeniously erred do make vs variable. I can from hence requite you wth no news wch hath made me fill pap wth the vanyty of myne owne discourse. it shall end in letting y^{o} know y^{t} in this place y^{o} are more vnacquaynted, then obscure. & so I wish vs a bette[r] world.

[1] *Shake* is evidently a mistake of the scribe for *spake*.

[2] The transcript states that this marginal note was in another hand from that of the letter itself (D 1). It looks as if the beginning of the letter had been lost.

[3] Adapted from Terence, *Andria*, ll. 96–8. Donne substitutes 'amicum' for 'gnatum'.

[4] *rather . . . in ye french then in ye spanish pace*, that is, too fast rather than too slowly.

[5] Cf. *Letters* (1651), p. 203: 'your company, that place, and my promise are strong inducements, but an Ague flouts them all, of which I have had two such threatenings, that I provide against it by a little Physick.'

[6] Livy's Preface, § 4, 'nulla unquam respublica . . . bonis exemplis ditior fuit'.

[7] Cf. Donne's verse letter 'To Sr Henry Wotton' (Grierson, i. 180–2), which denounces the evils found at court. There, however, the condemnation is a general one, forming part of Donne's contribution to a poetical dispute on the comparative evils of court, city, and country, in which Bacon, Wotton, and Thomas Bastard took part. Here Donne's dissatisfaction with the court is much more acute, probably owing to the disgrace of Essex.

[5]

I will answere y^{r} letter bycause I remember I had a promyse from y^{o} of many of y^{em}. wch is not easy for you to make me forgiue y^{o}. I vnderstand Sr Maurice Barkly[1] is in towne I haue sent my man vnto him cũ salute plurima, but dare not wish him where we shall meet at supꝑ least I com̄it some exces of gladnes: Wee are here yet not contented though the very lookes of princes be satisfactorie: but as honest minds are not apt to do wrong so no doubt they receaue ye deepest impressions of iniuries. I am glad of y^{r} frendship for many | causes & (f. 296.) amongst ye rest y^{o} shall giue me leaue to make this vse of it. y^{t} wee may sometymes togeather privately speake of ye course of these wor[l]dly things wch are governed wth[2] much instability. I will conclude y^{t} virtus is[3] in terris ꝑegrina in cælo civis.[4]

The two preceding letters probably belong to the early part of 1600, when Essex was in disgrace, and Wotton, who had returned in his train from Ireland, thought it prudent to withdraw into the country. Donne was now secretary to Egerton, the Lord Keeper, to whose custody at York House Essex was committed from October 1599 to July 1600. The sympathies of Donne and Wotton were, of course, with Essex, under whom they had both served in the Cadiz and Azores expeditions. Wotton, however, had been more closely associated with Essex than Donne, since he had followed Essex to Ireland and had been one of his secretaries. In these letters, and in those which are found on folios 296^{v}, 297, 298, 299^{v}, Donne sends Wotton news from court, expressing in discreetly veiled terms his dissatisfaction with the turn which affairs had taken.

[1] Sir Maurice Berkeley was knighted at Cadiz in 1596. Donne and Wotton probably made his acquaintance on that expedition. For his relations with Wotton, see Pearsall Smith, i. 22 n.

[2] Transcript 'wth wth'.

[3] Presumably Donne wrote 'est'.

[4] Douce made a note in the Bodleian copy of the first edition of the *Reliquiae Wottonianae* (Douce, W. 55): 'I have seen the following words written by Sir Henry Wotton in a German album: "Virtus in terris peregrina est, In caelo civis. Bono hospiti haec scripsi Henricus Wottonus, Anglo-Britannus, ex legatione Veneta domum rediens, Lutetiae Parisiorum Februarii xxvi, cɪɔɪɔcx".' The sentence was a favourite one with Wotton, who used it in a letter dated 25 Oct. 1592, and addressed to Lord Zouch: 'I imitate though not the nature, yet the fortune of virtue, which certainly is *peregrina in terris, in caelo civis*' (Pearsall Smith, i. 290).

[6]

(f. 296v.) Sr That loue wch went wth you followes & overtakes & meetes you. if words seald vp in letters be like words spoken in those frosty places where they are not heard till ye next thaw[1] they haue yet this advantage yt where they are heard they are herd only by one or such as in his iudgment they are fitt for. I am no Courtier for wthout having liued there desirously I cannot haue sin'd enough to haue deserv'd that reprobate name: I may sometymes come thither & bee no courtier as well as they may sometymes go to chapell & yet are no christians. I am there now where because I must do some evill I envy yr being in ye country not that it is a vice will make any great shew here for they liue at a far greter rate & expence of wickednes. but because I will not be vtterly out of fashion & vnsociable. I gleane such vices as the greater men (whose barnes are full) scatter yet I learne that ye learnedst in vice suffer some misery for when they haue reapd flattery or any other fault long there comes some other new vice in request wherein they are vnpracticed. only ye women are free from this charg for they are sure they cannot bee worse nor more throwne downe then they haue beene: they haue pchance heard that god will hasten his iudgment for ye righteous[2] sake. & they affect not that hast & therfore seeke to lengthen out ye world by their wickednes. The Court is not great but full of iollyty & revells & playes and as merry as if it were not sick. her mtie is well disposd & very gratious in publique to my Lo: Mountioy my lo: of Essex & his trayne are no more mist here then the Aungells wch were cast downe from heaven nor (for anything I see) likelyer to retourne. he withers still in his sicknes & plods on to his end in the same pace where yo left vs. the worst accidents of his sicknes are yt he conspires wth it & yt it is not here beleeved. that wch was sayd of Cato yt his age vnderstood him not I feare may be averted[3] of yr lo: that he vnderstood not his age: for it is a naturall weaknes of innocency. That such men want lockes for themselues & keyse for others.

This letter clearly belongs to 1600, as the reference to

[1] See Plutarch, *Moralia*, De profectibus in virtute, c. 7, and Rabelais, Bk. IV, c. 55. There is a reference to this passage of Rabelais in the verses headed 'Incipit Ioannes Dones' prefixed to Coryat's *Crudities*, 1611, sig. f 5 verso (ll. 11–13):

> It's not that *French* which made his *Gyant* see
> Those vncouth Ilands where wordes frozen bee,
> Till by the thaw next yeare they'r voic't againe.

[2] Transcript 'rigtheous'.

[3] *averted*. Perhaps a confusion with *adverted*, but the context implies 'reversed'.

Essex shows. Donne's words imply that Essex had already been some months in disgrace, and the letter was probably addressed to Wotton, as Essex is described as 'your lord', and Donne is writing from the court to a correspondent in the country.

[7]

S^{r}. Methinks y^{r} good discretion should not call ill fortunes faults. (f. 297.) nor threaten me wth y^{r} sylence because I wanted meanes to answere y^{r} last let^{r}. it is not an age to looke for faultlesnes in y^{r} frend it is well if wee err reasonably & excusably therefore if y^{o} coole not in frendship be not loath to write for letters are frendships sacraments. & wee should be in charyty to receaue at all tymes. I would bee loath to find a languishing or decay in my frends affections wch I feare ye lesse bycause theire good opinions are not built or sustaind by any my desert wch would soone fayle but by theire owne iudgments from wch euery mā is loath to depart. but if y^{t} should fall out it would well suite wth these tymes wch are ariued to y^{t} height of illnes y^{t} no man dares accuse them bycause every one contributes much himself to y^{t} accesse. Wee haue a new fashioned valor to suffer any thing rather then misery a new fashiond wisedome to cover imꝑfections: & envy (wch not exceeding the limits of emulacion & desire to equall worthy men ꝑchaunce is no fault) is now growne a ꝑfect vice. for heretofore it was but oposed to good fortune & so men might be thought to rich now it is oposd to vertue & a man may be to good: If vices bee extremities I wonder how every day such growth & addition: but if wee complayne no otherwise then former ages, that is, if because wee see & feele o^{r} owne tymes ꝑfectlyest, wee accuse most & that ye prophesy of Horace Etas parentū prior[1] etc belong also to o^{r} tymes, it may serve vs for some comfort (though a hard shift) y^{t} are already borne. and if as those wch travayle to ye pole call the english sothernly people so the world shall last to a tyme so wicked y^{t} o^{r} age shalbe thought good in respect of that as we do of former ages it is not 600 yeres nor 6000 wch will bring the world to his ꝑiod[2] o^{r} wickednes is to strong & stobborne to be so soone weakened why then should wee much desire lyfe or her delights since we see much ill & feare more: since to bee out of fashion is to bee rude & barbarous & to be in fashion is to be dishonest since poverty is dispised & hapines envyed? since vertue is not only not worne as a compleat royall garment but not

[1] *Prior* is clearly an error for *peior*. The words are quoted from Horace, *Odes*, III. vi: 'aetas parentum, peior auis, tulit | nos nequiores, mox daturos | progeniem vitiosiorem.'

[2] Transcript 'ꝑvod'.

(f. 297v.) as a color or a | skarfe: no man desiring now to cover his vice wth her shew. against these batteries Sr yo do well to frame yo an armor of yt mettall wch nature hath infused into yo, & the loue of learning hath ham̄erd & fashioned: & being so strong against these assaults as yo are why should yo hyde yr self in the Cuntrey when wee worse provided liue here in the Court & city in continuall battayle & yet I hope keep ye reputacon of honest men. but for my p̄ticular I do it not of iudgment or choyce as they wch purpose to conquer as the helvetians[1] as divers others destroyed first there owne townes & burnt theire ships to quench all hope of revenging, so am I in this warfare enforced to fight it out bycause I know not whether to rū: I can̄ot therefore honestly p̄swade you to abandon ye Country bycause if my fortunes fitted it I should p̄swade yo to stay there by my exsample. yet I desyre much sometyme to see you here & to haue yo a litle trip though not fall nor stumble att ambition or other distractions. least I seing an honest man happy should begin for yr sake to loue the world againe wch I would be loath to do.

This letter probably belongs to the period 1599–1600. Donne writes in the same tone of dissatisfaction with the court as in the previous letters, and the correspondent whom he addresses as living for the time in the country is probably Wotton.

[8]

(f. 298.) Sr. I promised a iorney like godfathers wch promise & vow three things for children before they know whether it bee in the childrens destiny to bee able to keepe there vowes or no. for I am since overtaken, & mett & inwrapd in busineses wch I could nether suspect nor avoyd: nothing else could haue made me com̄itt this omission. for wch yet I will not aske pardon bycause yo cannot giue it & my verie offence of not com̄ing is my punishment I meane the want of that good company yo haue & are. Sr. I would some great princes or men were dead so I might chuse them or some states or Countryes overthrowne so I were not in them yt I might haue some newes to ease this itch of writing wch travayles me for in or owne or in the d'amours Court[2] I know nothing worth yr reporting whereof I might iustyfy this

[1] Caesar, *De Bello Gallico*, lib. i, c. v.

[2] This seems to be a reference to the Christmas revel of the *Prince d'Amour* at the Middle Temple, when Richard Martin was the Prince, and John Hoskyns made 'a tuftaffeta speech'. This revel was probably acted during the Christmas season of 1597–8 (Chambers, *Elizabethan Stage*, i. 169, and L. B. Osborn, *John Hoskyns*, pp. 10–11).

reprobate headlong lett^r^. wch least I heape vp many sins I will here cut off.

alwayes & all wayes y^rs^.

This letter may have been written early in 1598.

[9]

S^r^. I am no great voyager in other mens works: no swallower nor devowrer of volumes nor pursuant of authors. ꝑchaunce it is because I find borne in my self knowledg or ap^r^hension enough for (w^th^out forfeiture or impeachment of modesty) I think I am bond to god thankfully to acknowledg it) to consyder him & my self: as when I haue at home a convenient garden I covet not to walk in others broad medows or woods especially because it falls not w^th^in that short reach wch my foresight embraceth to see how I should employ that wch I already know to travayle for inquiry of more were to labor to gett a stomach & then find no meat at home. To know how to liue by the booke is a pedantery, & to do it is a bondage. for both hearers & players are more delighted wth voluntary then wth sett musike. And he that will liue by p^r^cept shalbe long w^th^out ye habite of honesty: as he that would every day gather one or two feathers might become brawne wth hard lying before he make a feather bed of his gettings.[1] That Erle of Arundell[2] y^t^ last dyed (that tennis ball whome fortune after tossing & banding brikwald into the hazard[3]) in his impriso[n]-ment vsed more then much reading, & to him y^t^ asked him why he did so he answerd he read so much lest he should remember something. I am as far from following his counsell as hee was from petruccios:[4] but I find it true that after long reading I can only tell y^o^ how many leaves I haue read. I do therfore more willingly blow & keep awake y^t^ (f. 298^v^.)

[1] Cf. Pearsall Smith (*Wotton*, i. 401 n.): 'Wotton replied by reminding them [the authorities of Lucca] of a Venetian proverb, "*che chi bada ad ogni piuma non fa mai letto*".'

[2] Philip Howard, Earl of Arundel, died in 1595 after ten years' imprisonment in the Tower for his adherence to the Roman faith, and for supposed complicity in plots against Elizabeth.

[3] *Banding* is here used as the equivalent of *bandying*, cf. Fletcher, *Custom of the Country*, v. iv (folio 1647, p. 22): 'Our adverse fortune, Banding us, from one hazard to another.' *Brikwald*, past tense of brickwall, a corruption of *bricole* from Fr. *bricole*, associated by popular etymology with the *brick wall* of the tennis-court (*N.E.D.*). The substantive *bricole* was a technical term for the rebound of a ball from the wall of a tennis-court, and from it was formed the verb *bricole*, 'to cause to rebound'. Donne uses the substantive in a letter in the Tobie Mathew Collection, p. 65. *Hazard*, each of the winning openings in a tennis-court.

[4] *petruccios*. Perhaps Petruccio Ubaldini, an Italian pensioner of Elizabeth, man of letters and illuminator, in England 1562–86.

smale coole wch god hath pleased to kindle in mee[1] then farr off to (f. 299.) gather a faggott of greene sticks wch consume wthout flame or | heat in a black smoother: yet I read something. but indeed not so much to avoyd as to enioy idlenes. Even when I begun to write these I flung away Dant the Italian a man pert enough to bee beloved & to much to bee beeleeued: it angred me that Celestine[2] a pope far[3] frō the manners of other popes yt he left even there seat should by ye court of Dants witt bee attached & by him throwne into his purgatory. & it angred me as much. yt in ye life of a pope he should spy no greater fault, then yt in ye affectation of a cowardly securyty he slipt frō ye great burthen layd vpon him. alas? what would Dant haue him do? thus wee find the story related: he that thought himself next in succession by a trunke thorough a wall whispered in Celestines eare counsell to remoue ye papacy: why should not Dant be content to thinke that Celestine tooke this for as imediate a salutaciō & discourse of ye holy ghost as Abrahim did the cōmandment of killing his sonn? if he will needs punish retyrednes thus what hell can his witt devise for ambitiō? & if white integryty merit this what shall Male or Malū wch Seneca condems most,[4] deserve? but as ye chancell: Hatton[5] being told after a decree made yt his prdecessors was of another opinion he answered hee had his genius & I had myne: So say I of authors that they thinke & I thinke both reasonably yet posibly both erroniously; that is manly: for I am so far from ꝑswading yea conselling yo to beleeue others yt I care not yt yo beleeue not mee when I say yt others are not to bee beleeued: only beleeue that I loue you and I haue enough.

(In Parkhurst's hand.) I have studied philosophy therefore marvayle not if I make such accompt of arguments que trahuntr ab effectib9.[6]

[1] Cf. *Fifty Sermons*, 36. 326: 'If thou canst in those embers, those cold ashes, finde out one small coale, and wilt take the paines to kneell downe, and blow that coale with thy devout *Prayers*.'

[2] Pope Celestine V was persuaded by Cardinal Gaetano that it was against his soul's health to retain the Papacy, and solemnly resigned his office, Gaetano being elected to succeed him as Boniface VIII. Dante does not mention Celestine by name, but according to the early commentators, particularly Boccaccio, he referred to Celestine in Canto iii. 59–60 of the *Inferno*: 'Vidi e conobbi l'ombra di colui | Che fece per viltà lo gran rifiuto.'

[3] *far*, read [*so*] *far*.

[4] *Male or Malum*. The passage is corrupt. According to Seneca the worst of vices is to love vice (*Ep*. xxxix. 6). Donne may have written *malle malum* or have quoted Seneca's *malorum ultimum*.

[5] Sir Christopher Hatton (1540–91), Lord Chancellor from 1587 to 1591.

[6] Transcript 'trahunte ab affectib9.'

This long and interesting letter with its references to Italian literature was probably written by Donne to Wotton, who took a great interest in the subject. In 1598 Lombardelli, a learned Sienese, published a small book in the form of a letter to Wotton, *I Fonti Toscani*, in which he spoke of Dante as one of the masters of Italian literature. In a list of Italian authors drawn up by Wotton for the use apparently of some friend, we find this entry: '*Il Dante col Commentario di Landino*, in fol. Worthy the studying' (Pearsall Smith, ii. 485). Dante was little read in England during the sixteenth and seventeenth centuries, but Donne evidently studied him early in life, for we find an allusion in the fourth *Satire*: 'and a trance Like his, who dreamt he saw hell, did advance It selfe on mee' (Grierson, i. 164).

[10]

S^{r} if I had remembred y^{t} I should haue wanted y^{r} sight I would (f. 294^{v}.) not haue beene sick or at least I would not haue beene well by so ill a meanes, as taking phiseck: for I am bound by making myself loose. methinks now y^{t} y^{ey} err wittyly wch teach that saints see all mens action in god as in a mirror.[1] for I am sure y^{t} if I were but glorified wth y^{r} sight I should gather many ꝑticulars of carieres & altibaxos[2] (as y^{t} fryer sayes) wherein fortunes tumblers are exercised at & from ye Court, for I hunger to know who & why & when doth what. more then any thing else. S^{r} I long to see y^{o} when I haue drunk one potion more to my health & weakned my self I shalbee strong enough to find y^{o} att Essex or rather then not at all at Court where you shall find me (a miracle in y^{t} place) y^{r} honest frend.

This letter, which bears all the characteristic marks of Donne's style, was probably written by him to Wotton in 1600. The reference to his own honesty and the scarcity

[1] Cf. Donne's 'Obsequies to the Lord Harrington', ll. 31–4 (Grierson, i. 272):

> God is the glasse; as thou when thou dost see
> Him who sees all, seest all concerning thee,
> So, yet unglorified, I comprehend
> All, in these mirrors of thy wayes, and end.

[2] Transcript 'altibaros'. *Altibaxos* is a form of *altibajos*, plural of *altibajo*, a downright blow in fencing. In the plural it is used to mean 'vicissitudes, the ups and downs in life' (Velazquez, *Spanish–English Dictionary*).

of such a quality at court is in the tone of the letters on folios 296v and 297.

[11]

(f. 308v.) Sr. Only in obedience I send yo some of my paradoxes; I loue yo & myself & them to well to send them willingly for they carry wth them a confession of there lightnes. & yr trouble & my shame. but indeed they were made rather to deceaue tyme then her daughthr truth:[1] although they haue beene written in an age when any thing is strong enough to overthrow her: if they make yo to find better reasons against them they do there office: for they are but swaggerers: quiet enough if yo resist them. if pchaunce they be pretyly guilt, yt is there best for they are not hatcht: they are rather alarũs to truth to arme her then enemies: & they haue only this advantadg to scape frō being caled ill things yt they are nothings: therfore take heed of allowing any of them least yo make another. yet Sr though I know there low price except I receue by yr next lettr an assurance vpō the religion of yr frendship yt no coppy shalbee taken for any respect of these or any other my compositions sent to yo, I shall sinn against my conscience if I send yo any more. I speake yt in playnes wch becomes (methinks) or honestyes; & therfore call not this a distrustfull but a free spirit: I meane to aquaint yo wth all myne: and to my satyrs there belongs some feare & to some elegies & these phaps shame. against both wch affections although I be tough enough yet I haue a ridling disposition to bee ashamed of feare & afrayd of shame. therfore I am desirous to hyde them wth out any over reconing of them or there maker. but they are not worth thus much words in theyre disprayse. I will step to a better subiect yr last lettr to wch I need not tell I made no answere but I had need excuse it. all yr lettr I embrace & beleeue it when it speakes of yr self & when of me too if ye good words wch yo speake of me bee ment of my intentions to goodnes: for else alas! no man is more beggerly in actuall vertue then I. I am sory yo should (wth any great ernestnes) desyre any thing of P Aretius[2] not yt he could infect; but yt it seemes yo are alredy infected wth the cōmon opinion of him: beleeue me he is much lesse then his fame & was to well payd by ye Romā church in yt coyne wch he coveted most where his bookes were by the counsell of Trent forbidden wch if they had

[1] Aulus Gellius, *Noctes Atticae*, lib. xii, c. xi: Alius quidam veterum poetarum, cuius nomen mihi nunc memoriae non est, *veritatem temporis filiam* esse dixit.

[2] *P. Aretius*, i.e. Pietro Aretino. Probably the scribe has omitted a contraction mark over *Aretius*.

beene pmitted to haue beene worne by all long ere this had beene worne out: his divinyty was but a sirrops[1] to enwrapp his prophane bookes to get them passage yet in these bookes wch haue devine titles there is least harme as in his letters most good his others haue no other singularyty in them but that they are forbidden. the psalmes (wch y^o^ aske) If I cannot shortly procure y^o^ one to poses I can & will at any tyme borrow for you: In the meane tyme S^r^ haue the honor of forgiuing two faults togeather: my not writing last tyme and my abrupt ending now.

(The transcriber has added a note: 'Here follow Donne's Paradoxes "That all things kill themselues" etc.')

This letter, which is undoubtedly Donne's, was probably written by him to Wotton about 1600. Although we cannot date the *Paradoxes* exactly, they seem to be earlier than the *Problems*, and to belong to the period when Donne was a young man at court in the service of Egerton, and was in the habit of exchanging witty trifles in prose and verse with other clever young men of the day (*supra*, chap. vi). The reference to the *Satires* and *Elegies* would agree with this date. Grierson assigns the *Satires* to the years 1593–9, and the majority of the *Elegies* to the same period. In the present letter Donne shows that he already felt a certain shame about them, caused, perhaps, by the responsible post which he now held as secretary to the grave Lord Keeper, and also by his growing love for Ann More, whom he married in December 1601.

[12]

S^r^. In this sickly dotage of ye world where vertue languisheth in a banishment I must be glad shee hath found so holesome a dwelling in y^r^ mind y^t^ dares not only harbor her, but avouch it by y^r^ words & deeds. for it is as dangerous to haue vertue in this world as it wilbe to haue wanted it in the next & I am sure to find more sinners in heaven then honest mē vpon ye earth. yet S^r^ ye greatest harme y^t^ honesty doth y^o^ is y^t^ it arests my iudgment & suffers it not to go forward to consider y^r^ witt yor learnings & other worthineses. because methinks I haue taken a ritch prize & made a rare discouerie when I haue found an honest man: & therfore whatsoever y^o^ haue more then honesty is the wast & vnthriftynes of nature: I know it a fault to com̄end a thing (f. 298.)

[1] Donne probably wrote 'sirrope'.

so much out of fashion as honesty yet since I desire infinitely to contract a frendship wth you (bycause I know how far yo overstripp me in all other vertues) I stand most vpon honesty wth wch I haue had most acquaintaunce & society. I am best able to keepe wing wth yo in it though yo sore high. I haue now red one letter from yo since I saw yo & by it I see I should haue bee[n] glad of more: when yo think my letter or me worthy of offner salutations, write & when one of yr (f. 298v.) letters ꝑisheth wthout answere & thanks | lett me forfeit you. I had almost condemned you of forgetting me but yo are saved by yr booke. wch I will keep till it pleaseth to dispose it otherwise. Sr in a long & well studied oration no man shalbee able to com̄end to you an honester loue then this galloping letter doth: & therfore till ye next com̄odity of sending let me here kisse yr hand & vow to yu the observaunces of

yr servant & lover.

This letter probably belongs to 1600 or 1601, since Donne refers to the lack of virtue and honesty at court in the same tone which marks the letters which we know to have been written during Essex's disgrace. The correspondent addressed is not Wotton, however, but an acquaintance with whom Donne wishes to contract a friendship.

[13]

(f. 299v.) I send to yo now yt I may know how I do bycause vppon yr opinion of me all I depend: for though I be troubled wth the extremyty of such a sicknes as deserues att lest pitty if not loue yet I were as good to send to a coniurer for a good fortune as to a phisition for health. indeed I am oprest wth such a sadnes as I am glad of nothing but that I am oprest wth it: if it had pleased yo to haue norisht & brought vpp so much loue in yr brest as yo haue done greife ꝑchaunce I should haue as much loue in yr service as I haue done greif: yet I should accompt even sorrow good payment if by [it] myne yrs were lessoned: now I vene[1] & vrge my body wth phisick when my desperat mind is sick as they batter citty walls when the cittizens are stobborne: but by all this labor of my penn my mind is no more comforted then a condemned prisoner would bee to see his chamber swypte & made cleane: only yo know whethr ever I shalbee better & only yo can tell me (for yo are my destyny) whether I were best to dy now, or endevor to liue & keep ye great honor of being

yr servant.

[1] So in transcript.

This letter appears to have been written in February 1601/2 when Donne was in disgrace after the disclosure of his marriage. The letters printed from the Loseley Manuscripts by Kempe, and later by Gosse, are written in the same strain, complaining of the sickness which attacked Donne after his disgrace, and which was probably due to the anxiety and nervous strain which he underwent. Thus on 12 February he wrote from the Fleet Prison to Sir Thomas Egerton, the Lord Keeper:

'To excuse my offence, or so much to resist the just punishment for it, as to move your Lordship to withdraw it, I thought till now were to aggravate my fault. But since it hath pleased God to join with you in punishing thereof with increasing my sickness, and that he gives me now audience by prayer, it emboldeneth me also to address my humble request to your Lordship, that you would admit into your favourable consideration how far my intentions were from doing dishonour to your Lordship's house, and how unable I am to escape utter and present destruction, if your Lordship judge only the effect and deed. My services never had so much worth in them as to deserve the favours wherewith they were paid, but they had always so much honesty as that only this hath stained them. . . .' (Gosse, i. 105.)

On folio 283 of the Burley MS., Donne's fourth *Satire* was transcribed: 'Well, I may now receive, & die.' This was followed on folio 285ᵛ by the verse letter 'To Sir H. W. going to Venice', to which was added on folio 286 the following postscript:

[14]

Sʳ though ꝑchaunce it were nevʳ tryed except in Rabelais his land of tapistry[1] it may bee true yᵗ a pygmey vpon a Giant[2] may see further

[1] *land of tapistry*. The transcriber has queried this expression needlessly. Dr. C. T. Onions points out that it is a reference to Rabelais, Bk. V, ch. xxix, 'Comment nous visitasmes le pays de Satin . . . duquel les arbres et herbes ne perdoient fleur ne feuilles, et estoient de damas, et velours figuré: Les bestes et oiseaux estoient de tapisserie.' It is described also as 'le pays de tapisserie' both in this and in the following chapter. It is peopled mainly by fantastic and mythological creatures.

[2] *a pygmey vpon a Giant*. Professor C. C. J. Webb points out that this was a saying of Bernard of Chartres preserved by John of Salisbury in the *Metalogicon*, iii. 4 (p. 131, ed. Giles; Migne, *Patr. Lat.*, cxcix. 900 c): 'Dicebat Bernardus Carnotensis nos esse quasi nanos gigantium humeris insidentes,

then ye giant so after a long letter this postscript may see further into y^o then y^t if y^o will answere to 2 questions whether y^o haue y^r last despatches at court or whether y^o make many dayes stay there or at London. such a one as I may yett kisse y^r hand.

The verse letter must belong to July 1604, since it inquires whether Wotton had received his last dispatches before starting for Venice. Wotton was knighted on 8 July, and on 19 July he was at Dover, ready to embark for the journey to France and thence to Venice (Pearsall Smith, i. 45).

[15]

(f. 296.) Madam. I am intangled in a double affliction by being accused not only to haue heard (wch it is a forfeyture of my service & place in y^r favor) but to haue spoken dishonorably of y^o. I find not myself to be so spungy either to take in or powre out so easyly. and I am sure y^o would not thinke me worthy to bee pardoned for any fault if I should confessingly aske a pardon for this. it would moue me less y^t ye envious world should speake this, because envy (wch cannot be driuen from accompanying vertue) is foule spoken; & therfore naturally slaunderous. but I must wonder wth griefe y^t my lo: Latm̃[1] whose discretion & allowaunce of my loue to him I should much prise one by no meanes (knowne to me) interested in y^r honor or compassionate in y^r dishonor otherwise then generall nobility borne in him instructeth him should load Mr Davies wth ye op^{r}ssion of having dishonored y^o & deriue it from him to me. I heere y^r father hath taken it for good fuell of anger against m^r davis & ꝑchaunce me to. I do easylyer forgiue his anger then his credulity; for it is pitty he should haue beene any instrument in ye building of so fayre a pallace as y^o are and so furnishing it as his care hath done if hee would not be angry wth any defect. but (methinks) it cannot become y^t discretiō wch I think y^o inherit from him to vnbridle his suspiciō so much to ye p^{r}iudice of my vnderstanding & honesty. though my merites be not such as y^t they ever do works of superrogatiō, yet I durst vpon my conscience acquit him of ever

ut possimus plura eis et remotiora videre, non utique proprii visus acumine aut eminentia corporis, sed quia in altum subvehimur et extollimur magnitudine gigantea.'

[1] *Latm̃*, i.e. *Latimer*. The title of Baron Latimer was assumed wrongfully by Richard Neville of Penwyn, cousin of John Neville, fourth Baron Latimer, who died in 1577, leaving four daughters. Richard Neville died in 1590, and his son Edmund then assumed the title and held it during the rest of Donne's lifetime.

conceaving vnworthyly of you. but ye reverence & respect I haue alwayes loued[1] you com̄ands me to employ all my force in keeping myself in yr good thoughts & to leaue yo well assured not yt I ever spake but yt I never heard ill word from any man wch might be wrested to ye impeachment of yr honor wch here I sweare to yo by my loue & by yt fayre learned hand wch I humbly kisse. & take leaue.

The 'Mr. Davies' here mentioned is probably the poet, John Davies of Hereford. He is mentioned by Anthony à Wood as one of a group (including Ben Jonson, Drayton, Selden, William Browne, and Wither) who knew and admired Christopher Brooke, Donne's intimate friend. He moved in the same literary circles as Donne, for he dedicated *The Holy Roode* in 1609 to the Countess of Derby and her three daughters, and in 1612 he published *The Muses Sacrifice*, dedicated to Lucy, Countess of Bedford, Mary Countess-dowager of Pembroke, and Elizabeth Lady Carey. In the latter he referred to Donne's lately published elegy on Elizabeth Drury, and made the usual pun on his name.

[16]

Madam. I will haue leaue to speake like a lovor, I am not altogether (f. 295.) one: for though I loue more then any yett my loue hath not ye same marke & end wth others. How charitably you deale wth vs of these parts? yt at this tyme of ye yeare (when the sun̄ forsakes vs) yo come to vs & suffer vs not (out of yr mercy) to tast ye bitternes of a winter; but Madam you owe me this releif because in all that part of this som̄er wch I spent in yr presence yo doubled ye heat and I liued vnder ye rage of a hott sonn & yr eyes. that hart wch yo melted then no winter shall freise but it shall ever keepe that equall temper wch you gaue it soft enough to receaue yr impressions & hard enough to retayne them. it must not tast to yo as a negligence or carelesnes yt I haue not visited yr Lad: in these dayes of yr being here call it rather a devout humylyty yt I thus aske leaue & bee content to beleeue from him yt can as impossibly ly to yo as hate yo yt by com̄aundment I am sodenly throwne out of ye towne so dayly and diversly are wee tempested yt are not or owne. at my retourne (wch therfore I will hasten) I wilbee bold to kiss yt fayre vertuous hand wch doth much in receaving this letter & may do easyly much more in sending another to him whose best honor is that hee is yr leiuetenant of himself. Anonim9.

[1] Query, 'owed'.

If this letter is Donne's, it is probably addressed to the Countess of Bedford. The tone of devotion, which resembles that of a lover but is subtly differentiated from it, is the tone also of certain of Donne's poems addressed to that lady, e.g. the verse letters 'To the Countesse of Bedford' (Grierson, i. 189, 191, 195, 198, 218, 220, 227) and 'Twicknam Garden' (ibid. 28). The close of the letter may be compared with the last sentence of a letter addressed to the Countess in the 1651 *Letters*: 'Here therefore I humbly kisse your Ladiships fair learned hands, and wish you good wishes and speedy grants.'[1]

It is strange, however, that this letter should be marked out from the rest of the D 1 group by the signature *Anonimus*. Donne never disguised his Platonic admiration for Lady Bedford, and he sometimes sent a copy of his letters to her to Sir Henry Goodyer. I feel extremely doubtful whether we should be justified in ascribing the letter to Donne.

[17]

(f. 297^{v}.) S^{r}. as well in Loue as in greife why should not sylence be interpreted a signe rather of store then want? so if y^{o} construe myne at this tyme y^{o} shall not be mistaken. & besyds y^{r} frendly censure of me will deserve thanks: let me intreat y^{o} mayntayne this loue betweene vs by this meanes of sylent discoursing whereby I shall hold ye defect of absence half cured & made by conceit a well formed p^{r}sence vntill it may be so indeed. wch I will further. And although you can never receaue from me so worthy a loue as may iustly deserue yo^{rs} yet y^{o} shall haue mine what it is in the highest measure & if y^{r} gentle dispositiō can frame it pleasing to y^{r} self I shall hold myself happy because I haue my most ernest desyre satisfied in being reputed as I am

y^{r} honest frend.

[18]

(f. 300.) M.C.

To excuse where there is no trespas, is to speake what we could not what wee need: but if we do need a mutuall ꝑdon freeth vs both: such is Good Will. At my retorne out of North: I met wth y^{r} remembraunce, wch tould me of y^{r} travell abroad, & arrant to me: for y^{r} advauncem^{t}: for my advice. the former: I assure you y^{t} as I loue learning for it self where ere I find it. so much more a learned wise-

[1] *Letters* (1651), p. 68.

dome purchased by a travellers exꝑience I most admire, yea ꝑdon me wth a touch of envy. the lattr giues me certayne knowledg of yr error: but for t'is error amoris I will excuse it & wish it were not so. To giue you coũsell in these affayres were to offer much more then I cã giue: yet thus much I dare say in generall: that the course if yo go on good grounds, may be yr fayrest & I wish myself such oportunyty. yr body if I know it wth a spare diet & good excersise yo may keep sound. for yr mind take but such a prparatiue as yr Cosin Nay:[1] out of his exꝑiance can prscribe yo, & I doubt not yo shall go well instructed for ye best of knowledg. What yo know already I can tell yo, that abroad tis best being trusty to yr self, & keep all secrets at home lockt vp wth yo. Com̃on curtesies bring good acquaintaunce that againe. giues oportunyty to observe that wch happyly is not in vs: but in all keep distaunce still. to intrust as a secret yt wch is not, in some kind of people wins their loue: seeme to suspect none. seeme not to observe, be not covetuous of newes. nor lavish in report. to be factious in any religion where are many may breed yo daunger curtesy yo shall find much more com̃on there thẽ honesty prserve ye one, the other yo may requite wthout much cost. for yr private wth Sr. H. W. I can say nothing for I know not yr employment nor what course yo meane to hold wth him: In these kind of courses or the like we see so many hopes so many discontentments all such vncertaynteis crossing each other still in all, yt I find my self far below ye degree of a counseller to direct in any. ꝑ varios casus ꝑ tot discrimina rerũ tendimus in Latiũ sedes vbi fata quietas ostendunt.[2] Yr desire hath made me betray my weakenes. the messengr that brought yr note stays for this therfore no more. Loue me as yo were wont & I will nevr cease to bee

yr. Hl. S.

This letter must have been written after July 1604, when Wotton was knighted, since the writer refers to him as 'Sir H. W.' The gentleman addressed evidently wished to travel and to receive an introduction to Wotton, which the writer was unwilling to give him.

P. hand

[19]

Sr. you may thinke itt somewhat strang for me, being vnknowne, (f. 309v.) thus to molest yo vnacquainted: this fashion being never or not

[1] A corrector of the transcript has queried 'May:'. The name which might have given a clue to the recipient of the letter is abbreviated.

[2] Virgil, *Aen.* i. 204–6. Transcript 'tendring' for 'tendimus'.

comõnly vsed but where itt may be warranted wth some fore aquaitance:[1] but Sr I assure yo itt is only an extraordinary estimation of yr worth yt makes me rũ this extraordinary course: and iff itt be construed that my desire familiarly to know yr self, doth worke in me as good effects, as my longest familiarity wth others my meaning is not mistaken: yf out of what I write there be gathered any acceptable kindnes, yt, and what is due thereto I do assume vnto myself: if any overboldnes, yt burthen must be borne by or deare and worthy frend Mr. H. W. whose credit I haue in pawne yt yo shall accept these lines (as I offer them) kindly and lovingly. They haue nothing in charg but to tell yo yt the effect of yr vertue and worth besydes ye autority of or forenamed frends reports haue made you already knowne vnto me, but yt knowledg is as a tast wch doth rather stir vpp appetite thẽ satisfy itt: and yt therefore I do infinitly desire to increase itt by or acquaintance: and for yt purpose (being vnwilling to attend so long an occasion as or meeting) I do this according to the fashion of a soldier (wch occupation for a while I professe) charg yo wth this health: yt yo do me reason itt shalbee an argument of exceeding curtesy, a confirmation of yr frends iudgmẽt, & the world report & lastly itt shall tye vnto yo the loue though of an vnworthy yett of an honest & assured frend.

Perhaps from Donne to a gentleman—a friend of Wotton's—whose acquaintance he desires to make. If it is Donne's, it must belong to the earlier part of his career, as it was only before 1598 that he could speak of himself as professing the occupation of a soldier, and 1596, the year of the Cadiz expedition, or 1597, that of the Islands voyage, would be the most likely date.

[20]

(f. 302v cont.)

That increase of his greatnes although it were enough to warme his blood & the vessels of spirits in him yet certayne hath neither in his [2] nor minde made any new impressions wch I do the more wonder att, bycause methought I found that day myself a little raysed in myne owne conceipt: as servants clyme vpp vpõ theire masters fortunes.

This short letter, which in the transcript follows the preceding one immediately, affords no clear indication of its writer or date.

[1] Probably the contraction mark over 'ai' has been omitted.

[2] Here there is a blank in the transcript. In the margin a pencil query has been made '? owne behaviour'.

[21]

(f. 303.) S^{r}. I am come but a litle nerer to y^{o}, and I am already att my tropicke wch I canot yet transgresse: I made a promise to y^{o} of sending my footemā. and though ꝑchance y^{o} would easyly forgiue me this promise yet my love of a good conscience and zeale in this religion of keeping promise sends him. I always loued an innocence better then a pardon: and had rather haue true grace thē reputed. I do you a litle honor in this message: for I enable y^{o} to performe y^{t} wch a great conqueror out of his abondance promised to those y^{t} would come to him y^{t} those wch came footemē should retorne horsemē Att y^{r} last being att londō you tooke (as phisitians say wisemē should so of wine) generosū haustū a gallant full draught of o^{r} london pleasures: and therefore I do not hope to see y^{o} so dry as to tast vs againe: I must therefore haue leaue here at home & frō y^{o} to see y^{o} in y^{r}. E. wch. I desire much & by the goodnes of my loue am worthy y^{t} y^{o} desire itt too. Frō D. parke M^{r}. m house to whome wth m^{r}. S. & me all prayse & loue & remembrance of y^{o} be now & for ever most welcome Amen.

[22]

(f. 303^{v}.) S^{r}. I am so far frō telling y^{o} what day y^{o} may meete mee at London that I am not here suffered to resolue wth whome I dine to morrow: for I find here more kindnesses thē I can tell how to dispose off: wch is one of the happiest pouerties y^{t} I have yet falne into: beleeue me this is a place of much contentm̄t, Iuuenes et viri, occurrunt salutant, invitant Ingens messis est. y^{o} shall grace me wth the newest occurrents by this carrier of whome I will demand itt on saturday: In the meane while be satisfyed wth these few lines frō a mā that wheresoever he is doth languish wthout y^{o}.

[23]

(f. 300^{v}.) S^{r}. To write to you newes were to giue you a coppie of the original that you haue already receaued: yet some what I must tell you (though it may be suꝑfluous) only to lett you knowe that I doe not make daynty of my paines. ꝭ. I pray pardon my want of ceremony you shall find my loue wthin my lett^{r} & y^{r} Lp on the backe of my lett^{r}.

This short letter gives no certain indication of its date or authorship.

[24]

(f. 302^{v}.) S^{r}. I haue receaued a very kind lett^{r} frō y^{o} wch promiseth many more hereafter when this is more then ever I shall demerit. Howbeit

I am very content of them, as some men that loue to borrow money yet know not how to repay. Wherefore I would haue y^{o} first acquainted wth my estate lest when you thinke but to lend y^{o} in effect do giue: you cannot chuse but loose much by the bargaine, receaving empty lines for letters frought wth intelligence and matter[1] Y^{rs} shall serve as so many obligations wherein I stand bond vnto y^{o}; and the most y^{t} myne can serve is an acknowledgment and[2] confessiō of the debt; wch I shall then imagine y^{o} demand at my hands whensoever y^{o} giue over that wch y^{o} haue now begū.

Perhaps from Donne to a new friend. There is no clear indication of date.

[25]

(f. 302.) Ad bonitatem requiritur[3] integritas boni; ad malum sufficit singularis defectus.[4] To[5] make my letters acceptable I should admitt no discontinuitie, least, as the best of ill Divines (the Roman schoolemen) thinke that vppon every sinn of ours God returnes to his anger

[1] Cf. Donne's letter to Wotton, *Letters* (1651), pp. 120, 121: '. . . especially such Letters as mine, which (perchance out of the dulnesse of the place) are so empty of any relations, as that they oppresse not your meditations, nor discourse, nor memory. . . . How shall I then who know nothing write Letters? Sir, I learn knowledge enough out of yours to me. I learn that there is truth and firmnesse and an earnestnesse of doing good alive in the world. . . .'

[2] Transcript 'due' corrected by another hand to 'and'.

[3] Transcript 'requiritum'.

[4] For the sentiment expressed here, compare *Letters* (1651), p. 97: 'For vertue is even, and continuall, and the same, and can therefore break no where, nor admit ends, nor beginnings: it is not only not broken, but not tyed together. He is not vertuous, out of whose actions you can pick an excellent one. Vice and her fruits may be seen, because they are thick bodies, but not vertue, which is all light. . . .' Donne took the idea from St. Thomas Aquinas, *Summa Theologica*, 1–2^{ae}, qu. 19, art. 1, ad 1^{mum}: 'Ergo dicendum quod, sicut Dionysius dicit in 4 cap. de Div. Nom., bonum causatur ex integra causa, malum autem ex singularibus defectibus.' Ibid., qu. 20, art. 2: 'Est autem considerandum quod, sicut supra dictum est, ad hoc quod aliquid sit malum, sufficit singularis defectus; ad hoc autem quod est simpliciter bonum, non sufficit unum singulare bonum, sed requiritur integritas bonitatis.' The passage in Dionysius is in the old translation used by St. Thomas, cap. 4, lect. 22: 'Bonum ex una et tota est causa; malum autem ex multis et particularibus defectibus.' The Greek is *τὸ ἀγαθὸν ἐκ τῆς μιᾶς καὶ τῆς ὅλης αἰτίας· τὸ δὲ κακὸν ἐκ πολλῶν καὶ μεριστῶν ἐλλειψέων* (Dionysius, *de Div. Nom.*, iv, § 30; *Patr. Graec.*, iii, col. 729). For the above references I am indebted to Professor C. C. J. Webb.

[5] Transcript 'So'.

for all the old store, you should vppon my new negligences remember my old I write therefore now, rather Ne detur vacuũ then that I present anything worthy. His Maties: ə. of y^{r} particulars I haue to say now, and myself am not worthy of a line, not in myne owne letters, my best honor is that I have a roome in y^{r} frendship, and my best merit that I giue y^{o} one in my prayers.

The letter is clearly Donne's, and has the characteristic marks of his style. The reference to 'His Matie' shows that it was written after the accession of James I.

[26]

S^{r}. My Loue maks me write vnworthy lettres and yet you had (f 300^{v}.) wont to measure a lett^{r} by the loue of the writer: then haue I matter enough, for I know this assuredly that this lett^{r} hath loue enough to make it worthy, were he worth any thing that writes it therefore bycause he loues you. yet least I say nothing lett my[1] tell you S^{r}. that the sleeping preacher[2] is sent for againe to the king for y^{t} contrary to

[1] So in transcript. Read 'lett my letter'.

[2] *The sleeping preacher* was Richard Haydock or Haddock, of whom Arthur Wilson gives the following account (*History of Great Britain*, *Being the Life and Reign of King James the First*, 1653, p. 111): 'For in the beginning of his Reign, *Richard Haydock* of *New-Colledg* in *Oxford*, practised *Physick* in the *day*, and *Preached* in the *night* in his bed. His *Practice* came by his *Profession*, and his *Preaching* (as he pretended) by *Revelation*: For he would take a *Text* in his sleep, and deliver a good *Sermon* upon it, and though his *Auditory* were willing to silence him, by pulling, haling, and pinching, yet would he pertinaciously persist to the end, and sleep still. The *fame* of this sleeping *Preacher* flies abroad with a light *Wing*, which coming to the Kings knowledg, he commanded him to the Court, where he sate up one night to hear him: And when the time came that the *Preacher* thought it was fit for him to be asleep, he began with a *Prayer*, then took a *Text* of *Scripture*, which he significantly insisted on a while, but after made an *excursion* against the *Pope*, the *Cross* in *Baptism*, and the last *Canons* of the Church of *England*, and so concluded sleeping. The King would not trouble him that night, letting him rest after his *labours*, but sent for him the next morning, and in *private* handled him so like a cunning *Chirurgion*, that he found out the *sore*; making him confess not only his *sin* and *error* in the *act*, but the *cause* that urged him to it, which was, That he apprehended himself as a buried man in the *University*, being of a *low condition*, and if something *eminent* and *remarkable* did not spring from him, to give life to his *Reputation*, he should never appear anybody, which made him attempt this *Novelty* to be taken notice of.' See also the accounts in Anthony à Wood, *Annales*, ii. 284; and Nichols, *Progresses of James I*, i. 509, in which further particulars are given.

his promise he practises againe wch maks some report that his former confessiō was vntrue and extorted and y^{t} it was in him an act either natural or diuine: for my self I am assured that never Heriticke or any other Innovator of State or Religiō tooke a more dangerous course then hee doth or more powerfull to ꝑswade a people were not the king as ready to prevent. The particularities y^{o} shall haue by the next. In the meane tyme assure y^{r} self y^{t} y^{r} com̄ands shall nev^{r} be able to surprise or surcharge me.

This letter must belong to 1605, which was the year of the 'sleeping preacher's' appearance at court.

[27]

(f. 302.) If you please to write I will wth all gladnes answere y^{r} letters: yf you please to be sylent yet will I answere y^{r} affection wch need not be testified vnto me by letters; whereof myne owne sure knowledg and the cleernesse of my soule vnto you will not suffer me to haue the least doubt. You haue all liberty wth me, all authoritie ouer me. Only it doth very much trouble me that any thing (what I can̄ot ghesse) should depriue me of the happines I was wont to haue in y^{r} letters whereby I haue enioyed you at such distants: yt makes me doubt least I haue made some fayle in iudgment (for other it is impossible) if so, I desire you to shew it me, and chyde for I will take it kindly and amend; if not, then chyde y^{r} self in my behalf; for one of these in Justice I craue of you.

Probably from Donne to Wotton. There is no clear indication of date. 'Y^{r} letters whereby I haue enioyed you at such distants' might refer to the correspondence between Donne and Wotton when the latter was in Ireland, or to Wotton's letters during his first embassy in Venice.

[28]

(f. 301^{v}.) S^{r} y^{r} letter of ye 26 of Ma: came vnto my hands wthin the space of 20 dayes as if y^{r} goodnesse were not contented wth ye bare extending it self vnto y^{r} poore dependents, but wth ye rare company of expedition what comfort bysyds the honor it was vnto me I best know y^{t} haue felt ye effects, neither can it bee vnknowne to y^{r} self from whence the course hath so literally flowne, though what the advantage will bee I must refer to future event wch I hope shortly will fall out if it fall not in the meane tyme into the ordinarie Court apoplexie of forget-fullnes. I would gladly passe frō hence to the performance of some service of relatiō, if either my desyre or meanes of knowing the tymes evills did agree wth my forwardnes to serue you. Some things I haue learnd since my comīg of church affayres I will keep my self w^th^in my compasse. It is great pittie to see the distractions of it, on the one syde challenged for innovatiō, on the other accused of antiquitie that if it were not as it is placed in the saftie of mediocritie[1] there were small hope of endurance, and it might seeme strange that so many disagreements should brake out if the hand of God had not sett this as his owne marke vppō it. The Puritans increase frō theire discontents they receaue at the B^ps^. and the papists rise by theire disagreements: they be two new names invented by the diuel as visards to scarr mē frō all ancient learning and godly liveing.[2] meere names they are and words of tyme;[3] if you aske what the things are signified either y^r^ answere shalbe nothing or as many things as y^o^ haue answeres.[4] it will nev^r^ be agreed what they are. for my part I repent me of my paynes takē in my studie and am resolued to sett my self downe in myne Inn,[5] and neither medle nor make in the world further then by my prayers and good wishes. I make accompt to find some contentment at home or at the worst some such discontentm^t^ as may diuert myne eyes frō the publike. but whilst I rememb^r^ my self I forgett you. I growe

[1] Cf. *LXXX Sermons*, 5. 42: 'the overbending, and super-exaltation of zeale, and the captivity to the private spirit, which some have fallen into, that have not beene content to consist in moderate, and middle wayes in the Reformed Church . . . many times, an over-vehement bending into some way of our owne choosing, does not onely withdraw us from the left hand way, the way of superstition, and Idolatry, from which wee should all draw, but from the middle way too, in which we should stand, and walk.'

[2] Transcript 'liveving'. For the thought compare *LXXX Sermons*, 49. 493, in which Donne suggests that the words 'papist' and 'puritan' are used too loosely as terms of reproach, and asserts that he is willing to be called a papist for his devotions, and a puritan for his moral earnestness.

[3] Cf. *Letters* (1651), p. 29: 'You know I never fettered nor imprisoned the word Religion; not straightning it Frierly, *ad Religiones factitias* (as the *Romans* call well their orders of Religion), nor immuring it in a *Rome*, or a *Wittemberg*, or a *Geneva*; they are all virtuall beams of one Sun, and wheresoever they finde clay hearts, they harden them, and moulder them into dust; and they entender and mollifie waxen. They are not so contrary as the North and South Poles; and that they are connaturall pieces of one circle. Religion is Christianity, which being too spirituall to be seen by us, doth therefore take an apparent body of good life and works, so salvation requires an honest Christian.' These words are found in a letter written by Donne during his life at Mitcham.

[4] Query, 'answerers'.

[5] That is, settle down quietly. Cp. John Heywood, *Proverbs* (1562), pt. i, c. 5: 'To let the world wag, and take mine ease in mine inn'.

tedious. The Bp. of Glocester is remoued to London by the means of [1] as much for his instrumental as vocal fittnesse wch I name ye rather yt yo may see the wisedome of or Archbps in preferring wthout partialitie those whome they find fitt I say so bycause there is now a difference put betwixt fittnesse and worthinesse and many worthy there may bee to haue good place wch are not fitt to doe the (f. 302.) evills of them.[2] the Ar:[3] is a mā | compounded of puritanisme and policy the one in iudgment the other in state. I beginn to grow wild it is tyme to take vp my self and to committ yo to God and yr more waighty affayrs. so I rest.

This letter must have been written in 1607, since it was in May of that year that Thomas Ravis, Bishop of Gloucester, was transferred to the See of London. Although the passages quoted in the foot-notes show that the standpoint of the writer of the letter was similar to that of Donne, there are certain phrases, such as that about 'yr poore dependents', which suggest that he was not the author. Professor R. C. Bald conjectures that the letter may have been written by Nathaniel Fletcher (son of the bishop and brother of the dramatist), who was Wotton's chaplain during the first two years of his embassy, and returned to England towards the end of 1606. Wotton praised him warmly to Salisbury in a letter written from Venice on 22 Sept. 1606 (Pearsall Smith, *Wotton*, i. 363) and asked Salisbury to do something for him. This would explain the first sentence of the letter here printed.

[29]

(f. 301.) Sr. All this while like a silke worme I worke myself into a bottome or clew and by my former sylence and contemplation of yr honorable merits I am so increased in my inward loue and desire to doe you service, as when you shalbee pleased to vntwine me, you shall find

[1] There is a blank in the manuscript.

[2] Cf. *Letters* (1651), p. 279: . . . 'It was an impertinent jealousie that I conceived of that Gentlemans absence from my L. for he gives that full Testimonie of him, that he never discerned any kinde of unfitnesse in him for any imployment, except too much goodnesse; and Conscientiousnesse may sometimes make him somewhat lesse fit for some kindes of businesse, then a man of a looser raine.'

[3] *The Ar*: i.e. Archbishop Bancroft. The charge of Puritanism was not so often brought against him as against his successor Abbot.

length enough in my desires though perhaps my thred of performance be very small. If therefore in the accompts you cast of y^{r} frends you do not sum̄ me vpp amongst the rest it will very much greiue and molest me, bycause though others take me only for a cypher, to increase the number of theire frends yet I am ambitious to be reputed of some number wth you whose frendship I know and iudgment admitts no cypher. And bycause I cannot but communicate wth my frends y^{t} wch I know I will tell you y^{t} it did much reioyce my hart whē I heard my L^{d}. E by his ho^{ble}. testimony giue great reputatiō to the Ld Amb^{r} of Venice as to one of very great fidelitie and excellent dexterity and skill in publike businesses of wch he had giuē acceptable proofe and experience to his Mj^{tie}: now as I doubt not but your desyre to merit him, so (if y^{o} willbe pleased not to thinke I presume to advise you) besyds y^{t} satisfactiō of y^{r} excellent dispatches nothing wilbe more acceptable thē some such models and frames[2] & I speake this (w^{th}out comissiō) for y^{t} I know both y^{r} dispositions and I desire to encrease his good opiniō of y^{o}.

and I am content[1]

This letter is clearly addressed to Wotton during his tenure of the post of English ambassador at Venice. It implies that Wotton had already held the post long enough to give considerable proofs of his skill, but it also evidently belongs to his first embassy at Venice (1604–10), since his re-appointment in 1616 and again in 1621 afforded such evidence of the king's confidence in him as needed no support in the narration of casual remarks like that recorded in this letter. 'My L^{d}. E.' is probably Lord Ellesmere, who was made a baron on 19 July 1603, and Lord Chancellor on 24 July. Moreover, all the correspondence contained in these pages of the Burley MS. belongs to a period earlier than 1616.

The letter is probably from Donne; the opening sentence has the ring of his style; 1608 or 1609 would seem a likely date.

[30]

(f. 303.)

The Tyrrany of a suddaine raging sicknes (comfortable in nothing but ye violence of itt) assures y^{t} either itt or I are short liued[3] having

[1] These words are added in the margin. They should be inserted after 'frends'.

[2] Transcript 'ad [blank]', corrected in another hand to 'and frames'.

[3] Compare Donne's complaints of a sickness in a letter to Sir H. G. (Sir

found either vertue or stubbernes inough in me to disdaine all bitternes y^{t} itt can make against my body, now assayles my mind & shews me y^{t} (by imprisoning me in my chamber itt is able to depriue me of y^{t} happines wch by y^{r} grace was allowed me whē y^{o} gaue me the priueledg of having leaue to visit y^{o}. I confesse that this is my sicknes worst fitt & as fearefully ominous as Tamerlins last dayes black ensignes whose threatnings none scaped.[1] Let not y^{r} charity therefore desdayne to coyne wth me, in an honest deceit, to breake this tempest of my sicknes, and since this letter hath my name, and hand, and words, and thoughts bee content to thinke itt me, & to give itt leaue thus to speake to y^{o}, though y^{o} vouchsafe not to speake to itt againe. It shall tell you truly (for from me itt sucked no levin of flattery) wth what height or rather lownes of devotion I reverence you: who besides the com̃andm^{t} of a noble birth, and y^{r} perswasiue eloquence of beauty, haue the advantage of the furniture of arts and languages,[2] and such other vertues as might serve to iustify a reprobate fortune and ye lowest condition: soe that if these things whereby some few other are named are made[3] worthy, are to you but ornaments such might be left wthout leaving you vnperfect. To y^{t} treasure of y^{r} vertues whereof y^{r} fayre eyes curtesy is not the lest iewell I present this paper: and if itt be not to much boldnes in itt my excuse of not visiting y^{o}. And so kindly kissing y^{r} fayre hand y^{t} vouchsafes the receipt of these lines I take leaue.[4]

Henry Goodyer), *Letters* (1651), pp. 34, 37: 'I have often seen such beg-gers as my indisposition is, end themselves soon, and the patient as soon. . . . I have mending or dying on my side, which is two to one.'

[1] Cf. Marlowe, *Tamburlaine the Great*, pt. i, Act iv, sc. i, and Act v, sc. i. On the first day Tamburlaine's colours were white to signify mildness, on the second day red, but on the third and succeeding days his ensigns were black to signify that no quarter would be given.

[2] For this emphasis on the union of beauty, noble birth, and learning in the lady whom Donne addresses, compare his verse letter *To the Countesse of Bedford* (Grierson, i. 190), ll. 24–7:

> Your birth and beauty are this Balme in you.
> But you of learning and religion,
> And vertue 'and such ingredients, have made
> A methridate . . .

and again, *To the Countesse of Bedford. On New-yeares day* (Grierson, i. 200), ll. 36–7:

> Hee [i.e. God] will best teach you, how you should lay out
> His stock of *beauty*, *learning*, *favour*, *blood*.

[3] Query, 'and are made'.

[4] Cf. *Letters* (1651), p. 68 (in a letter addressed *To the Countess of Bedford*): 'Here therefore I humbly kisse your Ladiships fair learned hands.'

This letter is clearly Donne's, and it was probably addressed to the Countess of Bedford at some date between 1608 and 1614, the years during which he wrote most of his verse letters to that lady.

[31]

S^{r}. The relacō of occurrences heere I leaue to this gentlemā M^{r} W^{llm}. Strachey[1] allwayes my good frend (who is desirous y^{r} Lp: should know so much) and sometymes secretary to S^{r}. T. G:[2] I dare boldly say that the greatest folly he ever com̄itted was to submitt himself and parts to so meane a M^{r}. y^{o} may thinke this a preposterous course in steed of com̄ending a gentlemā to open his imperfections, but I know y^{r} Lp. so wise as out of contraries to draw / gather[3] true and necessarie conclusions: and to say but truth for me to opē my mouth in his com̄endations were but to play the owle or some other bird in a painted cloath in whose mouth some sentence is put wch most mē know: and so of his vertues. only this I shall intreat that bysyde his merit he may for my sake find himself welcome. (f. 301.)

[32]

S^{r}. I haue the honor of a letter from y^{r} Lp: and a testimony that though better then any other you know my infirmity yet you are not scandalized with my chang of habitt. I haue S^{r}. besydes many other internal advantages this also by itt, that besydes the obligations of (f. 255.)

[1] William Strachey sailed for Virginia in May 1609. With Sir Thomas Gates and Sir George Somers he was wrecked on the Bermudas during the great storm of July 1609. He wrote an account of the shipwreck in a letter which was published later in *Purchas his Pilgrimes* (1625), iv. 1734. In 1610 he reached Virginia, where he was appointed secretary and recorder of the colony. He returned to England in 1611 (*D.N.B.*).

[2] *Sr T. G.* Probably Sir Thomas Gates, who was knighted in 1596 on the Cadiz expedition. In 1609 he was made lieutenant-general of Virginia, and sailed on the Bermudas voyage. He went with Strachey to Virginia in 1610, and after a visit to England returned as governor of the colony, a post which he held from 1611 to 1614. Wotton refers once or twice to Gates in his letters, for example, when writing to Ralph Winwood in 1604 he says, 'I commend unto you the bearer hereof, Sir Thomas Gates, whom I entreat you to love, and to love me, and to assure yourself that you cannot love two honester men' (Pearsall Smith, *Wotton*, i. 320). In 1614 Wotton wrote to Winwood, 'The bearer is a servant to Sir Thomas Gates, and I hope hath learned some diligence from his master' (ibid., ii. 50).

[3] draw / gather } These alternative readings appear thus in the transcript.

frendship and services towards you wch binde mee alwayes to comēnd y^r^ fortunes to God in my prayers (having never had any other way of expressing myself) I am come now to doe itt by my office. And I may bee credible to do my frend that service with much ernestnes bycause as yet I haue no other charge. for I do not so much as enquire of myne owne hopes what the K. will do wth me: Hee forbad me at first and I obey him still, and forbeare so much as to remember him that hee forbadd mee.

This letter was evidently written by Donne soon after his ordination, which took place in January 1614/15. It was not till the spring of 1616 that Donne was presented to the living of Keyston, in Huntingdonshire, and later in the same year he became rector of Sevenoaks, in Kent.

In the Burley MS. the letter was separated from the other Donne letters by a considerable interval, as it was transcribed on folio 255, and the Donne poems began on folio 279, and the letters (except for the postscript on folio 286) on folio 294. It will be noticed that all the other letters seem to have been written during Wotton's first embassy at Venice or earlier. Later entries were often made on blank spaces in commonplace books, and this letter was probably added after the other pages had been filled.

Appendix to Chapter XII

Letters in the Burley MS. certainly not by Donne.

(f. 302.) Mille volte ringratio V. E. dell' efficacissimi pegni della sua benignita inverso[1] me. Prego Iddio tanto me ne rende degno quanto ella si compiocce (?) non hauer riguardo ad altra degnita che delle proprie sue virte. I must acknowledg I haue no defence for this and the rest then the infirmity of myne owne iudgment by wch it was as necessary for me to comitt many errors as it is proper for y^r^ goodnes to pardon them. And so wishing y^o^ many happie yeares wth y^t^ zeale wch is only worthy of y^r^ acceptance I rest.

This letter, certainly not by Donne, was addressed to Wotton, as is shown by the use of the term 'V. E.', i.e. 'Vostra Eccellenza'.

(f. 259.) I must wonder y^t^ since my cōming to Lon: I haue not many tymes heard from y^o^ frō whome I expected a truer representation of those

[1] Transcript 'inverto'.

parts where yō liue then frō any other vessell of lesse receipt. and indeed besyds y^{r} loue y^{o} should yeeld somwhat in this to o^{r} p^{r}sent humors wch if they haue not matter of truth to worke vppon are likely to breed in themselues some monstruous imaginations. wee are put into beamorris by ye scanting of the wind vpon vs wch to me is a p^{r}paratiue for Ir: st̂ May I after these kisse that fayre & learned hand of y^{r} m^{ris} then whome ye world doth posesse nothing more vertuous farwell sodenly. for if I should giue way to myself I should begin againe.

To this is added in another hand: 'S^{r}. It were not only a wrong but a kind of violence to put y^{o} in mynd of my busines and therefore the end of this is only to salute y^{o}. farwell. you must not forgett septies in hebdomada[1] to vesit my best and dearest att Thr:'

Since Donne did not embark on the Irish expedition, this letter cannot have been written by him, but it may have been addressed to him by Wotton. It has been printed among Wotton's letters by Mr. Pearsall Smith (i. 306), who adds: 'This letter, without date, address, or signature, occurs among a collection of Donne's letters (most of them apparently addressed to Wotton), and almost certainly belongs to the lost Wotton and Donne correspondence. The mention of Beaumaris gives the approximate date', i.e. 11–14 April 1599.

Right. Ho: L: It may seeme strang to y^{o} that vpon so short a (f. 300v.) comendatiō & lesse abylyty of desert in me I should so sodenly importune y^{or} Hon^{ors} favo^{r} but emboldned by the relatiō of the world in satisfying all excusable demands & p^{r}suming in ye necessary respect of this importunyty I hope my boldnes will find excuse or at least favorable censure: May it please y^{r} Ho: therefore I arrived in Raguza a month agoe where I remayned twenty daeys from whence to Parentio & so to Venice in a smale barke & potentos[2] from both places: yet I feare purgatory & therefore so farr as wth modesty I may I craue y^{r} Ho: favor in procuring absolution: & fearing to be tedious in further relatiō of my suite vnto y^{o} I besech y^{r} Hon: to send y^{r} secretary where

[1] Query, 'hebdomade'.

[2] So in the transcript. Dr. C. T. Onions suggests that the sense may be 'permits' or 'passports', to free the writer from quarantine up to that point of the journey. 'Potent' in the sense of a military warrant or order occurs in F. Markham's *Book of War*, 1622. See the *O.E.D.*

I am in a banke right over against the house of ye Sanito'[1] wth whose help I may wth lesse offence of circumstaunce recom̄end this my suite & service to y^{r} Ho: Thus least I should fold vp many errors in one I humbly take my leaue & vow the observaunces of him who is

y^{r} H^{rs}. most obliged.

This letter is clearly not by Donne. It seems to be addressed to Wotton by an Englishman who required his help to escape quarantine.

[1] The Venetian Board of Health, established in 1485, especially to take preventive measures against plague. The 'purgatory' to which the writer refers is quarantine.

APPENDIX A

LIST OF MANUSCRIPTS OF DONNE'S PROSE WORKS

1. Manuscripts of *Juvenilia* (Paradoxes, Problems, Characters, Essay of Valour), with the symbols used for them in this work:

A 18. Additional MS. 18647, British Museum.

A 25 (one problem, no paradoxes). Additional MS. 25707, British Museum.

Ash. 826. Ashmole MS. 826, Bodleian Library.

B. Bridgewater MS., formerly in the possession of the Earl of Ellesmere, and now in the Henry E. Huntington Library, Pasadena.

Bur. Burley MS., formerly in the possession of Mr. G. H. Finch at Burley-on-the-Hill, where it was destroyed by fire. The Delegates of the Clarendon Press possess a transcript.

Do. Dobell MS., formerly in the possession of Mr. P. J. Dobell, and now in Harvard College Library (Nor. 4506).

N. Norton MS., Harvard College Library (Nor. 4503).

O'F. O'Flaherty MS., formerly in the possession of the late Rev. T. R. O'Flaherty, now in Harvard College Library.

P. Phillipps MS., Bodleian Library, MS. Eng. poet. f. 9.

S. Stephens MS., Harvard College Library.

S 96. Stowe MS. 962, British Museum.

Tan. Tanner MS. 299, Bodleian Library (one problem only).

TCC. MS. R. 3. 12, Trinity College, Cambridge.

TCD. MS. G. 2. 21, Trinity College, Dublin.

W. Westmoreland MS., formerly in the possession of the late Sir Edmund Gosse, now in the New York Public Library.

Wy. Wyburd MS., formerly in the possession of the late W. Wyburd, from whom it passed to Mr. P. J. Dobell.

2. *Catalogus Librorum Aulicorum*

MS. B. 14. 22, Trinity College, Cambridge.

3. *Biathanatos*

MS. e Musaeo 131, Bodleian Library.

4. *Sermons*

A. Ashmole MS. 781, Bodleian Library.

C. Collier MS., formerly in the possession of the late J. Payne Collier, now in that of Mr. Wilfred Merton.

D. Dowden MS., formerly in the possession of the late Professor Edward Dowden, now in that of Mr. Wilfred Merton.

Do. Dobell MS. Harvard College Library (Nor. 4506). See above under *Juvenilia.*

L. Lothian MS., formerly in the possession of the late Rev. A. H. Jessopp, now in that of the Marquess of Lothian.

PC. MS. St. Paul's Cathedral Library, London.

5. *Letters*

British Museum. Additional MS. 29598, ff. 13, 15.
British Museum. Cotton MS. Cleop. F. vii; Jul. C. iii, ff. 153–4.
Bodleian Library. MS. e Musaeo 131 (accompanying *Biathanatos*).
Bodleian Library. MS. Tanner lxxiii, f. 305.
Harvard College Library. Charles Eliot Norton Collection, bound up with *Letters* (1651).
H. E. Huntington Library. MS. H.M. 7281.
State Papers Domestic, James I, cxxxiv, no. 59, and clxxvi, no. 28.
State Papers Domestic, Charles I, x, no. 28.
Bath MSS. ii. 59 (Hist. MSS. Comm. Rep. III, App., p. 196).
Fortescue MSS. (Hist. MSS. Comm. Rep. II, App., p. 59).
Loder-Symonds MSS. (Hist. MSS. Comm. Rep. XIII, App. iv, p. 383).
Loseley MSS. (Hist. MSS. Comm. Rep. VII, App., pp. 659, 670–1).
Portland MSS. III (Hist. MSS. Comm. Rep. XIV, App. ii, p. 6).
Powis MSS., Series II.
(Transcript only) Burley-on-the-Hill MS. Delegates of the Clarendon Press.

Note to Section 1. As this volume goes to press, Professor R. C. Bald sends word that the Long Island Historical Society, Brooklyn, N.Y., possesses a manuscript of Donne's *Juvenilia* contained in a volume of miscellaneous prose and verse dated approximately 1630.

APPENDIX B

A CHRONOLOGICAL ARRANGEMENT OF DONNE'S SERMONS

IT is evident that the lack of any chronological arrangement of the sermons is a serious stumbling-block in the way of any student who wishes to illustrate the course of Donne's life by reference to his sermons, or to trace any development in his theology and his inward experience during the sixteen years of his ministry.

In the *LXXX Sermons* of 1640 the sermons are arranged according to the festivals on which they were delivered. A certain number are dated, and these are generally arranged in order, e.g. the Christmas sermons are dated 1622, 1624, 1625, 1626, 1627, 1628, followed by an undated sermon. No conclusion can safely be drawn from the position of the undated sermon, as the Whitsunday sermons are thus arranged —1627, 1628, one undated, 1629, six undated. A gap in the series of sermons may sometimes be supplied from a later volume; thus in the series described as 'preached in Lent', and delivered, as the dates show us, on what Walton calls Donne's 'old constant day', the first Friday in Lent, the sermon missing for the year 1620/1 is found as the fourth sermon in the *XXVI Sermons* of 1660/1.

The *L Sermons* of 1649 are arranged as 'Sermons preached at Marriages', 'at Christenings', 'at Churchings', 'at Lincoln's Inn', 'at Whitehall', 'to the Nobility', 'at S. Paul's', 'at S. Dunstan's'. Many of the sermons are undated, and in one of them the date given is certainly incorrect.[1]

No arrangement is apparent in the *XXVI Sermons* of 1660/1, but they are all (with three exceptions) headed and dated.

A further problem is presented by the untrustworthy nature of a few of the headings. Such a heading as that of the thirteenth sermon in the *LXXX Sermons*, 'Preached in Lent, To the King, April 20, 1630', is manifestly incorrect, for 20 April fell that year on the Tuesday following the third Sunday after Easter. A sermon which appears twice in the *XXVI Sermons* (as Nos. 5 and 16) is dated at first 12 February 1629, and afterwards 22 February 1629. Here a reference to the ecclesiastical calendar for the year 1629/30 shows that the former date is probably correct, that being the first Friday in Lent.

[1] Sermon 35, which is dated 21 Feb. 1611, several years before Donne entered Holy Orders.

On the whole, however, if used with caution, the headings are of considerable help in making a chronological arrangement of the sermons. It is impossible to accept Gosse's conjecture that the *LXXX Sermons* are identical with those revised by Donne during his retreat at Chelsea from the plague in 1625,[1] and that therefore 'we may accept with confidence all the autobiographical touches which its headings supply'. Twenty-six of these sermons are dated subsequently to the letter in which Donne mentions this revision, and No. 71 is definitely connected by its heading with the last year of Donne's life—'At the *Haghe* Decemb. 19, 1619. I Preached upon this Text. Since in my sicknesse at *Abrey-hatche* in Essex, 1630. revising my short notes of that Sermon, I digested them into these two.'

It is possible that a few of the *XXVI Sermons* were among the eighty revised by Donne in 1625, for the majority of them belong to the earlier part of his career and their headings are sometimes unusually detailed.

Out of the hundred and fifty-four sermons contained in the three volumes, less than thirty offer us no clue as to their date. The headings of eighty-three contain either actual dates, or a clear reference to current events by which the sermon can be dated. By far the larger number of these belong to the later period of Donne's life, whilst he was Dean of St. Paul's. Only three sermons are dated as belonging to the two and a half years between his ordination and his wife's death, and two of these are dull and lifeless. Probably Donne felt in later years that his early sermons were unworthy of his subsequent reputation, and therefore he did not trouble to revise and preserve them.

Each of the years 1618, 1619, and 1620 has four sermons ascribed to it. Those preached in 1619 are of especial interest owing to the circumstances under which they were delivered. One was 'preached to the Lords, upon Easter Day, at the Communion. The King being then dangerously sick at Newmarket.' The second was the 'Sermon of Valediction', preached just before Donne's departure on the Bohemian Embassy with Lord Doncaster, and closely connected in thought and expression with the 'Hymn to Christ, at the Author's Last Going into Germany'. The third was preached in Heidelberg before the Princess Palatine, that unfortunate lady Elizabeth, daughter of James the First, who recalled in later years the 'delight'

[1] See the letter dated 25 Nov. 1625, quoted by Gosse in *Life and Letters of John Donne*, vol. ii, pp. 222–5, and his comment on p. 310. The impossibility of accepting this conjecture was pointed out in the *Cambridge History of English Literature*, vol. iv, pp. 240, 241, by Dr. F. E. Hutchinson.

and 'edification' with which she had listened to Donne; and the fourth was delivered at the Hague, where the States General presented Donne with a gold medal representing the Synod of Dort.

Donne was appointed Dean of St. Paul's in November 1621, and after this the number of sermons which have been preserved increases rapidly. Ten are dated as belonging to 1622, and two of these were considered sufficiently important to be published at once. One was delivered at St. Paul's Cross to explain 'some reasons, which His Sacred Majesty had been pleased to give, of those Directions for Preachers, which he had formerly sent forth'. James was delighted with this sermon, and desired to see it in print, saying 'that it was a piece of such perfection as could admit neither addition nor diminution'.[1] The other was preached to the Virginia Company, and is described by Dr. Jessopp as the first missionary sermon in the English language.

The sermons dated as belonging to 1623 are much less numerous. Donne's serious illness in the last months of the year deprived us of the Christmas sermon which it was his custom to preach at St. Paul's, but gave us instead the *Devotions upon Emergent Occasions*.

In 1624 Donne was appointed Vicar of St. Dunstan's, and we have several sermons preached in that church soon after his institution. The early part of 1625 is rich in sermons, amongst them being one preached a few days before King James's funeral and another in presence of his successor. No sermons date from the autumn of 1625, as the plague was then raging in London, and Donne was forced to retreat to Chelsea—at that time a remote village—where he spent some months in Sir John Danvers's house, in the congenial company of George Herbert and his mother, the saintly lady to whom Donne had already addressed several poems, and whose funeral sermon he was to preach not quite two years later.

Donne returned to London to preach the Christmas sermon at St. Paul's, and in January 1626 he delivered a striking sermon at St. Dunstan's on the plague which had so recently devastated the city. He was now at the height of his fame, and more of his sermons have been handed down to us as belonging to this year than to any other. The year 1627 was also marked by a large number of sermons, one of which incurred the suspicions of Charles the First and Laud, though Donne was able to clear himself to the King's satisfaction from all charge of disloyal Puritanism. Donne's letters show that he found it difficult to see how this sermon could have roused the King's

[1] Letter from Viscount Doncaster to Donne, in the Tobie Mathew Collection.

displeasure in any way, but there are phrases in it which might easily have been construed as an attack on Henrietta Maria and the 'Romanizing' policy which her influence was supposed to favour.[1] One of Donne's most interesting sermons of this year, 1627, is that preached on 1 July at Lady Danvers's funeral, in which he draws a striking picture of the home-life of the Herbert family.

During the years 1628 and 1629 Donne suffered from attacks of illness which for several months prevented him from preaching, but nevertheless we have a fair number of sermons dating from this time. It was not till the summer of 1630 that his health finally broke down. During his illness at Abury Hatch in the autumn of 1630 he revised some of his sermons, as we learn from the heading to no. 71 in the *LXXX Sermons*. He came to London again early in 1630/1 to preach before the King on the first Friday in Lent, when he delivered his last sermon, the famous 'Death's Duel', which was published in 1632. After the sermon he went back to his house, 'out of which', as Walton says, 'he never moved, till, like St. Stephen, "he was carried by devout men to his grave".' His death took place on 31 March 1631.

The following list includes only those sermons of which the date is clearly given in the heading. The dates in italics have been supplied from a comparison of the ecclesiastical and civil (Julian) calendars for the period.

[1] e.g. 'When they [the Apostles] came in their peregrination, to a new State, to a new Court, to Rome it selfe, they did not enquire, how stands the Emperour affected to Christ, and to the preaching of his Gospel; Is there not *a Sister*, or *a Wife* that might be wrought upon to further the preaching of Christ? Are there not some persons, great in power and place, that might be content to hold a party together, by admitting the preaching of Christ? This was not their way; They only considered who sent them; Christ Jesus: And what they brought; *salvation* to every soul that embraced Christ Jesus. . . . All Divinity that is bespoken, and not ready made, fitted to certaine turnes, and not to generall ends; And all Divines that have their *soules* and *consciences*, so disposed, *as their Libraries may bee*, (At that end stand Papists, and at that end Protestants, and he comes in in the middle, as neare one as the other) all these have a brackish taste; as a River hath that comes near the Sea, so have they, in comming so neare the Sea of Rome.' L, 27, p. 231.

Vol. and No.	Date	Place and Occasion
xxvi, 11[1]	1615 Apr. 30 (*3rd Sun. after Easter*)	At Greenwich.
„ 6	1616 Apr. 21 (*3rd Sun. after Easter*)	At Whitehall.
„ 24	1616/17 Mar. 24	'A Sermon Preached at Pauls Cross to the Lords of the Council, and other Honorable Persons. . . . It being the Anniversary of the Kings coming to the Crown, and his Majesty being then gone into Scotland.'
„ 7[2]	1617 Nov. 2 (*20th Sun. after Trinity*)	At Whitehall.
„ 18	„ Dec. 14 (*3rd Sun. in Advent*)	At Denmark House to Queen Anne.
„ 1	1617/18 Feb. 20 (*1st Fri. in Lent*)	At Whitehall.
„ 12	1618 Apr. 12 (*1st Sun. after Easter*)	„ „
„ 13	„ Apr. 19 (*2nd Sun. after Easter*)	„ „
„ 2	1618/19 Feb. 12 (*1st Fri. in Lent*)	„ „
lxxx, 27[3]	1619 *Mar.* 28 (Easter Sunday)	'To the Lords upon Easter-day, at the Communion, The King being then dangerously sick at New-Market.'
xxvi, 19	„ Apr. 18 (*3rd Sun. after Easter*)	At Lincoln's Inn. 'A Sermon of Valediction at my going into Germany.'
„ 20	„ June 16	'Two Sermons, to the Prince and Princess Palatine, the Lady Elizabeth at Heydelberg, when I was commanded by the King to wait upon my L. of Doncaster in his Embassage to Germany. First Sermon as we went out.'[4]

[1] This is the earliest of Donne's sermons which we possess, for L, 35, which is headed 21 Feb. 1611, must be incorrectly dated, as Donne was not ordained till Jan. 1614/15.

[2] If L, 48 is the sermon on Lam. iii. 1 mentioned by Walton as Donne's first after his wife's death, it must belong to Aug. 1617 and should be inserted here.

[3] The heading of this sermon does not give the year, but the mention of the King's illness at Newmarket points conclusively to 1619.

[4] The second sermon to the Prince and Princess Palatine has apparently been lost.

Vol. and No.	Date	Place and Occasion
lxxx, 71 & 72	1619 Dec. 19 (*4th Sun. in Advent*)	At the Hague. 'Since in my sicknesse at Abrey-hatche in Essex, 1630, revising my short notes of that Sermon, I digested them into these two.'
„ 14	1619/20 Mar. 3 (*1st Fri. in Lent*)	At Whitehall.
xxvi, 9[1]	1620 Apr. 2 (*5th Sun. in Lent*)	„ „
lxxx, 74	„ Apr. 30 (*2nd Sun. after Easter*)	„ „
„ 42	„ *June* 11 (Trinity Sunday)	At Lincoln's Inn.
l, 30	1620/1 Jan. 7 (*1st Sun. after Epiphany*)	'To the Countesse of Bedford, then at Harrington house.'
xxvi, 4	„ Feb. 16 (*1st Fri. in Lent*)	Before the King at Whitehall.
„ 14[2]	1621 Apr. 2 (*Easter Monday*)	At Whitehall.
lxxx, 70	„ Apr. 8 (*1st Sun. after Easter*)	„ „
l, 36	„ *Dec.* 25 (Christmas Day)	At St. Paul's.
lxxx, 15	1621/2 Mar. 8 (*1st Fri. in Lent*)	At Whitehall.
xxvi, 25	1622 *Apr.* 22 (Easter Monday)	At the Spital.
„ 23	„ *May* 30 (Ascension Day)	At Lincoln's Inn.
l, 37	„ *June* 24 (Midsummer Day)	At St. Paul's.
„ 31	„ Aug. 25 (*10th Sun. after Trinity*)	'At Hanworth, to my Lord of Carlile, and his company, being the Earles of Northumberland, and Buckingham, etc.'
Published separately in 1622	„ Sept. 15 (*13th Sun. after Trinity*)	The Cross (i.e. St. Paul's Cross). 'Wherein occasion was justly taken for the publication of some reasons, which His

[1] Numbered erroneously as 10 in the 1660/1 edition, no. 9 being omitted, and this and the following sermon (which is on the same text) being both numbered as 10. I believe that Sermon 10, which is clearly a continuation of 9, though undated, should be inserted here, as it probably followed at an interval of one or two weeks.

[2] This sermon is evidently a continuation of xxvi, 13, which is dated 19 Apr. 1618, since it is called 'A Second Sermon preached at Whitehall' and allusion is made in it to the foregoing one. It is difficult to believe that Donne would have reminded his hearers of a sermon preached three years before. One of the two dates is probably incorrect.

Vol. and No.	Date	Place and Occasion
		Sacred Majesty had been pleased to give, of those Directions for Preachers, which he had formerly sent forth.'
L, 38	1622 Oct. 13 (*17th Sun. after Trinity*)	At St. Paul's.
,, 43	,, Nov. 5	'The Anniversary celebration of our Deliverance from the Powder Treason. Intended for Pauls Crosse, but by reason of the weather, Preached in the Church.'
Published separately in 1622	,, Nov. 13	Preached to the Honourable Company of the Virginian Plantation.
LXXX, 1	,, *Dec.* 25 (Christmas Day)	At St. Paul's.
,, 16	1622/3 *Feb.* 28 (1st Fri. in Lent)	At Whitehall.
,, 18	1623 *Apr.* 13 (Easter Day)	At St. Paul's, 'in the Evening'.
Published separately in 1623	,, *May* 22 (Ascension Day)	'Encænia. The Feast of Dedication Celebrated At Lincolnes Inne. . . . At the Dedication of a new Chappell there.'
LXXX, 19	1624 *Mar.* 28 (Easter Day)	At St. Paul's '. . . in the Evening'.
L, 45	,, Apr. 11 (*2nd Sun. after Easter*)	At St. Dunstan's. 'The first Sermon in that Church, as Vicar thereof.'
,, 46	,, Apr. 25 (*4th Sun. after Easter*)	'The second Sermon Preached by the Author after he came to St. Dunstanes.'
LXXX, 43	,, *May* 23 (Trinity Sunday)	At St. Dunstan's.
L, 32	,, June 13 (*3rd Sun. after Trinity*)	'To the Earl of Exeter, and his company, in his Chappell at Saint Johns.'
LXXX, 2	,, *Dec.* 25 (Christmas Day)	At St. Paul's, 'in the Evening'.
L, 49	1624/5 Jan. 1 (*Circumcision*)	At St. Dunstan's.
LXXX, 46	,, *Jan.* 30 (*4th Sun. after Epiphany*)	'At S. Paul's, The Sunday after the Conversion of S. Paul, 1624.'
,, 17	,, Mar. 4 (*1st Fri. in Lent*)	At Whitehall.

Vol. and No.	Date	Place and Occasion
Published separately in 1625	1625 Apr. 3 (*5th Sun. in Lent*)	'The First Sermon preached to King Charles, At Saint James.'
lxxx, 20	„ *Apr.* 17 (Easter Day)	At St. Paul's, 'in the Evening'.
l, 33	„ Apr. 26	'At Denmark house, some few days before the body of King James was removed from thence, to his buriall, Apr. 26, 1625.'
lxxx, 65	„ May 8 (*3rd Sun. after Easter*)	At St. Paul's. 'The first of the Prebend of Cheswicks five Psalmes.'
„ 3	„ *Dec.* 25 (Christmas Day)	At St. Paul's.
xxvi, 21	1625/6 Jan. 15 (*2nd Sun. after Epiphany*)	At St. Dunstan's. 'The First Sermon after Our Dispersion by the Sickness.'
lxxx, 66	„ Jan. 29 (*4th Sun. after Epiphany*)	At St. Paul's. 'The second of my Prebend Sermons upon my five Psalmes.'
Published separately in 1626	„ Feb. 24 (*1st Fri. in Lent*)	'A Sermon Preached to the Kings M[tie] at White-hall.'
lxxx, 21	1626 *Apr.* 9 (Easter Day)	'The first Sermon upon this Text, preached at S. Pauls, in the Evening.'
„ 73	„ Apr. 18	'Preached to the King in my Ordinary wayting at White-hall.'
xxvi, 8	„ Apr. 30 (*3rd Sun. after Easter*)	To the Household at Whitehall.
lxxx, 77	„ May 21 (*Sun. after Ascension Day*)	At St. Paul's.
„ 78	„ June 21	„ „
„ 67	„ Nov. 5	St. Paul's '*In Vesperis*'. 'The third of my Prebend Sermons upon my five Psalmes.'
„ 80	„ Dec. 12	'Preached at the funerals of Sir William Cokayne, Knight, Alderman of London.'
„ 4	„ *Dec.* 25 (Christmas Day)	At St. Paul's.

Vol. and No.	Date	Place and Occasion
lxxx, 68	1626/7 Jan. 28 (*Sexagesima Sun.*)	At St. Paul's. 'The fourth of my Prebend Sermons upon my five Psalmes.'
„ 22	1627 *Mar.* 25 (Easter Day)	At St. Paul's.
l, 27	„ Apr. 1 (*1st Sun. after Easter*)	To the King, at Whitehall.
„ 41	„ May 6 (*Sun. after Ascension Day*)	At St. Paul's Cross.
lxxx, 28	„ *May* 13 (Whitsunday)	At St. Paul's.
„ 44	„ *May* 20 (Trinity Sunday)	At St. Dunstan's.
Published separately in 1627	„ July 1 (*6th Sun. after Trinity*)	'A Sermon of Commemoration of the Lady Danvers, late Wife of Sir John Danvers. Preached at Chilsey [i.e. Chelsea] where she was lately buried.'
l, 1	„ Nov. 19	'At the Earl of Bridgewaters house in London at the mariage of his daughter, the Lady Mary, to the eldest sonne of the L. Herbert of Castle-island.'
lxxx, 5	„ *Dec.* 25 (Christmas Day)	At St. Paul's.
„ 47	1627/8 Jan. 27 (*3rd Sun. after Epiphany*)	'At S. Paul's, The Sunday after the Conversion of S. Paul.'
xxvi, 15	„ Feb. 29 (*1st Fri. in Lent*)	At Whitehall.
lxxx, 54	1628 Apr. 5	'To the King at Whitehall, upon the occasion of the Fast.'
„ 23	„ *Apr.* 13 (Easter Day)	At St. Paul's.
„ 75	„ Apr. 15 (*Easter Tuesday*)	'To the King at Whitehall.'
„ 29	„ *June* 1 (Whitsunday)	At St. Paul's.
l, 42	„ Nov. 23 (*24th Sun. after Trinity*)	St. Paul's 'in the Evening'.[1]
lxxx, 6	„ *Dec.* 25 (Christmas Day)	At St. Paul's.
„ 48	1628/9 Jan. 25 (Conversion of St. Paul)	'At S. Pauls in the Evening, Vpon the day of S. Pauls Conversion, 1628.'

1 This is the heading of the sermon, though the pages are headed 'At Saint Pauls Crosse'. The printer has carried on the headline of the previous sermon.

Vol. and No.	Date	Place and Occasion
xxvi, 3[1]	1628/9 Feb. 20 (*1st Fri. in Lent*)	At Whitehall.
lxxx, 24	1629 *Apr.* 5 (Easter Day)	Probably at St. Paul's (no place given).
l, 28[2]	" Apr. —	'Preached to the King, at the Court in April, 1629.'
lxxx, 31	" *May* 24 (Whitsunday)	At St. Paul's.
l, 44	" Nov. 22 (*25th Sun. after Trinity*)	At St. Paul's Cross.
lxxx, 49	1629/30 *Jan.* 25[3] (Conv. of St. Paul)	At St. Paul's.
xxvi, 5[4]	" Feb. 12 (*1st Fri. in Lent*)	To the King at Whitehall.
lxxx, 25	1630 *Mar.* 28 (Easter Day)	At St. Paul's.
" 13	" Apr. 20	[5]'Preached in Lent, to the King.'
xxvi, 26 (published separately in 1632 as 'Death's Duel')	1630/1 *Feb.* 25[6] (1st Fri. in Lent)	At Whitehall before the King.

[1] This sermon is repeated as xxvi, 17, where no date is given.

[2] Before its appearance in the *L Sermons*, this was published in 1634 by the University of Cambridge as one of *Six Sermons upon Severall Occasions* preached by Donne.

[3] Should this sermon be dated 24 Jan. or 31 (the Sundays preceding and following the Feast of St. Paul's Conv.) rather than 25 Jan., the actual date of the Feast? See Donne's remarks on his habit of celebrating festivals on the Sunday preceding or following, in lxxx, 47. The place is not mentioned in the title, but from Donne's words 'I have, for divers yeares successively, *in this place*, determined my selfe upon this Book', it is clear that the sermon was preached at St. Paul's.

[4] This sermon is repeated as xxvi, 16, where the date is given as 22 Feb. Since that date fell on a Monday, it is evident that xxvi, 5 gives the correct date, the first Friday in Lent being, as Walton tells us, Donne's 'old constant day'.

[5] There is an error in this title, for in 1630 Easter fell on 28 Mar., so that 20 Apr. could not possibly have been in Lent. Gosse dates the sermon 23 Apr. and adds a footnote 'Misprinted "April 20" in the 1640 edition (p. 127). Dr. Jessopp points out that the third Sunday after Easter fell on the 23rd' (*Life and Letters of John Donne*, vol. ii, p. 263). This emendation only increases the confusion, for as a matter of fact, 23 Apr. was a Friday, and moreover was not in Lent.

[6] The *XXVI Sermons* give no date for this sermon, but Walton tells us that it was preached on the 1st Friday in Lent. The separate edition (1632) says that it was delivered 'in the beginning of Lent 1630' [i.e. 1630/1].

Conjectural and approximate dates

LXXX, 7. 'Preached upon Christmas Day.' As Dean Donne was required to preach at St. Paul's on Christmas Day we have sermons for every Christmas from 1621 to 1628 inclusive, except for 1623 when he was recovering from his dangerous sickness. He was too ill to preach on Christmas Day 1630, when he was lying sick at Aldborough Hatch. It is probable that this sermon, therefore, belongs to 1629.

LXXX, 9. 'Preached upon Candlemas day.' The heading of this sermon tells us that the text (Rom. xiii. 7) formed 'part of the Epistle of that day, that yeare'. The text occurs in the Epistle for the Fourth Sunday after Epiphany, and the sermon must therefore belong to 2 February 1616/17, or 1622/3, those being the only years during Donne's ministry in which the Fourth Sunday after Epiphany fell on 2 February. Of the two dates, 1622/3 seems to me to be preferable.

LXXX, 10. 'Preached upon Candlemas day.' At the beginning of this sermon Donne says, alluding to his text (Rom. xii. 20), 'It falls out . . . that those Scriptures which are appointed to be read in the Church, all these dayes, (for I take no other this Terme) doe evermore afford, and offer us Texts, that direct us to patience.' This indicates that Donne was preaching in the week of the Third Sunday after Epiphany, in the Epistle for which this text is found. The only years during Donne's ministry in which Candlemas Day fell in this week were 1621/2 and 1627/8. References in the sermon to 'the miseries of our brethren round about us', and 'the aimes and plots of our adversaries upon us' (p. 97) make the year 1621/2 seem probable, as men's minds were then much disturbed by the sufferings of the Protestants in Germany.

LXXX, 11. 'Preached upon Candlemas day.' The last sentence runs 'And therefore since all the world shakes in a palsie of wars, and rumors of wars, since we are sure that Christs Vicar in this case will come to his *Dimittuntur peccata*, to send his Buls, and Indulgences, and Crociatars for the maintenance of his part, in that cause, let us also, who are to do the duties of private men, to obey and not to direct, by presenting our diseased and paralytique souls to Christ Jesus, now, when he in the Ministry of his unworthiest servant is preaching unto you, . . . let us endeavour to bring him to his *Dimittuntur peccata*, to forgive us all those sins, which are the true causes of all our palsies, and slacknesses in his service; and so, without limiting him, or his great Vicegerents, and Lieutenants, the way, or the time, to beg of him, that he will imprint in them, such counsels and such resolutions, as his wisdome knows best to conduce to his glory, and the maintenance of his Gospell.' This might refer to the agitation felt in England over the defeat of the Elector Palatine at Prague in October 1620. Public opinion was strongly in favour of war; men were anxious that James I should take up arms on behalf of his son-in-law the Elector, and thus defend the Protestant cause on the Continent against that of Roman Catholicism.

Thus 2 February 1620/1 seems a probable date for this sermon. If LXXX, 10 is correctly dated as belonging to 2 February 1621/2, and LXXX, 9 as 2 February 1622/3, these years are excluded. 2 February 1623/4 is excluded by Donne's illness at that time. 2 February 1624/5 is also a possible date.

LXXX, 26. 'Preached upon Easter-day.' It was Donne's duty as Dean of St. Paul's to preach in the Cathedral on Easter Day. He was elected Dean in November 1621, and we possess Easter sermons preached at St. Paul's for 1623 and all the succeeding years of his life. This sermon probably belongs therefore to Easter 1622.

LXXX, 30, 32, 33, 34, 35, 36, 37. 'Preached upon Whitsunday.'

As Dean, Donne was required to preach at St. Paul's on Whitsunday. We have sermons for 1627, 1628, and 1629 (LXXX, 28, 29, 31). Six of these sermons may therefore be assigned to the Whitsundays of 1622, 1623, 1624, 1625, 1626, 1630. There would then remain one sermon not accounted for. This might be LXXX, 30, which is inserted between the Whitsunday sermons of 1628 and 1629. We cannot, however, assume that sermons 32–7 are placed in the order in which they were preached, for the whole series of ten sermons begins with those for 1627 and 1628, after which there is an undated sermon followed by that for 1629. The date of any of the undated sermons can be settled by internal evidence only. With some hesitation I assign no. 32 to 1623, for it contains less anti-Roman matter than any of the others. During the negotiations in 1623 for the Spanish match, the King ordered preachers to refrain from violently controversial sermons.

LXXX, 38, 39, 40, 41. 'Preached upon Trinity Sunday.' A careful examination of these sermons shows that they form a course, announced by Donne in no. 38, as intended to deal, not in a controversial spirit but in one of devotion and edification, with the Three Persons of the Trinity and with sins directed against each Person. No. 38 takes as its subject God the Father, no. 39 sins directed specially against Him, no. 40 God the Son, and no. 41 sins directed specially against Him. Donne's introductory words in no. 38 indicate that the course was preached at Lincoln's Inn not on separate Trinity Sundays, but on successive Sundays after Trinity during the summer term.[1] It was

[1] 'I have bent my meditations, for those dayes, which this Terme will afford, upon that, which is the character and mark of all Christians in generall,

Donne's duty as Reader of Lincoln's Inn—a post which he held from October 1616 to February 1622—to preach 'every Sabbath day in the term, both forenoon and afternoon, and once the Sabbath days before and after every term, and on the Grand Days every forenoon'. We possess a sermon preached at Lincoln's Inn on Trinity Sunday 1620 (LXXX, 42), and in 1619 Donne was in Germany with Doncaster's embassy. Thus it seems that this course of sermons should be ascribed to the Trinity season of 1617, 1618, or 1621, and of these dates 1621 is, in my opinion, to be preferred.

LXXX, 50, 51, 52, 53, 55. 'Preached upon the Penitentiall Psalmes.' These are arranged with LXXX, 54 to form a series on Psalm vi. LXXX, 54, which is headed 'Preached to the King at White-hall, upon the occasion of the Fast, April 5, 1628', is on verses 6 and 7. It is unlikely that Donne, preaching before the King on the occasion of a special Fast, would merely continue a series of sermons which he had been preaching for some time, and therefore we need not suppose that the undated sermons necessarily belong to 1628. Internal evidence suggests that nos. 50–3 were preached much earlier, for nos. 50 and 52 are closely linked with the *Essays in Divinity* (see pp. 213–14 *supra*), and the last sentence of no. 52 shows that no. 53 was to follow quickly: 'And so we have done with our first Part, which was the Prayer it selfe; and the second, which is the Reasons of the Prayer, we must reserve for a second exercise.' On the other hand, no. 55 (on verses 8, 9, 10 of Psalm vi) shows no such links with the *Essays*. I suggest that nos. 50–3 should be assigned to the period between 1615 and Donne's departure for Germany in 1619.

LXXX, 69. 'The fifth of my Prebend Sermons upon my five Psalmes: Preached at S. Pauls.'

This must be later than 28 January 1626/7, when the fourth of Donne's prebend sermons was preached (LXXX, 68). The prebend sermons followed one another at intervals of a few months, so this sermon may be safely assigned to 1627.

LXXX, 76. 'Preached to the Earle of Carlile, and his Company, at Sion.'

Viscount Doncaster was created Earl of Carlisle in September 1622, so the sermon was probably preached after that date.

LXXX, 79. 'Preached at S. Pauls.'

Political references in this sermon seem to date it as belonging to 1620–2.

the Trinity, the three Persons in one God.' LXXX, 38, p. 376. Had the sermon been preached anywhere but at Lincoln's Inn, Donne would hardly have mentioned the term.

E.g. 'I may have a full measure in my selfe, finde no want of temporall conveniencies, or spirituall consolation even in inconveniencies, and so hold up a holy alacrity and cheerefulnesse for all concerning my selfe, and yet see God abandon greater persons, and desert some whole Churches, and States, upon whom his glory and Gospel depends much more then upon me, but this is a prayer of charitable extension, *Satura nos*, not *me*, but *us*, all us that professe thee aright.'[1]

'But he may derive help upon us, by meanes that are not his, not avowed by him, He may quicken our Counsels by bringing in an *Achitophell*, he may strengthen our Armies by calling in the Turke, he may establish our peace and friendships, by remitting or departing with some parts of our Religion; at such a deare price we may be helped, but these are not his helps.'[2]

'God does all that he can for us; And therefore when we see others in distresse, whether nationall, or personall calamities, whether Princes be dispossest of their naturall patrimony, and inheritance, or private persons afflicted with sicknesse, or penury, or banishment, let us goe Gods way, all the way.'[3]

'Our Ancestors who indured many yeares Civill and forraine wars, were more affected with their first peace, then we are with our continuall enjoying thereof, And our Fathers more thankfull, for the beginning of Reformation of Religion, then we for so long enjoying the continuance thereof.'[4]

The references here are probably to Frederick, Elector Palatine, and his expulsion from the Palatinate. In 1620 James I was moved to anger by a rumour that Frederick had invited the Turks into Hungary to help him in his Bohemian campaign.[5] Feeling in England ran high in favour of Frederick, and great impatience was manifested at the reluctance of James to assist his son-in-law.

L, 3. 'Preached at a Marriage.' This was also published in 1634 in the *Six Sermons*, and it is found in the manuscript in St. Paul's Cathedral Library, where it has the heading 'Preached at St. Clements at Mr. Washingtons Marriage'.

L, 8. 'Preached at Essex House, at the Churching of the Lady Doncaster.'

Doncaster married, as his second wife, Lucy Percy, daughter of the Earl of Northumberland. The marriage took place in November 1617.

[1] LXXX, 79, p. 805.
[2] Ibid., p. 806.
[3] Ibid., p. 808.
[4] Ibid., p. 811.
[5] Tillières's dispatch, April 6/16, Raumer, *Briefe aus Paris*, ii. 299, as quoted by S. R. Gardiner, *History of England*, 1603–42, vol. iii, p. 344.

Doncaster was created Earl of Carlisle in September 1622. This sermon therefore belongs probably to 1618–22. From May 1619 to January 1620 Doncaster and Donne were abroad on the Bohemian Embassy. It seems therefore that 1618 is the most probable date for this sermon.

L, 9. 'Preached at a Churching.'

10. 'Preached at the Churching of the Countesse of Bridgewater.'

These two sermons have the same text, and the second is evidently a continuation of the first, if indeed the two do not form one sermon, divided by Donne when he revised his notes, as we know to have been the case with LXXX, 71 and 72.[1]

The Earl and Countess of Bridgewater had a numerous family, consisting of four sons and eleven daughters, of whom two sons and three daughters died in infancy. The occasion of L, 10 must have been afforded by the birth of one of the younger members of the family, perhaps that of John[2] (born 1622), the eldest surviving son, who succeeded to the title in 1649. The sermon cannot be later than 1623, when the youngest child of the Earl and Countess was born.

L, 11. 'Preached at Lincolns Inne, preparing them to build their Chappell.'

This sermon probably belongs to the spring or summer of 1618.[3]

L, 12–23. 'Preached at Lincolns Inne.'

These sermons evidently belong to the period during which Donne held the office of Reader at Lincoln's Inn (October 1616–February 1621/2), a post which involved, so Dr. Jessopp computes, the preaching of not less than fifty sermons a year. During term he was required to preach twice every Sunday.

Of this group nos. 12 and 13 are closely connected and were apparently preached on the same day, one in the morning and the other in the evening.[4] Donne's words in no. 13 imply that he had already been Reader for more than a year.[5]

[1] The conjecture that the two sermons are really one is supported by the absence of any reference in L, 9 to the occasion on which it was preached.

[2] John, Viscount Brackley, played the part of the Elder Brother in the performance of Milton's *Comus* at Ludlow Castle in 1634.

[3] See G. R. Potter, *A Sermon Preached at Lincoln's Inn by John Donne*, pp. 5–7. He shows that Gosse was wrong in stating that 'In 1617 he [Donne] laid the first stone of their new chapel'.

[4] These two also appeared in 1634 in the *Six Sermons*.

[5] 'In such an appearance doth this Text differ from that which I handled in the forenoon, and as heretofore I found it a usefull and acceptable labour, to employ our Evening exercises upon the vindicating of some such places of Scripture, as our adversaries of the Roman Church had detorted in some point

Nos. 14 and 15 are similarly connected.

No. 16 may be one of the course of controversial sermons mentioned in no. 13. If so, it preceded nos. 13–15, and must have been preached in an earlier term.

Nos. 17 and 18 both take as their text St. Matt. xviii. 7 and no. 18 is evidently a continuation of no. 17. It is probable that they belong to the winter of 1620–1, for there are passages in no. 18 which seem to point to the dismay in England at the news of the Elector Palatine's defeat at Prague, and to the general impatience for war on his behalf.[1]

Nos. 19–23 form a series preached on Ps. xxxviii, and of these nos. 21–3 take ver. 4 as their text.

L, 26. 'Preached to the King, at White-Hall, the first Sunday in Lent.'

1626/7 seems a probable date for this sermon, as that is the only year from 1617/18 till Donne's death for which we possess no sermon preached at Whitehall on the first Friday in Lent. (There is no sermon for 1623/4, when Donne was recovering from his dangerous illness.) It is hardly probable that the King would have ordered

of controversie between them and us, and restoring those places to their true sense (which course I held constantly for one whole year) so I think it a usefull and acceptable labour, now to employ for a time those Evening exercises to reconcile some such places of Scripture, as may at first sight seem to differ from one another; In the morning we saw how Christ judged all [no. 12 has as its text "The Father judgeth no man, but hath committed all judgment to the Son"]; now we are to see how he judges none: *I judge no man.*' L, 13, p. 101.

[1] Speaking of the man who is easily scandalized, Donne says, 'Hee stays not to give men their Law, to give Princes, and States time to consider, whether it may not be fit for them to come to leagues, and alliances, and declarations for the assistance of the Cause of Religion next year, though not this. But *continuò scandalizatur*, as soon as a *Catholique army* hath given a blow, and got a victory of any of our forces, or friends, or as soon as a *crafty Jesuit* hath forged a Relation, that that Army hath given such a blow, or that such an Army there is, (for many times they intimidate weake men, when they shoote nothing but Paper, when they are onely *Paper-Armies*, and *Pamphlet-Victories*, and no such in truth) *Illico scandalizatur*, yet with these forged rumours, presently hee is scandalized.' L, 18, p. 147.

Prof. S. R. Gardiner says 'The first news of Frederick's defeat reached London on November 24 [1620]. The agitation was great. It was easy to see that, in their hearts, the citizens laid the blame of all that had taken place upon the King. Not a few took refuge in incredulity. The story, it was said, had come through Brussels, and had probably been invented by the Papists. Many days passed before the unwelcome news was accepted.' *History of England*, 1603–42, vol. iii, p. 385.

Donne to preach before him on the 1st Sunday in Lent as well as on the 1st Friday.

L, 29.[1] 'Preached to the King, at the Court.' This is evidently a continuation of L, 28 which was preached to the King in April 1629 on the same text, Gen. i. 26.

L, 35. This was certainly preached before Donne's departure to Germany in April 1619. In the Dobell MS. (Harvard College, Norton 4506) it is accompanied by a copy of Donne's letter to the Countess of Montgomery which was printed in the *Letters* of 1651, pp. 24–6, in which Donne says that he is 'goinge out of the kingdome'. It is probable that the sermon had been preached a few weeks earlier, for the Countess had heard the sermon and had asked Donne for a copy. It has always been recognized that the heading prefixed to the sermon in *L Sermons* must be an error, 'Preached February 21, 1611', for Donne was not ordained till 1615, but Gosse in his note (ii. 122) made confusion worse by stating that the sermon 'was probably identical with the discourse printed as preached on the 21st February 1623, in the Folio of 1649'. The sermon is found also in *Six Sermons* (printed 1634), and in the Lothian MS.

L, 47, 48, 50. 'Preached at St. Dunstans.' These sermons probably belong to the period when Donne was Vicar of St. Dunstan's. He preached his first sermon there as vicar on 11 April 1624.

No. 47 is headed 'An Anniversary Sermon preached at St. Dunstans, upon the commemoration of a Parishioner, a Benefactor to that Parish'.

No. 48 has as its text Lam. iii. 1. 'I am the man that hath seen affliction by the rod of his wrath.' This is the text on which, according to Walton, Donne preached his first sermon after his wife's death. On this evidence Gosse[2] has identified this sermon with the one described by Walton, though the latter expressly states that the one to which he refers was preached 'where his [Donne's] beloved wife lay buried—in St. Clement's Church, near Temple Bar, London', whereas L, 48 is headed 'Preached at St. Dunstans', and is included among a number of sermons preached at that church. It is possible, of course, that Gosse is right in regarding Walton's statement as one of his numerous inaccuracies, or the heading of L, 48 may be incorrect; on the other hand, as Gosse has remarked, there is nothing in L, 48 which has any clear reference to Donne's bereavement, or makes it in any sense a funeral sermon.[3] During his ministry Donne preached an

[1] Also published in 1634 in the *Six Sermons*.

[2] *Life and Letters of John Donne*, vol. ii, p. 94.

[3] Walton says, 'And indeed his very words and looks testified him to be

enormous number of sermons, and it is possible that the sermon described by Walton has not been preserved, and that as Vicar of St. Dunstan's, at least seven years having elapsed since his wife's death, Donne used the same text and treated it somewhat differently.

In no. 50 Donne refers to a previous sermon on the text 'Jesus wept'.[1] We possess a sermon (LXXX, 16) on this text preached at Whitehall on the first Friday in Lent (28 February), 1622/3.

XXVI, 10. This is a continuation of XXVI, 9 (see pp. 277–8 *supra*), which is dated 2 April 1620. This sermon may therefore safely be dated as belonging to 1620.

Thus there remain only the few following sermons to which as yet no date can be assigned. Further investigation will probably lessen their number still further.

LXXX, 8.	'Preached upon Candlemas Day.'
12.	'Preached upon Candlemas Day.'
30.	'Preached upon Whitsunday.'
45.	'Preached upon All-Saints Day.'
56–64.	'Preached upon the Penitentiall Psalmes' (56–63 form a series on Ps. xxxii).
L, 2, 3.[2]	'Preached at a Mariage.'
4–7.	'Preached at a Christning.'
24, 25.	'Preached at White-Hall.'
34.	'To the Nobility.'
39, 40.	'Preached at Saint Pauls.'
XXVI, 22.	'Preached at the Temple.'

truly such a man ['as had seen affliction']; and they, with the addition of his sighs and tears, expressed in his sermon, did so work upon the affections of his hearers as melted and moulded them into a companionable sadness.'

[1] 'We reade in the Naturall Story, of some floating Islands, that swim, and move from place to place; and in them a Man may sowe in one place, and reape in another: This case is so farre ours, as that in another place we have sowed in tears, and by his promise, in whose tears we sowed them, when we handled those two words, *Jesus wept*, we shall reape in Joy.' p. 466.

[2] No. 3 also appeared in 1634 in the *Six Sermons*.

APPENDIX C

PROSE WORKS ATTRIBUTED TO DONNE

THERE are two books, *Polydoron* and *The Ancient History of the Septuagint*, which have been frequently attributed to Donne, though their real author seems to have been a certain John Done, of whom little is known. He was probably the writer of a long letter on alchemy, preserved in the Bodleian Library in Ashmole MS. 1415, fol. 19 verso, 'on the author's practice about Alchemy by John Done'.

Polydoron is a small volume in duodecimo, first published in 1631 with the title 'Polydoron: or a miscellania of Morall, Philosophicall, and Theological sentences. By John Done. Printed at London by Tho. Cotes, for George Gibbes dwelling in Popes-head Alley at the signe of the Flower de Luce. 1631.' Dr. Keynes notes (*op. cit.*, p. 152) that some copies have a leaf with dedication to the Earl of Dover and with an extra signature A 3 inserted between A 2 and A 3.

In 1650 the book was reissued with the following title: 'A miscellania of morall, theologicall, and philosophicall sentances; Worthy observation. (Ornament between rules.) Printed for Iohn Sweeting, At the Angel in Popes-head-alley, 1650.' It contained a dedicatory epistle *To the Right Honourable Henry, Earl of Dover*, signed *John Done*, while the remainder of the book consisted of sheets A 3–K 4 of the 1631 edition.

The Ancient History of the Septuagint appeared in 1633. The title runs thus: 'The Auncient History of the Septuagint. Written in Greeke, by Aristeus 1900. Yeares since. . . . Newly done into English By I Done. *Tempora, Tempera, Tempore.* London: Printed by N. Okes. 1633.' In 1685 a new edition was published by W. Hensman and Thomas Fox, who described the book on the title-page as 'First English'd from the Greek, by the Learned and Reverend Dr. John Done, late Dean of St. Pauls. Now Revised, and very much Corrected from the Original.'

This assertion of Donne's authorship, made for the first time more than fifty years after his death, has of course no authority, but it was accepted and repeated by the successive editors of Walton's *Lives* during the eighteenth and early nineteenth centuries. In 1855 Dr. Jessopp in his edition of the *Essayes in Divinity* (p. lxxi) wrote thus: 'The History of the Septuagint attributed to Donne by *all* the editors of Walton is not his; it was by one *John Done*, a poor and flimsy writer, the author of two or three other trifles.'

This translation has none of the marks of Donne's style. It is plain that if the original publisher could have claimed the book as Donne's, he would have done so in 1633—the year of the publication of the *Poems* and *Juvenilia*. John Donne the younger made no mention of it or of *Polydoron* in the petition which he sent to Laud asking for an injunction against those publishers who had issued works ascribed to his father without his permission, nor did he reissue either book among his later collections of his father's works.

In *Notes and Queries* (6th Ser., vi. 47) a question was asked about the authorship of *Polydoron*. This was answered on page 95 of the same volume by Dr. Jessopp: 'The bookling mentioned by Mr. Wilson is not the only work produced by John Done. *The Auncient History of the Septuagint*, which appeared in 1633, is frequently to be met with, and seems to have had a somewhat wide circulation. . . . It is a trumpery production, and could never be set down to the great dean by any one at all familiar with his writings. I tried to find out something about the man Done twenty-five years ago, but I cannot lay my hand on my notes; my impression is that he was a needy schoolmaster, who was employed by the booksellers.'

In a letter to *The Times Literary Supplement*, 7 July 1921, Professor S. G. Dunn argued that John Donne the younger might have had a hand in both *Polydoron* and *The History of the Septuagint*. Professor Dunn notes passages in *Polydoron* which remind him of the *Paradoxes and Problems* and others which recall the *Sermons*; he conjectures that the poet may in his early days have jotted down a number of reflections in a 'table-book' to which his son later had access.[1] He also conjectures that the younger Donne may have employed his leisure at Christ Church to produce the translation of *The History of the Septuagint*.

The parallels which Professor Dunn adduces are not at all convincing. The author of *Polydoron* lacked the biting wit and morbid fancy of the poet, and he was far graver and more moral than that 'atheistical buffoon', John Donne the younger, whose only original work, *Donne's Satyr* (1662), consists of 'somewhat obscene, though not

[1] 'There is about some of these "sentences" a distinct flavour of Donne, but we can confidently say that he was not the author of "Polydoron". . . . I would suggest, then, that John Donne the younger was the author of "Polydoron". It is the kind of book a man of his stamp would be likely to produce. Wood, who did not approve of him, allows him to be "a man of sense and parts", and the author of "Polydoron" was no fool. The "Sentences" are put together carelessly, there are numerous misprints; but there are shrewd things said and there is evidence of fairly wide reading. According to my theory the younger Donne had his father's early notes to draw upon, but was too indolent and unscholarly to make any better use of them.'

very amusing, pleasantries' (Keynes). The writer of *Polydoron* occupies much of his space in denouncing drunkenness, gaming, and stage-plays.[1] He has what seems to be a contemptuous reference[2] to the famous Mermaid Tavern, the haunt of Shakespeare and Ben Jonson; and he professes profound hatred of 'the paradoxion babling wit shewers',[3] among whom Donne should certainly be reckoned. His condemnation of 'desperate foredoers of themselve' on page 129 is in opposition to Donne's more charitable judgement in *Biathanatos*. A link with the letter on alchemy by the unknown 'John Done' is furnished by the frequent references to that science.[4] I cannot agree with Professor Dunn's statement that 'there is nothing in his language to indicate that he practised it himself'.[5] His attitude towards women also differs from Donne's. On page 147 he platitudinizes thus: 'God saw it was not good for man to live alone, and therefore made him a helper, *viz.* woman: Wherefor in consequence a woman ought not onely to bee a companion, but also a helper.' This should be contrasted with a mordant saying in the *Devotions upon Emergent Occasions* (1624), Meditation 21: 'God saw that Man needed a Helper, if hee should be well, but to make Woman ill, the Deuill saw, that there needed no third.'

[1] *Polydoron*, pp. 6, 10, 16, 18, 19, 21, 23, 26, 49, 51, 77, &c.

[2] Ibid., p. 72: 'Give a drunkard that hath learned to reele of the tap-spinning Mearmaide, and a divell bomm-e Ruffian (*sic*), the wall, in any case; for the one needes it, the other in right should have wall on all sides of him, *viz.* Newgate.' According to a letter of Thomas Coryat, Donne himself had been one of the 'Right Worshipful Fraternity of Sireniacal Gentlemen that meet the first Friday of every month, at the sign of the Mermaid.'

[3] Ibid., p. 40.

[4] Ibid., pp. 43–5, 64, 70, 71, 83, 85, 124.

[5] Note particularly p. 44: 'The children of this Arte ("occult philosophy") understand the Language of the parents; onely, to the rest they speake in obscure riddles: for as cocks the birds of the Sunne crow and are onely answered by other cocks, so in this divine mysterie the intelligent must be a bird of the Sunne also.' Also p. 70: '*Mars* his concubinarie lying with *Venus* in *Ouid*, signifieth iron changed into copper; *Vulcan's* finding them, and discouering the false play; is the fire, and tryall; for iron is not transmuted, as some suppose, but the coppresse or vitrioll, corporated into a metalline forme by the power of *Mars* or iron, his lustfull and fiery sulphur. The Gods laughing, is Truth discerning the Alchymist mistake; for the like is betwixt *Mercury* and *Saturne*.' P. 83: 'Alchymie is the knowledge of things hidden in nature, the revelation thereof the gift of God.' In view of such passages it seems clear that the sentences which Professor Dunn quotes express the dislike of the learned occultist for the vulgar practitioner: e.g. p. 85: 'A mettall-monging Alchimist is but a hors-keeper to a coyner, however he curries his tromperie. . . .'

But the most conclusive piece of evidence against Donne's authorship of *Polydoron* is to be found in the preliminary address 'To the Reader', in which the author speaks of 'these my Miscellanies' as 'the first acknowledged thrust out issue of my braine'. Professor Dunn admits that this could not have been written by Donne, but he ascribes the preface to Donne's son, and remarks, 'it is no violent supposition to believe that he embellished his own "first thrust out issue" with his father's learning'. He does not, however, adduce one scrap of evidence to connect the book with the younger Donne, and he does not attempt to explain how that worthy could have made arrangements to publish a book of scraps stolen from his father's notebooks while that father was still alive and in full mental, though not physical, vigour. *Polydoron* was entered in the Stationers' Register on 1 December 1630, four months before Donne's death. On that date we find the entry: 'George Gibbes. Entred for his Copie vnder the handes of master Buckner and master Kingston warden, A booke Called *Polydoron or A Miscelania* by John Done. vj^{d}.'

INDEX

PRINTED IN
GREAT BRITAIN
AT THE
UNIVERSITY PRESS
OXFORD
BY
CHARLES BATEY
PRINTER
TO THE
UNIVERSITY

Date Due

DEC 6 1957
NOV 29 '68
APR 15 1970